MW00795927

MRS. (OSCAR HERBERT) ELIZABETH M. RIXFORD

Families Directly Descended from

All the Royal Families in Europe
(495 to 1932)

and

Mayflower Descendants

bound with Supplement

By Their Lineal Descendant
Mrs. (Oscar Herbert) Elizabeth M. Leach Rixford

"Happy he, who with bright regard looks back upon his father's fathers,
who with joy recounts their deeds of grace, and in himself,
valued the latest link in the fair chain of noble sequence."
—GOETHE.

"Remember the days of old, the years of many generations:
ask thy father and he will shew thee:
thy elders and they will tell thee."
—DEUT., 32:7.

CLEARFIELD

Originally published
Burlington, Vermont, 1932
Supplement published 1943

Consolidated and reprinted for
Clearfield Company, Inc. by
Genealogical Publishing Co., Inc.
Baltimore, Maryland
1992, 1993, 1999, 2000, 2001, 2002

International Standard Book Number: 0-8063-4945-X

Made in the United States of America

Dedicated

to

My Beloved Husband

Oscar Herbert Rixford

PREFACE

This genealogy is a study in the old world as well as the new. Extensive references have been given, countless books have been consulted, nearly all procured from New England Historical and Genealogical Society, and to "Colonial Families," compiled by the New York Historical Society, and to them I acknowledge my indebtedness. I have placed dependence on printed records, and when authorities differ a conclusion has been reached by critical comparison and weighing of evidence. Many family records never printed before have been used.

I have traced from Cerdic, first of the West Saxon Kings, 495, through Alfred the Great, 849, Robert Bruce, King of Scotland, King Henry I, II and III, King Edward I, II and III, also many other royal lines through Charlemagne, Louis I, Earls of Warren, Dukes of Normandy, Royal House of Portugal, House of Capet, Counts of Anjou, Kings of Jerusalem, and many other royal families too numerous to name. This book also includes several Mayflower lines connected to all members of the Vermont Society of Mayflower Descendants, who are direct descendants of these lines. Those with ancestry to the Earls of Warren have been connected up to the royal families. The book also includes the ancestry of Gen. George Washington, the first President of the United States, traced back 1,000 years to the Earl of Orkney Isles, the founder of the Washington family. It also contains the ancestry of Gen. Nathaniel Greene, who ranked next in military fame to George Washington.

As a foundation for my "Genealogy of Royal Descent," Vol. I, and "Families with 200 Puritan Ancestors," Vol. II, I have used the four Mayflower lines to Francis Cooke, James and Susannah Chilton, and daughter Mary, and two lines to the National Society Founders and Patriots of America, to Lawrence Leach and William Phelps, these seven lines being traced by my brother F. Phelps Leach. The Author has three lines to the Huguenot Society to Hon. John Washburn, John Bissell, and James Eno; ten lines to the Daughters of the American Revolution to Ephraim Leach, Samuel Shattuck, Aaron Field, Samuel Hungerford, Isaiah Hungerford, Samuel Nash, James Hawley, Joel Phelps, Stephen Mead, and Samuel Brown; three lines to the United States Daughters of 1812; forty-seven lines to the Colonial Daughters of the 17th Century; one hundred forty supplemental lines to the National Society Daughters of the American Colonists in Vermont.

Colonial ancestors of (Mrs. Oscar H.) Elizabeth M. Rixford, which have been accepted by the National Society of Daughters of

American Colonists, and for which Ancestral Bars have been received
(see "Daughters of American Colonists Lineage Book," 1931-1932) :

Francis Cooke, James Chilton, John Winslow, Robert Latham, Lawrence
Leach, Giles Leach, Benjamin Leach, Esq., Sergt. Solomon Leach, John Leach,
William Phelps, Lieut. Timothy Phelps, Lieut. Samuel Phelps, Ensign Samuel
Phelps, Joel Phelps, Thomas Nash, Lieut. Timothy Nash, Lieut. John Nash,
Samuel Nash, Esq., William Mead (Author), Joseph Mead, Sr., Dea. Edward
Griswold, Joseph Mead, Jr., Capt. Stephen Mead, Richard Bidwell, James
Eno, Sr., James Eno, Jr., Samuel Hungerford, Thomas Hungerford, Thomas
2nd Hungerford, Thomas 3rd Hungerford, Samuel Barber, Sergt. Thomas
Barber, Rev. Samuel Stone, John Stone, Nathaniel Merrill, Huguenot, John
Merrill, Dea. Abraham Merrill, Jonathan Graves, Capt. John Graves, Benjamin
Graves, Capt. Benjamin Graves, John Washburn, Capt. Matthew Smith, Lieut.
Matthew Smith, Capt. Nathaniel Turner, Abraham Brown, Nathaniel Frary,
Samson Frary, Samuel Gregory, John Gregory, Jachan Gregory, William
Latham, Dea. John Watson, Lieut. Joseph Kellogg, Stephen Tery, Dea. Samuel
Chapin ("The Puritan"), Ebenezer Field, Samuel Field, Centinel Aaron Field,
Lieut. Thomas Gilbert, Thomas Sanford, Ezekiel Sanford, Capt. Ezekiel San-
ford, Capt. Ephraim Sanford, Capt. John Bissell, Samuel Bissell, Robert Hins-
dale, Col. William Shattuck, Dr. Philip Shattuck, Dr. Joseph Shattuck, Samuel
Shattuck, Capt. Joseph Clesson, Capt. Matthew Clesson, John Hawks, Sergt.
Obadiah Dickinson, Anthony Thompson, John Drake, John Drake, Jr., Mariner
John Thompson, Peter Woodward, Sr., Capt. Christopher Stanley, John Frary,
Robert Daniel, William Cheney, Capt. Humphrey Johnson, Hon. John Johnson,
Col. Samuel Hinsdale, Jonathan Reynolds, John Reynolds, John Hoare, Thomas
Holcomb, Thomas Sherwood, Dea. Richard Platt, Nicholas Baker, John 1st
Cutler, James St. John, Mathias 1st St. John, Mathias 2nd St. John, Issaac
Johnson, Esq., Gov. Thomas Wells, Joseph Hawley, John Green, John Lawrence,
Enoch Lawrence, Capt. Daniel Lawrence, Isaac Lawrence, Capt. Abraham
Brown, Jonathan Brown, Dea. Samuel Hyde, Job Hyde, John Hewitt, Ensign
John Fuller, Andrew Stephenson, John Whitney, John Whitney, Jr., James Pat-
terson, Robert Seabrook, Rev. John Mayo, Henry Chamberlain, William Cham-
berlain, Rev. Henry Smith, Dea. Thomas Judd, Sergt. William Judd, Thomas
Judd, Stephen Freeman, Capt. John Astrode, William Comstock, John Steele,
Dea. Nathaniel Phelps, John Rogers, Thomas Moore, Thomas Thomson,
Robert Reynolds, Capt. Edmund Goodenow, Nathaniel Dickinson, Thomas
Hewitt, Lieut. Joseph Washburn, Moses Cleveland, Samuel Cleveland, Richard
Hildreth.

Rev. A. A. Chapin, D.D., at the unveiling of the Deacon Samuel
Chapin Monument, "The Puritan," at Springfield, Mass., said:

"To preserve the memory of our ancestors is one of the marks of a high
state of civilization." "Among enlightened people if a child is born a record is
made of it. A man dies, the fact is set down with day and date in a public
register. In this way men may trace the history of families and individuals.
Among barbarians no such records are kept. Hence, too, among all enlightened
people, monuments are reared and the chisel of the sculptor and the palette of
the painter are put into requisition to hand down to posterity the form and
features of the departed."—CHARLES EAGAN CHAPIN.

ELIZABETH M. LEACH RIXFORD.

East Highgate, Vermont,
    March 18, 1932.

EXPLANATORY

The contest between arbitrary and constitutional government, which had never ceased in England after King John signed the Magna Charta, raged with unusual violence while the throne was occupied by the Stuarts. The reign of the Tudors had been a period of comparative rest; the Wars of the Roses having so weakened the great barons, who in earlier times made and deposed kings at their pleasure, and the introduction of artillery having so strengthened the monarch against an enemy destitute of these engines of destruction, that, from Henry the Seventh to Elizabeth, there was but faint resistance to the will of the sovereign by the hereditary lords who sat in the upper house of Parliament. By the transfer of the supremacy of the Church, another check on the royal prerogative had been removed; so that the lords spiritual, who in the olden time had been as little dependent on the king as the lords temporal, were now subservient to the power which placed them in office. The Tudors, therefore, transmitted to their successors a more arbitrary sceptre than had been wielded by earlier kings.

But the time of the Stuarts was less favorable than that of the Tudors for maintaining a theory and practice of government which contravened the rights of the subject. Formerly the great barons had come to Parliament followed by hundreds of archers and spearmen ready to back their lords in any contest which might occur; but the barons only, and not their retainers, had presumed to put to question the conduct of the overlord. Out of the decay of this feudal baronage, there had gradually grown up a new antagonist to despotism, which, exhibiting considerable power in the reign of Elizabeth, vigorously encountered the house of Stuart at its accession, and suffered no permanent defeat till it had brought a king of England to the scaffold.

Beginning about the twelfth century, March 25 was considered the first day of the year. It was not until 1752 that England and the countries under its jurisdiction adopted the Gregorian Calendar, and January 1 became the first of the year; therefore, my records before this date would be reckoned as by the old calendar.

Julius Cæsar made a reform in the calendar 46 years before Christ. Solar year 365 days, 6 hours, and the sixth hour was taken into account by making every fourth a leap year. The true solar year is 11 minutes and some seconds short of 365¼ days. A new style was made in 1582 by taking 10 days from October by act of Parliament.

HERALDRY

Heraldry, the act of science of blazoning or describing in appropriate technical terms coats of arms and other heraldic and armorial insignia, was largely employed during the feudal ages to display the exploits of chivalry, and to reward as well as commemorate its triumphs over oppression and violence. But the system is of very ancient origin, long antedating the Christian era.

In its modern sense, however, the heraldic art dates from the time of the Crusades, and was reduced to its present perfect system by the French. It was not until the time of the Crusades that the crest or cognizance was generally adopted. Originally the crest was an ornament chiefly worn by kings, knights, and warriors. At first these badges were placed on the summit of the helmet, to render them more plainly visible, or on the arm; but in later times were transferred to the shield or armor. The crest served to distinguish the bearers in battle, and as a mark for their followers or supporters. In the ages of the past, the crest enjoyed the place of honor.

An erroneous idea is entertained by some that heraldic symbols denote an aristocratic or exclusive class, and are undemocratic in their origin and permanency. On the contrary, these badges of distinction were the reward of personal merit, and could be secured by the humblest as well as the highest. They are today the testimonials and warrants of bravery, heroism, and meritorious deeds of our ancestors.

Modern armies have inherited the idea. British regiments have always used them. They did not come into "official" use in our own army until 1919, when the War Department authorized them and prescribed in detail their general characteristics.

The Quartermaster General's Office has a number of reproductions of corps and division insignia dating back to the Civil War. In the World War, they were not adopted officially for divisions until the summer of 1918 in France. It seems that the 81st Division—the Wild Cat—arrived in France with the familiar shoulder patch which was then unauthorized. Authorities in the A. E. F. were quick to see its possibilities as a means of identification and the value in developing the spirit of the division, and directed all division commanders to adopt distinctive shoulder patches.

At the present time all Regular Army regiments, many National Guard and Reserve organizations have adopted distinctive insignia. The War Department approves the design to prevent duplication. Each insignia perpetuates in heraldic form the notable achievements of the outfit. The documents in the Office of the Quartermaster General dealing with the subject of the military coats of arms are: "War Department Circulars," Nos. 444 and 527, 1917; and "Quartermaster Review," Volume VII, No. 6, May-June, 1928, pages 26 and 28. These are on file in room 229, State War Building, Washington, D. C.

Among other army services which have adopted distinctive coats of arms, for their various units is the field artillery.

We indulge the hope that an interest in heraldic science may increase, that parents, instructors of youth, and the leaders in the progress of modern endeavor may give it the place to which it is so eminently entitled.

CONTENTS

LIST OF ABBREVIATIONS

bapt., baptized; b., born; bur., buried; d., died; dau., daughter; m., married; unm., unmarried.
Figures are members of generations.
Colonial Daughters of the 17th Century.
*Charter members.
N. E. H. R., New England Historical Register.
U. S. D. 1812, United States Daughters of 1812.
N. S. D. A. C., National Society Daughters of the American Colonists.
N. S. D. A. R., National Society Daughters of the American Revolution.
N. S. D. F. P. A., National Society, Daughters of Founders and Patriots of America.

LIST OF CHARTS

LIST OF ILLUSTRATIONS

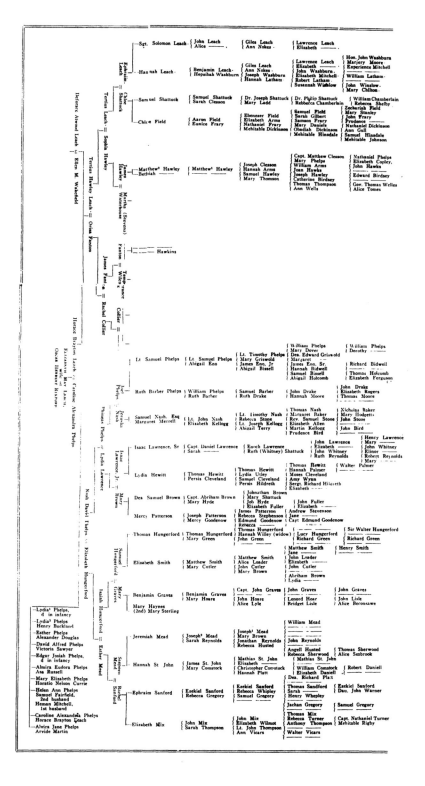

{ John Washburn
{ Martha Stevens
{ Robert Moore
{ Ellen Taylor

{ John Washburne ·
{ Jone Bushell

{ John Washburne
{ Emme ————·

{ John Washbourne ·
{ Joan Milton
{ William Milton,
{ Lord of Weston

{ Norman Washbourne ·
{ Elizabeth Knivton ·

{ John Washbourne ·
{ Margaret Poher, heiress
{ of Witchenford
{ Henry Knivton

{ Edward Winslow
{ Madeline Oliver
{ James Chilton ·
{ Susanna ————
{ Henry Chamberlain
{ Jane ————

{ Kenelyn Winslow ·
{ Katherine ———— ·

{ William Winslow
{ ———— ————

{ Thomas Winslow ·
{ Heiress of Tousley ·

{ John Winselow
{ Agnes Thorkmorton

{ Christopher Stanley
{ Susanna ————

{ John Stanley
{ Widow ————

{ Roger Stanley
{ ———— ————

{ William Stanley
{ ———— ————

{ John Stanley
{ ———— ————

{ Thomas Stanley
{ ———— ————

{ William Gull
{ Elizabeth Smith
{ Robert Hinsdale
{ Ann Woodward
{ Capt. Humphrey Johnson
{ Ellen Cheney

{ Peter Woodward

{ Hon. John Johnson
{ Marjory ————
{ William Cheney
{ Margaret ————

{ Isaac Johnson
{ John Cheney
{ Elizabeth ————

widow, mother of Copley the celebrated artist

{ John Tomes
{ ———— ————

Note—For other Royal Lines see Chart, page 1; also
Royal Line of forty-eight generations, Pedigree A,
pages 2 to 5; Pedigree B, page 5; Pedigree C, page 6;
Pedigree D, pages 6 to 7; and other Royal Lines given
in this Genealogy

{ James Phelps
{ Joan ————

{ Richard Phelps
{ ———— ————

{ William Drake
{ ———— ————
{ John Rogers
{ ———— ·
{ Thomas Moore
{ ———— · ————

{ Robert Drake
{ ———— ————
{ Walter Moore
{ Alice ————

{ John Drake
{ Anne Grenville
{ William Moore
{ Margaret Brenchley,
{ dau and coheir

{ John Drake
{ Margaret Cole
{ Agnes Austin, dau. and
{ heir to Robert Austin
{ John Brenchley, Esq.
{ Margaret Golding, dau. and
{ heir to Richard Golding

{ John Drake
{ Agnes ————
{ Thomas Moore
{ Catherine Ancher, dau. and
{ heir to Anthony Ancher, Esq

{ John Drake
{ ————Cruwys
{ William De More

{ John Lawrence
{ ———— ————
{ Thomas Whitney
{ Mary Bray

{ John Lawrence
{ ———— ————
{ Robert Whitney
{ Elizabeth Guillims

{ Robert Lawrence
{ ———— ————
{ Sir Robert Whitney
{ Sybil Baskerville

{ John Lawrence
{ ———— ————
{ Robert Whitney
{ Margaret Wye (see Wye)
{ Sir James Baskerville
{ Katherine Deverox

{ Thomas Lawrence
{ ———— ————
{ James Whitney
{ Walter Deverox, lineally descended
{ from King Edward I

{ John Lawrence
{ ———— ————

{ Sir Edward Hungerford
{ ———— ————
{ Robert Green
{ Sir Hugh Smith
{ ———— ————

{ Sir Walter Hungerford
{ ———— ————
{ John Green

{ Robert, Lord Hungerford
{ ———— ————

{ Robert, Lord Hungerford
{ ———— ————

{ John Graves
{ ———— ————
{ Anthony Lisle
{ Elizabeth Dormer

{ William Graves
{ ———— ————
{ Thomas Lisle
{ ———— Moore

{ John Graves
{ ———— ————
{ Lancelot Lisle
{ Anne Wroughton

{ George Lisle
{ Anna Montgomery

{ Sir John de Insula
{ Margaret Bremshot

{ William de Insula
{ ———— ————

{ William de Insula
{ ———— ————
{ Walter de Insula
{ Florence ————

{ Walter de Insula
{ Margaret ————

{ John de Insula
{ ———— ————

{ Baldwin de Insula
{ ———— ————

{ Walter de Insula
{ Margaret ————

{ Geffrey de Insula
{ ———— ————

{ Jordan de Insula
{ Hawise ————

{ Robert Seabrook
{ Alice Goodspeed

{ Nicholas Goodspeed
{ ———— ————

{ Thomas Sanford
{ Friswith Eve

{ Richard Sanford
{ ———— ————

{ John Gregory
{ Humphrey Turner
{ Lydia Gamer or Garnet
{ Edward Rigby

{ Henry Gregory
{ ———— ————

{ John Gregory
{ Alicia ————

{ Thomas Gregory
{ Dorothy Breslau

{ Sligo Gregory
{ Maria ————

{ William Gregory
{ Dorothy ————

MR. AND MRS. HORACE BRAYTON LEACH
Parents of the author of this book.

(Burke's "Royal Families," Vol. II, Pedigree CCIII)

Pepin the Old, Mayor of Austrasia, d. in 639.
=

Doda, son of Pepin. = Anchises, dau. of St. Arnold, Bishop of Metz, d. in 640.

Pepin d'Heristal, Duke of Austrasia, d. in 714. = Elphide.

Charles Martel, Duke of Franks, d. in 741. = Robrude.

Pepin the Short, King of France, d. 768. = Bertra de, dau. of Caribert, Count of Laon.

Charlemagne, Emperor of the West, d. 814. = Hildegarde, of Swabia.

ANCIENT ROYAL ARMS OF

France

Lewis le Bebonaire, King of France. = Judith, dau. of Guelph I.

Charles the Bold, King of France. = Hermentrude, dau. of Vodon, Earl of Orleans.

Baldwin, 1st Count of Flanders. = Judith, widow of King Ethelwold.

Baldwin, 2nd Count of Flanders, d. 918. = Alfretha, dau. of Alfred the Great, King of England.

Arnolf, 3rd Count of Flanders. = Alice, dau. of Herbert, 2nd Count of Vermandois.

Baldwin, 4th Count of Flanders. = Maud, dau. of Conrad I.

Arnolf, 5th Count of Flanders, d. in 988. = Rosalie, dau. of Beranger II, King of Italy.

Baldwin, 6th Count of Flanders. = Eleanor, dau. of Richard, 2nd Duke of Normandy.

Baldwin, 7th Count of Flanders, d. 1017. = Adela, dau. of Robert I, King of France.

Matilda, dau. of Baldwin, Count of Flanders, d. in 1083. = William the Conqueror, King of England.

Henry I, King of England, d. in 1135. = Matilda, dau. of Malcolm III, King of Scotland.

Maud (widow of Henry V), Empress of Germany. = Geoffrey Plantagenet, son of Fulk, King of Jerusalem.

Henry II, King of England. = Eleanor, dau. of William, Duke of Aquitaine.

Twenty-five generations from here to Oscar A. Rixford, only son of the Author of this book. (See Royal Descent Line to Elizabeth M. Rixford.)

1

PEDIGREE A

ROYAL DESCENT FROM CERDIC, FOUNDER OF THE WEST SAXON KINGDOM, 495

("Colonial Families," by New York Historical Society, 1928, pages 104-107)

1. · CERDIC, founder of the West Saxon Kingdom, or Wessex, is described in ancient records as an "ealdorman," who in the year 495 landed with his son Cynric in Hamptonshire, England, where he was at once attacked by the Britons. In the year 508 he defeated the Britons with great slaughter, and again in 519, aided by fresh arrivals of the Saxons, gained another decisive victory and took the title of King. His last work was the conquest of the Isle of Wight.
2. CYNRIC, succeeded his father as King of Wessex, and defeated the Britons at Salisbury in 552, and again at Beranbury, probably Barbury Hill, in 556. At his death in 560 he was succeeded by his son, Ceawlin.
3. CEAWLIN, King of the West Saxons, is first mentioned in the Anglo-Saxon Chronicle under the date 556 as fighting with his father, Cynric, against the Britons at Barbury Hill. On becoming King in 560, he began a career of conquest, and extended his kingdom greatly. In 591 he suffered defeat and lost the northern part of his kingdom. In 592 he was driven from Wessex, and in the following year killed, possibly in an attempt to regain it.
4. CUTHWIN.
5. GEOWALD.
6. CENRED.
7. ·INGILD.
8. ·EOPPA.
9. ·EOFA.
10. ·EALHMUND, King of Kent, is mentioned in a charter dated 784.
11. ·EGBERT, King of West Saxon, or King of Wessex, reigned in 802, and d. in 836. He conquered the lands south of the Thames, and by his great conquests became Lord of England up to the River Firth. He m. the Lady Redburga, and had a son *Ethelwulf*, of whom further.
12. ·ETHELWULF, son of Egbert, and his successor to the kingdom, was deeply honored by his subjects, his name meaning noble wolf. He m. Osburga, and had four sons:
    1. ·*Ethelred.*
    2. ·*Ethelbald.*
    3. ·*Ethelbert.*
    4. ·*Alfred,* of whom further.

Œdward III.,
OF ENGLAND

13. ·ALFRED "the Great," son of Ethelwulf, was b. in 849, and d. in 901. He was King of Wessex, and is famous for founding the British Navy and for bringing culture and civilization to England. He broke the power of the Danes, and kept them subdued during his reign. He m. Alswitha, and had *Edward,* of whom further.

14. ·EDWARD the Elder's third wife was Edgiva, dau. of the Earl of Sigelline, Lord of Meapham, Culings, and Lenham, in Kent, and the issue of this marriage were three sons:

Edmund, who succeeded his brother ·Athelstan.

Edred, successor to Edmund.

Elfred, who was the especial favorite of his father, by whom he was made copartner in the kingdom. He d. young, and was bur. at Winchester.

·Edward d. in 925, and was succeeded by his eldest son.

15. ·EDMUND the "Elder," who was crowned at Kingston; but his reign, a vigorous one, endured only six years. In 946, at a banquet given in celebration of the feast of St. Augustine, he was stabbed by a noted outlaw, Leolf.

·Edmund had m. Elgiva, a princess of exemplary piety, and left two sons, ·*Edwy* and ·*Edgar,* of whom presently as kings of England. At the decease of Edmund, the childhood of his sons rendered them incapable of directing the government, and in an assembly of the prelates, thanes, and vassal princes, their uncle.

16. ·EDGAR the "Peaceful," one of the most distinguished monarchs in the early annals of England and, perhaps, the most powerful. The Saxon Chronicles relate that in 973, he received at Chester, the homage of eight princes: Kenneth, of Scotland; Malcolm, of Cumberland; Mac Orric, of Anglesey, and the Isles; Iukil, of Westmoreland; Jago, of Galloway; and Howell, Dyfnwal, and Griffith of Wales; and they farther narrate how the ceremony was opened by a splendid procession by water on the Dee, wherein the royal barge was rowed by the vassal kings.

·Edgar m. (1) Elfleda, dau. of Ordmer, a nobleman of East Anglia, by whom he had a son, *Edward,* his successor; and (2) Elfrida, the beautiful dau. of Ordgar, Earl of Devon, by whom he had another son, *Ethelred.*

This great and good king d. in 975.

17. ·ETHELRED II, surnamed the "Unready," whose coronation was performed at Kingston on Apr. 14, 978. He d. in 1016. He m. (1), in 984, Elgiva, dau. of Thored, an English Earl, and by her (who d. in 1003), was father with other issue, of *Edmund,* his heir, and *Edwy,* slain by the orders of Canute. Ethelred m. (2), in 1003, Emma, called for her beauty, "the Pearl of Normandy," dau. of Richard I, Duke of that province, and by her (who wedded (2), King Canute) had two sons: *Alfred* and *Edward.*

18. EDMUND, "Ironsides," son of Ethelred, became King in 1016. He was murdered in 1017. He m. Algitha.

19. ·EDWARD "the Exile," son of Edmund, m. Agatha, dau. of Henry II, Emperor of Germany.

20. ·MARGARET, dau. of Edward "the Exile," m. Malcolm III, King of Scotland.

21. ·EDITH MATILDA, of Scotland, dau. of Malcolm III and Margaret, m. Henry I, son of William the Conqueror. Henry I reigned from 1100 to 1135, and was called a "fine scholar."

22. ·MATILDA (MAUD), dau. of Henry I and Edith Matilda, d. in 1167. She m. (1) the Emperor Henry V; she m. (2), in 1127, Geoffrey Plantagenet, Count of Anjou (see William the Conqueror III), and had a son, *Henry Plantagenet,* of whom further. She battled for her rights, and is one of the heroines of romantic history.

23. ·HENRY PLANTAGENET (Henry II of England), son of Geoffrey Plantagenet and Matilda, was b. Mar. 25, 1133, and reigned in England as Henry II until 1189. He m. in 1152, Eleanor, of Aquitaine, and had a son, *John,* of whom further.

24. JOHN PLANTAGENET (King John of England), son of Henry Plantagenet, was b. in 1167, and m. Isabella Taillefer, of Angouleme. (See Taille-

fer IX and Edward III of England.) They had a son, *Henry*, of whom further.
25. HENRY PLANTAGENET (Henry III of England), m. in 1236, Eleanor, dau. of Raimond Berenger IV, of Provence. (See Provence VII.) They had *Edward*, of whom further.
26. EDWARD I, King of England, son of Henry III, m. (1) Princess Eleanor, of Castile; he m. (2) Margaret, of France, and had *Edward*, of whom further.
27. EDMUND PLANTAGENET, of Woodstock, Earl of Kent, youngest son of Edward I, King of England, and his second wife, Margaret; m. Margaret, dau. of John, Lord Baron Wake.
28. JOAN PLANTAGENET, dau. of Edmund, of Woodstock, and Margaret Wake, was known as "the faire Maid of Kent." She m. Thomas Holland, second son of Robert, first Baron Holland. (See Holland II.)
29. THOMAS HOLLAND, son of Thomas and Joan (Plantagenet) Holland, was Earl of Kent, Baron of Holland, Woodstock, and Wake, and Earl Marshal. He m. Alice Fitz-Alan, dau. of Richard, Earl of Arundel. (See Fitz-Alan VII.)
30. THOMAS HOLLAND, son of Thomas and Alice (Fitz-Alan) Holland, was Earl of Kent, Duke of Surrey, Baron of Holland, Woodstock, Earl Marshal, and Lord Lieutenant of Ireland. He was taken prisoner and beheaded at the Battle of Cirencester in 1400, on account of his loyalty to his cousin, the deposed King Richard III. At the time of his death he was bethrothed to Constance, dau. of Prince Edmund de Longley, fifth son of Edward III and Duke of York.
31. JOHN TOUCHETT, son of James Touchett, had livery of all his father's castles, lordships and lands. He was summoned to Parliament as baron until his death. He m. (1) Margaret, dau. of William, Lord Roos, of Hamloke, by whom he had *John*, son and heir. He m. (2) Eleanor Holland, natural dau. of Thomas Holland, Earl of Kent, by Constance, dau. of Edmund de Longeley, Duke of York. (See Holland V.) John and Eleanor (Holland) had three sons and three daus., of whom one was *Constance*, of whom further.
32. CONSTANCE, dau. of John and Eleanor (Holland) Touchett, m., as second wife, Sir Robert Whitney, Knight. (See Whitney English Pedigree X.) Sir Robert Whitney, son of Sir Eustace Whitney, was probably a knight and was an active participant in the War of the Roses, and was attainted as a Yorkist in 1459. He was probably at the Battle of Mortimer's Cross in 1461. He was the subject of a poem by Lewis Glyn Cothi, on the occasion of his marriage to Alice, the great-granddaughter of Sir David Gam. He m. (1) Alice Vaughan, dau. of Thomas Vaughan; (2) Constance Touchett, who was the mother of his sons. She was descended from William the Conqueror, through the second wife of Edward I, King of England.
33. JAMES WHITNEY, son of Sir Robert Whitney, m. Blanche Milbourne, dau. and heir of Simon Milbourne. (See Milbourne IV.)
34. ROBERT WHITNEY, son of James Whitney, was of Icomb, and in charge of other confiscated estates. Died in 1541; m. Margaret Wye.
35. SIR ROBERT WHITNEY, son of Robert Whitney, m. Sybil Baskerville.
36. ROBERT WHITNEY, son of Sir Robert Whitney, m. Elizabeth, dau. of Morgan Guillims, or Duglim.
37. THOMAS WHITNEY, Gentleman, son of Robert Whitney, was of Westminster. He m. Mary Bray, dau. of John Bray, of Westminster.
38. JOHN WHITNEY, son of Thomas and Mary (Bray) Whitney, was b. in England in 1583, and d. June 1, 1673. He emigrated from London, England, in 1635, and settled in Watertown, Mass., the first of the name in America. He m. in England, Elinor ———, who was b. in 1599, and d. in Watertown, May 11, 1659. He m. (2), in Watertown, Sept. 29, 1659, Judith Clement, who d. before her husband.

OSCAR A. RIXFORD
(SON OF THE AUTHOR OF THIS GENEALOGY)

Born at East Highgate, Vt., August 4, 1890. Attended graded school East Highgate, Vt. Swanton High School, Swanton, Vt. (1 year). Lower Canada College, Montreal, Que. (2 years). Goddard Seminary, Barre, Vt. (2 years). Graduated from Goddard in 1908. Entered employ of Rixford Manufacturing Company in 1908. (Great-grandson of Luther Rixford who founded the business in 1812.) Became Vice-President of the Company in 1911 and upon the death of his father, O. H. Rixford in 1926, was elected President of the Corporation, which position he still holds.
Was Town Auditor 1918 to 1924. Selectman from 1925 to 1931 and again in 1933-1934. He represented the Town of Highgate in the State Legislature in 1915-1916. Was one of the first in Vermont to join the Progressive Party in 1912 and was State Committeeman for Franklin County from 1912 to 1916, and under his leadership Theodore Roosevelt carried Franklin County in the Presidential Election of 1912. He was a Delegate from Vermont to the National Convention of the Progressive Party at Chicago in 1916. He has been a member of the Board of Civil Authority of the Town of Highgate since 1925 and Chairman since 1930. In 1917 he was elected Moderator of the Town and has served every year since then with the exception of one year when illness prevented his serving. In 1942 the Townspeople presented him with a very fine gavel, made of rosewood trimmed with sterling silver, commemorating his having served as Moderator for twenty-five years. In 1935 Mr. Rixford was appointed a member of the State Highway Board by the late Governor Charles W. Smith for a six-year term. In 1941 he was reappointed for another six-year term by Governor William H. Wills.
Charter member of the Society of Mayflower Descendants and served as Governor of the Society from 1943 to 1946. A member of the Vermont Society of Sons of Colonial Wars and the Vermont Society of Sons of the American Revolution. Mr. Rixford was appointed a Lay Reader of the Episcopal Church by the late Bishop Arthur C. A. Hall, Bishop of Vermont, in 1919, and has served continuously since then in Swanton and Highgate. He has been a member of the Vestry of St. John's Church since 1912 and has been Treasurer for several years. He was elected a Lay Member of the Executive Council of the Diocese of Vermont when that body was formed by the Diocesan Convention of 1931 and has served as Treasurer of that Council ever since. He has twice been chosen a Lay Deputy to the Provincial Synod of the Episcopal Church and was elected a Lay Deputy to three General Conventions of the Church held in Washington 1928, Atlantic City 1934 and Philadelphia 1946.

39. John Whitney, Jr., son of John and Elinor Whitney, was b. in England in 1624; m. Ruth Reynolds, of Boston. He d. Oct. 12, 1692, and his wife d. later.
40. Ruth Whitney, b. Apr. 15, 1645; m. (1) a Shattuck; m. (2) Enoch Lawrence, Mar. 6, 1676-7. He was b. Jan. 5, 1648, and d. Sept. 28, 1744.
41. Capt. Daniel Lawrence, b. Mar. 7, 1681; d. 1777; m. Sarah ———, who d. probably at Canaan, Conn.
42. Isaac Lawrence, Sr., b. Feb. 25, 1704-5; d. Dec. 2, 1793; m. Lydia Hewitt, who d. Nov. 14, 1765.
43. Isaac Lawrence, Jr., of Canaan, Conn.; m. May 8, 1760, Mary Brown, 7th child of Dea. Samuel Brown.
44. Lydia Lawrence, b. 1761-2; d. Sept. 20, 1813; m. at New Haven, Vt., Phineas Phelps, b. Apr. 10, 1767; d. Apr. 20, 1813.
45. Nash David Phelps, b. Oct. 4, 1796; d. Apr. 15, 1884; m. Apr. 20, 1821, Elizabeth Hungerford, b. Feb. 7, 1798; d. Jan. 7, 1878.
46. Caroline Alexandria Phelps, b. July 3, 1840; d. Mar. 29, 1921; m. Sept. 8, 1863, at Stanbridge, Que., Horace Brayton Leach, b. Sept. 25, 1836; d. May 6, 1919.
47. Elizabeth May Leach, b. Jan. 7, 1866; living Jan. 1, 1932; m. Sheldon, Vt., Sept. 8, 1889, Oscar Herbert Rixford, b. Dec. 27, 1859; d. Sept. 11, 1926.
48. Oscar Adelbert Rixford, b. Aug. 4, 1890; m. Jan. 18, 1919, Montreal, Que., Mary Carolyn Hefflon, b. June 6, 1899; both living Jan. 1, 1932. They have two children:
    Mary-Elizabeth Lenora, b. Oct. 6, 1922.
    Oscar Theodore, b. July 21, 1925; both living Jan. 1, 1932.

References : 1 to 37 generations—"Colonial Families," 1928.
38 to 43 generations—"Watertown, Mass.," Bond, Vol. 1, 2nd Ed.
"Gen. Conn.," Vol. 2, pages 831-832.
Records of Elizabeth M. Rixford.
Lineage of Elizabeth M. Rixford, "D. A. C. Book," 1931.
44 to 48 generations—Family Records.

PEDIGREE B

("Colonial Families," 1928, pages 26-28)

1. A Danish Knight, founder of the line.
2. Gunnora, his dau., became the wife of Richard, Duke of Normandy.
3. Richard, Duke of Normandy, son and heir of Richard, Duke of Normandy, and Gunnora, his wife, was the father of *Richard,* Duke of Normandy, who, dying without issue, was succeeded in the dukedom by his brother Robert.
4. Robert, Duke of Normandy, son of Richard, Duke of Normandy, was known as Robert the Devil.
5. William, Duke of Normandy, and King of England, was surnamed the Conqueror, the son of Robert, Duke of Normandy. (See William the Conqueror I.)
6. Gundred, dau. of William the Conqueror, was m., in France, to William de Warren, first Earl of Warren and Surrey, who accompanied the Conqueror to England, and was the recipient of bounteous favors at his hands. (See Warren Pedigree 5-15, Stanley 11.)

Oscar A. Rixford, 34th in direct descent from (1) A Danish Knight.

PEDIGREE C

Generations 1-6 same as House of Capet 1-6. (See House of Capet.)

7. ·HUGH, Earl of Vermandois, was son of Henry I, King of France, and brother of Philip, King of France. He was fifth Earl of Vermandois, by right of his wife Adela, who was the dau. and heiress of Herbert, fourth Earl of Vermandois. (See Vermandois I.)

8. ·ISABEL, dau. of Hugh the Great and Adela (dau. of the fourth Earl of Vermandois), was m. to William de Warren, second Earl of Warren and Surrey, in England. Through this alliance, the Warrens were connected with the bloodroyal of France. (See Warren Pedigree 6.)

Oscar³ A. Rixford is 29th in direct descent from Henry I, King of France.

PEDIGREE D

(Descent of Gundred, daughter of William the Conqueror, the wife of William, first Earl of Warren and Surrey, from the Emperor Charlemagne, most illustrious member of the Carolingian dynasty, which appears in history in the year 613, and gained the throne of France in 751, holding it for more than two hundred years, or until 987, when it was ousted by the Capetian dynasty.)

1. ·PEPIN I, who d. in 640, was the founder of the line. He was mayor of the palace to the youthful Dagobert I, whom Clothaire II had placed over the kingdom of Austrasia. He returned from Aquitaine (where he had sought refuge when Dagobert became sole king in 629), at the latter's death (639), and governed Austrasia, in Sigebert's name, until his death in the following year.

2. ·BEGGA, dau. of Pepin I, m. Adalgiselus, son of Arnolf, Bishop of Metz, and was the mother of Pepin II.

3. ·PEPIN II, son of Adalgiselus and Begga, was for many decades almost the entire master of Gaul, extending widely the Frankish suzerainty. He was a great churchman, and did much to spread Christianity. He d. Dec. 16, 714.

4. ·CHARLES MARTEL, 688-741, Frankish ruler, was a natural son of Pepin II, and one of the most famous figures in medieval history; he d. at Quierzy, Oct. 22, 741, shortly after having divided the Frankish kingdom between his two sons. He was a fearless and able leader, and under his rule vast strides were made in the system of government, and Christianity was spread to a greater extent than ever before. The deed of conquest and bravery of Charles Martel and his grandson, Charlemagne, are immortalized in the Chansons de Geste, where, however, the two are often confused, so striking were the points of resemblance in their characters. To the elder of his two sons, Charles Martel gave Austrasia, Alemania, and Thuringia, with suzerainty over Bavaria; the younger, Pepin, received Neustria, Burgundy, and Provence.

5. ·PEPIN, son of Charles Martel, surnamed the Short, d. in 768. In 747 the abdication of his brother, Carloman, left Pepin sole master of the Frankish kingdom, although he was not its king. In 751 he removed the feeble Childeric III from the throne to a monastery, and had himself crowned by St. Boniface, a ceremony new to France, which had hitherto elected its monarchs, and which gave him an

immense prestige. His reign was marked by many important religious and civil events, and he headed many notable ecclesiastical reforms. Pepin d. on Sept. 24, 768, leaving two sons: *Charles* (Charlemagne), and *Carloman.*

6. ·CHARLEMAGNE (Charles the Great), Roman Emperor, and King of the Franks, was the elder son of Pepin the Short, King of the Franks, and Bertha or Bertrade, dau. of Charibett, Count of Laon. Some authorities give the date of his birth as Apr. 3, 742. On the death of his brother, Carloman, in Dec., 771, Charlemagne was at once recognized as King of all the Franks. In 775, after conquering Desiderius, King of the Lombards, he took to himself the title of King of the Lombards, to which he added the dignity of "Patrician of the Romans," which had been granted to his father. In 800, Charlemagne entered Rome for the stated purpose of restoring discipline in the church, in which strife was rampant. His interest in ecclesiastical affairs was continuous. On Christmas Day, 800, he was crowned in St. Peter's by Pope Leo III, Emperor and Augustus, amid the acclamations of the crowd. For several decades previous he had been the real ruler of Rome, however. His rule was well ordered, and everywhere beneficial, and under it great progress was made in civilization. In 806, he made a division of his territories among ·his three legitimate sons, which, however, was nullified by the death of Pepin in 810, and Charles in the following year. He then named the remaining son, Louis, as his successor. On Jan. 28, 814, he d., and on the same day his body was bur. in the Church of St. Mary, at Aix.

He was a regular observer of religious rites, and a generous almsgiver. Charlemagne took a prominent part in the theological controversies of the time, and was responsible for the addition of the clause filioque in the Nicene Creed. Innumerable legends have grown up around Charlemagne, in which he is represented as a warrior performing superhuman feats, a ruler dispensing perfect justice, and even as a martyr to the cause of religion.

7. ·LOUIS I, surnamed "The Pious," Roman Emperor, third son of the Emperor Charlemagne and his wife Hildegarde, was b. in Chasseneuil, in Central France, in 778. He was prominent in ecclesiastical affairs, although an able military leader, and earned the title of "Pious" by his attempt to purify and reform monastic life, and by his great liberality to the church. In 819 he m. Judith, dau. of Welf I, Count of Bavaria, who in 823 bore him a son, *Charles,* after called the Bald. He d. June 20, 840.

8. ·CHARLES THE BALD, Roman Emperor and King of the West Franks, was the son of Louis I and Judith, and was b. in 823. In 840 he m. Ermuntrude, dau. of the Count of Orleans, and she d. in 869. He was a prince, of excellent education, and a friend of the church. Opinons differ widely as to his ability as a military leader and ruler.

9. ·JUDITH, dau. of Charles the Bald, m. Baldwin I, of Flanders. (See Ancient Counts of Flanders I.)

10. Generations 10-16 same as Ancient Counts of Flanders 2-8. (See Counts of Flanders.)

17. ·GUNDRED, dau. of William the Conqueror and Maud of Flanders, his wife, became the wife of William (2) de Warren, first Earl of Warren and Surrey, in England. (See Warren Pedigree V, William the Conqueror II, Stanley 11.)

F. Phelps Leach, brother of the Author, is 44th in direct descent from (1 Pedigree C) Pepin, who d. in 640.

AQUITAINE

Arms—*D'or a l'aigle de sin.; a la bord. d'azur semee de fleurs-de-lis de champ.* (Or, an eagle vert; a bordure azure semee of fleurs-de-lis of the field.)

The name Aquitaine is probably a form of Auscetani, which in turn is a lengthened form of Ausces and is thus cognate with the words Basque and Wasconia (Gascony). The extent of this ancient Province of France has varied considerably. About the time of Julius Cæsar, Aquitaine comprised that part of Gaul lying between the Pyrenees and the Garonne, but during the time of the Roman Emperor Augustus it included the whole of Gaul south and west of the Loire and the Allier. Parts of it were held by the Visigoths for a time, but the Frankish Clovis took possession in 507. In 781 Charlemagne gave Aquitaine (then referred to as a kingdom) to his young son Louis. When Louis became Emperor he gave Aquitaine to his son Pepin. A little before 845 the title Duke of Aquitaine was revived, and in 893 King Charles III ordered that Count Rainulf II, who then held Aquitaine, should be poisoned, after which the King bestowed the duchy upon William the Pious, Count of Auvergne, founder of the Abbey of Cluny. He was succeeded by his nephew, Count William II, in 918, and there followed a long line of dukes, among whom William IV fought against Hugh Capet, King of France; William VI added Gascony; and William IX became famous as a crusader and troubadour.

William X, who died in 1137, had a daughter, Eleanor, who married (first) Louis VII, King of France, from whom she was divorced. She married (second) in 1152, Henry II, of England. (See Royal Descent No. 23.)

Mary-Elizabeth L. Rixford and Oscar Theodore Rixford are 27th in direct descent from William X, Duke of Aquitaine.

ANGOULEME

("Colonial Families," 1928, page 109)

Angouleme is a city in southwestern France, capital of the Department of Charente, formerly the old Province Angoumois, of which also it was the capital. The Countship of Angouleme dated from the ninth century, the most important of the early counts being William Taillefer.

1. WULGRIN, Count of Perigord and Angouleme, d. in 886. He m. Rogerlinde, dau. of Bernard, Duke of Toulouse.
2. ALDWIN, Count of Angouleme, d. in 916, and was succeeded in the Countship of Angouleme by William Taillefer. (See Taillefer I.)

Mrs. Henrietta Read Buker is 35th in direct descent from (1) Wulgrin.

MARY ELIZABETH RIXFORD

S H (Y) 3/C

TOWER CONTROL OPERATOR, U.S.N.T.S.
QUONSET POINT, R. I., 1944

OPERATIONS, N.A.A.F.
GROTON, CONN., 1945

OSCAR THEODORE RIXFORD
RADAR MAN 3/C on the
U. S. S. Quincy, HEAVY CRUISER
ON BOTH INVASIONS IN FRANCE

ANJOU

("Colonial Families," 1928, page 111)

Arms—Per fesse argent and gules, over all an escarbuncle knobbed and flory or.

Ancient Counts
of
Anjou

    Anjou is the old name of a French territory, the political origin of which is traced to the ancient Gallic state of the Andes, on the line of which was organized, after the conquest by Julius Cæsar, the Roman civitas of the Andecair. This was afterwards preserved as an administrative district under the Franks with the name first of Pagus, then of Comitatus, or Countship of Anjou. It occupied the greater part of what is now Maine-et-Loire, and included other territory to the North, South, and East.

1. ·FULK THE GREAT, Count of Anjou, being stung with remorse for some wicked action, went on a pilgrimage to Jerusalem and was scourged before the Holy Sepulchre with broom twigs, plant-de-genet. Thereafter the family used the name Plantagenet.
2. FULK THE RED, d. in 938.
3. FULK II, surname "The Good," m. Gerverga, surname unknown.
4. GEOFFREY I received for gallant services a grant from King Robert of the offices of Seneschal of France. He m. Adelais, of Vermandois, dau. of Robert, Count of Troyes.
5. FULK III, surname "The Blac," Count of Anjou.
6. ERMENGARD, dau. and heiress of Fulk III, m. Geoffrey, Count of Gastinois (surnamed Ferole).
7. FULK IV, son of Ermengard and Geoffrey, Count of Gastinois, succeeded as Count of Anjou.
8. ERMENGARD, dau. of Fulk IV, m. (1) William, Duke of Aquitaine; (2) Alan, Count of Bretaign.
9. FULK V, son of Ermengard, became Count of Anjou. He m. (1) Ermengard, dau. of Helias, Count of Maine.
10. · GEOFFREY, Count of Anjou, m., in 1127, Maud (some records say Matilda), dau. and heiress of Henry I. (See Royal Descent No. 22.)

    Elizabeth-Mary L. and Oscar[4] Theodore Rixford, grandchildren of the Author, 38th in direct descent from (1) Fulk the Great, Count of Anjou.

BASKERVILLE

Arms—Argent, a chevron gules between three hurts.

Crest—A wolf's head erased argent, holding in its mouth a broken spear, staff or, head argent, imbued gules.

Motto—*Spero ut fidelis* (I hope in order to be faithful).

The surname Baskerville originated in Bascreville, now Bacqueville, in the arrondissement of Dieffe, Department of Seine Inferieure, Normandy. The founder of the English family came in with the Conqueror, and is recorded on the Roll of Battle Abbey. The family was for many generations after the Conquest one of the most important in England. ("Colonial Families," 1928, pages 177-179.)

1. ·RAUFF BASKERVILLE, of Eardisley, County Hereford, in the time of Henry II, was living in 1194. He m. Anne St. Owen.
2. ·SIR ROGER BASKERVILLE, son of Rauff and Anne (St. Owen) Baskerville, m. Bridget de Gros.
3. ·WALTER BASKERVILLE, of Eardisley, son of Sir Roger and Bridget (de Gros) Baskerville, m. Elizabeth Penbrugge, dau. of Sir Richard Penbrugge.
4. ·WALTER BASKERVILLE, living in 1272, son of Walter and Elizabeth (Penbrugge) Baskerville, m. Susanna Crigdon, dau. of Sir John Crigdon.
5. ·SIR RICHARD BASKERVILLE, third son of Walter and Susanna (Crigdon) Baskerville, was high sheriff of Herefordshire in the eighth year of Edward II. He m. —— Solers. They had a son, *William*.
6. ·SIR WILLIAM BASKERVILLE, son of Sir Richard Baskerville, d. about the twelfth year of Edward II. He m. Sibilla Corbet, dau. of Peter Corbet, of Caus.
7. ·SIR RICHARD BASKERVILLE, son of Sir William and Sibilla (Corbet) Baskerville, d. about the fifteenth year of Edward III (1342); having m. in 1340, Jane Payntz., dau of Sir Nicholas Payntz or Paynings.
8. ·RICHARD BASKERVILLE, son of Sir Richard and Jane (Payntz) Baskerville, m. Isabella Hampton, dau. of Sir Richard Hampton.
9. ·RICHARD BASKERVILLE, son of Richard and Isabella (Hampton) Baskerville, d. Sept. 16, 1394. He m. Joan Everingham, dau. of Adam Everingham.

10. ·SIR JOHN BASKERVILLE, son of Richard and Joan (Everingham) Baskerville, m. Elizabeth Brugge, dau. and heir of John Brugge, of Letton and Staunton.
11. ·RALPH BASKERVILLE, second son of Sir John and Elizabeth (Brugge) Baskerville, b. Oct. 21, 1410; m. Anne Blackett, dau. of Sir John Blackett.
12. ·JANE BASKERVILLE, dau. and heir of Ralph and Anne (Blackett) Baskerville, m. Simon Milbourne, and had *Blanche,* and twelve other daus. (See Milbourne III.)
12. SIR JAMES BASKERVILLE, son of Sir John· and Elizabeth (Touchett) Baskerville, was sheriff of Hereford; was made Knight Banneret for extraordinary valor at the Battle of Stoke, 1487; and Knight of the Bath at the coronation of Henry VII. He m. Katherine Devereux, dau. of Walter Devereux, Lord Ferrers, of Chartley, lineally descended from Edward I. (See Devereux XVII.)
13. ·SIR WALTER BASKERVILLE, son of Sir James and Katherine (Devereux) Baskerville, sheriff of Hereford, was made Knight of the Bath at the marriage of Prince Arthur in 1501. He m. Anne, dau. of Morgan ap Philip, of Pencoyd.
14. ·SIR JAMES BASKERVILLE, son of Sir Walter and Anne (of Morgan ap Philip) Baskerville, m. Elizabeth Breynton, dau. and coheir of John Breynton, by Sybil, dau. and coheir of Simon Milbourne, and sister of Blanche, who m. James Whitney.
15. · SYBIL BASKERVILLE, dau. of Sir James and Elizabeth (Breynton) Baskerville, m. Sir Robert Whitney, who d. Aug. 5, 1567, son of Robert and Margaret (Wye) Whitney. (See Whitney English Pedigree XIII.)
    See Royal Descent No. 35—Lottie E. Martin is 27th in direct descent from (No. 1) Rauff Baskerville. She was b. Sept. 4, 1865; d. Aug. 10, 1901; m. Oct. 30, 1900, at Clarenceville, Que., to F. Phelps Leach. She is the dau. of Arvide Martin (he was a merchant at Bedford, Que.) and Alvira Jane[10] (Phelps) Martin, her mother being the dau. of Nash David and Elizabeth (Hungerford) Phelps). She was a graduate of Feller Institute, Grand Ligne, Que. Mr. Leach received his education at Brigham Academy, Bakersfield, and St. Albans Academy, St. Albans, Vt. He is a life member of the New England Historical Genealogical Society. He is a member of the Vermont Society of Mayflower Descendants, State No. 42, General No. 9855. They had one dau., *Lottie Lydia,* b. Aug. 3, 1901; d. Oct. 21, 1901.

BEAUCHAMP
("Colonial Families," 1928, page 26)

Arms—Vair.

Normandy, using Beauchamp geographically, gave a surname to a notable family.

1. ·ROBERT BEAUCHAMP is the first of the Somerset family of whom mention is made. He was sheriff of the counties of Somerset and Dorset in 1163, and d. in 1212. He m., wife's name unknown.
2. ·ROBERT BEAUCHAMP, son of Robert Beauchamp, d. about 1252, leaving a son, who m., wife's name unknown.
3. ·ROBERT BEAUCHAMP, son of Robert Beauchamp, was the founder of the priory of Frithelstoke, in Devonshire. He left a son, *John,* who m., wife's name unknown.
4. ·JOHN BEAUCHAMP, son of Robert Beauchamp, m. Cicely, dau. and coheiress of Maud de Kyme (who was dau. of William de Ferrers, Earl of Derby), by her second husband, William de Vivonia.

5. ·JOHN BEAUCHAMP, son and heir of John and Cicely (de Vivonia) Beauchamp, had summons to Parliament, 1299 to 1337. He m., wife's name unknown.
6. ·JOHN BEAUCHAMP, son and heir of John, Baron Beauchamp, had summons to Parliament, 1337 to 1344. He m. Margaret, surname unknown. Children:
    1. ·*John*, who m. Alice, dau. of Thomas Beauchamp, Earl of Warwick; no issue.
    2. ·*Cecily*, of whom further.
    3. ·*Eleanor*, who m. —— Meriet.
7. ·CECILY BEAUCHAMP, dau. of John, third Lord de Beauchamp, and Margaret, his wife, m. (1) Sir Roger St. Maur, or Seymour, and brought the manors of Hache and Shepton-Beauchamps to the Seymours. (See Seymour 4-9, and Winslow No. 4.)

Mary-Elizabeth L. Rixford and Oscar Theodore Rixford are 28th in direct descent from Robert Beauchamp (1).

BRAY

Arms—Quarterly, 1st and 4th argent, a chevron between three eagles' legs sable, erased a la cuisse, their talons gules; 2nd and 3rd vair argent and azure, three bends gules.
Crest—A flax breaker or.

The surname BRAY originated from the parish of Bray, probably the one in the Department Eure, Normandy. The name of Sieur de Bray occurs on the Roll of Battle Abbey, among the associates in arms of William the Conqueror, 1066, and its right to be there is confirmed by the fact that William de Bray is one of the subscribing witnesses to the charger of 1088, conferred by the Conqueror on the abbey he had founded in commemoration of his triumph at Hastings. The family supplied sheriffs to Northamptonshire, Bedfordshire Bucks, etc., between 1202 and 1273. Ralph de Bray was sheriff of these counties between 1202 and 1234. ("Colonial Families," 1928, pages 179-180.)

1. ⸱WILLIAM DE BRAY, in 1260 was possessed of two knights' fees in Wollaston, Northamptonshire.
2. ·SIR ROBERT DE BRAY, son and successor of William de Bray, was summoned to attend Edward I in his wars in Scotland, and again by Edward II.
3. ·SIR JAMES DE BRAY, son of Sir Robert de Bray, lived in the reign of Richard I and of John.
4. ·ANSELM DE BRAY, son of Sir James de Bray.
5. ·WILLIAM DE BRAY, son of Anselm de Bray.
6. ·THOMAS DE BRAY, son of William de Bray, m. (2) —— Braxby.
7. ·WILLIAM BRAY, son of Thomas de Bray.
8. ·EDMUND BRAY, son of William Bray.
9. ·SIR RICHARD BRAY, son of Edmund Bray, was probably of the Privy Council of Henry VI, and was bur. in Worcester Cathedral. He m. (1) Margaret Sandes, dau. of John Sandes; (2) Joan, surname unknown. Sir Reginald Bray, son of Sir Richard and Joan Bray, was made a knight banneret at Bosworth in support of Henry VII, who gave him large grants of land, and conferred upon him the Order of the Bath and finally that of the Garter, but most of his estate he devised to his nephew.

10. · Sir John Bray, son of Sir Richard and Joan Bray, and younger brother of Sir Reginald, was bur. in the church at Chelsea. He had three sons and a dau., among whom was *Sir Edmund.*

11. Sir Edmund Bray, second son of John Bray, was one of the knights appointed to accompany Henry VIII to Calais to meet the King of France. He m. (1) Elizabeth Levell; and (2) Beatrice Shirley, of Wiston, Sussex, by whom the Surrey Brays. He was sheriff of Surrey and Sussex in 1539, and member of Parliament for Surrey under Queen Mary. He d. in 1588. The male line of his elder brother, heir of Sir Reginald, failed in the male line in the third generation. His younger brother, Reginald, founded the Gloucestershire Brays, of Barrington, etc.

1. · John Bray, of Westminster, "taylor," was probably of a line from a younger son of the Brays of Surrey. He m., but the name of his wife is unknown; he d. in 1615. As there was no law for parish registration until 1538, his parentage is probably not on record.

2. . Mary Bray, dau. of John Bray, was bapt. at St. Margaret's Church,˙ the official church of the British House of Commons, adjacent to Westminster Abbey, and was bur. at St. Margaret's, Sept. 25, 1629. She m. May 12 (license May 10), 1583, Thomas Whitney, of Lambeth Marsh, father of John Whitney, of Watertown, Massachusetts. (See Whitney, English Pedigree XV.)—See Royal Descent No. 37.

M. Lydia Phelps Buckland, children of Henry and Lydia Buckland, two sons, Arthur and Henry, are 11th in direct descent to (1) John Bray, of Westminster.

BULKELEY

Arms—Sable, a chevron between three bulls' heads cabossed argent.
Crest—Out of a ducal coronet or, a bull's head argent, armed of the first.
Motto—*Nec temere, nec timide.* (Neither rashly nor timidly.)

1. Robert de Buklogh, Lord of the Manor of Buklogh; in the reign of King John (1199-1216), Buclough; in 1120, Bucclogh; in County Chester, about nine miles northwest of Nantwich, Robert's ancestors, little known, were Lords of Buclough, in the reign of King John.

2. William de Bulkeley.

3. Robert de Bulkeley, m. a dau. of Butler, of Bewsey, in Warrington.

4. William de Bulkeley, 1302, m. Maude, dau. of Sir John Davenport.

5. Robert Bulkeley had Eaton in Davenham and Alstanton. He m. Agnes, surname unknown.

6. Peter Bulkeley, of Houghton, m. Nicola, dau. and heir of Thomas Bird.

7. John Bulkeley, m. Arderne, dau. of John Fitley, of Shropshire.

8. Hugh Bulkeley, of Woore, m. Helen, dau. of Thomas Wilbraham, of Ware, in Shropshire.

9. Margery Bulkeley, dau. of Hugh and Helen (Wilbraham) Bulkeley, according to Warren pedigree, m. Sir Lawrence Warren. (See Warren 14, and Stanley No. 11.)

Adelbert Horace Leach, youngest brother of the Author, 27th in direct descent from (1) Robert de Buklogh.

HOUSE OF CAPET

Arms—Azure, semee of fleurs-de-lis or.

𝕳𝖔𝖚𝖘𝖊 𝖔𝖋 𝕮𝖆𝖕𝖊𝖙

For nearly nine centuries, the kings of France and many of the rulers of the most powerful fiefs in that country belonged to the family of Capet, and it mingled naturally with several of the other royal races of Europe. The original significance of the name remains in dispute, but the first of the family to whom it was applied was Hugh, who was elected King of the Franks in 987. The real founder of the house, however, was Robert the Strong, who received from Charles the Bald, King of the Franks, the countships of Anjou and Blois, and who is sometimes called Duke, and he exercised some military authority in the district between the Seine and the Loire. According to Aimoin of Saint German-de-Pres, and the chronicler, Richer, he was a Saxon, but historians question this statement. Descent is traced as follows:

1. ROBERT THE STRONG, Count of Anjou and Blois, sometimes called Duke of Anjou and Blois.
2. ROBERT, second Count or Duke of Anjou and Blois, also King Robert I of France, or more accurately, King of the Franks, was the younger son of Robert the Strong, Count of Anjou, and the brother of Odo (or Eudes), who became King of the Western Franks in 988. He was himself crowned King of the Franks at Reims, June 20, 922, but Charles III marched against him, and he was killed in a battle near Soissons, June 15, 923.
3. HUGH THE GREAT, son of Robert I, became Duke of France, and the Franks of Burgundy, and Count of Paris, his domain extending from the Loire to the frontiers of Picardy; was one of the founders of the Capetian house and its power in France. He m. Hedwiga, dau. of Henry I of Germany. He had a son, *Hugh,* of whom further.
4. HUGH CAPET, son of Hugh the Great, was crowned King of the Franks at Reims, in 987, reigned to 996. The house of Capet continued to rule in France from 987 to 1328. He m. Adelaide, dau. of William III, Duke of Aquitaine. (See Counts of Flanders No. 7 and Henry I, King of England.)

   Oscar A. Rixford is 33rd in direct descent from No. 1 Robert the Strong.

HOUSE OF CASTILE
("Colonial Families," 1928, page 116)

Arms—Gules, a tower triple-towered or.

Crest—The tower.

Castile
ANCIENT ROYAL ARMS

An ancient kingdom of Spain, Castile is said to have derived its name from the numerous frontier forts (castilles) erected in the Middle Ages as a defence against the Moors. The transformation of Castile from a small county in the north of what is now old Castile into an independent monarchy was one of the decisive events in the re-conquest of Spain from the Moors. Ferdinand I of Castile (1035-65), by his marriage with Sancha (Sancia), widow and heiress of the last king of Leon, was enabled to unite Leon and Castile in a single kingdom with its capital at Burgos. The arms described herewith are the ancient royal arms of Castile.

1. FERDINAND I, m. Sancha, heiress of Leon. The had a son, *Alphonso,* of whom further.
2. ALPHONSO VI, son of Ferdinand I and Sancha, reigned in Castile from 1065 to 1109. He m. Constance, dau. of Robert, Duke of Burgundy.
3. URRACA, dau. of Alphonso VI and Constance, m. (2) Alfonso I of Aragon and VII of Castile and Leon. They were the parents of *Alfonso,* of whom further.
4. ·ALFONSO VIII, son of Alfonso I of Aragon and VII of Castile and Leon, and of Urraca, reigned in Castile from 1126 to 1157. He m. Berengaria, dau. of Raymond of Barcelona. They were the parents of *Ferdinand II,* of whom further.
5. ·FERDINAND II, son of Alfonso VIII and Berengaria, reigned from 1157 to 1188. He m. Urraca, dau. of Alfonso I of Portugal. (See line of Portugal VI.) They were the parents of *Alfonso IX,* of whom further.
6. ALFONSO IX, son of Ferdinand II and Urraca of Portugal, reigned in Castile from 1188 to 1230. He m. Berengaria, surname unknown.
7. FERDINAND III of Castile, son of Alfonso IX and Berengaria, reigned from 1230 to 1252. He m. (2) Joanna, dau. of Count of Aumale and Ponthieu. They were the parents of *Eleanor,* of whom further.

8. ELEANOR, dau. of Ferdinand III of Castile and Joanna, m. King Edward I of England. (See Royal Descent of Elizabeth M. Rixford No. 6; Edward 1.).

Edwin Francis Currie, grandson of Nash David and Elizabeth Hungerford Phelps, is 30th in direct descent from Ferdinand I.

CHENEY FAMILY

Cheney.

Ancestral line to Sir John Cheney, Knight, of Fen Ditton, County Cambridge, England.

1. · SIR JOHN CHENEY, Knight, of Fen Ditton, County Cambridge, England; m. Katherine, dau. and coheir of Sir Laurence Pabenham, Knight, by Elizabeth, dau. and coheir of Sir John Engaine, Knight.
2. · LAWRENCE CHENEY, of Fen Ditton, m. Elizabeth, dau. of John Cockayne, of Hatley.
3. · SIR JOHN CHENEY, Knight, of Fen Ditton, m. Elizabeth, dau. and coheir of Sir Thomas Rempston, Knight.
4. · WILLIAM CHENEY, of Thorngumbald in Holderness, County York, j.u., d. 1 Edward VI; m. Anne, dau. and coheir of John Holme of Paul Holme, County York.
5. · WILLIAM CHENEY, bur. at Boston, 43 Eliz.; m. Frances, natural dau. of Sir Thomas Cheney, K. G. Lord Warden of the Cinque Ports; bur. at Boston. Will dated Nov. 25, 1604; proved Aug. 4, 1608.
6. · JOHN CHENEY, of Bennington, b. Boston; mar. lic. Nov. 28, 1614, then ae. 46; bur. Mar. 16, 1623-4; m. (1) Elizabeth, dau. of ——; d. between June and Nov., 1614; m. (2) Alice, widow of —— Skiner, of Frieston, ae. 46 in 1614; rem. Richard Kelsey, Fishtoft (mar. lic. Aug. 10, 1627), 2nd wife.
7. · WILLIAM CHENEY, bapt. at Bennington, Feb. 5, 1598-9; d. June 30, 1667, Roxbury, Mass.; m. Margaret —— in England and settled in Roxbury, Mass. In Roxbury he served as constable. He was the policeman on disagreeable occasions; the messenger of the selectmen sometimes; but his chief care was collecting taxes. He had a "rate" committed to him, with a sum to be obtained from each adult male inhabitant; and he had authority to pay out sums of money on selectmen's orders. At the end of the year he made a detailed report. William

Cheney was one of the two constables in 1654-5 and his final account was approved Feb. 13, 1655-6. Jan. 19, 1656-7 he was elected a member of the board of selectmen. Jan. 18, 1663, he was made one of a committee to inspect Peter Gardner's "leanetoo" and "the fence that doth range from it" to see that they did "not intrench upon the highway." He was chosen one of the trustees of the Free School in 1664, and on the town records we find him written down "as Feoffee" in an agreement touching some money belonging to the school fund and affixing (his X mark) to the page along with half a dozen regular signatures Jan. 25, 1666-7. He was a member of the Roxbury, Mass., Militia in 1647. He was a resident in Roxbury before 1640. Then had a dau., Ellen.

8. ELLEN CHENEY, b. in England about 1626; m. Mar. 20, 1642-3, at Roxbury, Mass., Capt. Humphrey Johnson, b. about 1620.
9. MEHITABLE JOHNSON, b. 1644; d. Aug. 4, 1689; m. Oct. 31, 1660, Samuel Hinsdale.
10. MEHITABLE HINSDALE, dau. of Samuel and Mehitable (Johnson) Hinsdale, was b. Oct. 18, 1663, at Medfield; m. Obadiah Dickinson.
11. MEHITABLE DICKINSON, b. 1696; m. Jan. 26, 1715-6, at probably Deerfield, Mass., Nathaniel Frary, b. Nov. 29, 1675; d. Apr. 30, 1737.
12. EUNICE FRARY, b. Nov. 30, 1721; d. Oct. 28, 1813; m. May 26, 1743, at Deerfield, Mass., Aaron Field, b. Mar. 17, 1721-2; d. Mar. 17, 1800.
13. CHLOE FIELD, b. Dec. 29, 1743; d. Apr. 10, 1781; m. Nov., 1764, at Greenfield, Mass., Samuel Shattuck, b. Sept. 18, 1741; d. Sept. 1, 1827.
14. CHLOE SHATTUCK, b. Nov. 22, 1766; d. Jan. 22, 1845; m. Nov. 17, 1785, at Greenfield, Mass., Ephraim Leach, b. Dec., 1761; d. Feb. 28, 1840.
15. TERTIUS LEACH, b. Nov. 21, 1786; d. Feb. 4, 1864; m. Jan. 1, 1812, at Sheldon, Vt., Sophia Hawley, b. Aug. 17, 1795; d. Jan. 7, 1879.
16. TERTIUS HAWLEY LEACH, b. Mar. 19, 1813; d. Sept. 19, 1881; m. Feb. 28, 1835, at Sheldon, Vt., Orissa Fanton, b. May 1, 1812; d. June 24, 1890.
17. DEFORACE ATWOOD[8] LEACH (*Tertius Hawley*[7], *Tertius*[6], *Ephraim*[5], *Sergt. Solomon*[4], *John*[3], *Giles*[2], *Lawrence*[1]), twin brother of Horace Brayton Leach, b. at Sheldon, Vt., Sept. 25, 1836; d. at Eden, Vt., Dec. 13, 1906. He m. at Lowell, Vt., Mar. 10, 1856, Ellen M. Wakefield, b. Feb. 9, 1837; d. at Eden, Vt., Sept. 14, 1910, dau. of Calvin and Marian Wakefield. Children b. in Lowell, Vt.
   1. Henry Deforace[9], b. Feb. 4, 1858; m. Elizabeth LeVine. Had four sons and two daus.
   2. Hattie S., b. Nov. 9, 1867; m. Sherman Cammett, Newport, Vt. Children: Horace B., Sherman, Bertie E., Perley P., Dell A.
   3. Brayton Horace, b. Dec. 21, 1870; d. May 20, 1920; m. May 24, 1898, Lillian Tracy, b. June 4, 1880, and had one child: Roy Nelson, b. Oct. 30, 1899, who m. Nov. 10, 1920, Beatrice Gillen, b. Oct. 23, 1899, and have one son, Lloyd Leach.

References: 1 to 12 generations—Records of Elizabeth M. Rixford.
13 to 15 generations—"Leach Genealogy," by F. Phelps Leach.
16 to 17 generations—Family Record.

CHENEY FAMILY—Pope
Part 1, William of Roxbury and His Descendants

(Page 17) WILLIAM CHENEY was a very early resident of Roxbury in the Colony of Massachusetts Bay, in New England (now included in the city of Boston). The oldest records of that town which have been brought down to modern times are contained in a volume whose opening sentence says that The Book Was bought in

1639 for the purpose of recording various matters relating to the inhabitants. . . . These records demonstrate the fact that "William Cheney was a land-holder and resident in Roxbury before 1640"; and they do no more.

The settlement at Roxbury was begun in 1630, a little later than those at Dorchester and Boston; but there was no church organization for a year (page 18) and no pastor till 1632. In the records of the church of Roxbury, written by the first pastor, who was that remarkable "Apostle to the Indians," Rev. John Elliot, there is a very interesting list of the members, giving many personal sketches.

(Page 20)   And an acre of land commonly called the wolf trapp bought of Humphrey Johnson lying on the north of the land of John Gorton, and west upon the highway. And halfe of sixteene accres of woodland lately the land of Richard Sutton, but bought by him of John Johnson.

The deed of this "Wolf Trapp" is not on record, though there are deeds recorded whereby lands adjoining this piece were conveyed and called "Wolf Trap," showing that the name applied to quite a large tract, perhaps a valley where many wolfes had been taken. We find two deeds of William Cheney's, one of land he bought, the other of some he sold; and we give them here:

"29.3.1648. Humphrey Johnson of Roxbury granted unto Willim Chenie of Roxbury twenty Acres of land in Roxbury bounded with the highway that leads to the fresh meddow on 'the East, the land of the heires of John Levens south, the Schoole lands & Richard Peacocks north west, & Giles Pason & the highway Northerly & This was by an absolute deed of sale 2 (1) 1647. Wth all priviledgs there to belonging.

HUMPHREY JOHNSON and a seale.

Sealed & dd in P'sence
of WILLIAM ASPINWALL
NICHOLAS BUTLER."

William Cheney of Roxbury and Margaret his wife sell to John Peirpoint "One entire quarter or fourth part of a Water Mill in Roxbury, and one quarter part of a piece of Marish ground esteemed to be one Acre more or less being all that is his, or that belongeth to his said part of the said Mill."

(Page 22)   One of the offices that called for promptness and energy and for good faculty of dealing with men was the position of constable. He was the policeman on disagreeable occasions; the messenger of the selectmen sometimes; but his chief care was collecting taxes. He had a "rate" committed to him, with a sum to be obtained from each adult male inhabitant; and he had authority to pay out sums of money on selectmen's orders. At the end of the year he made a detailed report. If he did not possess a good education he must have a sharp faculty of reckoning and a strong memory of names and numbers. William Cheney was one of the two constables in 1654-5 and his final account was approved Feb. 13, 1655-6.

But the citizens were not content to have him simply perform the toilsome work of a constable. Jan. 19, 1656-7, he was elected a member of the board of selectmen, associated with men of education and rank.

ELEVENTH GENERAL CONGRESS OF MA

Septen

When the Vermont Society was admitted to the National Society those who attended from the Vermont Society were the Founder and Governor, Mrs. Guy B. Horton of Montpelier; Deputy Governor and Treasurer, Dr. Henry A. Elliot; and the Secretary, Mrs. Elizabeth M. Rixford.

At this Congress, Mrs. Horton was elected Governor General of the Vermont Society and Dr. Henry A. Elliot was elected Deputy General.

Those from the Vermont Society who attended the Twelfth General Congress, September 2, 3 and 4, 1930, were the Governor, Mrs. Guy B. Horton; Secretary, Mrs. Elizabeth M. Rixford; Historian, Mrs. Samuel H. Mills; Treasurer, Dr. Forrest A. Slader. At this Congress Mrs. Horton was reelected Governor General for Vermont and Mrs. Mills was elected Deputy Governor.

At the annual meeting held at Montpelier, February 26, 1931, Mrs. Horton withdrew as Governor. Dr. Forrest A. Slader was elected Governor of the Vermont Society and Mrs. M. C. Lovell of Springfield was elected Deputy Governor.

The General Congress is held at Plymouth, Mass., every three years.

YFLOWER DESCENDANTS AT PLYMOUTH, MASS.

ber 5 to 8, 1927

Jan. 18, 1663, he was made one of a committee to inspect Peter Gardner's "leanetoo" and "the fence that doth range from it" to see that they did "not intrench upon the highway."

We have already seen that he was chosen one of the feofees of the Free School in 1664; and on the town records we find him written down "as Feoffee" in an agreement touching some money belonging to the school fund, and affixing (his $\times$ mark) to the page along with half a dozen regular signatures, Jan. 25, 1667-7.

May 23, 1666, he was made a "freeman of the Colony," which made him eligible to colonial office and capable of voting on matters relating to the general government. But he did not live to make use of this franchise. He fell sick in the spring of 1666-7, as we learn from the opening phrases of his will; and after a few weeks he passed beyond the reach of care or pain. The town clerk made this entry in his list of persons deceased:

"William Cheney aged 63 yeares died June the 30 day, 1667"; and the hand of Rev. John Eliot or Rev. Samuel Danforth wrote in the church book among the burials: "1667. Moneth 5 day 2 Willian Cheany sen."

His will is in the hand of some expert penman, one of the pastors, it may be, or some tried friend and associate in public affairs; but though he could not pen it, he gave it marks of individuality, showing that he really composed it.

(Page 32)   Children of William and Margaret Cheney:

1. ELLEN[2], b. in England about 1626; m. at Roxbury, Mass., Mar. 20, 1642-3, Humphrey Johnson, a son of John and grandson of Isaac Johnson who was one of the chief men in the founding of Roxbury. Humphrey Johnson resided in Roxbury many years, then removed to Hingham; was a man of affairs, a soldier in Capt. Isaac Johnson's Co. in the war against King Philip in 1675.
   Children:
   (1) *Mehitable Johnson,* bapt. at Roxbury, Mar. 29, 1646.
   (2) *Martha Johnson,* bapt. Sept. 12, 1647.
   (3) *Deborah Johnson,* bapt. Jan. 20, 1649.

Marguerite Cheney Burges, widow of Wm. Cheney, Roxbury, 1639.

JAMES CHILTON, WIFE SUSANNAH AND DAUGHTER MARY OF THE MAYFLOWER

1. JAMES CHILTON, Passenger on the *Mayflower,* d. on Cape Cod soon after signing the Mayflower Compact. His wife, Susannah, d. soon after landing at Plymouth. His dau., Mary, reputed to be the first Pilgrim woman to step on Plymouth rock, m. John Winslow and was the grandmother of Hannah Latham Washburn, widow of Joseph W.[1] ("Society of Colonial Wars," page 558)—James Chilton, Signer of Mayflower Compact on the *Mayflower;* was in Capt. Miles Standish Company.

2. MARY CHILTON, of the *Mayflower,* d. in Boston, 1679, and is bur. in Kings Chapel Burying Ground. She m. Dec. 10, 1624, John Winslow, b. Apr., 1597, in England; d. 1673-4.

3. SUSANNAH WINSLOW, m. 1649, Robert Latham.
4. HANNAH LATHAM, b. Bridgewater, Mass.; d. Apr. 14, 1750; m. at East Bridgewater, Mass., Joseph Washburn, b. July 7, 1683.
5. HEPZIBAH WASHBURN, b. Bridgewater, Mass.; d. Apr. 14, 1750, Bridgewater, Mass.; m. Sept. 8, 1702, at Bridgewater, Mass., Benjamin Leach, b. at West Bridgewater, Mass.; d. July 13, 1764.
6. HANNAH LEACH, b. Mar. 4, 1725; m. at Bridgewater, Mass., Aug. 6, 1743, Sergt. Soloman Leach, b. Feb. 19, 1712.
7. EPHRAIM LEACH, b. Dec., 1761; d. Feb. 28, 1840; m. Nov. 17, 1785, at Greenfield, Mass., Chloe Shattuck, b. Nov. 22, 1766; d. Jan. 22, 1845.
8. TERTIUS LEACH, b. Nov. 21, 1786; d. Feb. 4, 1864; m. Jan. 1, 1811, at Sheldon, Vt., Sophia Hawley, b. Aug. 17, 1795; d. Jan. 7, 1879.
9. TERTIUS HAWLEY LEACH, b. May 19, 1813; d. Sept. 19, 1881; m. Feb. 28, 1833, at Sheldon, Vt., Orisa Fanton, b. May 17, 1812; d. June 24, 1890.
10. HORACE BRAYTON LEACH, b. Sept. 25, 1836; d. May 6, 1919; m. Sept. 8, 1863, at Stanbridge, Que., Caroline Alexandria Phelps, b. July 3, 1840; d. Mar. 29, 1921.
11. FRANKIE ORISA LEACH, b. Oct. 11, 1870; m. June 5, 1895, at Fairfield, Vt., Homer Jessie Cutler, b. Jan. 5, 1870. Both living Jan. 1, 1932.
   Children (surname *Cutler*, b. at East Highgate, Vt.) :
      Horace Leach, b. Apr. 19, 1898; m. Dec. 22, 1919, Gertrude Sarah Loukes, b. at Highgate, Vt., Oct. 21, 1897. They have children:
      1. Earl James Cutler, b. May 19, 1922.
      2. Horace Leslie Cutler, b. July 14, 1923.
      Alberta Irene, b. Mar. 2, 1904.
   (All of generation No. 11 mentioned here living Jan. 1, 1932.)

   References: "Ebenezer Washburn, His Ancestors and Descendants."
               "Mayflower Descendants," Vol. 1 and Vol. 2.
               "Lawrence Leach of Salem, Mass., and His Descendants,"
                  Volumes 1, 2 and 3, by F. Phelps Leach.
               Records of Elizabeth M. Rixford.

   The following members of the Vermont Society of Mayflower Descendants trace their ancestry to James Chilton, wife Susannah, and daughter Mary:

      Miss Alberta Irene Cutler, East Highgate, Vt., State No. 24, Gen. No. 9596; noble grand of Highgate Rebecca Lodge.
      Mrs. Frankie Leach Cutler, East Highgate, Vt., State No. 23, Gen. No. 9595.
      Mr. F. Phelps Leach, East Highgate, Vt., State No. 42, Gen. No. 9855.
      Oscar T. Rixford, 4th, East Highgate, Vt., State No. 73, Gen. No. 10723.
      Miss Jessie A. Southard, Fairfax, Vt., State No. 39, Gen. No. 9771.
      *Mrs. Elizabeth M. Rixford, East Highgate, Vt., State No. 18, Gen. No. 7881.

      * Charter member.

FRANCIS COOKE, MAYFLOWER PASSENGER

("The Bassett-Preston Ancestry,"—Preston, page 71)

10. · FRANCIS[1] COOKE was born in England about 1583. He went to Leyden, Holland, where he was married June 30, 1603. The marriage record at Leyden reads: "Francis Cooke, wool comber, unmarried, from England, with Hester Mayhieu, unmarried, from Canterbury, Eng., accompanied by Jennie Mayhieu, her mother, and Jennie Mayhieu, her sister." The Mayhieus were Walloons and

THE LEACH HOUSE ON SUMMER STREET

Built in 1679, one of the "Old Houses" still standing at Plymouth, Mass.

Huguenots. Francis and his son John were on the *Speedwell* when it sailed from Delftshaven, July 20, 1620, with some of the Pilgrims bound for America. At Southampton they joined the *Mayflower* and set sail on August 5. The *Speedwell* began to leak, but although the ships put into Dartmouth for repairs and sailed again August 21, new leaks compelled the *Speedwell* to return to London, with such immigrants as could not be taken in the *Mayflower,* which then went on alone. Francis and his son were on the *Mayflower,* and he was the seventeenth signer of the Mayflower Compact. His son John was living in 1694, probably the oldest male survivor of the *Mayflower.* His wife, Hester, and the rest of their children, came in the *Ann* in 1623. Winslow recorded "The wife of Francis Cooke being a Walloon, holds communion with the church at Plymouth, as she came from the French, by virtue of the communion of churches."

SERVICE

Francis Cook, 17th Signer of the Mayflower Compact, m. at Leyden, Holland, Hester Mahieu.
"King Philip's War," August 28, 1676, Francis Cook, Credit 2, items 04-04-04.

He was freeman, 1633; a member of Myles Standish's Company, 1643, and in the expedition against the Indians; on a committee to lay out roads in Plymouth. Bradford called him "a very old man" in 1650. He died April 7, 1663, aged 80, and was buried in the old Plymouth Burying Ground. His will of 1659 names his wife, Hester, and son, John, executors. An agreement of the heirs in June, 1666, showed the surviving children were John, Jacob, Hester Wright and Mary Thompson. Hester, his widow, died in 1675.

Children, four born in Leyden, one in Plymouth:
JANE, b. 1608; d. before 1666; m. 1627, Experience Mitchell.
JOHN, b. 1612; d. 1695; m. 1634, Sarah Warren (·Richard[1]).
JACOB, b. 1618; d. 1676; m. (1) ·Damaris Hopkins, 1646; (2)·Elizabeth (Lettice) Shurtleff.
HESTER, b. 1620; m. 1644, Richard[1] Wright.
·MARY, b. 1626; d. 1715; m. 1645, John[1] Thompson.

SEE THOMPSON

MARY[2] COOKE, m. John[1] Thompson.
JACOB THOMPSON, m. Abigail[3] Wadsworth.
HANNAH THOMPSON, m. Ebenezer[4] Reed.
BARNABAS REED, m. Silence[5] Sprague.
SARAH REED, m. John[7] Ford.
MEHITABLE FORD, m. Francis[7] Bassett.
CHARLES R. BASSETT, m. Elvira[7] Rogers.
EDWARD M. BASSETT, m. Annie R.[8] Preston.
References: "Munsey Hopkins Family," Lowell, 1920.

1. FRANCIS COOKE, b. in England about 1583; m. at Leyden, Holland, June 30, 1603, Hester Mayhieu, from Canterbury, England. He d. Apr. 7, 1663, and was bur. in the old Plymouth Burying Ground. His will of 1659 names his wife, Hester, and son, John, executors. An agreement of the heirs in June, 1666, showed the surviving children were: *John,*

Jacob, Hester Wright and Mary Thompson. Hester his widow, d. in 1675.
2. JANE COOKE, b. 1608; d. before 1666; m. 1627, Experience Mitchell.
3. ELIZABETH MITCHELL, b. 1629; m. 1645 at Duxbury, Mass., John² Washburn, who was b. about 1621.
4. JOSEPH³ WASHBURN, b. 1655 in Bridgewater, Mass.; m. at East Bridgewater, Mass., Hannah Latham.
5. HEPZIBAH WASHBURN, b. at West Bridgewater, Mass.; d. Apr. 14, 1750; m. Sept. 8, 1702, at Bridgewater, Mass., No. 20 Benjamin Leach, Esq., b. at West Bridgewater, Mass.; d. July 13, 1764.
6. HANNAH LEACH, b. Mar. 4, 1725, at West Bridgewater, Mass.; m. Aug. 6, 1743, at Bridgewater, Mass., Soloman Leach, b. Feb. 19, 1712.
7. EPHRAIM LEACH, b. Dec., 1761; d. Feb. 28, 1840; m. Nov. 17, 1785, at Greenfield, Mass., Chloe Shattuck, b. Nov. 22, 1766; d. Jan. 22, 1845.
8. TERTIUS LEACH, b. Nov. 21, 1786; d. Feb. 4, 1864; m. Jan. 1, 1811, at Sheldon, Vt., Sophia Hawley, b. Aug. 17, 1795; d. Jan. 7, 1879.
9. TERTIUS HAWLEY LEACH, b. May 19, 1813; d. Sept. 19, 1881; m. Feb. 28, 1835, at Sheldon, Vt., Orisa Fanton, b. May 17, 1812; d. June 24, 1890.
10. HORACE BRAYTON LEACH, b. Sept. 25, 1836; d. May 6, 1919; m. Sept. 8, 1863, at Stanbridge, Que., Caroline Alexandria Phelps, b. July 3, 1840; d. Mar. 29, 1921.
11. FAYETTE PHELPS LEACH, b. in Bakersfield, Vt., Nov. 17, 1864. He m. (1) Josie L. Brown, Sept. 3, 1887, b. at Sheldon, Vt., Feb. 3, 1870; d. at East Fairfield, Vt., Nov. 22, 1894. They had children:
  1. *Beatrice Josie,* b. Aug. 16, 1889, at Milton, Vt.; d. 1919; m. Apr. 27, 1914, Frank A. Young. One child:
    Kathleen Mary Young, b. Aug. 22, 1918.
  2. *Hazel May,* b. Oct. 14, 1891, at East Fairfield, Vt.; m. Oct. 26, 1914, James E. Allard. Children:
    (1) Viola Beatrice Allard, b. Aug., 1916.
    (2) James Leach Allard, b. June, 1918.
    (3) Conrad Milton Allard, b. June 5, 1928.
  Mr. Leach m. (2) Sept. 6, 1896, Emma L. McManimon, and had one dau.:
    Edith Emma, b. Sept. 16, 1897, at East Fairfield, Vt.; m. Aug. 22, 1917, Claude Clesson Macy. Children:
    (1) Fern Alice Macy, b. July 13, 1918.
    (2) Keith Sherwood Macy.
    (3) A dau., d. young.
    (4) Beverly, b. 1930.
  Mr. Leach m. (3) Oct. 30, 1900, Lottie E. Martin at Clarenceville, Que., b. Sept. 4, 1865; d. Aug. 10, 1901. They had one child:
    Lottie Lydia, b. Aug. 3, 1901; d. Oct 21, 1901.
  Mr. Leach is a member of the General Society of Mayflower, being General No. 9855, and also No. 42 of the Vermont Society of Mayflower Descendants. He is a life member of the New England Historic Genealogical Society, and for forty-one years has devoted much of his leisure time to genealogy. In 1924 he published "Hungerford Genealogy," first and second edition, and "Leach Genealogy," Volume I. In 1925 he published "Leach Genealogy," Volume II, and in 1926, "Leach Genealogy," Volume III.

Reference: "Lawrence Leach and His Descendants," by F. Phelps Leach.

The following members of the Vermont Society of Mayflower Descendants trace their ancestry to Francis Cooke:

Miss Stella Frankie Buker, Jeffersonville, Vt., State No. 79, Gen. No. 11012.

Adah E. G. Grant (Mrs. V. A.), Randolph, Vt., State No. 58, Gen. No. 8241.

Miss Fleda L. Grant, Randolph, Vt., State No. 59, Gen. No. 8242.

Mrs. Vollie H. Griffith, Danby, Vt., State No. 63, Gen. No. 10112.
Cora Baker Hunt (Mrs. Geo. W.), Antrim, N. H., State No. 65, Gen. No. 10427 (deceased).
Mrs. Edward B. Huling, Bennington, Vt., State No. 30, Gen. No. 9425.
Mr. F. Phelps Leach, East Highgate, Vt., State No. 42, Gen. No. 9855.
Ephraim Smith Read, Jeffersonville, Vt., State No. 25, Gen. No. 9597.
Miss Mary-Elizabeth L. Rixford, East Highgate, Vt., State No. 43, Gen. No. 9856.
Mabel A. Tabor (Mrs. H. G.), Danby, Vt., State No. 75, Gen. No. 10910.
*Mrs. Frederick C. Negus, Proctor, Vt., State No. 7, Gen. No. 5273.
*Dr. Percy M. Williams, Rutland, Vt., State No. 9, Gen. No. 4101.
*Mrs. O. M. Rowell, South Albany, Vt., (p. o., West Glover), State No. 11, Gen. No. 6565.
*Mrs. Elizabeth M. Rixford, East Highgate, Vt., State No. 18, Gen. No. 7881.
*Oscar A. Rixford, East Highgate, Vt., State No. 22, Gen. No. 9594.

* Charter member.

THE COMPACT

Signed in the Cabin of the "Mayflower," Nov. 11th, Old Style, Nov. 21st, New Style, 1620

"In the name of God, amen, we whose names are underwritten, the loyall subjects of our dread soveraigne Lord, King James, by the grace of God, of Great Britaine, Franc and Ireland king, defender of the faith, &c., haveing undertaken, for the glorie of God, and advancemente of the Christian faith, and honor of our king and countrie, a voyage to plant the first colonie in the northerne parts of Virginia, doe by these presents solemnly and mutualy in the presence of God, and one of another, covenant and combine ourselves together into a civill body politick, for our better ordering and preservation and furtherence of the ends aforesaid; and by vertue hereof to enacte, constitute and frame such just and equall laws, ordenances, acts, constitutions and offices, from time to time, as shall be thought most meete and convenient for the general good of the colonie, unto which we promise all due submission and obedience. In witness whereof we have hereunto subscribed our names at Cap-Codd the 11 of November, in the year of the raigne of our soveraigne lord, King James of England, Franc and Ireland the eighteenth, and of Scotland the fifty-fourth, ANo Dom 1620."

JOHN CARVER,	EDWARD TILLEY,	DEGORY PRIEST,
WILLIAM BRADFORD,	JOHN TILLEY,	THOMAS WILLIAMS,
EDWARD WINSLOW,	FRANCIS COOKE,	GILBERT WINSLOW,
WILLIAM BREWSTER,	THOMAS ROGERS,	EDMUND MARGESON,
ISAAC ALLERTON,	THOMAS TINKER,	PETER BROWN,
MYLES STANDISH,	JOHN RIDGDALE,	RICHARD BRITTERIDGE,
JOHN ALDEN,	EDWARD FULLER,	GEORGE SOULE,
SAMUEL FULLER,	JOHN TURNER,	RICHARD CLARKE,
CHRISTOPHER MARTIN,	FRANCIS EATON,	RICHARD GARDINER,
WILLIAM MULLINS,	JAMES CHILTON,	JOHN ALLERTON,
WILLIAM WHITE,	JOHN CRACKSTON,	THOMAS ENGLISH,
RICHARD WARREN,	JOHN BILLINGTON,	EDWARD DOTEY,
JOHN HOWLAND,	MOSES FLETCHER,	EDWARD LISTER.
STEPHEN HOPKINS,	JOHN GOODMAN,	

COURTENAY FAMILY

("A Genealogical History of the Noble and Illustrous Family of Courtenay," by E. Cleaveland, B.D.—printed by Edw. Farley, at Shakefpear's Head near Eaft-gate, 1735) page 111. Note that this Genealogy was printed about 200 years ago.

To the Honourable Sir William Courtenay, Bt.:
When I had the Honour to Affift you in your Studies in Oxford, Couriofity put me upon enquiring into the Antiquity and Greatnefs of your Family: I had heard before (as all that have heard any Thing of the Family muft) that it is truly Great and Noble; and I had feen fome fhort Account of it in "Camden, Dugdale," and other modern Authors; but when I made a particular Search into the Hiftories of our Nation, and other Hiftories, I found a great deal which did tend to fhew forth the Greatnefs and Luftre of it; and having made a Collection of all that I found relating to the Family, I have put it in the beft Method I could and do here prefent it to you.

I had for my Patron, by your Recommendation, that generous and noble-fpirited Gentleman your Grandfather, and I have fince received many Favours from you; and I was glad of an Opportunity of fhewing my Gratitude, and of doing what Service I could for the Family: And I hope by laying before your Children the Lives of their Noble Anceftors, and fhewing of them the Pictures of their Minds, they will be as well pleafed as to fee the Pictures of their Bodies placed up in their Houfes; and that by reading an Account of their Noble Actions, they and their Pofterity will be induced to practife those Virtues for which their Anceftors were famous, by which they got great Renown, and raifed themfelves high in the World. And feeing your Children by your Noble and Virtuous Lady (whofe Death was an unfpeakable Lofs to the Family, and of whom to give a juft Character it would require the Pen of that famous Poet, that made an Elegy upon that Excellent Lady her Mother) have the Blood of the Berties and Norris's mixed with that of the Bourtenars, we have great Reafon to hope that they will fhew themfelves Nobly Defcended by their Noble and Generous Actions.

Of the Firft of thefe Families, via. the Berties, was Leopold de Bertie, who was Conftable of Dover Caftle in the Time of King Etheldred, and from whom was defcended Richard Bertie, who in Queen Mary's Reign was forced with his Lady, the Dutchefs of Suffolk, to fly from his Native Country for the Sake of his Religion; and when he was in Exile, having a Son born, he named him Peregrine, which Name does continue in the Family to this Day, to put thofe that are of it in Mind what their Anceftors did and fuffered for the Proteftant Religion; which Peregrine was Lord Willoughby of Erefby, by Defcent from his Mother Catherine Willoughby, Heirefs of that Family and Dutchefs of Suffolk, Widow of Charles Brandon Duke of Suffolk. This Lord Willoughby was, as Mr. Camden faith, made Governour of Berwick by Qu. Elizabeth, and in France and the Low Countries went through all the Offices of a Commander with great Commendation; and there goes this Story of him, that having a Challenge fent him when he was ill of the Gout, he returned this Anfwer, "That he was lame in his Hands and Feet, yet he would meet his Challenger with a Piece of Rapier in his Mouth." Robert his Son fucceeded him, and by the Lady Vere his Mother, Sifter and Heirefs to Edward, Earl of Oxford, became Hereditary Lord Great Chamberlain of England, and was created Earl of Lindfey by Charles I, and was General of his Army in the Fight at Edgehill, and being there mortally wounded, and taken Prifoner by the Rebels, did with his laft Breath exhort them to return to their Duty and Allegiance. And as in this Robert the Family received an additional Honour in his becoming Lord Great Chamberlain of England, and in his being made an Earl, for it has received a greater Luftre in being honoured with the Title of Duke, which Title was conferred by King George I, upon Robert late Duke of Ancafter and Keftevan.

Of the other Family, viz. that of Norris, there were Six brethren, Sons of James Lord Norris of Ricot, who by their warlike Actions in Ireland, France, and the Low Countries, rendered themſelves famous, and raiſed themſelves to great Honours and Preferments in the Reign of Queen Elizabeth: and from the Heireſs of this Family, married to Montague Earl of Lindſey, Son of the firſt Robert, came James Bertie, who was Lord Norris of Ricot, as deſcended from his Mother, and was made Earl of Abigdon by King Charles II, the Father of your Right Honourable Lady.

And ſeeing, as I ſaid, your Children have ſuch Noble Anceſtors, we may very well hope, that they and their Poſterity will imitate them in their Courage, Generoſity, Love for their Country, Zeal for their Religion, and all other good and noble Qualities: And as the Family has continued in Splendour, and Flouriſhed for many Generations back, ſo that it may ſtill proſper, and continued to all ſucceeding Generations, is the Prayer of, Honoured SIR,
Your moſt Obedient
And moſt obliged Humble Servant
EZRA CLEAVELAND.

(Page 278, Part III, Chap. IV) Sir Philip Courtenay, ſecond of that Name, of Powderham-Caſtle, was born in the Year 1404: He was very young when his Father died, and was not full Eleven Years old when his Uncle the Biſhop of Norwich died. He married Elizabeth Daughter of Walter Lord Hungerford, and had with her the Manour of Molland-Botreaux in Devonſhire: It is called Molland-Botreaux, to diſtinguiſh it from another Manour called Molland-Sarazen in the ſame Pariſh; and it is called Molland-Botreaux from the Family of Botreaux that were Lords of it, and did ſometime live there, and ſometime at Botreaux-Caſtle in Cornwall; and Molland continued in the Family of Botreaux until the Reign of Henry VI when it came to the Family of Hungerford by Margaret Daughter of William Lord Botreaux, who married to Robert Lord Hungerford: And Sir Philip Courtenay marrying the Daughter of Walter Lord Hungerford had it with his Lady in Marriage. This Walter Lord Hungerford was Lord High-Treaſurer of England in the Reign of Henry VI and he did by his Teſtament, bearing Date July 1, 1449, 27 Henry VI give to Elizabeth his Daughter, Wife of Sir Philip Courtenay, Knight, a Cup of Gold.

Sir Hugh Courtney, died 1340. At the age of 17 married Agnes, daughter of Sir John St. John, Knight. Thomas Courtney, of Southpole, fourth son, married Muriel, daughter and heiress. Margaret Courtney, first daughter, married Thomas Peverell, of Park, County Cornwall.

Ancestral line to Reginald de Courtenay who was first of that family that came into England.

1. ATHON, who fortified the Town of Courtenay about the year 1000, and gave that name to his Family.
2. SEIGNEUR DE COURTENAY, m. Isabel, dau. of Guy, Seign. de Montlebery, and had three children: 1. *Miles;* 2. *Joſceline,* Count of Adeffa, and Jeofry Courtenay de Chaplay.
3. MILES DE COURTENAY, m. Emengarde, dau. of Renaud, Count de Nevers. They had three children: *Joſceline, Reginald* and *William.*
4. REGINALD DE COURTENAY, m. Hawiſe, dau. of Robert de Aincourt. They had four children: *Robert, Henry, Reginald* and *Egeline.*

5. •ROBERT DE COURTENAY, m. Mary de Redvers, dau. of Wi.Iam, Earl of Devonshire. Children: *John, William* and *Hawife.*
6. •JOHN DE COURTENAY, m. Ifabel, dau. of Hugh, Earl of Oxford.
7. HUGH COURTENAY, Baron of Okehampton, m. Eleanor, dau. of Hugh Defpenfer, Earl of Winchefter.
8. HUGH COURTENAY, Earl of Devon, m. Agnes, dau. of John, Lord St. John.
9. THOMAS COURTENAY, of Southpole, fourth son, m. Muriel, dau. and heiress of Sir John de Noels, Knight.
10. MARGARET COURTENAY, first dau., m. Thomas Peverill of Parke, Hamatethy, Penhale, etc., County Cornwall and had
11. CATHERINE PEVERILL, m. before Sept. 18, 1402, Walter Hungerford, who was b. about June 22, 1378. He was nominated Knight of the Bath in 1399. She was living as late as June 14, 1426.
12. •ROBERT, LORD HUNGERFORD, m. at Heytesbury, Wilts, Margaret, only dau. and heiress of William, Lord Botreau, by Elizabeth, dau. of John, Lord Beaumont. He d. May 18, 1459, and was bur. in Salisbury Cathedral. His wife d. Feb. 7, 1477-8.
13. •ROBERT, LORD HUNGERFORD, and Lord Moleyns, son and heir, b. prior to 1429. Beheaded May 18, 1464, at Newcastle, Northumberland. He m. before Nov. 4, 1440, Eleanor, dau. and heiress of Sir William de Moleyns, of Stoke Pogis, County Bucks, by Anne, dau. of John Whalesborough, of Cornwall.
14. SIR WALTER HUNGERFORD, younger son, d. 1516, m. Jane, widow of Thomas Bulstrode and had
15. SIR EDWARD HUNGERFORD, of Heytesbury Wiltshire and of Farleigh Hungerford, Somersetshire, m. (1) Jane, dau. of John Zouche, Lord Zouche, of Harringsworth, and had
16. SIR WALTER HUNGERFORD, of Heytesbury, Wilts and of Farleigh Hungerford, Sommerset, son and heir of Sir Edward Hungerford by first wife, was b. probably about 1502. He m. (1) Susan, dau. of Sir John Danvers, of Culworth Northants, by Anne, dau. of Sir John Stradling, of Dauntsey Wilts. She d. before Mar. 22, 1526-7. He was beheaded July 28, 1540.
17. •LUCY HUNGERFORD, widow of Sir John St. John, m. Sir Anthony Hungerford, b. 1564; d. 1627.
18. THOMAS HUNGERFORD, landed on the shores of New England in 1628; bapt. probably at Bremhill Parish, England, in 1602; d. at New London, Conn., 1663; who m., name unknown, and had
19. THOMAS HUNGERFORD, b. 1648; d. 1714; m. before June 6, 1671, Mary Green, of Narragansett, and had
20. THOMAS HUNGERFORD, b. about 1673; d. 1750; m. 1699, Elizabeth, dau. of Mathew Smith and Mary Cutler, and had
21. SAMUEL HUNGERFORD, b. about 1713; d. at New Fairfield, Conn.; m. June 23, 1746, Mary Graves, b. probably at Hatfield, Aug. 20, 1722, and had
22. •ISAIAH HUNGERFORD, b. Jan. 23 1757; d. June 16, 1833; m. Esther Mead, b. Aug. 11, 1760; d. Dec. 22, 1836, and had
23. •ELIZABETH HUNGERFORD, b. Feb. 7, 1797; d. Jan. 7, 1878; m. Nash David Phelps, b. Oct. 4, 1796; d. Apr. 15, 1884, and had
24. CAROLINE ALEXANDRIA PHELPS, b. July 3, 1840; d. Mar. 29, 1921; m. Sept. 8, 1863, Horace Brayton Leach, b. Sept. 25, 1836; d. May 6, 1919, and had
25. ELIZABETH MAY LEACH, b. Jan. 7, 1866; m. Sept. 8, 1889, Oscar Herbert Rixford, b. Dec. 27, 1860; d. Sept. 11, 1926.
26. OSCAR ADELBERT RIXFORD, b. Aug. 4, 1890; m. Jan. 18, 1919, Mary Carolyn Hefflon, b. June 6, 1899.
27. MARY-ELIZABETH LENORA RIXFORD, b. Oct. 6, 1922.
    OSCAR THEODORE RIXFORD, b. July 21, 1925.

References: 1 to 17 generations—Records of Elizabeth M. Rixford.
18 to 21 generations—"Thomas Hungerford and His Descendants," by F. Phelps Leach.
22 to 27 generations—Family Record.

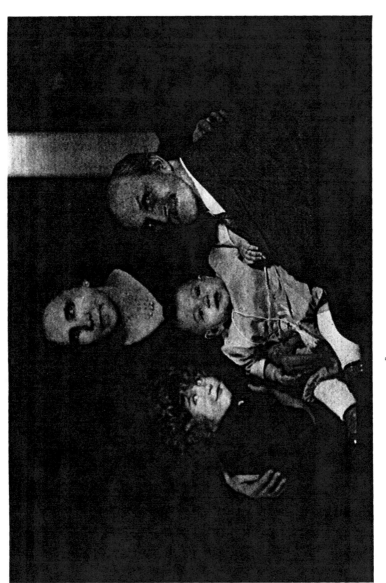

MR. AND MRS. OSCAR[2] HERBERT RIXFORD AND GRANDCHILDREN
Mary-Elizabeth L. Rixford and Oscar[4] Theodore Rixford.

THE ROYAL AND BARONIAL ANCESTRY OF ELIZABETH M. RIXFORD FROM THE ILLUSTRIOUS FAMILY OF DE VERE AND HUNGERFORD

Compiled by John S. Wurts, "Hedgefield" Germantown, Pa., editor of 9th edition of "Americans of Royal Descent."

CHILPERIC, King of the Burgundians, 450 A. D.
CHARLES MARTEL, Duke of Austrasia, 732.
CHARLEMAGNE, Roman Emperor and King of France.
EGBERT, King of Wessex.
ALFRED THE GREAT, King of Wessex.
GARCIA XIMENES, King of Navarre, 880.
MALCOLM "CAENMOHR," King of Scotland.
His and all the Magna Charta Barons.

A. ALBERIC DE VERE, 1066.
B. ALBERIC DE VERE.
C. SIR AUBREY DE VERE.
1. SIR ROBERT DE VERE, a Surety for Magna Charta.
2. HUGH DE VERE.
3. ROBERT DE VERE.
4. ALPHONZO DE VERE.
5. ·JOHN DE VERE.
6. ISABEL DE VERE.
7. SIR HUGH DE COURTENAY.
8. SIR HUGH COURTENAY.
9. THOMAS COURTENAY.
10. ·MARGARET COURTENAY.
11. CATHARINE PEVERILL.
12. ·ROBERT, Lord Hungerford.
13. ROBERT, Lord Hungerford.
14. SIR WALTER HUNGERFORD.
15. SIR EDWARD HUNGERFORD.
16. SIR WALTER HUNGERFORD.
17. LUCY HUNGERFORD.
18. THOMAS HUNGERFORD.
19. ·THOMAS HUNGERFORD.
20. ·THOMAS HUNGERFORD.
21. SAMUEL HUNGERFORD.
22. ·ISAIAH HUNGERFORD.
23. ·ELIZABETH HUNGERFORD.
24. CAROLINE ALEXANDRIA PHELPS.
25. ELIZABETH MAY RIXFORD.
26. OSCAR ADELBERT RIXFORD[3], a life member of the Sons of Runnemede.
   Mary-Elizabeth L. Rixford.
   Oscar Theodore Rixford[4].
   Both successive life members.

THE ROYAL AND BARONIAL DESCENT OF HUNGERFORD FROM THE ILLUSTRIOUS FAMILY OF DE VERE AND THE ENGLISH LINE OF HUNGERFORD

A. • ALBERIC DE VERE, or "Count Aubrey, Sanglier," Count de Ghisnes, or Guines, was the founder in 1066 of this celebrated family in England. This famous house, the noblest in England, and indeed, as Englishmen loved to say, the noblest in Europe, is the very first, most historic, most illustrious, of our ancient nobility and derives its title through an uninterrupted male descent from a time when the families of Howard and Seymour were still obscure, when the Nevilles and Percys enjoyed only a provincial celebrity and when even the great name of Plantagenet had not yet been heard in England. Alberic de Vere was a cousin of William the Conqueror and a descendant of many early kings and potentates including Hugh Capet; Hugh Magnus; Kings Henry and Charles of France; Louis IV of France; Otto I of Saxony; Crinan; Vladimer, Czar of Russia; Bazil, Emperor of Constantinople; Egbert, First King of England; and Charlemagne, Emperor of the West. At the time of the great survey of England, Alberic de Vere possessed numerous lordships in different shires, and had his principal residence at his castle of Hedingham, in Essex. In the latter end of his days he assumed the cowl, and died in 1088, a monk, and was buried in the church of Colne Priory, which he founded.
Alberic de Vere, m. before 1139, Beatrix de Gand, or Ghent, heiress and dau. of Henry de Gand, Castellan of Bourbourg Castle, and his wife, Sibylla, dau. and heiress of Manasses, Count of Guines, and had

B. • ALBERIC DE VERE (or Aubrey), eldest son, who, being in high favor with King Henry I, was constituted great high chamberlain of the kingdom, in 1133, to hold the same in fee to himself and heirs. In 5 Stephen, while a joint sheriff with Richard Basset, justiciary of England, of several counties, he was slain in a popular tumult at London, in 1140, having issue by his wife, Adeliza, or Alice de Clare, sister of Richare Fitzgilbert, first Earl of Hertford (see Round's "Geoffrey de Mandeville," page 388).

C. • SIR AUBREY DE VERE, eldest son, b. before 1120, third baron by tenure, of Kensington, Count of Ghisnes. For his fidelity to the Empress Maud, he was confirmed by her in his inheritance of the lord chamberlainship and all his father's possessions. He was given also the choice of several earldoms, and selected that of Oxford, and was so created by Henry II in 1155, and d. in 1194. He m. (2) Lucia, dau. and heiress of Henry de Essex, or of William, second or third Baron d'Abrincis, of Folkstone, in Kent, and had

1. • SIR ROBERT DE VERE, the Surety, who succeeded as fifth Baron, by tenure, and third Earl of Oxford, second son. Earl Robert, although hereditary lord great chamberlain of the kingdom, was one of the principal barons in arms against King John, and was elected *one of the Sureties for the observance of the Magna Charta*, a party to that covenant which resigned to the barons the custody of the city and Tower of London, and one of those excommunicated by the Pope. In the beginning of the reign of Henry III, having made his peace with the young monarch after the Battle of Lincoln, he was received into his favor, and was, in 1220-1, appointed one of the judges in the Court of King's Bench, but d. a few months afterwards, and was bur. in the priory of Hatfield, Broad Oak, in Essex in Oct., 1221. Sir Robert, third Earl of Oxford, m. Isabel, and had

2. • HUGH DE VERE, fourth Earl of Oxford, Great Chamberlain of England, b. circa, 1210; d. Dec., 1262. He m. after Feb. 11, 1223, Hawise, and had

3. · ROBERT DE VERE, fifth Earl of Oxford and sixth Lord Great Chamberlain of England, m. Alice, dau. and heiress of Gilbert de Saundford, and had
4. · ALPHONZO DE VERE, second son, who had
5. JOHN DE VERE, seventh Earl of Oxford, m. Maud de Badelsmere, dau. of Bartholomew, first Baron Badelsmere, and had
6. · ISABEL DE VERE, m. John, fourth Baron Courtenay, and had
7. · SIR HUGH DE COURTENAY, fifth Baron Courtenay and third Baron of Okehampton, m. Eleanor, dau. of Hugh de Spencer, and had
8. · SIR HUGH COURTENAY, d. 1340. At age seventeen m. in 1292, Agnes, dau. of Sir John St. John, Knight, and sister of Lord St. John, of Basing, and had (a) *Sir Hugh de Courtenay,* m. Margaret Bohun, great-grand-dau. of Edward I, King of England, and (b) his brother
9. · THOMAS COURTENAY, of Southpole, fourth son, m. Muriel, dau. and heiress of Sir John de Moels, Knight, and had
10. · MARGARET COURTENAY, first dau., m. Thomas Peverill, of Parke, Hamatethy, Penhale, etc., county Cornwall, and had
11. · CATHERINE PEVERILL, m. before Sept. 18, 1402, Walter Hungerford, fourth but first surviving son and heir of Sir Thomas H. [Speaker of the House of Commons, d. Dec. 3, 1397 (not 1398). He was chief steward to John of Gaunt and constable of Grosmont and Monmouth Castles. His family never wavered in its loyalty to the House of Lancaster.], of Farleigh and Wellow, Somerset, and of Heytesbury, Wilts, by his second wife, Joan, dau. and coheiress of Sir Edmund Hussey, of Holbrook, Somerset, and widow of John Whyton, who was b. about June 22, 1378. He was nominated Knight of the Bath in 1399; returned to Parliament 1400. He was preeminently distinguished in the French wars. He fought at the Battle of the Agincourt, Oct. 25, 1415. In May, 1416, he was one of the ambassadors nominated to treat with the Archbishop of Cologne. In Aug., 1416, he commanded the naval expedition to Harfleur. As Steward of the Household to Henry V he was appointed Nov. 1, 1417, Constable of Windsor Castle. In 1418 he was one of the English Commissioners sent to Rouen and received for his many services a grant of the castle and lordship of Hommet in Normandy. Installed Knight of the Garter, May 3, 1421. He was one of the executors of the will of Henry V and was on the Council of Regency in 1422. In 1424 he was Steward of the Household to Henry VI and from 1426 to 1432 Lord High Treasurer. He was summoned to Parliament from Jan. 7, 1425-6 to Jan. 2, 1448-9, by writs directed Waltero Hungerford Chivaler whereby he is held to have become Lord Hungerford. Catherine Peverill, who was living as late as June 14, 1426, and was bur. in Salisbury Cathedral, had by her husband Walter Hungerford: (a) *Sir Edmund Hungerford,* of Down Ampney, whose descendant m. No. 17 Lucy Hungerford, and (b)
12. ROBERT, LORD HUNGERFORD, second but first surviving son and heir by first wife; proposed going on a pilgrimage to the Holy Land about 1423. Served in the French wars and was in the retinue of the Duke of Bedford in 1435. He was summoned to Parliament from' Sept. 5, 1450 to May 26, 1455, by writs directed Roberto Hungerford seniori Militia. He m. at Heytesbury, Wilts, Margaret, only dau. and heiress of William, Lord Botreau, by Elizabeth, dau. of John, Lord Beaumont. He d. May 18, 1459, and was bur. in Salisbury Cathedral. Will dated Apr. 22 and proved July 7, 1459. His widow on the death of her father, May 16, 1462, became suo jure Baroness Botreaux. She survived both her son and grandson. Dying Feb. 7, 1477-8, she was bur. with her husband in Salisbury Cathedral. Will dated at Heytesbury, Aug. 8, 1476. They had
13. ROBERT, LORD HUNGERFORD and Lord Moleyns, son and heir, b. prior to 1429. Presumably in consequence of his marriage he was summoned v.p. to Parliament from Jan. 13, 1444-5 to Jan. 20, 1451-2, whereby he

is held to have become Lord Moleyns. He served in France and was taken prisoner, remaining in the Duchy of Aquitaine for several years not being released until a large ransom had been paid. He appears to have returned not long after his succession to the barony of Hungerford. On Mar. 31, 1460, he dealt with a great deal of his family property and in the same year was present with Lord Scales in defence of the Tower of London, whence he escaped and a license was obtained for him to go to Florence. In 1461 he was in France, on behalf of Queen Margaret, and for a time under arrest. On Nov. 4, 1461, he was attainted and his possessions forfeited as from Mar. 4, 1460-1. In 1462 he joined the Queen in Scotland and thereafter shared her fortunes. After the Lancastrian defeat at Hexhan, May 15, 1464, he was taken prisoner and beheaded forthwith May 18, 1464, at Newcastle Northumberland. He was bur. at Salisbury Cathedral. He m. before Nov. 4, 1440, Eleanor, dau. and heir of Sir William de Moleyns, of Stoke Pogis, County Bucks, by Anne, dau. of John Whalesborough, of Cornwall, and had (a) *Thomas,* who succeeded as fourth Lord Hungerford, m. Anne Percy, and d. in 1469, and (b) his brother,

14.   Sir Walter Hungerford, younger son, d. 1516; m. Jane, widow of Thomas Bulstrode, and had

15.   Sir Edward Hungerford, of Heytesbury Wiltshire and of Farleigh Hungerford, Somersetshire, m. (1) Jane, dau. of John Zouche, Lord Zouche, of Harringsworth, and had

16.   Sir Walter Hungerford, of Heytesbury, Wilts and of Farleigh Hungerford, Sommerset, son and heir of Sir Edward Hungerford of the same by his first wife, Jane, dau. of John (Zouche), Lord Zouche, of Harryngworth, was b. probably about 1502. As esquire of the body he had livery of the lands of his father and grandfather July 15, 1523. He m. (1) Susan, dau. of Sir John Danvers, of Culworth Northants, by Anne, dau. of Sir John Stradling, of Dauntsey Wilts. She d. before Mar. 22, 1526-7. He was Sheriff of Wilts, 1534, and about this time became intimate with the King's Minister, Thomas Cromwell. Summoned to Parliament from Apr. 27, 1536 to Mar. 1, 1538-9, whereby he became Lord Hungerford, of Heytesbury. Thomas Cromwell, then Earl of Essex, was attainted and perhaps in consequence of this fault a bill of attainder against Lord Hungerford, of Heytesbury, was introduced in July, 1540. The Hungerford estates then became forfeited and the barony extinct. He was beheaded with Earl of Essex on Tower Hill, July 28, 1540. His widow m., 1544, Sir Robert Throckmorton, of Congleton, Worcestershire. Sir Walter and Lady Susan had (a) *Sir Walter Hungerford,* of Farleigh; and (b) three daus., one of whom,

17.   Lucy Hungerford, dau. and coheiress of Sir Walter Hungerford, and widow of Sir John, son of Nicholas St. John and Elizabeth Blount, his wife, m. Sir Anthony Hungerford (the son of her fifth cousin, Anthony Hungerford, Sr.), b. 1564; d. 1627, of Black Bourton or Bourton Inges, who by his wife Lucy had:

(a)·*Sir Edward Hungerford,* first son, of Cadenham, K. B., b. 1596; d. 1648, a spendthrift.

(b)·*Sarah Hungerford,* who m. Sir John Carew.

The American Line of Hungerfords

Anne Hungerford, of Boston, sister of Thomas Hungerford, m. John Lee or Leigh of the General Lee family.

18.   (d) Thomas Hungerford, of Hartford and New London, Conn., according to Mr. J. J. Murphy, who in his "Life of Colonel Daniel Elihu Hungerford," written in 1869, says that Thomas, brother of Sir Edward Hungerford, K.B., landed on the shores of New England in 1628. The said Col. Daniel Elihu Hungerford was b. in Herkimer County,

N. Y.; d. in Rome, Italy, 1896, and had a dau. who m. John W.
Mackey, of California, residing in Paris. Both she and her father
have spent much time in England and have given especial attention to
the genealogy of the Hungerfords. Thomas Hungerford was bapt.
probably at Bremhill Parish, England in 1602. [See the book,
"Thomas Hungerford, of Hartford and New London, Conn., and Some
of His Descendants with Their English Ancestors," by F. Phelps
Leach (1924)]; d. at New London, Conn., 1663; who m. name unknown. Service: "History of New London," by Caulkins, 1860, page
68—Thomas Hungerford and Jonathan Brewster of the Cape Ann
Party, 1650, on the pen. where the 1st Trading Post Stood.

19. · THOMAS HUNGERFORD, b. at Hartford, Conn., 1648; d. at East Haddam,
Conn., 1714, who m. before June 6, 1671, Mary Green, of Narragan-
sett. Service: Bodges' "King Philip's War," Leominster, Mass., 1896
No. 140 being Thomas Hungerford.

20. ·THOMAS HUNGERFORD, b. at New London, Conn., about 1673; d. 1750;
who m. 1699, Elizabeth, dau. of Mathew Smith and his wife Mary
Cutler. Service: Bodges' "King Philip's War"—List of Volunteers
who drew Cedar Swamp Lots. No. 163 being Thomas Hungerford.

21. · SAMUEL HUNGERFORD, b. probably at East Haddam, Conn., about 1713; d.
at New Fairfield, Conn.; represented New Fairfield, Conn., in the
Legislature in 1777. He m. June 23, 1746, Mary Graves, b. probably
at Hatfield, Aug. 20, 1722.

Aug., 1763, he obtained of Gov. Benning Wentworth grants of three
townships on the N. E. of Lake Champlain, chartered by the names of
Fairfield, Smithfield, and Hungerford (now Sheldon). ("Mrs. Hemen-
way's Gazetteers.")

Data from "Index to the Papers of the Surveyors-General of Vermont" (page 85 of Index).

Hungerford, N. H., Grant to Samuel Hungerford and associates,
Aug. 18, 1763; name changed to Sheldon, Nov. 8, 1792.

Charter—Registered by I. A., S-G, 19:208; Variation of Bounds
from Ms. S. P. 31:72: A. J., 1796:115.

Fairfield, N. H. (page 69) Grant to Samuel Hungerford and Associates, Aug. 18, 1763; parts from Smithfield and to Bakersfield, 1792;
parts to and from Swanton, 1829, etc.

Ferdinand, N. H., Grant to Thos. Hungerford and associates, Oct.
12, 1762; parts from Wenlock and Brighton, 1853.

Charter—original, 2:134A; copy registered by I. A., S-G, 19:199. (S-G—
means Surveyor-General.)

Proprietors—Names, 41:46; 41-79, etc. (page 71).

Vol. of Field Books, shows Town lines of 1783-7, ... Hungerford, etc.

Vol. 10 of Field Books of Survey of Town Lines made by the
Surveyor-General or his Deputies, compiled and attested by James
Whitlaw, Surveyor-General, gives systematically a part or all of the
surveys of the lines of . . . , Averill, Avery's Gores (3), Barre, Berlin,
Chelsea, Ferdinand, Highgate, ... Hungerford . . . . Lemington, Mont-
pelier, Newbury, Norwich, Orange, Rocock, Pocock Leg, Washington,
Wildersburg, Williamstown, etc. (Only a partial list is copied.)

22. · ISAIAH HUNGERFORD, b. at New Fairfield, Conn., Jan. 23, 1757; d. at Stanbridge, P. Q., June 16, 1833. Private, was in Captain Hubbell's Co.;
pay roll for horse travel Capt. William Hubbell's Co., in the 16th Reg.
Militia commanded by Nehemiah Beardsley, Esq., Co. 1, in expedition
to Fairfield, Norwalk and Stamford; New Fairfield, Conn., July 8, 1779.
He m. Esther Mead, b. Aug. 11, 1760; d. Dec. 22, 1836.

23. · ELIZABETH HUNGERFORD, b. Feb. 7, 1797; d. Jan. 7, 1878; who m. Nash
David Phelps, b. at New Haven, Vt., Oct. 4, 1796; d. Apr. 15, 1884.

24. · CAROLINE ALEXANDRIA PHELPS, b. July 3, 1840; d. Mar. 29, 1921; who m. Sept. 8, 1863, Horace Brayton Leach, b. Sept. 25, 1836; d. May 6, 1919.

25. · ELIZABETH MAY LEACH, who was b. at Bakersfield, Vt., Jan. 7, 1866; and m. at Sheldon, Vt., Sept. 8, 1889, Oscar Herbert Rixford, b. Dec. 27, 1860; d. Sept. 11, 1926. Mrs. Rixford is a member of the following societies:

A life member of the Huguenot Society, being a descendant of Hester Mahieu, wife of Francis Cooke. Two supplemental lines.

A member, No. 7881, of the National Society of Mayflower Descendants, being a descendant of James and Susanna Chilton, through their dau. Mary; and of Francis Cooke, through his dau. Jane.

A member, D. C. No. 430, State No. 18, of the Vermont Society of Mayflower Descendants, of which Society she is the State Secretary.

A member, No. 1922, of the National Society, Daughters of Founders and Patriots of America, of which Society she is State Historian, being a descendant of Lawrence Leach a Founder and of Ephraim Leach a Patriot. Vt. Chairman, Committee on Preservation of Records of D. F. P. A.

A member, No. 1404, of the Massachusetts Society of the Colonial Dames of America in Vermont, being a descendant of Samuel Chapin.

A member of the Daughters of Vermont.

A member, No. 193195, of the National Society of the Daughters of the American Revolution, through Ephraim Leach, with ten supplemental lines.

A member, No. 9183-215, of the Daughters of 1812, being a descendant of James Hawley, with three supplemental lines.

A member, No. 226, of the Massachusetts Society Daughters of the Colonial Wars, being a descendant of Francis Cooke.

A member of the Magna Charta Dames, through Robert de Vere, third Earl of Oxford, and State Regent for Vermont.

A member, No. 2, of the Vermont Society of the Daughters of the American Colonists, being a descendant of John Winslow, with one hundred and thirty-seven supplemental bars for different Ancestors who gave their service for the New England Colonists. She is Vice-President of this Society, also Vice-President, Colonial and General Records Committee for the Atlantic Coast Section.

A member, No. 772, of the Colonial Daughters of the Seventeenth Century, through Deacon Samuel Chapin.

A member, No. 992, of the National Society Daughters of the Union.

A member, No. 85, of the Ancient and Honorable Artillery Co., through Hon. John Johnson.'

A life member of the Washington Headquarters Association for the Preservation of Virginia Antiques.

The first woman appointed on the State Committee for the First District in Vermont at the Roosevelt State Convention, held at Rutland, Nov. 20, 1912.

One of the State Advisory and Educational Committee of the Republican Party of Vermont during the Hoover campaign.

The founder of the Saxe Literary Club of Highgate, Vt., organized 1928 to commemorate the memory of the poet, John B. Saxe, who was born in this town.

The founder, No. 1, of Highgate Colony of New England Women, organized May 6, 1929. At the National Congress held at Boston, May 5-6-7-8, 1930, Highgate Colony won the National Marshall Cup, presented for the greatest increase in membership during the year. The cup has been held by Syracuse, N. Y., 1925-6; Detroit, Mich., 1926-7; Detroit, Mich., 1927-8; St. Petersburg, Fla., 1928-9; Meriden, Conn., 1929-30; Highgate, Vt., 1930-1. At the meeting held at Burlington, Vt., Aug., 1931, it was voted to plant a Washington Elm, near the home

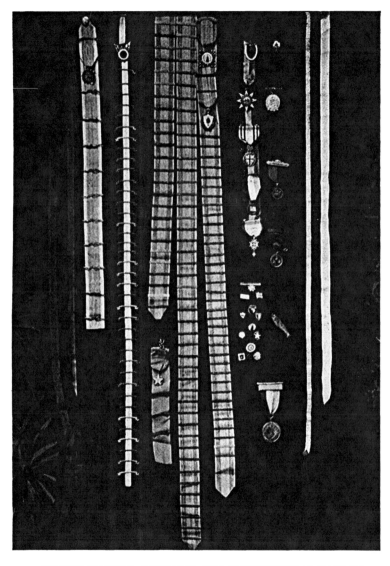

REGENT RIBBONS, INSIGNIAS AND SUPPLEMENTAL BARS OF
ELIZABETH RIXFORD
Of which societies she is a member.

of the Founder, and place a bronze tablet on the tree to commemorate the founding of the Society in that place. Endorsed at a meeting of the Board, Feb. 25, 1932 Honorary President for life.

Nominated as a candidate for Director General of the National Society of New England Women, February, 1932.

A member of the Washington Bicentennial Committee in Vermont, appointed by the Governor of the State. She is a direct descendant of the Washington Family. Also member of the American Tree Association of Washington, D. C.

Appointed Co-chairman for Vermont of the National Woman's Committee for Washington Cathedral, announced by the Rt. Rev. James E. Freeman, Bishop of Washington, February, 1932.

Pages 27 to 33 compiled by John S. Wurts.

THE FAMILY OF THE HUNGERFORDS IN ENGLAND

("Hungerfordiana," pages 33, 122-123)

This ancient family which extends itself so widely over the western circuits of our island.

1. Hungerford of Hysterbury.
2. Hungerford of Farley Castle.
3. Hungerford of Down Ampney.
4. Hungerford of Cadenham or Studley.
5. Hungerford of Windrush.
6. Hungerford of Black Bourton.

(Page 108) Formal bearings of the family of Hungerford.

1. Heytesbury.   3. Fitz-John.   5. Botreaux.
2. Hussay.   4. Peverell.   6. Molyns.

In the succeeding years ten more divisions were added to their coat of arms (copies from "Farley-Hungerford," by Gray, of England).

1. Cornwall.   4. Botreaux.   8. Burnell.
2. Cobham.   5. Moels.   9. Botrurt.
3. Courtney.   6. Manduit.   10. Lister.
                7. Molyns.

Arms—Quarterly: 1st and 4th, sa., two bar arg., in chief three plates, for Hungerford 2nd and 3rd, or on a chevron sa., cetised gu., three martlets of the field a chief vaire, for Heldich.

Crests—1st, out of a ducal coronet or, a pepper garb of the first between two sickles erect ppr., for Hungerford; 2nd, a martle sa., in front of a cross pates fitches between two branches palm or, for Heldich.

Mottoes—*Et dieu mon appui*, for Hungerford; *Stot fortuna domus*, for Heldich.

Seat—Hurley Cottage, Hurley, Gt. Marlow.

Clubs—St. James and Turf.

The sickle was the original coat of arms and still can be seen in Salisbury Cathedral (built by the Hungerfords and later remodeled and name changed). The crest was taken from St. George in 1611.

The brasses and shields in Salisbury Cathedral (the site of the Hungerford Church) abound with the sickle, in various forms, single, double and treble and we find the same device in the numerous churches and mansions attached to their former property and it is well known that crests were very frequently taken and adopted from facts of the Asmoral berings. From a pedigree of this family by La Weir among the Lansdown MSS. in the British Museum we learn that the old sinister of the Barons Hungerford were dexter, a griffin, sable, sinister, a bird with a long tail and wings.

The ancient seat of the Castle of St. Donets Corinth, of Glamorgan, Sir Edward Stradley married Elizabeth Hungerford, daughter of Sir Anthony Hungerford. John Hungerford, Manor of Studley. Danford Hungerford Dunford Magna. Chelsia, Highgate, Fairfield, Penshore, Sumerford, Keynes, White Parish (Wiltz). Walter, son and heir of Sir Thomas, Sheldon, Great Chiverell, Lollydown, Biddleston, Winterborn, Stoke, Bapton, Mildenhall, Merston, Over and Vether Stratton, Upton Sendamore, etc. Other of their mansions were Biddensden of Warminster, Shydmore of Opton, Skydmore of Little Sutton, of West Codford, of Winterborn, Stoke of Teffout, of Lyle, Cheverill, Wales Cheverill and Cheverell Burnell, of Mildenhall near Marlboro, and the Manor of Westwell one mile distant from Farleigh. Kirbie Castle and Bednall Green in the County of Middlesex. John Hungerford, died 1673. Chester House, Hinton (Somerset), 1594. Anthony Hungerford, died 1594. Weston Underwood (Buebs). Elizabeth Hungerford, died 1571.

Some other castles, estates and mansions of the Hungerfords are: Beduyn, Falne, Huytesbus, Fuicklade, Wotten Basset, Marlborough, Chippenham, Chicklade, Malmsbury, Farley.

About 64 miles out of London, where you follow the quaint old Bath Coach Road you will arrive at the village of Hungerford, the ancient seat of the Hungerford Family, in Pastoral, Berkshire, and extending into Wiltshire. Hungerford is well off the well traveled tourists' routes but it holds more than passing interest to the traveler who likes to linger long in quaint byways of the world, studying customs of olden days where they are still observed in all the simple ingenuousness. Such a traveler would delight in the observance of Hock Day. The holiday occurs the Thursday, Easter week. Hungerford is also a favorite hunting center. John of Gaunt, Duke of Lancaster, presented to the citizens the manoral rights including Kennit and other streams in the locality which are numerous, and carefully preserved in the town hall. One of their town houses was located next to Buckingham Palace on the Thames River.

Farley-Hungerford was distinguished from the other places of the same name by the appellation of Farley Montfort, which estate was purchased of the Montfort family. Spoken of in Girling's "English History," page 126, Simon de Montfort was the Earl of Leicester who was in the War of the Barons, 1264.

James Hungerford Smithson (1765-1835), English chemist, and founder of the Smithsonian Institution, Washington, D. C., was a son of Hugh Smithson, the first Duke of Northumberland, and Mrs. Elizabeth Reate Malie, a granddaughter of Sir George Hungerford, of Studley (or Cadenham) branch of Hungerfords. Mr. Smithson died without issue and left at his death $508,318.46 to the Institute.

References: "Hungerfordiana, or Memoirs of the Hungerford Family," collected from the College of Arms, Parish Registers, Monumental Inscriptions, and various records, collected by Sir Richard Colt Hoar, Bart., Southhold, England, in 1823.
"Shakespeare's Poems," Vol. VI, Part III, page 162.
"Encyclopædia Britannica," 11th English Edition.

HUNGERFORD, Lord Hungerford, created 28[c] Henry VIII, extinct 31 Henry VIII (originally 4 Henry VI). This last creation was in a younger branch, after the first creation had gone into the Hastings family. The name was taken from the town of Hungerford in Wiltshire, in which county it was very ancient. Sir Walter de Hungerford, was father of Sir Thomas, Speaker of the House of Commons, 51 Edward III. He died December 3, 1398, and was buried in the chapel of Farley Castle, leaving (by Joan, daughter and coheir of Sir Edmund Hussey) Sir Walter Hungerford, son and heir, K. G. who was summoned to Parliament as Lord Hungerford, from 4 to 26 Henry VI, and died August 9, 1449 (27 Henry VI), leaving two sons, Sir Robert, his heir, and Sir Edmund.

Sir Edmund Hungerford, second son, married Margaret, daughter and heir of Edmund Burnel, and had the manor and seat of Downe-Ampney, County Gloucester, of which he died seized, 2 Richard III. He left a son, Sir Robert, father of Sir Anthony, father of John, whose son, Sir John, died seized of Downe-Ampney, March 18, 1634, ae. 69, having married Mary, daughter of Sir Richard Berkley. By her he had issue, Sir Anthony, his son and heir, who married Elizabeth, daughter of Sir Thomas Lucy, and left issue by her, Bridget, his sole daughter and heir, married to Edmund Dunch, Esq., father of Hungerford Dunch, Esq., who succeeded to Downe-Ampney, father of Edmund, whose three daughters and coheirs married Lord Charles Montague, Sir George Oxenden, and Mr. Thompson.

Sir Robert, eldest son, succeeded as second Lord Hungerford, and died 31 Henry VI, leaving by Margaret, daughter and sole heir to William, Lord Botreaux, Sir Robert Hungerford, commonly called Lord Molines, on account of his marriage with Aleanor, daughter and heir to William, Lord Molines. He was beheaded for his activity in the Lancastrian cause, 3 Edward IV. His son and heir, Thomas, fourth Lord Hungerford, suffered death in the same cause, 8 Edward IV. By Lady Anne, daughter of Henry, Earl of Northumberland, he left Anne, his sole daughter and heir, who brought a very large estate[d] to her husband, Edward, second Lord Hastings.

I now come to the issue of the second marriage of the second Lord Hungerford, who by his second wife, Catherine, daughter of

[c]—This should have preceded one or two of the last peers.
[d]—The rental is given in Dugdale. It lies in seven counties, and on casting it up, it amounts to £10,991/2s./2d.

Reginald West, Lord Delaware, had two sons, Walter and Leonard, which Walter, being active on the side of Henry at the Battle of Bosworth, had his share in the benefit of that glorious victory. He married Jane, daughter of Sir William Bulstrode, and left issue, Sir Edward Hungerford, of Heytesbury in Wiltshire, who, by Jane, daughter of John, Lord Zouche, had issue, Walter, who had summons to Parliament as Lord Hungerford, 28 Henry VIII, but in 31 Henry VIII, was attainted in Parliament and suffered death the following year on Tower-hill. He had two wives, first, Susan, daughter of Sir John Danvers, Kt., who by Anne, daughter of Sir William Dormer, had one son, Edward, who died young, and three daughters, Susan, married to Michael Earnley, Esq., of Corning, in Wilts; Lucy, to Sir John St. John, of Lydiard; and Jane, to Sir John Carne, of Glamorganshire. Lord Hungerford married secondly Alice, daughter to William, Lord Sands, by whom he had two sons, Sir Walter, who died 1586, and who had a son, Edward, who died without issue before him, and a daughter, Lucy, who married Sir Anthony Hungerford, of Black-Borton, in Oxfordshire. Sir Edward, the other son of Lord Hungerford, succeeded to the estate at Farley, etc., He was one of the gentleman pensioners to Queen Elizabeth, and married Jane, daughter to Sir Anthony Hungerford, of Downe-Ampney, but died without issue. The estate then went to Sir Edward Hungerford, K. B., son of Lucy Hungerford (she is stated on her monument to be the last of the Farley branch), by Sir Anthony, of Black-Borton (a Sir Anthony Hungerford, of Black-Borton, died in 1657, and was buried there). This Sir Edward died October 23, 1648, ae. 52, having married Margaret, daughter and coheir of William Holladay, alderman of London, by whom he had another Sir Edward, K. B., who died 1711, having foolishly dissipated the estate of his ancestors.

(Page 291) ANNE PERCY (probably youngest daughter of Henry, second Earl of Northumberland) was born at Dugnanis (so it seems written in Cavell's Roll, but is thought to mean Dungeness in Scotland) on February 3, anno MCCCC. As she lived to the year 1522, it is most credible that she was one of the youngest of the second Earl's children, and most probably born after 1428. She was married first, to Sir Thomas Hungerford, son of Robert, Lord Hungerford and Molyns, and had issue by him of one daughter, wife of Sir Edward Hastings, Knt., and mother of the first Earl of Huntingdon; secondly, to Sir Laurence Raynsford, Knt.; and thirdly, to Sir Hugh Vaughan, Knt. She lived to an extreme old age, according to Dugdale, who says she died July 5, 1522, and was buried in St. Michael's Chapel, within the church of St. Margaret, Westminster.

References: Collins' "Peerage of England." From chart "Peerage of England," Vol. IX.

10. MARGARET COURTENAY, first dau., m. Thomas Peverill, of Parke, Hamatethy, Penhale, etc., County Cornwall, and had

11. CATHERINE PEVERILL, m. before Sept. 18, 1402, Walter Hungerford, who was b. about June 22, 1378. He was nominated Knight of the Bath in 1399. She was living as late as June 14, 1426.

CHART 1

A GENEALOGICAL TABLE OF THE FAMILY OF JOFCELINE DE COURTENAY, COUNT OF EDEFFA

ATHON, who fortified the Town COURTENAY about 1000, and gave that Name to his Family

1ſt wife, Hildegarde, dau. of Jeofry Ferrole, Count of Gaftinois. = Jofeline de Courtenay = 2nd wife, Ifabel. dau. of Guy, Seigneur de Montlehery.

1. Dau., named Hodierr e = Jeofry Count de Joigny.
1. Miles, Seigneur 1ſt wife, a dau. of a Prince of = 2. Jofceline, 1ſt Count of Edeffa. = 2nd wife, a dau. of Roger, 3. Jeofry de Courtenay.
de Courtenay.   Armenia.   Prince of Antioch.

Jofceline, 2nd Count of Edeffa = Beatrix, widow of William de Saona.   Stephania de Courtenay, Abbefs of St. Mary-major in Jerufalem.

1. Jofceline, 3rd Count of Edeffa = Agnes, dau. of Henry de Buffle.   2. Elizaleth. who d. young.   3. Agnes = Almerick, King of Jerufalem.
                                                         —She had 3 other husbands.

1. Beatrix = Court Alimond.   2. Agnes = William de Mandalee.

        1. Baldwin 4, King of Jerufalem.   2. Silylla, Queen of Jerufalem = 1. William, Marquefs of Montferrat.
                                                                 2. Guy of Lufignan, King of Jerufalem.
        Baldwin 5, King of Jerufalem. d. an infant.

CHART 2

(A Genealogical Hiſtory of the Noble and Illuſtrious Family of Courtenay in Three Parts, by E. Cleveland. B.D.—Printed by Edw. Farley, at Shakeſpear s
Head near Eaſt-gate, 1/35:—Book 1, pages 1 and 113.)

A GENEALOGICAL TABLE OF THE FAMILY OF REGINALD DE COURTENAY WHO WAS THE FIRST OF THAT FAMILY THAT
CAME INTO ENGLAND

ATHON, who fortified the Town COURTENAY about the year 1000, and gave that name to his Family

Hildegarde, dau. of Jeofry Ferrole, Count of Gaftinois = Jofeline 1, Seigneur de Courtenay = Ifabel, dau. of Guy, Seigneur de Montlehery.

Hodierne = Jeofry 2, Count de Joigny.
Emengarde. dau. of Renaud. Count de Nevers = 1. Miles.   2. Jofceline. Count of Edeffa.   3. Jeofry Courtenay de Chaplay.

1. Jofceline. A ſifter cf Guy du Donjon = 2. Reginald = Hawife, dau. of Robert de Aincourt.   3. William. = Matilda. dau. of Robert Fitz-Ede.

Peter, ſon of Lewis le Groffe, = Elizabeth.   1. William = Ada.   2. Robert = Alicia de Romeli.   3. Reginald.
King of France.

1. Robert = Mary de Redvers. dau. of William, Earl of Devonshire.   2. Henry.   3. Reginald.   4. Egeline = Gilbert Baffet.

1. John = Ifabel, dau of Hugh, Earl of Oxford.   2. William = a dau. of William Baffet.   3. Hawife = John de Nevil.

Hugh Courtenay, Baron of Okehampton = Eleanor, dau. of Hugh Defpenfer. Earl of Winchefter.

1. Hugh, Earl of = Agres, dau. of 2. Philip of Moreton.   3. Margaret = John Mules.   4. Aveline = John Giffard.   5. Ifabel = John, Lord St. John.
Devon.   John, Lord St. John.   6. Egeline = John Scales.

1. Hugh. Earl of Devon = Marg. de Bohun.   2. Robert.   3. John Abbott of Taviſtock.   4. Thomas = Muriel de Mulis.   5. Eleanor.   6. Elizabeth
                                                        Ancestor of Elizabeth Rix-
                                                        ford. through the Hungerford
                                                        line.

1. Hugh = Elizabeth,   2. Thomas.   3. Edward.   1. Hugh d. without iffue.   2. Margaret = Thomas Peverel.   3. Muriel = John Dinham.
dau. of   Emma, dau of 4. William.   5. Philip = Anne, dau. of   6. John.   7. Peter., 8. Humphry. 9. Elizabeth.
Guy de Brian.   Sir J. Dauney   Sir Thomas   10. Margaret. 11. Joan. 12. Catherine.
                                                  Wade.   13. Matilda. 14. Eleanora. 15. Guinora.
                                                                  16. Ifabel. 17. Philippa.

Hugh = Joan. dau. of Thomas Holland.   1. Edward. Earl of Devonfhire.   1. Richard, Bifhop of Norwich. 2. Sir John. 3. Sir William.
Earl of Kent. d. without iffue.   2. Hugh of Haccomb.

ELIZABETH HUNGERFORD PHELPS

Whose lineage gives her granddaughter (Mrs. Oscar H.) Elizabeth M. Rixford, membership in the National Society of Magna Charta Dames traced to Robert de Vere, the 3rd Earl of Oxford. Mrs. Rixford is Regent for the State of Vermont.

12. ·ROBERT, LORD HUNGERFORD, m. at Heytesbury, Wilts, Margaret, only dau. and heiress of William, Lord Botreau, by Elizabeth, dau. of John, Lord Beaumont. He d. May 18, 1459, and was bur. in Salisbury Cathedral. His wife d. Feb. 7, 1477-8.

13. ·ROBERT, LORD HUNGERFORD, and Lord Molyns, son and heir, b. prior to 1429. Beheaded May 18, 1464, at Newcastle, Northumberland. He m. before Nov. 4, 1440, Eleanor, dau. and heir of Sir William de Moleyns, of Stoke Pogis, County Bucks, by Anne, dau. of John Whalesborough of Cornwall.

14. SIR WALTER HUNGERFORD, younger son, d. 1516; m. Jane, widow of Thomas Bulstrode, and had

15. SIR EDWARD HUNGERFORD, of Heytesbury, Wiltshire, and of Farleigh Hungerford, Somersetshire, m. (1) Jane, dau. of John Zouche, Lord Zouche, of Harringsworth, and had

16. SIR WALTER HUNGERFORD, of Heytesbury, Wilts, and of Farleigh Hungerford, Somerset, son and heir of Sir Edward Hungerford by first wife, was b. probably about 1502. He m. (1) Susan, dau. of Sir John Danvers, of Culworth Northants, by Anne, dau. of Sir John Stradling, of Dauntsey, Wilts. She d. before Mar. 22, 1526-7. He was beheaded July 28, 1540.

17. LUCY HUNGERFORD, widow of Sir John St. John, m. Sir Anthony Hungerford, b. 1564; d. 1627.

18. THOMAS HUNGERFORD, landed on the shores of New England in 1628; bapt. probably at Bremhill Parish, England, in 1602; d. at New London, Conn., 1663; who m., name unknown, and had

19. THOMAS HUNGERFORD, b. 1648; d. 1714; m. before June 6, 1671, Mary Green, of Narragansett, and had

20. THOMAS HUNGERFORD, b. about 1673; d. 1750; m. 1699, Elizabeth, dau. of Mathew Smith and Mary Cutler, and had

21. SAMUEL HUNGERFORD[1], b. about 1713; d. at New Fairfield, Conn.; m. June 23, 1746, Mary Graves, b. probably at Hatfield, Aug. 20, 1722, and had

22. ISAIAH HUNGERFORD, b. Jan. 23, 1757; d. June 16, 1833; m. Esther Mead, b. Aug. 11, 1760; d. Dec. 22, 1836, and had

23. SAMUEL HUNGERFORD[2], b. Aug. 12, 1799, at New Fairfield, Conn., brother of Elizabeth Hungerford Phelps; d. Nov. 21, 1883, at Farnham, Que.; m. (1) Mirabah Phelps; d. May 6, 1850; m. (2) Mar. 23, 1858, Mary Wilson.

24. SAMUEL JAMES HUNGERFORD[3], of Montreal, Que., b. at Farnham, Que., July 16, 1873; m. at Winnipeg, Man., Apr. 13, 1893, Alberta, dau. of Rev. J. W. Demorest.

Mr. Hungerford, when a boy of 14 at Farnham, Que., became acquainted with the railway locomotive; metaphorically speaking, he boarded it then and made it carry him from the lathe of the machinist's apprentice, to the chair of the vice-president of the Grand Division of the Canadian National Railways, the world's greatest railway. Mr. Hungerford is a man of quick action who never seems to be in a hurry. He has a wide circle of friends in the railway world, friends that he made while mastering his various jobs in the mechanical department at important railway points clear across the country. First as a machinist's apprentice and then in the mechanical department of the Canadian Northern Railroad of the Western Lines. At the end of five years the mechanical line of the road was in first-class shape and S. J. Hungerford's jurisdiction was extended over the Eastern Lines of the system. In 1915 when a vacancy occurred in the management of the Eastern Lines of the Canadian Northern, Mr. Hungerford was appointed vice-president of operating and maintenance activities. On Feb. 20, 1924, the three Grand Divisions of the Atlantic, Eastern and West Regions consolidated and Mr. Hungerford was made vice-president in charge of operations and maintenance. After the roads were consolidated the name was changed to Canadian National Railways. Those who know Mr. Hungerford well, have complete

confidence in his capacity.   He is regarded as one of those men, who
with the president, will set new standards of devotion to duty and
loyalty to employers; in this case the general public of Canada.
Children:
 Alice, b. 1894, at Farnham, Que.
 Ethel, b. 1895, at Montreal, Que.; m. at Montreal, Apr. 14, 1931,
  William Bernard Schon.
 Beryl Maryion, b. 1898, at Farnham, Que.; m. A. E. Romeril, of
  Toronto, Ont. She d. Nov. 3, 1931. They had one dau., Arline.
 Stewart James, b. 1908, at Winnipeg, Man., a graduate of McGill
  University, Montreal, 1931.

Mrs. Reginald Clare Snyder, Norwalk, Ohio, a direct descendant
of this house and an accepted member of the Magna Charta Dames
from records furnished by Mrs. Elizabeth M. Rixford, author of this
genealogy. Mrs. Snyder is historian of the Ohio Society of the Daughters of the American Colonists.

Mrs. Leon C. (Lillian Soule) Butterfield, 167 South Oxford St.,
New York, N. Y., a direct descendant of this house and an accepted
member of the Magna Charta Dames from records furnished by the
author of this genealogy.

References : 1 to 18 generations—Col. by Elizabeth M. Rixford.
              18 to 23 generations—"Thos. Hungerford and His Descend-
               ants," by F. P. Leach.
              24 generations—Col. by Elizabeth M. Rixford.

(Page 16)   Some of the other descendants who are entitled to
this Royal Line through the Hungerfords are the children and
descendants of Nash David and Elizabeth Hungerford Phelps,
namely: Mrs. Henry Buckland, Mrs. Alexander Douglas, David
Alfred Phelps, Mrs. Asa Russell, Mrs. Horatio Currie, Mrs. Heman
Mitchell Fairfield, Mrs. Horace B. Leach, Mrs. Arvide Martin and
their descendants.

 (Pages 11-12)   Eunice Hungerford, sister of Samuel Hungerford[1], born in New Fairfield, Conn., 1751; died in Fairfield, Vt.,
August 19, 1839, aged 88 (gravestone); m. Joseph Soule (Mayflower Ancestry from George Soule), b. 1747, in Dover, Dutchess
County, N. Y., and went to Fairfield, Vt.

See "Thomas Hungerford and His Descendants," by F. Phelps
Leach.

Both families and their descendants are entitled to the Royal
Ancestry of the Hungerford Family, also all the descendants of
Thomas Hungerford (page 7).

FARLEIGH-HUNGERFORD CASTLE

The ruins of an ancient building generally set the mind of the
observer reflecting on the history, strange and eventful as it may be,
that the old walls enshrine.   And the curiosity thus aroused is deep-
ened when the remains contemplated are those of a castle, because
they at once carry the thought back to feudal days, when the owner
of the fortress ruled like a petty sovereign over his tenants and
dependants, and when

> A thousand vassals muster'd round,
> With horse and hawk, and horn and hound,

SCHON-HUNGERFORD WEDDING GROUP

Mr. William Bernard Schon, and his bride, Miss Ethel Gertrude Hungerford, with their attendants. The wedding having taken place on Tuesday evening, April 14, 1931 in Dominion-Douglas Church. From left to right: Mrs. L. M. Hart, Mr. Stewart Hungerford, Miss Arline Romeril, of Toronto, flower girl, Mr. Allan Matthews, Mrs. George M. Grant, of Ottawa, the bride, Mr. Philip Allison, of Toronto, who was best man, Mrs. A. E. Romeril, of Toronto, who was her sister's matron of honor, Mr. E. Faret Mason, Miss Alice Hungerford, Mr. A. F. McLachlin, and Mrs. J. W. Baldwin, of Halifax, N. S., sister of the groom. The bride is the daughter of Mr. and Mrs. Samuel Hungerford, and the groom a son of the late William Schon and Mrs. Schon, of Halifax. Mr. Hungerford, the father of the bride, is Vice-President of the Canadian National Railways.

FARLEIGH-HUNGERFORD CASTLE
Chapel and Gatehouse looking east.

or at other time were marshalled to follow their lord in tournay or in war. During its long existence in grim strength the seat of the Hungerfords must often have been the center of such scenes as these, as well as of tournament and joust, with now and then gay hunting and hawking cavalcades passing out of its chief gateway to enjoy the sport the surrounding country afforded, unless war's alarms and dynastic struggles compelled the raising of the drawbridge and the garrison to keep watch and ward on the battlement. How different is the aspect now! Shapeless walls, a couple of time-worn towers, the gateway, chapel, and priests' house, are all that remain of this once great stronghold, supplying with its greensward a delightful haven for picnic parties and school treats.

For three centuries the Hungerfords lorded over the castle and retainers. Their wealth was great, acquired mainly by the ruling habit of wooing and winning well-endowed heiresses in successive generations. Their success in this branch of the matrimonial market explains how it was they were enabled to boast that they could ride from Farleigh to Salisbury on lands of their own, though there were one or two breaks in the continuity implied. Among the predecessors in the ownership of the manor was Smewin, a Saxon thane, who held it in the time of Edward the Confessor. Long, however, before the advent of the Saxons, the Romans had a settlement here, as in so many other beautiful spots, and traces of their occupation have been revealed in coins, baths, and a tesselated pavement (removed to the Ashmolean Museum) from time to time unearthed. Like so many of his class, Smewin was deprived of his patrimony at the time of the Conquest, when it was bestowed on Sir Roger de Curcelle, who came over with the Conqueror. At his death it passed to the Crown, and in due time it was granted by William Rufus to Hugh de Montfort, another of William's Norman followers. His descendant sold it *temp.* Edward III to Bartholomew Lord Burghersh who distinguished himself by his valor in the wars of his day, particularly at the Battle of Cressy. The next owner by purchase was Sir Thomas Hungerford, who took possession in 1369. It was in the early part of this century that the family came to the surface. Deriving their name from Hungerford, in Berkshire, they appear to have had some property there, but soon became identified with Salisbury, where they owned a house or two. Walter Hungerford was bailiff of the town in 1333, and his elder brother, Sir Robert, was a justice in Eyre, and represented the county in Parliament; he died in 1352. Sir Thomas, a son of Walter, was steward to John of Gaunt, and for a short time was the first speaker of the House of Commons. He it was who purchased Farleigh and some estates at Heytesbury, being then described as a "citizen and merchant of New Sarum," for the See of which he was special attorney in 1357. His son Walter was the great man of the family. He was Lord High Treasurer of England in the reign of Henry VI. He had served at Agincourt under Henry V and obtained a good share of the spoils of war, including the Barony of Homet, in Normandy, which he held under the Crown by one of those singular tenures, not uncommon at the period, of rendering every year at the Castle of Rouen, one lance with a fox's brush hanging to it.   The duty was less strange than one which governed the holding of a manor in Essex; there, scalding the King's pigs gave the noble possessors their title. Lord Hungerford stood high in the favor of Henry, who made him a Knight of the Garter, Constable of Windsor Castle, Captain of Cherbourg, in France, and Lord Steward of the Household; he was also one of the executors of the King's will.   The wealth he amassed from these sources was further augmented by marrying a rich heiress, who brought him as her dower the great estates of the Peverells, of Devonshire.

In the meantime the house built by the Montforts had been converted into a castle.   Sir Thomas Hungerford, in 1383, obtained a royal license to make the conversion, at the same time he changed the name from Farleigh Montford, as hitherto called to Farleigh Hungerford.   At his death the castle was left unfinished, but it was completed by his son Walter.   During the Wars of the Roses the Hungerfords changed sides, first fighting for York and then for Lancaster, sacrificing in the cause of the latter many of their estates. Indeed, the manor of Farleigh was held for a time by the Crown, and was then bestowed on the Duke of Clarence, whose daughter Margaret, Countess of Salisbury, was born in the castle in 1473. She perished on the scaffold in 1541, one of the many victims of Henry VIII's tyranny.   Such was the sad fate of the last of the Plantagenets, a niece of Edward IV and Richard III.

It was about the time of the above tragedy that Leland was perambulating Wiltshire.   In his Itinerary he gives a fair, if quaint description of the castle as he then saw it.   He says (modernizing his spelling):   "Before I came to the castle I crossed Frome water, which, passing through a rocky valley and bottom, breaketh into armlets, making islands, but soon meeting again, join the principal stream.   This water runneth close to the fortress and there driveth a mill.   The castle, set on a rocky hill, is partly surrounded by a moat; it hath divers pretty towers in the outer court, where is an ancient chapel and a new one (a chantry) annexed to it.   There were two priests officiating in the chapel, at the end of which they had a pretty mansion.   The gatehouse of the inner court is fair, and bears the arms of the Hungerfords, richly carved in stone.   The hall, and three chambers within the second court, are stately.   There is a common saying that one of the Hungerfords built this part of the castle by the prey of the Duke of Orleans whom he had taken prisoner."   To this account a few more details may be added.   The two courts mentioned ran north and south, and were separated from each other by a crenellated walk, and a gateway flanked by two circular turrets.   In the outer were the stables and offices; in the inner, the residential portion.   This court measured 180 feet in length from east to west, and 144 feet in breadth, the four towers that flanked it were sixty feet in height, with walls five to eight feet thick.   Here

EAST WINDOW OF FARLEIGH CHAPEL

There is some fine old glass in the east window of fifteenth century date, said to have been brought from abroad, and believed to be Spanish. The subjects are Moses and the Brazen Serpent, Job and His Wife, St. Francis and St. Clare, St. Luke, and the Madonna and Child, and the Resurrection. There are other fine specimens of old Flemish glass.

FARLEIGH-HUNGERFORD CASTLE
East Gatehouse from the west.

were the great hall or armory, as well as the state apartments, which were sumptuously furnished. Round the walls of the former were hung the armor worn by its martial possessors, and spoils brought ·from Cressy, Poitiers, Agincourt and Calais. Some of the armor was removed to the chapel as well as an old chest containing sundry papers, including letters of Oliver Cromwell, one of which was framed and hung on the wall, but it was stolen by a visitor in 1789, who offered to restore it to Colonel Houlton on receipt of £10. What became of it and the other contents of the chest is not known. The chief entrance of the building was through the gatehouse, still remaining; it bears the crest of the family—a wheatsheaf and two sickles, also the letters "E. H."

When the castle was erected the Parish Church was included in its precincts in order to form the domestic chapel of the family. Another was built in its place by Lord Walter and still stands. In fact one of the characteristics of the Hungerfords was their devotion to the Church, as attested by the churches they built in Wiltshire and Somerset, their liberality to various religious houses, and the chantries founded by them in Salisbury Cathedral, at Chippenham, Wellow, as well as at Farleigh. In 1427, Lord Hungerford purchased the manor and advowson of Rowley, and a few acres of land at Iford, the latter being of importance to him as it enabled him to enlarge his park considerably.

DEVEREUX

Arms—Argent, a fesse gules in chief three torteaux.
Crest—Out of a ducal coronet or, a talbot's head argent, eared gules.
Motto—*Virtutis comes invidia.* (Envy is the companion of virtue.)

The surname Devereux originated as D'Evreux, from Evreux, an arrondissement in the Department Eure, in Normandy, France. ("Colonial Families," 1928, pages 183-185.)

1. WALTER DEVEREUX, Court of Rosmor, aided William the Conqueror in the conquest of England, and received for his valiant service the lordships of Salisbury and Amesbury in Wiltshire. His sons were: *Geruld*, b. in Normandy, who became Earl of Rosmor, whose line became extinct in the third generation; *Edward*, ancestor of the Earls of Salisbury; and *Robert*, of whom further.
2. ROBERT D'EVREUX, son of Walter D'Evreux, was Court of Rosmor.
3. REGINALD D'EVREUX, only son and heir of Robert D'Evreux.
4. WILLIAM D'EVREUX, only son and heir of Reginald D'Evreux, m. Halewyse.
5. ·EUSTACE D'EVREUX, only son and heir of William D'Evreux.
6. STEPHEN D'EVREUX (or D'EBROIS), only son of Eustace D'Evreux, attended King John in his expedition into Poitou in the fifteenth year of his reign, and also served King Henry III in his wars against the Welsh. He m. Isabel, surname unknown.
7. ·WILLIAM D'EVEREUX, son of Stephen and Isabel D'Evereux, was one of the baron's marchers against the Welsh; but at the Battle of Lewes, May 14, 1264, he sided with Simon Montfort, against the King, and was slain in the Battle of Evesham, Aug. 4, 1265. He m. Maud Gifford, sister to Walter Gifford, Bishop of Bath and Wells.
8. WILLIAM D'EVEREUX, only son of William and Maud (Gifford) D'Evereux,

had summons to Parliament as baron, A. D. 1298. He m. Alice, surname unknown.

9. ▪SIR WILLIAM D'EVEREUX, son of William and Alice D'Evereux, m. Alice, surname unknown.
10. ▪SIR WALTER DEVEREUX, son of Sir William and Alice D'Evereux, m. Margery, surname unknown.
11. SIR WILLIAM DEVEREUX, second son of Sir Walter and Margery Devereux, was seated at Bodenham and Whitechurch in Herefordshire; and was sheriff of County Hereford in 1371 and 1376. He m. Anne Barre, dau. of Sir John Barre.
12. SIR WALTER DEVEREUX, son of Sir William and Anne (Barre) Devereux, was sheriff of Herefordshire, and in 1383 m. Agnes Crophull, dau. of Thomas Crophull, and had four sons and two daus.
13. WALTER DEVEREUX, oldest son of Sir Walter and Agnes (Crophull) Devereux, m. Elizabeth Bromwich, dau. of Sir Thomas Bromwich.
14. SIR WALTER DEVEREUX, son and heir of Walter and Elizabeth (Bromwich) Devereux, m. Elizabeth Merbury, dau. and heir of Sir John Merbury.
15. ▪SIR WALTER DEVEREUX, oldest son of Sir Walter and Elizabeth (Merbury) Devereux, m. Anne Ferrers, sole dau. and heir to William, Lord Ferrers of Chartley, and by the special favor of Henry VI had livery of her lands. By this marriage he laid the foundation for the great honors the family afterward attained. In 1456, he was sheriff of Herefordshire; and on July 26, 1461, was summoned to Parliament by the title of Lord Ferrers. In 1470 he had a grant for life of County Caenarvon, and was installed Knight of the Garter; but adhering afterward to Richard III he was slain with him Aug. 22, 1485, at Bosworth Field, leaving three sons and a dau.
16. ▪JOHN DEVEREUX, oldest son of Sir Walter and Anne (Ferrers) Devereux, was summoned to Parliament as Lord Ferrers of Chartley from the third year of Henry VII to the eleventh. He m. Cecilie Bourchier, dau. of Henry Bourchier, and sister and sole dau. of Thomas Plantagenet, Duke of Sussex, maternally descended from Thomas Plantagenet, Duke of Gloucester, youngest son of Edward III; and thus from Edward I.
17. ▪WALTER DEVEREUX, only son of John and Cecilie (Bourchier) Devereux, was third Lord Ferrers, and served King Henry VIII in his wars with France, and for gallant behavior was elected on July 13, 1523, one of the Knights Companions of the Garter; and on Feb. 2, 1549-50, was advanced to the dignity of Viscount Hereford and to his heirs male forever. He d. Sept. 27, 1558. He m. (1) Mary Grey, a dau. of Thomas Grey, Marquis of Dorset.
18. ▪KATHERINE DEVEREUX, dau. of Walter and Mary (Grey) Devereux, m. Sir James Baskerville. (Burke's "Royal Families," Vol. I, says "Sybil," instead of Katherine. This follows Banks and Collins.) (See Baskerville XII.)

Mrs. (James) Hazel May Leach Allard is 31st in direct descent from (1) Walter D'Evreux, Court of Rosmor.

(Burke's "Royal Families,"

HENRY III, King of England = Eleanor, dau. and coheir of Raymond

Edward I, King of Eng- = Margaret, dau. of Philip'   Blanche, Queen Dowager
land. | III, King of France.   of Navarre.

Edmund Plantagenet,   = Margaret, sister and   Maud, dau. and heir of
surnamed "of Woodstock," | heir of Thomas, Lord   Sir Patrick Chaworth.
Earl of Kent, 2nd son. | Wake.

Edward, the   = Joan Plantagenet, the   = Sir Thos. de Hol-
Black Prince, 3rd | "Fair Maid of Kent," | land, K. G. Lord
husband. | m. 1st William Mon- | Holland, 2nd hus-
                  | tacute, Earl of Salis- | band
                  | bury.

King Richard II, d.s.p.   Thomas de Holland, 2nd Earl =
                                 of Kent.

John Beaufort, Marquess of Dorset, = Lady Margaret Holland, 2nd =
son of John of Gaunt. Duke of Lan- | dau. and eventual coheir of
caster, by Katherine Swynford, 1st hus- | Thomas, Earl of Kent.
band.

Lady Joan Beauford, eldest dau. of John, Marquess of Dorset.   =

The Princess Jane Stuart, dau. of James I, King of Scotland, and relict of =
James Douglas, Earl of Morton.

Lady Elizabeth Gordon, 5th dau. of George, 2nd Earl of Huntly.   =

Lady Agnes Keith, dau. of William, 3rd Earl Marischal, 1st wife.   =

Sir William Douglas, of Glenbervie, s. his kinsman as 9th Earl of Angus =
in 1588.

Sir Robert Douglas, 2nd son, had Glenbervie from his father, knighted by =
King James VI.

The Rev. George Douglas, D.D., 2nd son.   =

William Douglas, of Airdit.   =

The Rev. Sir Robert Douglas, of Airdit, D.D., Rector of Stepney, s. his =
cousin as 4th Baronet of Glenbervie, d. 1750.

Sir Robert Douglas, 5th Bart. of Glenbervie, author of the "Peerage and =
Baronage of Scotland."

Janet, dau. and eventual heir of Sir Robert Douglas.   =

Sir Kenneth Mackenzie, a General in the army, created a Baronet in 1831, =
d. Nov. 22, 1833.

Sir Robert   = Martha   Kenneth,   Alexander, an officer in the army, m.
Andrews | Elizabeth, Lieut., 58th Ester Phelps, sister of Mrs. Caroline
Douglas, | eldest dau. Regt., d. in Phelps Leach, and dau. of David Nash
2nd Bart., | of Joshua   1830.   and Elizabeth Hungerford Phelps.
b. in 1807: | Rouse, Esq.   had issue.
d. Nov. 1,
1843

SIR ROBERT DOUGLAS, 3rd and present Baronet of Glenbervie,
EDWARD I, King of England, 17th from Robert Bruce. King
CERDIC, first of the West Saxon Kings, began reign in A. D. 500.

Berenger, Count of Provence.   ROBERT BRUCE, King of Scotland.

= Edmund, Earl of Lancaster.

= Henry, Earl of Lancaster.

Walter, Lord High Steward of Scotland. = The Princess Margery, dau. of Robert Bruce.

Richard Fitzalan, Earl of Arundel K. G. = Lady Eleanor Plantagenet, widow of John, Lord Beaumont.

Robert II, King of Scotland =

Lady Alice Fitzalan, dau. of the Earl of Arundel.

: Thomas Plantagenet. Duke of Clarenece, son of Henry IV, 2nd husband.

Robert III, King of Scotland. =

: James I, King of Scotland.

: George Gordon, 2nd Earl of Huntly, Lord High Chancellor of Scotland, d. in 1507.

: William Keith, 3rd Earl Marischal, d. about 1530.

: Sir Archibald Douglas, of Glenbervie, knighted by King James V, only son of the Hon. Sir William Douglas, of Glenbervie, 2nd son of Archibald, 5th Earl of Angus.

Giles, dau. of Sir Robert Graham, of Mortphy.

Elizabeth, dau. of Sir George Auchinleck, of Balmanno.

Cicely, dau. and coheir of Sir Robert Drury, of Rougham.

Agnes, dau. of Sir Patrick Scot, of Ancrum.

Jane Paterson, Lady Dunmure, 2nd wife.

Margaret, eldest dau. of Sir James Macdonald, of Macdonald, Bart.

Mackenzie a younger son of Donald Mackenzie, Esq., of Kilcoy, Co. Ross.

Rachel, only child and heir of Robert Andrews, Esq., of Hythe, in Kent.

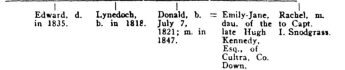

| Edward, d. in 1835. | Lynedoch, b. in 1818. | Donald, b. July 7, 1821; m. in 1847. | = Emily-Jane, dau. of the late Hugh Kennedy, Esq., of Cultra, Co. Down. | Rachel, m. to Capt. I. Snodgrass. |

b. July 19, 1837; 18th in a direct descent from of Scotland, and 44th in direct descent from ("Colonial Families," 1928, pages 181, 182.)

ALEXANDER DOUGLAS, born December 25, 1817; died Stanbridge, Que., November 22, 1871; married Esther Phelps, born August 8, 1827; died November 23, 1905. They had children born in Stanbridge, Que.:

1. HEBERT DOUGLAS.
2. JOHN DOUGLAS, b. Mar., 1851; d. Sept., 1920.
3. BERTHA DOUGLAS, b. Aug., 1853; d. July 1, 1871, unm.
4. IDA DOUGLAS, b. Mar. 31, 1855.
5. NANCY DOUGLAS, b. July 31, 1859; d. June 27, 1909; m. —— Roark.
6. CHARLES A. DOUGLAS, b. 1860; d. Feb., 1921.
7. CAROLINE DOUGLAS, b. Oct. 3, 1862.
8. LESLIE DOUGLAS, b. 1867; d. Dec., 1901.
9. ·ALFRED E. DOUGLAS, b. Sept. 15, 1869.

2. ·JOHN DOUGLAS, married and had two children:

(1) ·MABEL DOUGLAS, b. May, 1874; m. —— Futboye.
(2) ·ALFRED DOUGLAS, b. Apr., 1876; d. 1924.

4. ·IDA DOUGLAS, married first, —— Hauver. She married second, Burt Jenkins. By her first husband she had the following children:

(1) ELLA M. HAUVER, b. Mar. 15, 1877; m. —— Hood.
(2) ELSIE M. HAUVER, b. Dec. 22, 1882; m. —— Cross.
(3) ·BERTHA E. HAUVER, b. Dec. 30, 1884; d. Aug. 28, 1885.

(1)·ELLA M. HAUVER HOOD had children as follows:

a. ESTER HOOD, b. Mar. 6, 1898; m. —— Gibbons.
b. ALLAN HOOD, b. Mar. 2, 1900.
c. LESLIE HOOD, b. Mar. 23, 1906.

6. ·CHARLES A. DOUGLAS, married and had children as follows:

(1) BERTHA DOUGLAS, m. —— Garnet.
(2) ·GRETA.
(3)·ESTER, m. Charles H. Armstrong, of Arlington, Mass.

(1) ·BERTHA DOUGLAS GARNET had children as follows:

a. CHARLES DOUGLAS GARNET, b. Sept. 28, 1925.
b. ELINOR BERTHA GARNET, b. June 13, 1927.

References: Family Records of Elizabeth M. Rixford.

THE DRAKE FAMILY

By Louis Stoughton Drake, 1896

INTRODUCTION—HOME OF THE DRAKES—pages 1 to 16

Mount Drake, the original home of the Drakes, is situated in the manor of Musbury, Axminster, Devon County. Musbury is a pure Saxon name, "Maest Barrow," or "The Biggest Hill." The British name of the place was "Mae Dun," of which Maist Barrow is a translation. The old name, Mae Dun, survives in a cluster of houses about a quarter of a mile from the present village, where it is corrupted into "Mayden-hayne."

Mount Drake is a tableland or plateau of about 160 acres, half way up the great ridge which goes by the name of Musbury Castle. It was once the seat of a British, and then of a Roman encampment, and was a fortified camp, quite capable of accommodating two hundred persons or more. It was defended on three sides by a natural ravine, and on the upper side by bogs and a tangle of brushwood, part of which still remains.

There are no records existing to show when or by whom the present church at Musbury was built, but early in the days of Queen Elizabeth, if not before, the Drakes had a mortuary chapel attached to it. In the latter part of her reign, or in that of James I, they lengthened this mortuary chapel into an aisle called the Drake Aisle, which was appropriated by their family, retainers and servants. The church records show that, in the time of Charles I, the rector of the church was a Drake, and, with the exception of a few artisans and laborers, all the inhabitants of Musbury, probably about 160, were Drakes, or had married into the Drake family.

John Drake, at the time of his marriage to Christian Billett, although living at Mt. Drake, and presenting to the living of Musbury, was engaged in trade and shipping at Exmouth, nearby. His son John, who succeeded him, was engaged in the same business at Otterton, and his successor, John Drake, although making his home at Mt. Drake, where both he and his son jointly presented to the living of the Musbury Church, was a shipowner and trader at Exmouth.

There was a fortified house at Mt. Drake, before Ashe—an ancient seat in the parish of Musbury, adjoining Mt. Drake—was built. Ashe is about one mile and three-quarters to the south of Axminster, in the eastern confines of Devon County, the barton belonging thereto comprising about 180 acres, lying partly in the parish of Axminster, and partly in the parish of Musbury. It was bought into the Drake family, together with the Kilmington estate of Hampton or Kampton, about sixty acres, by the marriage (1420) of John Drake of Mt. Drake and Exmouth—the first from whom lineal descent can be traced—to Christian, daughter and heiress of John Billett of Ashe, and remained in the family for about 400 years. John Prince, in his "Worthies of Devon" (1701), gives the following in regard to the ancient history of Ashe:

"Ashe was sometimes the dwelling of Quandus de Ash, the most ancient inhabitant that I find there, who gave to, or took name from the place, after whom it was given by John Lord Courtenay, Lord of the manor of Musbury, unto Henry de Esse, or Ash, who gave it to Julian (likely his daughter), wife of John de Orway, or Orway, in the parish of Kentisberr, nigh Cullompton, in this shire; whose son Thomas had issue: John, o.s.p., and two daughters, Joan, wife of John Stretche; and Phillipa, wife of Warren Hampton. Stretche left issue, that died without issue, upon which Ash fell to Hampton, who had issue: First, Joan, thrice married, to Bonvile, Sachvile and Farrington; and, secondly, Alice, wife of John Billett, unto whom Ash was allotted; John Billett and Alice, his wife, had issue: Christiana, their sole daughter and heiress, who married John Drake of Exmouth."

Ashe was not inhabited by the family until the time of Sir Barnard Drake, Kt., who, during his youth, lived at Mt. Drake, and his father, John, although possessing Ashe, apparently lived at Exmouth. This John Drake was acting as steward of Newnham Abbey at the time of its dissolution, and he enriched himself by the purchase of some of the Abbey lands, both in Musbury and across the Axe. Two of his sons were then Abbey tenants, and they both became freeholders. One of them, Robert Drake, married into the family of Prideaux, and John Drake either gave or sold to him an Abbey estate in the parish of North Leigh, about eight miles distant.

On the death of his father, Barnard Drake rebuilt Ashe, and what remains of the house today bears witness that it was built with the stones of the ancient Abbey of Newnham, close by. During the construction of the house he lived at Colyton, and on his removal to Ashe, Mt. Drake was occupied by Henry Drake, a relative. The latter, however, was only a tenant, as were all the subsequent residents at Mt. Drake, till the house was pulled down about seventy years ago.

The estate of Trill, about a mile distant in the parish of Axminster, was acquired by Sir John Drake, of Ashe, who married Elinor Butler, or, as sometimes called, Helen Boteler. He was the godfather of John Prince, Vicar of Pomroy, born 1643, author of "Worthies of Devon." At the present time this is a lovely estate, mostly heath and moorland. The house, which still stands, is about the size of a modern English farmhouse, and it had a walled court, lodge and loop-holed towers. At the death of John Drake, in 1636, he left the estate of Trill to his eldest son, Sir John Drake, knighted by James II. His will may still be seen, in which he left the rest of his property to his widow, Elinor, with certain provisions to be made for his large family at his death.

Prince seems to be incorrect in his account of the destruction of Ashe during the civil wars, and that it "long lay in ruins."

At the death of John (9) Drake, in 1636, his widow, Elinor, remained at Ashe with her numerous family, her eldest son, Sir John Drake, first baronet, then occupying Trill. On the breaking out of the civil war she took zealously the side of the Parliament, and in 1644 sent for soldiers from Lyme and began to fortify her house, whereupon Lord Paulet came and attacked the house, and took it, firing the chapel and destroying the fortifications. The wing of the house, which touched the chapel was set on fire and much damaged, but was extinguished on the surrender of the Lady, which, as she had ten small children with her, she was very glad to make.

That Elinor Drake did not then make her abode at Trill, as stated by Prince, is proven by the parish register of Musbury, which gives positive evidence that she was residing at Ashe, in 1646, when she applied to Parliament to be reimbursed for the damage to her house, and that she resided there as late as 1668.

In 1648, her granddaughter, Arabella, child of her daughter Elizabeth and Sir Winston Churchill, who were then living with her, was baptized in the hall of Ashe House, and John, the illustrious Duke of Marlboro, son of the same Elizabeth and Sir Winston Churchill, was baptized in the chapel of Ashe House in 1650, by which time it had been repaired. Thus the family never went to Trill, and Sir John Drake, first baronet, never lived at Ashe.

At her death, in 1668, Elinor Drake left Ashe House to her nephew, Sir John Drake, second baronet, eldest son of Sir John of Trill, who spent his short tenancy beautifying Ashe and, as Prince says, "bringing it to greater perfection than it was ever before. He enclosed the park adjoining the house with a good wall, made fish ponds, walks, and gardens well furnished with a great variety of choice fruits, so that now it may vye for beauty and delight with most other seats in those parts."

Sir William Drake, sixth baronet, having no issue by his marriage with Ann, eldest daughter of William Peere Williams, the baronetcy, at his death in 1733, became extinct. There being no surviving male descendant of Sir John, first baronet, Sir William left the whole of his property of Mt. Drake, Ashe, Trill, Hampton, etc., to his widow, in her free and absolute disposal, to the exclusion of his own family. About four years after his death she married George Speke, Esq., of Whitelackington, in Somerset, by whom he had a daughter, who married Frederick, Lord North. Soon after his death, which occurred in 1793, the Ashe property, the advowson of the living, and all the estates which had been bequeathed to his widow by Sir William Drake, sixth baronet, were sold by Lord Guilford in parcel, and passed into various hands.

JOHN DRAKE, Esq., of Mount Drake and Exmouth in the County of Devon, "a man of great estate, and a name of no less antiquity," says Prince in his "Worthies of Devon," married in the time of Henry V (1413-22 A. D.), Christiana, daughter and heiress of John Billett, of Ashe. By this alliance the estate of Ashe, in the parish of Musbury, came to the Drake family, and was handed down in the name from father to son for fully four hundred years, although the most usual residence was Mount Drake, a mansion previously built by them in the same parish, and undoubtedly the original home of the Drakes, they having occupied it before the coming of William the Conqueror. This John Drake, or possibly his father, was reported in Exmouth in 1360.

At the death of John, his widow married second, Richard Frankcheney, thus unlawfully excluding from the estate of Ashe her son, John Drake[5] by a suit at law, recovered Ashe, which had been so long and unjustly withheld from his father, grandfather and great-grandfather.

2. JOHN DRAKE[2], numbered in the hundred of East Budleigh, Devon. On the second marriage of his mother, he settled at Otterton, about sixteen miles from Ashe. He m. Christiana, dau. and heiress of John Antage, and had:

3. JOHN DRAKE[3], of Otterton, who m. a dau. of John Crews, or Cruwys, representative of Crews Morehard, an ancient Saxon family of impor-

tance, their name occurring frequently in the old Devonshire rhyming legend concerning Saxon families who were prominent before the coming of William the Conqueror. This John was succeeded by his son:

4. ·JOHN DRAKE[4], of Otterton, in the County of Devon, Esq., who by his wife Agnes, dau. of John Kailway, had:
   5. I.　·*John,* his heir.
      II.　·*Johan,* who m. William Poole.
      III.　·*Robert,* second son.
      IV.　·*Gilbert,* third son.
      V.　·*Thomas,* of Hertford, in the County of Devon, who m. Ellin, dau. of Bennet Hillen, of Fenawtrie, in County of Devon, by whom he had six children, as given in "Visitations of Devon," page 292. His descendants lived in Hertford, Whytecombe Raleigh, Colebrooke, and Musbury.

5. ·JOHN DRAKE[5], ESQ., of Ashe, Exmouth, in the County of Devon, having recovered Ashe, as before stated, m. Margaret, dau. and heiress of John Cole, of Rill, in the parish of Whytecomb Raleigh, Devon, near Exmouth, which he gave, together with the Manor of Whytecomb, aforesaid, unto a younger son, John, whose daughter and heiress brought it to her husband, Thomas Raymond, of Chard. John has issue as follows.
   6. I.　·*John,* his heir.
      II.　·*John,* second son. He was receiver of Exeter, in the defense of which city he was shot through both cheeks by an arrow (Vowell's "Hist. Exeter," page 62). He was bur. Nov. 9, 1554, in St. Petrock, Exeter (St. Petrock, Exeter, Parish Register). He m. Feb. 7, 1540-1, Margaret, dau. and co-heiress of William Hurst, or Auert, as some authorities have it, of Exeter. She was bur. Apr. 6, 1570, in St. Petrock, Exeter.
      III.　·*Alice,* the second wife of Walter Raleigh, father of Sir Walter Raleigh.

DRAKE FAMILY

·JOHN DRAKE, JR.[2], m. Hannah Moore, November 30, 1648; was one of the first settlers at Simsbury; inventory presented September 12, 1689; Simsbury property amounted to £393/15s.; had a son John (now of Danbury) who in 1708 chose a guardian; she d. February 16, 1686.

Children:

JOHN[3], b. Sept. 14, 1649.　　ENOCH[5], b. Dec. 8, 1655.
JOB[4], b. June 15, 1651.　　·RUTH, b. Dec. 8, 1657.
HANNAH, b. Aug. 8, 1653.

' (Page 582) Arms—Argent; a wivern with wings displayed; gules. It is a maxim with the heralds, that the more simple a coat of arms, the more ancient it is; this is too obvious to need any other proof in support of it, than the repetition of the maxim; which eminently applies to the arms of DRAKE.

The crest of this coat, as given by Guilim, is an "Eagle displayed," which seems to have been laid aside for the "dexter arm erect, holding a battle-axe," some ages ago, but wherefore does not appear. The motto has always been: *Aquila non capit muscas.*

The figure in the shield, or escutcheon, is called by heralds a Wivern, which is another name for the fabled Dragon of antiquity. Draco or Drago, is the Roman name of Drake, and as late as the the time of Sir Francis Drake, writers frequently coupled his name with that of Dragon. Lope de Vega calls him by no other name throughout his long poem of ten books, which he composed about him; and Sir Winston Churchill (who married a DRAKE) says, Sir Francis found no Dragon more terrible than himself to guard the treasures of the Spaniards; and surely the Spaniards had reason, if any people could have, to imagine that Sir Francis Drake was descended, and that, too, in no remote degree, from the old master of all that was terrible.

The Romans had among their legions DRACONARII, who were the bearers of their standards; hence the name DRAKE may have been derived from that Roman officer. The Romans got the name from the Greeks, and it seems to have been known other than an ideal one, from the Mediterranean to the Baltic, in earlier and later times.

We find that the DRAGON was displayed in the banners of the Britons as early as 1448, and that churches have borne the emblem from time immemorial.

Another coat of arms was granted by Queen Elizabeth to Sir Francis, the great navigator.

The family of Drake has been distinguished in England from the earliest ages by a long array of noble men—soldiers, navigators, clergymen, martyrs and authors. But our limits forbid us from entering more into details; the curious reader will find these items in the little work from which we have made the preceding extracts. It is sufficient for our purpose to say that among the many noble families of the name, in Great Britain, the family who held their seat at Ashe were ever prominent, and from them it is supposed that the Drakes of New England were descended.

Of this family was JOHN, one of the Council of Plymouth, a member of the original company established by King James, in 1606, for settling New England. Several of his sons came hither and settled, *viz.: Richard,* who came over with two or more sons, and nine daughters, and settled at Hampton, N. H.; and *John,* who came to Boston in 1630 and settled in Windsor. From these are descended all of the name in America.

("History of Windsor, Conn.," 1859, page 583)

JOHN DRAKE, the father of Ruth, was descended from the illustrious English family of that name, which had its seat at Ashe. In England the name has long been borne by many distinguished as navigators, clergymen, martyrs, and authors. Among the foremost of these English families is that which has its seat at Ashe, County Devon, and from it descended the greater portion of the Drakes of Massachusetts and Connecticut. The line of ancestry of the Windsor (Conn.) Drakes may be thus summarized:

ROYAL LINE TO DRAKE FAMILY

, EDWARD I, King of England.   = ·Eleanor, dau. of ·Ferdinand III, King of Castile.

, Lady Elizabeth Plantagenet.   = ·Humphrey de Bohun, Earl of Hereford and Essex.

, Lady Margaret de Bohun, m. in 1325.   = ·Hugh de Courtenay, 2nd Earl of Devon.

·Margaret, dau. of Hugh, Earl of Devon.   = ·Theobald Granville, son of Sir Theobald Granville.

·William Granville, of Stow, in Cornwall, d. about 1450.   = ·Philippa, dau. of William Lord Bonville.

·Sir Thomas Granville, of Stow, High Sheriff, 21 Edward IV.   = ·Elizabeth, sister of Sir Theobald Gorges.

·Sir Thomas Granville, of Stow, K. B., d. 6 Henry VIII.   = ·Isabel, dau. of Sir Otes Gilbert, of Compton.

·Roger Granville, Esq., of Stowe, Sheriff, Temp. Henry VIII, d. in 1524.   = ·Margaret, dau. and coheir of Richard Whitley, of Efford.

·Amyre, dau. of Roger Granville, of Stow.   = ·John Drake, Esq., of Ash, Co. Devon, d. 1558.

See DRAKE ancestry No. 6, John Drake.

(See Burke's "Royal Families," Vol. II, Pedigree cxxix.)

1. JOHN, of Exmouth, Eng., b. 1360; m. Christian, dau. of John Billet; he acquired the estate of Ashe. His widow m. (2) Richard Francheyney.
2. JOHN, m. Christian, dau. of John Antage, and settled at Otterton; founded the Otterton family of Drake, through his son. He was unlawfully excluded from Ashe by his half-brother, Christopher Francheyney (son of his mother by her second marriage).
3. JOHN, inherited Otterton; m. a Cruwys, of Cruwys Morchand.
4. JOHN, of Otterton; m. Agnes, dau. of John Killoway.
5. JOHN, settled first at Axmouth, and by a suit-at-law recovered Ashe. He m. Margaret, dau. of John Cole of Rill.
6. JOHN, inherited Ashe; m. Anne, dau of Roger Greenville; his son, Bernard, inherited Ashe.
7. ROBERT, settled at Wiscomb, parish of South Leigh, County Devon.
8. WILLIAM, of Wiscomb, County Devon.
9. JOHN, b. at Wiscomb, County Devon about 1590 or 1600; m. Elizabeth Rogers. He came to Boston about 1639; he d. from the result of an injury, Aug. 17, 1659. His widow d. Oct. 7, 1681, it is stated, "at 100th year of age." If so, she must have been several years older than her husband, or else, which is more probable, he was b. at a considerably earlier date than stated above.

10. JOHN, b. about 1635; m. Hannah, dau. of Thomas Moore. ("Soc. Col. Wars," page 151—John Drake, Jr., 1656-1739, deputy to General Court Assembly of N. J., 1698; King Philip's War, page 450—John Drake credit 02-1400.
11. RUTH, b. Dec. 1, bapt. Dec. 6, 1657; m. Samuel Barber, of Windsor, Jan. 25, 1677; Samuel Barber was bapt. Oct. 1, 1648.
12. RUTH BARBER, b. July 24, 1683; m. (2) Apr. 18, 1706, William Phelps, who was b. Feb. 4, 1668-9.
13. LIEUT. SAMUEL² PHELPS, b. Apr. 5, 1708; d. Aug. 14-17, 1754; m. 1731, Ruth Phelps, who was b. Jan. 23, 1713.
14. JOEL PHELPS, b. 1732; m. Sept. 8, 1757, Jerusha Nash, b. Oct. 5, 1734; d. Sept. 20, 1813.
15. PHINEAS PHELPS, b. Apr. 10, 1707; d. Apr. 20, 1813; m. Lydia Lawrence, who was b. Jan. 15, 1762, and d. Sept. 20, 1813.
16. NASH DAVID PHELPS, b. Oct. 4, 1796; d. Apr. 15, 1884; m. St. Armand West, Que., Apr. 20, 1821, Elizabeth Hungerford, b. Feb. 7, 1798, and d. Jan. 7, 1878.
17. CAROLINE ALEXANDRIA PHELPS, b. July 3, 1840; d. Mar. 29, 1921; m. at Stanbridge, Que., Sept. 8, 1863, Horace Brayton Leach, b. Sept. 25, 1836; d. May 5, 1919.
18. ELIZABETH MAY LEACH, b. Jan. 7, 1866; living May 6, 1931; m. at Sheldon, Vt., Sept. 8, 1889, Oscar Herbert Rixford, b. Dec. 27, 1859, and d. Sept. 11, 1927.
19. OSCAR ADELBERT RIXFORD, b. Aug. 4, 1890; living May 6, 1931; m. Jan. 18, 1919, at Montreal Que., Mary Carolyn Hefflon, b. June 6, 1899; living May 6, 1931. Children:
    Mary-Elizabeth Lenora, b. Oct. 6, 1922.
    Oscar Theodore, b. July 21, 1925; both living May 6, 1931.

(Page 25)   Children of Ruth Drake and Samuel Barber.

By 1st marriage, born at Windsor:
1. THOMAS, b. Oct. 7, 1671; bur. Oct. 31, 1673.
2. SAMUEL, b. Jan. 26, 1673; m. Martha Ponder.
3. JOHN, probably d. young.

By 2nd marriage:
4. WILLIAM, b. 1678; m. Esther Brown.
5. HANNAH, b. Oct. 4, 1680-1, probably d. young, as she is not mentioned in either her father's, mother's or sister Mindwell's wills.
6. JOSEPH, b. 1681; m. Mary Loomis
7. RUTH, b. July 24, 1683; m. William Phelps.
8. MARY. (See explanation below regarding date of birth.)
9. ELIZABETH, b. Feb. 9, 1684-5; m. Daniel Loomis.
10. DAVID, b. May 12, 1686; m. Hannah Post.
11. SARAH, b. Aug. 28, 1688.
12. BENJAMIN, b. 1690; m. Hannah Lewis.
13. MINDWELL, b. Dec. 3, 1691; unm.
14. JOHN, b. probably about 1694; m. Jane Alvord.

References: "Barber Genealogy"—Desc. of Thomas Barber of Windsor, Conn., and John Barber of Worcester, Mass.
    1 to 11 generations—Records of Elizabeth M. Rixford.
    12 to 14 generations—"Thomas Hungerford Genealogy," by F. Phelps Leach.
    15 to 19 generations—Family Records.

EATON

Arms—Argent, a chevron between three eagles displayed with two heads gules.

The surname Eaton originated from a parish or township Eaton, of which there are several in the Midlands and West of England. The following family probably derives its name from Eaton Township, in Cheshire.

1. SIR NICHOLAS DE EATON, m. Margaret or Margery, dau. and heiress of Sir William Coleville, Knight. He had Nicholas, but outlived him.
2. SIR NICHOLAS DE EATON, JR., became Baron of Stockport, in Cheshire, adjoining Lancashire, by right of his wife, Joan, elder dau. of Sir Richard de Stockport and his wife, Cicely. Joan de Stockport was b. A. D. 1291, and her father d. in 1294. She outlived her husband. They had *Nicholas* and *John,* both of whom died without issue; also *Robert* and *Cicely,* b. at Poynton.
3. CICELY DE EATON, dau. of Sir Nicholas, Jr., and Joan (de Stockport) de Eaton, m. (1) Sir John Arderne, by whom no issue; (2) Sir Edward (2) Warren, son of Sir Edward (1) and Maud (de Skeyton) Warren. (See Warren 12-15, and Stanley 11.)

    Henrietta Read Buker and Ephraim Smith Read, only children of (Mrs. Charles J.) Albert Leach Read, sister of the Author, 25th in direct descent from (No. 1) Sir Nicholas de Eaton.

FERRERS

("Colonial Families," 1928, page 26)

Arms—Argent, six horseshoes sable, pierced or, three, two and one.

The family name Ferrers is usually derived from the occupation of farrier, originally a maker of horseshoes, but in the wars became an important office. Roger le Ferur is on record in the Hundred Rolls of County Dorset. But the de Ferrers, according to Burke, originated from Ferriers or Ferrieres, a small town in the Gastinois (now Le Gatinais), a district near Paris, named from its iron mines.

1. WALCHELIN DE FERRERS, or FERRARIIS, a Norman, was the founder of this family.
2. HENRY DE FERRERS, son of Walchelin de Ferrers, came into England with William the Conqueror, and obtained a grant of Tutbury Castle in County Stafford and large possessions in other counties, including one hundred and fourteen manors in Derbyshire. He m. Bertha, surname unknown, and had three sons, of whom *Eugenulf* and *William* d. before him.
3. ROBERT DE FERRERS, son of Henry and Bertha de Ferrers, was created, in 1138, Earl of Derby, by King Stephen, in consideration of his great services in the famous Battle of Northallerton, commonly called the Battle of the Standard, in which he commanded the Derbyshire men. He d. in 1139. He m. Harvise, surname unknown, and had a son, and three daus., of whom *Isolda,* m. Stephen de Beauchamp; *Maud,* m. Bertram de Verdon; and the third dau. m. Walchelin de Maninot.
4. ROBERT DE FERRERS, son of Robert and Harvise de Ferrers, was second Earl of Derby.

5. WILLIAM DE FERRERS, son of Robert de Ferrers, was the third Earl of Derby, and m. Margaret Peverel, dau. and heiress of William Peverel, of Nottingham, and had *Robert,* and *Walchelin.*
6. ·ROBERT (Heylin says William) DE FERRERS, son of William and Margaret (Peverel) de Ferrers, was fourth Earl of Derby, and m. Sibilla, dau. of William de Braose, and had *William,* and two daus., of whom *Millicent,* m. Roger, Lord Mortimer, of Wigmore.
7. ·WILLIAM DE FERRERS, son of Robert and Sibilla (de Braose) de Ferrers, was the fifth Earl of Derby, but d. soon after his father, in 1192, at the siege of Acre, in the Holy Land, whither he had attended King Richard. He m. and had a son.
8. ·WILLIAM DE FERRERS, son of William de Ferrers, was confirmed Earl of Derby, by special charter of King John in 1199; and in 1233 m. Agnes, one of the sisters and coheirs of Ranulph, Earl of Chester; William and his wife both d. in 1247, leaving issue.
9. ·WILLIAM DE FERRERS, son and heir of William and Agnes de Ferrers, in 1248 had also livery of Chartley Castle and of all the other lands of his mother's inheritance. He was the seventh Earl of Derby, and d. in 1254. He m. (1) Sibyl, or Sibil, dau. and coheiress of William Mareschal, or Marshal, Earl of Pembroke. (See Marshall IV.) He m. (2) Margaret, dau. and coheiress of Roger de Quinci, Earl of Winchester.
    Children by first marriage:
    1. ·*Agnes,* m. William de Vesey.
    2. ·*Isabel,* m. (1) Gilbert Basset; (2) Reginald de Bohun.
    3. ·*Maud,* of whom further.
    4. ·*Sibyl,* m. Franco de Bohun.
    5. ·*Joane,* m. (1) William Aguillon; (2) John de Bohun.
    6. ·*Agatha,* m. Hugh Mortimer, of Chelmarsh.
    7. ·*Eleanor,* m. (1) William de Vallibus; (2) Roger de Quinci, Earl of Winton; (3) Roger de Leyburne.
    ·Children by second marriage:
    ·8. *Robert,* eighth and last Earl of this family.
    9. ·*William,* granted by his mother, Groby Manor, in Leicestershire.
10. ·MAUD DE FERRERS, dau. of William and Sibil (Marshall) de Ferrers, m. (1) William de Kyme; (2) William de Vivon, or Vivonia; (3) Emmeric de Rupelanardi.
11. ·CICELY DE VIVONIA, dau. of William de Vivon, or Vivonia, and Maud, widow of William de Kyme, m. John, son of Robert Beauchamp. (See Beauchamp 4 to 7; Seymour 4-9 and Winslow No. 4.)

Helen Ann Phelps is 34th in direct descent from Robert de Ferrers.

HEMAN MITCHELL, born in East Highgate, Vt., April 14, 1822; married in East Highgate, Vt., May 2, 1857, Helen Ann Phelps (daughter of Nash David), born in Stanbridge, Que., December 21, 1837; died at Monticello, Ind., October 27, 1920. He died at Stanbridge, Que., July 29, 1869.
Children of Heman Mitchell and Helen Ann Phelps:
DAVID NASH MITCHELL, b. Stanbridge, Que., Oct. 2, 1859; d. Pittsfield, Wis.; m. Etta L. Currie at Jacksonville, Ill., June 16, 1886. They have five children as follows: (Dr. Alvin E.) *Mabel Bleck,* of Milwaukee, Wis.; *A. R. Mitchell,* of Madison, Wis.; (Mrs. Harry) *Bertha Franson,* of River Forest Ill.—they have one son, H. Eugene Franson; *Eugene* and *Ronald,* both of Pittsville, Wis. He was a graduate of Bedford, Academy, Bedford, Que. He was a jeweler at Waltham, Mass., and later at Pittsville, Wis. He was register of deeds at Grand Rapids, Wis., elected 1891. He was a member of the Wood County

Jury Commission, He was secretary for many years of the Masonic
Lodge at Pittsville, Wis., where his body reposed in state; under the
auspices of the Pittsville Lodge F. and A. M., of which he had long
been a member.

·HEMAN LESLIE MITCHELL, b. Stanbridge, Que., June 13, 1862; d. Stanbridge, Que., Mar. 21, 1863.

·HOBERT MITCHELL, b. Stanbridge, Que., Apr. 28, 1865; he was a goldsmith;
d. Waltham, Mass., July 1, 1883.

·FLORENCE MAY MITCHELL, b. Stanbridge, Que., Sept. 28, 1868; m. E. R.
Abbot, of 612 American Bank Bldg., 2nd and Spring St., Avelon, Calif.

Children of Helen Ann Phelps and second husband, Samuel
Fairfield, of St. Sebastien, Que. He was born November 9, 1841;
married January 23, 1873, at Stanbridge, Que. He died October 21,
1914, at Mystic Que.

JAMES FREDERICK FAIRFIELD, b. Stanbridge, Que., Aug. 14, 1875; m. Aug.
30, 1894, at Laconia, N. H., Etta Jane Hughey. They had one son,
Clayton George, b. Bedford, Que., Sept. 12. 1895. She d. Sept. 20,
1895. He m. (2) to Edna Marion Miller, North Stanbridge, Que.,
Oct. 21, 1897. She was b. at Pike River, Feb. 11, 1877. They had
children, *Claude Wesley Fairfield,* b. North Stanbridge, July 18, 1898.
Thelma Ruth Fairfield, b. at North Stanbridge, Que., Mar. 26, 1903.
She m. John F. Emms, 4832a Park Ave., Montreal, Que., by whom
she had a dau.

FITZ-ALAN

Arms—Gules, a lion rampant or, enraged azure.

Fitz-Alan as a family, which for some two centuries held Arundel, the premier earldom of England, came of the same Breton house
from which was derived the Royal House of Stuart. Henry I granted
to his second wife the "honour" of Arundel, of which the castle was
the head and which comprised a large portion of County Sussex.
After the death of Henry I, she married William "de Albini" (*i.e.,*
d'Aubigny), who from about 1141 is variously styled Earl of Sussex,
of Chichester, or of Arundel, or even Earl William de Albini. His
male line became extinct in 1243, and in the partition of his estates
the castle and honour of Arundel went to his second sister's
son, John, of whom further. ("Colonial Families," 1928, pages
182-183.)

1. ·JOHN FITZ-ALAN, Baron of Clun and Oswaldestry, in Shropshire, m.
Isabel, dau. of William ᴖe Albini, Earl of Arundel, and sister and
coheir to Hugh, Earl of Sussex and Arundel, the last Earl of the
Albini line, of Arundel.

2. ·JOHN FITZ-ALAN, son of John and Isabel (de Albini or D'Aubigny)
Fitz-Alan, succeeded, by right of his mother, Nov. 27, 1243, to the
Castle and Honor of Arundel, and on May 26, 1244, obtained possession of his paternal estates in Shropshire. He m. Maud, dau. of
Theobald le Botiller (second Baron Butler), and d. between Oct. 1,
and Nov. 10, 1267 (according to some early accounts he m. Maud
de Verdon, dau. of Rhys de Verdon).

3. JOHN FITZ-ALAN, only son of John Fitz-Alan, was Lord of Clun and
Oswaldestre, and de jure Earl of Arundel, was b. Sept. 14, 1246, and

d. Mar., 1272. He m. Isabel de Mortimer, dau. of Roger de Mortimer, Lord of Wigmore.

4. · RICHARD FITZ-ALAN, only son and heir of John and Isabel (de Mortimer) Fitz-Alan, was feudal Lord of Clun and Oswaldestre, and after attaining his majority in 1289 became in fact Earl of Arundel, being summoned to Parliament by a writ directed to the Earl of Arundel. He fought in the Welsh wars, 1288; in Gascony, 1295-97; and in the Scottish wars, 1298-1300. He m. before 1285, Alasia, dau. of Tommaso I, Marquis of Saluzzo, in Piedmont (1244-1299). She d. Sept. 25, 1292, and he d. Mar. 9, 1302, in his thirty-sixth year.

5. · EDMUND FITZ-ALAN, ninth Earl of Arundel and second de facto Earl of Fitz-Alan line, was b. in the Castle of Marlborough, May 1, 1285. He was summoned to Parliament, Nov. 9, 1306, as Earl of Arundel. In 1323 he was chief justiciar of North and South Wales. He m., in 1305, Alice de Warenne, only dau. of William de Warenne, who was only son and heir of John, Earl of Surrey and Sussex. Edmund was beheaded without trial, Nov. 17, 1326, and his castle and honor given to Edmund, Earl of Kent, who was himself beheaded Sept. 3, 1330.

6. RICHARD FITZ-ALAN, called "Copped Hat," third Earl de facto of Arundel in the Fitz-Alan line, being son and ,heir· of Edmund and Alice (de Warenne) Fitz-Alan; and succeded June 30, 1347, to the vast Warenne estate, by the death of his mother's brother, John, Earl of Surrey and Sussex, on the death of whose widow, Joan, in 1361, he assumed the title of Earl of Surrey. He was made justiciar of North Wales for life, 1334; sheriff of Shropshire for life, 1345. He m. (1) Feb. 9, 1320-21, Isabel, dau. of Sir Hugh le Despenser, the younger; (2) Feb. 5, 1344-45, Eleanor, widow of John de Beaumont, and dau. of Henry, Earl of Lancaster. He d. Jan. 24, 1375-76. He had by the second marriage: *Richard,* his successor; *Sir John,* who m. the sister and heir to Henry, Lord Maltravers; *Thomas,* Archbishop of Canterbury; and four daus.

7. · ALICE FITZ-ALAN, oldest dau. of Richard and Eleanor (Plantagenet) Fitz-Alan, m. Thomas Holland, Earl of Kent, son of Thomas and Joan (Plantagenet) Holland. (See No. 29 Royal Descent line.)

Mary-Elizabeth L. Rixford and Oscar Theodore Rixford are 27th in direct descent from (1) John Fitz-Alan.

FLANDERS

Arms—Or, a lion rampant sable, armed and langued gules.

Crest—Between a pair of wings or, the lion affrontée sejant.

Motto—*Vlaandeeren den leeuw* (Flanders to the lion).

Ancient
Counts of Flanders

The territorial name Flanders is derived from the Flemish Vlaandeeren, and was originally applied only to Bruges and its immediate neighborhood, but in the eighth and ninth centuries it was gradually extended to the whole of the coast region from Calais to the Scheldt. In the Middle Ages, it was divided into two parts, one with Bruges as capital, the other as Ghent as capital.

The ancient territory of Flanders comprised not only the modern provinces known as East and West Flanders, but the southernmost portion of the Dutch Province of Zeeland, and a considerable district in northwestern France. In the time of Cæsar, it was inhabited by the Morini, Atrebates, and other Celtic tribes, but in the centuries that followed, the land was repeatedly overrun by German invaders and finally became a part of the dominion of the Franks. On the break-up of the Carolingian empire, the River Scheldt was by the treaty of Verdun (843) made the line of division between the Kingdom of East Francia (Austrasia) under the Emperor Lothaire, and the Kingdom of West Francia (Neustria) under Charles the Bald. In virtue of this compact Flanders was henceforth attached to the West Frankish monarchy (France). It thus acquired a position unique among the provinces of the territory known in later times as the Netherlands, all of which were included in that northern part of Austrasia assigned on the death of the Emperor Lothaire (855) to King Lothaire II, and from his name called Lotharingia or Lorraine.

I. BALDWIN I, Count of Flanders (858-879), the first ruler of Flanders of
    whom history has left any record, was known as Baldwin Bras-de-
    fer (Iron-arm). This man, a brave and daring warrior under
    Charles the Bald, fell in love with the king's dau., Judith, the
    youthful widow of two English kings, m. her, and fled with his
    bride to Lorraine. Charles, though at first very angry, was at last
    conciliated and made his son-in-law margrave (Marchio Flandriæ)
    of Flanders, which he held as an hereditary fief. The Northmen
    were at this time continually devastating the coast lands, and Bald-
    win was entrusted with the possession of this outlying borderland of
    the West Frankish dominion in order to defend it against the in-
    vaders. He was the first of a line of strong rulers, who at some
    date early in the tenth century exchanged the title of margrave for
    that of count. He m. Judith, dau. of Charles the Bald (see descent
    from Charlemagne), and they were parents of *Baldwin II.*

II. BALDWIN II, Count of Flanders, from his stronghold at Bruges main-
    tained, as did his father, a vigorous defense of his lands against
    the incursions of the Northmen, and took an active part in the
    struggles in Lorraine between the Emperor Otto I and Hugh Capet.
    He m. Aelfthryth, dau. of Alfred the Great, and on his death, in
    918, his possessions were divided between his two sons:
    1. *Arnulf the Elder,* of whom further.
    2. *Adolphus.*

III. ARNULF, son of Baldwin II and Aelfthryth, inherited, after the death
    of Adolphus, the whole of his father's possessions.

IV. BALDWIN III, son of Arnulf I, d. in 962, when the countship reverted
    to his father for a short time and then passed to the son of Bald-
    win III.

V. ARNULF II, son of Baldwin III, held the countship from 965 to 988,
    when the title passed to his son, Baldwin IV; m. Adela.

VI. BALDWIN IV, son of Arnulf II, was Count of Flanders from 988 to 1036.
    He was called Barbatus or the Bearded. He fought successfully
    both against the Capetian Kings of France and the Emperor Henry II,
    from the latter of whom he received the Valenciennes in fief, the
    burgraveship of Ghent, the land of Waes and Zeeland. The Count
    of Flanders thus became a feudatory of the Empire as well as of the
    French crown. The French fiefs are known in Flemish as Crown
    Flanders (Kroon-Vlaanderen), the German fiefs as Imperial Flanders
    (Rijks-Vlaanderen).

VII. BALDWIN V (1036-1067), son of Baldwin IV, was known as Debon-
    naire. He was an active, enterprising man, and greatly extended his
    power by wars and alliances. He obtained from the Emperor Henry
    IV the territory between the Scheldt and the Dender as an imperial
    fief, and the margraviate of Antwerp.

    See Royal Descent Line No. 13. Twenty-nine generations from
    here to Oscar A. Rixford, son of the Author of this book. (See
    Royal Descent Line to Elizabeth M. Rixford.)

ANCIENT COUNTS OF FLANDERS

At the time of Cæsar the Flemish region was inhabited by the
Menapii and the Morini, and at the end of the Roman dominion was
all in the Province of Belgica Secunda. At that period great numbers of Franks established themselves in the country. The name
Flanders did not appear until the seventh century, and at first was
applied only to the city of Bruges and the surrounding territory.

Charles the Bald, of France, to whom the treaty of Verdun was given in 843, granted Flanders to a warrior named Baldwin and surnamed Bras de Fer.

1. BALDWIN I, Count from 858 to 879, m. Judith, dau. of Charles the Bald, and widow of Aethelwulf, King of England (839-857). The realm then consisted of the present East and West Flanders, and the Departments Du Nord and Pas de Calais in Northern France; the county being a vassal of France during the Middle Ages.
2. BALDWIN, called the Bald, was Count of Flanders, 879-918, and m. Aelfthryth, dau. of Alfred the Great, of England. (See Warren Pedigree C, X and D, XIV.)
3. ARNULF, son of Baldwin II and Aelfthryth, was Count, 918-964, and m. Adela, dau. of Herbert II, of Vermandois.
4. BALDWIN III, son of Arnulf I, according to George, d. in 962, but French history makes him Count, 964-968.
5. ARNULF II, son of Baldwin III, was Count, 965-988.
6. BALDWIN IV, called Barbu, son of Arnulf II, was Count, 988-1036.
7. BALDWIN V, son of Baldwin IV, was Count, 1036-1067, and m. Adela, dau. of Robert, King of France, a son of Hugh Capet.
8. MATILDA (French Maud), dau. of Baldwin V, Count of Flanders, m. William I, King of England, called the Conqueror. (See William the Conqueror I.)

Mary-Elizabeth L. Rixford and Oscar Theodore Rixford are 36th in direct descent from Baldwin I. Royal Descent No. 11—Henry I, King of England.

GRAVES FAMILY
J. C. Graves, 1896, Vol. I

INTRODUCTION, CREST, COAT OF ARMS AND MOTTOES
(Pages 7 and 8)

The distinctive arms of the Graves Family are "Gu. and eagle displayed or ducally crowned arg."

The crest—"A demi-eagle displayed and erased or enfiled round the body and below the wings by a ducal coronet arg."

By the alliance of members of the family with other families, and the marshalling of different arms in the same composition, variations are frequently found; they almost invariably retain, however, as quarterings, the distinctive arms of the family, the eagle displayed or.

Various mottoes have been adopted, some of which have been used by the members of the family exclusively, and others by this and other families.

The following are the mottoes used, as far as can be ascertained, and translations. There are fourteen mottoes, one of which is: "*Suprema Quaero.*" I seek the highest.

SKETCH OF THE GRAVES FAMILY IN ENGLAND

(Page 9) The family of Graves is one of the most ancient in England. It went in with the Norman army, and its members have been De Grevis, De Greves, Greve, Grave, Greaves, Greeves, and Graves. In the portion of Doomsday Book for Lincolnshire it is recorded:

(Page 10) The family lived in early days in that part of England now known as counties Lincoln, Nottingham, Derby and York, occupying the northern part of the three first named and the southern part of York. The first recorded family seat was known as Greves or Greaves, in the parish of Beeley, near Chatsworth, in the northern part of Derbyshire, and a few miles from the southerly boundary of York, where the family resided as early as the reign of Henry III (1216-1272). John Greaves, a descendant, in the reign of Elizabeth (1558-1602), became a purchaser of "Beeley," a quaint old house with an enclosed court, on the hill above Beeley, and now known as "Hilltop," and it was occupied as a family seat until about 1664, when it was sold to John, Earl of Rutland.

In the little church at Beeley, within the altar rails, is a fine flat stone on which are cut the coat of arms of the family, the motto *"Suprema Quaero,"* and the following inscription:

"This marble stone doth presse but not oppresse the body of John Greaves of Greaves, Esq. The 13th day of October in the year of our Lord (page XI) 1694. Ann his wife, b. of Geo. Bird, of Stenley Hall, Gent, ob. May 25, 1700."

"History of Norfolk, 1744-1900," page 721—Capt. John Graves, Guildford, Conn. Ensign 1665—C2P74, Captain 1669-1690—C4P25.

(Page 11) From the visitations of Derbyshire, in the College of Arms, and from MSS. in the British Museum, the following descent of the early founders of the family is extracted:

I.   JOHN DE LA GREVES.
II.   HUGO DE LA GREVIS, vixit temp. Henry III (1216-1272).
III.   WILLIAM DE LA GREVIS, filius Hugonis, temp. Edward I (1272-1307).
IV.   EGIDRUS DE LA GREVES, Letitia uxor ejus. 1316.
V.   THOMAS DE LA GREVES, filius Egidri, temp. Edward III (1327-1377).
VI.   JOHANNES DE LA GREVIS, fil. Thomas, fil. Egidri, temp. Edward III.
VII.   JOHN.
VIII. WILLIAM and wife Agnes.
IX.   JOHN, 1497; bur. Dec. 30, 1546.
X.   JOHN, of Greaves; bur. Dec. 30, 1595.
XI.   JOHN, of Greaves and Beeley.
XII.   JOHN, of Greaves, Beeley and Woodhouse, bapt. Sept. 17, 1581, and living 1634; had eight sons and three daus.
XIII. JOHN, of Beeley, bur. Feb. 6, 1673-4.
XIV.   JOHN, of Stanton Hall and Biggin, b. in 1644; d. without issue Oct. 13, 1694.

The family had early scattered over the surrounding country. As early as 1574 members of it are mentioned as at Kings Norton in Worcester County, where in the chapel is found a large monument to Sir Richard Greves, Kt., with crest; he died in 1631. In the rolls of the Exchequer Lay Subsidies for Buckingham and Northampton Counties, there are found taxes laid against different members of the family as early as 1522, and from that time forward.

John Graves was a resident of Cleckheaton, in the parish of Birstall, and Wapentake of Morley, in the West Riding of Yorkshire, as early as the time of Edward IV (1461-1483), and from him descend several of the most prominent families in Great Britain.

GRAVES ANCESTRY—Genealogy by F. Phelps Leach (1931)

(Page 55) JOHN GRAVES[1], born in England, came to the American Colonies with his wife in 1635 and settled in Concord, Mass. He soon after became a member of the church of which Rev. Peter Buckley was teacher. He was one of the signers of the petition to the General Court in 1643 in favor of Ambrose Martinmand; in 1644, his name was attached to a document pledging to signers nearly every head of a family in Concord, to the support of the Government. One of these signatures, probably the first, is now in the New England Historical Society in Boston. He had two sons, Benjamin and John.

References: "History of Norfolk, 1744-1900," page 721—Capt. John Graves, Guildford, Conn. Ensign 1665—C2P74. Captain 1669-1690—C4P25.

Benjamin, born in Concord, Mass.; married Mary Hoar, daughter of Benjamin Graves[2] was a member of Captain Wheeler, Vs. Co. John[1], of Concord, against the Indians, in Vol. 38, "New England Genealogical and Historical Register." He was given credit September 28, 1675, and again February 29, 1676, for service in King Philip Vs. War. He and John Graves, of Sudbury, Mass., with other purchased on May 20, 1681, from Christopher Hall, "all the mines and minerals of one kind and another, found or that may be found on his land in Groten, Mass., at a place called Cold Spring, near William Longley Vs. house with Liberty to dig, delve or use the land and to errect buildings, etc. He moved to Saybrook, Conn., in 1703 when he purchased January 25, 1703, of Nicholas Stoughton by consent of William Shipman at a place called Pottaconk, whatever the division of whichever part is agreed upon is made. Stroughtan to have first choice." Also the one-half of eleven acres of planting land, 10 pounds, 10 shillings.

(Page 56) "Now a resident of Killingworth, a messanger or tenament at Pottaconk with all the buildings, etc., bounded westerly by land of Joseph Graves, it being understood that Benj. is to retain the life use of the same." March 18, 1715, Benjamin Graves "for love and affection, to son, Joseph" deeded "one half the farm I now dwell upon the Westerly half."

BENJAMIN GRAVES[2] (*John[1]*), married October 21, 1668, Mary Hoar, daughter of John[1].

Their children were:

MARY GRAVES, b. Jan. 18, 1669; m. Apr. 1, 1691, Benjamin Rice, b. Dec. 22, 1668, son of Edward and Anna Rice, of Sudbury.

RUTH GRAVES, b. Nov. 25, 1671; m. Jan. 15, 1699, John Webb.

BENJAMIN[3], b. Mar. 2, 1676-7; d. 1752; m. (1) Mary Sterling; (2) Mary Haynes.
JOSEPH, b. Sept. 2, 1679.
JOHANNA, b. Feb. 2, 1681.
JOHN, b. 1683.

Benjamin[2] moved to Saybrook, Conn., where he died between 1716 and 1724.

BENJAMIN[3] (*Benjamin[2], John[1]*), born March 3, 1676-7, in Concord, Mass. He was descended as from New London, Conn., in a deed given to him of lands, purchased at Colchester, Conn., in 1709 where he had just moved. He was admitted inhabitant of latter place at town meeting January, 1716, chosen lister at town meeting December, 1727. He lived two and one-half miles from the village of Colchester (page 57) on the road to Lynn. He held several Colonial offices. He was buried in the churchyard in the village, the tombstone after standing 150 years (when visited by J. C. Graves), was in as good condition as it naturally would be after exposure of but a few years.

The children of Benjamin[3] and first wife, Mary Sterling, were:

BENJAMIN[4], b. 1699; m. (believed) Mary Jones, dau. of Thomas Jones.
RUTH GRAVES, bapt. Oct. 25, 1702, New London. Her parents owned the Covenant at Lyme, Conn.
MARY, bapt. Oct. 29, 1704, New London; m. Oct. 29, 1724, Ebenezer Daniels.
JONATHAN.
JEDEDIAH, b. 1708; m. 1728, Jerusha Ackley, East Haddam.

Children of Benjamin[3] and second wife, Mary Haynes, were:

JAMES, m. Hastins.
PETER.
HAYNES.
ELIZABETH, m. June 2, 1741, Ebenezer Hyde.
DEBORAH.
ABIGAIL, m. Oct., 1785, Nathan Dodge.
MARGARET, m. Oct. 28, 1744, Jonathan Loomis.
MARY GRAVES, b. Jan. 20, 1728; m. June 23, 1746, Samuel Hungerford[4].

All this above history of the Graves Family is received from Mrs. C. W. Brown, of Washington, D. C., who is a descendant of JAMES GRAVES[4] (*Benjamin[3], Benjamin[2], John[1]*) (page 17 note). Benjamin[3] Graves, born at Concord, March 2, 1676-7; died at Colchester, Conn., December 30, 1752 (Concord births).

COPY OF WILL OF BENJAMIN GRAVES, 1752

In the name of God, amen, This 11 day of Dec. 1752, and the 21st year of the Reign of our Sovereign Lord George of Great Brittain and King.

I, Benjamin Graves of Colchester, in the Co. of Hartford, and Colony of Connecticut in New England being sick and weak in body, but of sound and disposing mind and memory (thanks be to God for same), and being desirous to settle my affairs, do mark and ordain this my last will and testament in manner following: First and principally, I resign my soul into the hands of Almighty God, my Creator hoping and believing in and through it above merits of Jesus Christ, my only Lord and Saviour to obtain everlasting happiness in His eternal Kingdom my body I commit to the earth from which it was taken in faith of a resurrection, willing the same to be decently buried at the direction of my Executrix and Executor hereafter named, and as to such temporal goods, estate as it has pleased God to bestow upon me after my funeral charges and just debts are discharged which my will is that it be done with all convenient speed after by decease by my Executrix and Executor herein after named, I give and dispose them of in manner following (that is to say) I give devise and bequeath to my dear wife, Mary Graves, the whole use of all my real estate with all the privelege and apportentes there unto belonging during her natural life or so long as she shall remain my widow for her to use and dispose of in that way that she shall.

Think most for her advantage and also all my personal estate I give unto my wife so long as she shall remain my widow, and then to be equally divided to my two daughters, viz. Deborah and Abigal, that is to say all my personal estate excepting our Gun and that I give to my Son, Peter, and also two cows and then I give unto my children hereafter named, five shillings, old tenor, apiece, that is to say, Benjamin, Jedeiah, Jonathan, Ruth and Mary Daniels, James, Hayes, Elizabeth, Margaret and Mary Hungerford to be paid to them out of my personal estate by my Executors hereafter named and I do hereby constitute, appoint and ordain my wife, Mary Graves and my son Benjamin Graves of East Haddam, Executrix, and Executor to this my last will and testament and do hereby utterly disallow, revoke, disannull all and every other former testament, will legacy and Executrix and Executor by me in any way before named, confirming this and no other to be my last will and testament for witness whereof I hereunto set my hand and seal of day and year above written in presence of

his
BENJAMIN X GRAVES.
mark and seal

Witnesses:
ALICE RANSOM,
AMY RANSOM,
JABES JONES RANSOM.

References: Vol. 2, Probate Records, page 213, Colchester, Conn.

Old tenor—Paper money issued at different periods by the Colonial Government.

GRAVES

From the visitations of Derbyshire, in the College of Arms, and from MSS. in the British Museum, the following descent of the early founders of the family is extracted:

1. JOHN DE LA GREVES.
2. HUGO DE LA GREVIS, vixit temp. Henry III (1216-1272).
3. WILLIAM DE LA GREVIS, filius Hugonis, temp. Edward I (1272-1307).
4. EGIDRUS DE LA GREVES, Letitia uxor ejus. 1316.
5. THOMAS DE LA GREVES, filius Egidri, temp. Edward III (1327-1377).
6. JOHANNES DE LA GREVIS, fil. Thomas, fil. Egidri, temp. Edward III.
7. JOHN.
8. WILLIAM and wife Agnes.
9. JOHN, 1497; bur. Dec. 30, 1546.
10. JOHN, of Greaves, bur. Dec. 30, 1595.
11. JOHN, of Greaves and Beeley.
12. JOHN, of Greaves, Beeley and Woodhouse, bapt. Sept. 17, 1581; living in 1634; had eight sons and three daughters.
13. BENJAMIN GRAVES, m. Oct. 21, 1668, Mary Hoar, dau. of John[1].

14. BENJAMIN GRAVES, m. (1) Mary Sterling; (2) Mary Haynes. He was b. Mar. 2, 1676-7; d. Dec. 30, 1752.
15. MARY GRAVES, dau. of Benjamin and Mary (Haynes) Graves, b. Jan. 20, 1728; m. June 23, 1746, probably New Fairfield, Conn., Samuel Hungerford, who was b. about 1713; d. 1790.
16. ISAIAH HUNGERFORD, b. Dec. 26, 1756; bapt. Jan. 23, 1757; d. June 16, 1833; m. about 1777 at New Fairfield, Conn., Esther Mead, b. Aug. 11, 1760; d. Dec. 22, 1836.
17. ELIZABETH HUNGERFORD, b. Feb. 7, 1798; d. Jan. 7, 1878; m. Apr. 29, 1821, at St. Armand West, Que., Nash David Phelps, b. Oct. 4, 1796; d. Apr. 15, 1884.
18. CAROLINE ALEXANDRIA PHELPS, b. July 3, 1840; d. Mar. 29, 1921; m. Sept. 8, 1863, at Stanbridge, Que., Horace Brayton Leach, b. Sept. 25, 1836; d. May 6, 1919.
19. ELIZABETH MAY LEACH, b. Jan. 7, 1866; living May 6, 1931; m. Sept. 8, 1889, Sheldon, Vt., Oscar Herbert Rixford, b. Dec. 27, 1859; d. Sept. 11, 1927.
20. OSCAR ADELBERT RIXFORD, b. Aug. 4, 1890; m. Jan. 18, 1919, at Montreal, Que., Mary Carolyn Hefflon, b. June 6, 1899; both living May 6, 1931; had children:
    Mary-Elizabeth Lenora, b. Oct. 6, 1922; living May 6, 1931.
    Oscar Theodore, b. July 21, 1925; living May 6, 1931.

References: 1 to 12 generations—Records of Elizabeth M. Rixford.
13 to 15 generations—Records of F. Phelps Leach.
16 to 20 generations—Family Records.

THE DIM PERIOD OF GREENE HISTORY

FROM LORD ALEXANDER TO LORD THOMAS, 1202-1296 (Chapter 2)

("The Greene Family and Its Branches, 861 to 1904,"
by Lora S. La Mance)

Inquire I pray thee of the former age, and prepare thyself to the search of their fathers.—Job VIII, Verse 8.

Arms—Argent, on a fess azure between three pellets, each charged
with a lion's head erased of the
first, a griffin passant between
two escallops or.

Crest—A Woodpecker picking a staff
couped, ragules, and erect, all
proper.

All branches of the family are
entitled to use the three Bucks Trippant, Or, on an azure field, as it was
borne by the Founders of the Line.
The Crescent, a mark of cadency de-
noting the line of a second son, is
used by all the Warwick and Quid-
nesselt Greenes.

NEC TIMEO, NEC SPERNO.

Greene

All that we really know of the first Lord de Greene may be
summed up in this brief paragraph. Alexander, a Knight at the
King's court, was the great-grandson of one of the Norman nobles
who invaded England with William the Conqueror, 1066. King
John bestowed the estate of Boughton in Northampton upon him in
1202.

Lord Alexander assumed a surname after his chief estate, de
Greene de Boketon, *i.e.,* the Lord of the Park of the Deer Enclosure.
A green in the early day was a park. Boketon is an old, old word
meaning the bucks' (bokes) "ton" or paled in enclosure. Centuries
ago the terminal syllable "ton" had lost its original sense, and meant
a town. So that Boketon, still used in the original sense, shows
Lord Alexander came to an estate named long before, and noted
for its extensive parks and deer preserves. Boketon became Bucks
and Buckston, and later Boughton, its present name. It lies in
Northampton.

For a long time the full name de Greene de Boketon was used
in legal documents. Naturally in everyday speech it was shortened
to de Greene. During the reign of Henry VI, 1422-1471, with its
attendant French wars, the patriotic de Greenes dropped the patrician

de as too Frenchy in sound for Englishmen, as they now considered themselves.

The title of the early de Greenes was strictly Sir (Militis), and their wives were Dame. Familiarly they were called Lord, or the Right Honorable Lord, and their wives Lady. Lord Alexander was a great baron. He had a power in his estates almost as a petty king. He had to furnish so many men for the king's wars, pay a portion toward the dowry of the princesses, and entertain the king when in his territory. He had to pay homage, also to show that he held his estate from the crown. We are expressly told of how each of the Lords de Greene did this, 1202-1506, "by lifting up his right hand toward the King yearly on Christmas day, in what place soever the King is." ("Halstead's Genealogy," A. D. 1585.)

The Lords de Greene lived in state. They wore rich apparel, belted with a gold or silver girdle to which was attached a purse, a rosary, a pen and inkhorn, a set of keys and an elaborately chased dagger. These showed their rank. When they rode they wore gold spurs. Their armor was magnificent. They wore robes in Parliament, hats and plumes at court, and at the king's coronation they wore a crimson velvet cap, lined with ermine, and having a plain gold band. Their servants wore the Greene livery, which was blue laced with gold.

Thirteen years after Lord Alexander settled at Boughton, the Lords rose against King John. They met at Runnymede, only a few miles from the family seat of the de Greenes. Only seven barons adhered to John, and he was not one of them. Therefore, he must have been enrolled among the two thousand nobles who put their united protests in the hand of twenty-five lords who presented the Magna Charta to the king, and forced him to sign that document that guaranteed both the lives and the property of his subjects from arbitrary spoilation. It will interest a branch of Rhode Island Greenes who have the blood of the LaValleys as well, to know that two of the Magna Charta signers were Gilbert DeLaval and William de Lanvalley. Another signer was Roger, Earl of Winchester, whose great-great-granddaughter, Lucie de la Zouche, married Sir Alexander de Greene's great-great-grandson, Lord Thomas[5]. John revenged himself "like a devil," as one old historian puts it, burning castles and doing other foul deeds. He died the next year, 1216, and his old favorite fortunately escaped his fury.

Lord Alexander's son, the second Lord, was probably a crusading knight in the seventh Crusade, which ended in 1240. His grandson was almost undoubtedly one of the knights that accompanied Edward I on the last great Crusade, and died in the Holy War.

The Crusades brought about the use of coats of arms. A coat of arms has been from the first a badge of good birth.

ADDENDA

Notes to Chapters II and III

The second baron of the line, as listed in old rolls of 20th year of Henry III (1236), and 45th year of the same king (1261), was Sir Walter de Boketon. The same properties or affairs listed again in a roll of the 7th year of Edward II (1314), repeat the name of Sir Walter, and also give name of John de Boketon, whom we may consider the next heir. As the fourth lord was certainly Sir Thomas, who received the title in his infancy, at the beginning of the reign of Edward I (1272), this (Sir) John de Boketon was doubtless the young crusading knight who perished in Palestine in 1271. This completes the names of the lords of the line.

Ambitious family antiquarians are always proud if they can claim a royal descent. The Greenes find no trouble in presenting their royal tree, as their lineal line to the Capet Kings of France is complete without a break or an uncertain ancestor. We have followed Halstead's "Genealogy," Browning's "Americans of Royal Descent," and Rev. S. Beal's "D. C. L. Account of Greene's Norton," together with the known genealogy of the Capetian Kings of France, all of which agree with each other. Halstead's "Genealogy" stands at the head of English works of this kind. It was written in 1585 by the second Earl of Peterborough, himself of the blood of Greene.

King John was succeeded by weak, irresolute Henry III, who reigned fifty-six long, dreary years. Sir Thomas, the fourth Lord de Greene de Boketon, was born in the closing years of this reign. In 1270, Prince Edward, afterward known as The Hammer of Scotland, set forth on the last of the great Crusades. The flower of the nobility attended the Prince as knights. The second Lord de Greene was yet alive. His heir was a young man whose rank entitled him to accompany the Prince. Edward reached the Holy Land and won some victories, but at a frightful cost of life. Young de Greene is supposed to have perished in Palestine, leaving in far-off England a little son so young that his own heir was not born until twenty years after Prince Edward became king, which was in 1272. The old Lord, the child of Sir Thomas' grandfather, died a few years after his crusading son. "Sir Thomas flourished," says Halstead, "about the beginning of King Edward I," *i.e.*, he came to his title about this time. Halstead continues: "Sir Thomas we find recited in ancient catalogue of the knights who accompanied Henry I against the Scots in 1296." Sir Thomas' wife was Alice, daughter and co-heir of Sir Thomas Bottisham, of Braunston. Sir Thomas de Greene was mentioned in the records of 1319 as then alive.

Sir Thomas, the fifth Lord, was born in 1292. He contracted a high marriage with one of royal descent, and when about 40 was made High Sheriff of Northampton (1330-1332), in the early part of the reign of Edward III. "The office was not as in these days, but esteemed equal to the care of princes, an office of great trust and reputation, and justly esteemed *'honos sine onere.'* "

One chronicler continues: "He married Lucie the daughter of Eudo de la Zouche and Millicent, one of the sisters and heirs of George de Cantelupe, Lord of Abergavenny (on the River Usk in Wales), with whom he had in free marriage nine Messuages (houses with adjoining lands), one Toft (a grove), and fout Virgates of land (yard lands of from 15 to 40 acres each), with their appurtenances in Harringworth. The House of de la Zouche was lineally descended from Alan, the famous Earl and Sovereign of Little Britain." Sir Thomas[5] by Lady Lucie had one son, Sir Henry de Greene[6], afterward Lord Chief Justice of England.

Lady Lucie had royal blood. From her only son have descended the Earls of Wiltshire, Montague, Peterborough and Sandwich, as well as a host of good Americans, including the Warwick and Quidnessett Greenes. For their benefit Lady Lucie de la Zouche's pedigree is given.

Charles the Bald, the grandson of Charlemagne, was King of France from 823-877. When at war with his brothers and in sore straits, he called to his aid Robert the Strong, a Saxon leader in Germany, and rewarded him with rich territorial grants and titles of Count of Anjou and Duke of Ile de France. This was in 861. Duke Robert was every inch a military man, and won renown for his victories over the Norsemen, after they were successful almost everywhere else. It is from him that the martial ·spirit came that has blazed out anew now and then down the centuries, among his descendants, as in Lord Montague and the Earl of Sandwich in England, and our own Gen. Nathaniel Greene of Revolutionary War fame.

Robert the Strong fell in battle with the Norsemen. A son, Hugh, was later killed in a Norse battle also. Robert's two sons, Duke Eudes and Duke Robert, are by some reckoned among the kings of France, as they exercised the power of a ruler. Eudes long fought the Norsemen with dogged courage. Robert[2], who succeeded this brother, had civil wars to contend with. When Robert's son, Count Hugh the White, or Hugh the Great, became Duke of France, there was nominally a descendant of Charlemagne on the French throne. In reality Hugh was king in all but name. His son, Hugh Capet, in 987, wrested the throne from the weak puppet upon it, and was crowned king at Rheims. Hugo Capet married a sister of Guilhem Fier-a-Bras (William of the Iron Arm), the Duke of Aquitaine.

Their son, Robert the Pious, came to the throne in 996 and reigned until his death in 1031. He was a good man, but weak king. He obediently put away his first wife at the Pope's command, and married Constans of Provens, by whom he had Henry, who became king in 1031. For nearly 900 years this line of kings sat upon the throne of France. Henry, this third Capetian king, found it an uneasy seat. The whole of his 29 years' reign was a constant struggle with his great nobles. Guerrilla warfare was carried so far that the Church proclaimed a "Truce of God," by which no hostilities could take place from Thursday evening until Monday morning, or on feast days, or during Lent and Advent. King Henry's children were by his second wife, Anne of Russia. She was the daughter of Grand Duke Jaroslav, and was lineally descended from Jaroslav the Great, a famous Russian of 1000 years ago.

King Henry's second son was Hugh Magnus, Count of Vermandois, who is better known as the Great Crusader.

The Count's daughter, Lady Isabel, married Robert de Bellemont, Earl of Mellent and first Earl of Leicester. They had Earl Robert the Second, who married Aurelia de la Waer, the daughter of Ralph, Earl of Norfolk. This second Earl of Leicester was Lord Chief Justice of England also. Robert, the next and third Earl of Leicester, married Petronella, the daughter of Hugh de Grantes-Mismil.

The daughter of Earl Robert and Countess Petronella was Lady Margaret de Bellemont, who married Sieur de Quincy. This nobleman was the first beside kings and princes to assume a crest to his coat of arms. Newton, in his "Display of Heraldry," says the honor was conferred upon him because he was an eminent commander in the Holy Wars. This crest of his was noted for its extraordinary size. Sieur de Quincy was in the Crusade of 1188-1192, under Richard Coeur de Lion, King of England. One of his fellow crusaders was Robert, third Earl of Leicester, afterwards his own father-in-law. In 1207 King John created this nobleman Earl of Winchester. Nevertheless, when the barons rose against King John, eight years later, he was one of the twenty-five great barons who signed Magna Charta, and compelled the king to do likewise. His · son, Roger, second Earl of Winchester, married Helen, a daughter of Alen, Lord of Galloway.

Earl Roger's daughter, Lady Elene de Quincy, married Alen, Lord de la Zouche, Governor of the Castle of Northampton, who died in 1269. Eudo de la Zouche was the next in the line. He married Lady Millicent de Cantelupe. It was their daughter, Lady Lucie, that married the fifth Lord de Greene. She was the fifteenth in lineal descent from Robert the Strong, eleventh from Hugh Capet, eighth from Count Hugh the Crusader, and fourth from Earl Winchester, who signed Magna Charta. She had the blood of lords, earls, counts, dukes, grand dukes and princes, and of three kings in her veins. Those who descended from her need not feel unduly elated. There have been nineteen generations since her day, and whatever royal blood she transmitted to her line must be pretty effectually diluted by now.

To return to the de Greenes. Both Sir Thomas[5] who married Lady Lucie, and their son, Sir Henry[6], the Lord Chief Justice, received high honors from the hand of King Edward III, one of the best and strongest kings England ever had, and whose long reign of 50 years allowed him to bring about many reforms. He was a warrior and statesman, with a lawyer-like bent of mind. More important laws were passed in his reign than in 300 years before. He created justices of the peace; made the rank of a duke; established the Order of the Garter; divided Parliament into the House of Commons and the House of Lords, and had its powers first clearly defined. He ordered the use of the English language in Court and Parliament instead of French. An energetic, change-working king such as he, had particular need of trained judicial qualities.

One of the Lord Chief Justice's enterprises was the establishment of a Fair, held each year upon the spacious green or park at Boughton. A charter (the original text of King Edward's Charter is in Medieval Latin and is as follows: "Sir Henry Greene, Lord of Buckton and other Lands and Lordships: *Carta pro Feria in Buckton. Anno 25° Regis Edwards: Tertii*) was granted to him to hold a three days' fair on the "virgin day and morrow" of the Day of Saint John the Baptist, *i.e.*, the 24th, 25th and 26th of June each year.

The Boughton Fair became second only to the London Fair itself.

The Lord Chief Justice died in 1370, a little under 60, and was buried at Boughton. He was the last Lord of the line to be buried there. He was early married to Katherine, the daughter of Sir John, and only sister of Sir Simon Drayton, of Drayton. They had four sons and two daughters, Sir Thomas[7], the heir; Henry, afterwards knighted by King Richard II, and made heir to his uncle, Sir Simon Drayton; Nicholas and Richard, who never married, and supposedly died young; Margaret, who married Lord de la Zouche; and Amabila, who married Lord Ralph Raynes, of Clifton.

According to the English law, the title and estate should have been the oldest son's, but as Jacob of old loved Joseph above his other sons, so the Lord Chief Justice favored his second son above all the rest. There must have been something particularly engaging about Henry de Greene. The King afterwards advanced him to high honor; his uncle left him his title and estate, and the heir himself, Thomas[7], consented to the extraordinary and almost unheard of thing, to alienating an entailed estate, and passing the major part of it on to the second son. A special license was given by the King, Boughton remained to the heir's portion, and Green's Norton was purchased and added to it. With that and large moneys, the older son was content.

THE LORD GREENES OF GREEN'S NORTON, 1359 TO 1570

Norton was a beautiful manor as far back as Richard Coeur de Lion's day. He bestowed it on a favorite soon after his return from the Crusades. From Earl this and Earl that it passed for 165 years. Several who held it died young. Three died childless, and three left only daughters, so that each time the property passed to collateral lines. Baron Morley, to whom it came, was afraid of it. Lord

Chief Justice de Greene broke the entail for him, and acquired it himself, changing the name to Green's Norton. It was ever after the seat of the Lords de Greene, instead of Boughton.

The Lord Chief Justice's son, Sir Thomas[7], married Sir John Mablethorpe's daughter. Only one son survived. There is an old and handsome church at Green's Norton. Here the Greenes, from Sir Thomas[7], are buried. The family took a pride in the magnificence of their tombs. Some of their tombs had rare brasses, which were inlaid panels of fine brass with raised letterings. Others had altar tombs of finest marble, supporting effigies or recumbent statues representing those buried beneath. Canopies, recessed arches, and carved coats of arms were used wherever they could heighten the effect.

In the church at Green's Norton at the east end of the north aisle, is a depressed arch, under which was once a handsome tomb, now sadly mutilated. This is shown to sightseers as the Lord Chief Justice's tomb. It is really that of Sir Thomas[7] and his wife.

Sir Thomas[8] was born in 1369 and died in 1417. His only son, Sir Thomas[9], had a large family by Phillipa, daughter of Baron Ferrars. His wife was descended from William the Conqueror, through the Earl Spencers.

Sir Thomas[10] lies with his wife in the center of the nave of the church. The brass of their tomb-slab bears this inscription, that I commend to those who would like to try a specimen of middle-age Latin.

"Hic jacet Thomas Greene miles. D'n's de Norton et Matilda ux ejus, qui vero. Thomas fuit filius et heres Thome Greene Militis. D'ni de ead'm et Philpoe ux's ejus filie Roberti D'ni Ferras de Charteley et Elizabeth uxoris ejus filie Thomas Le Spencer, qui quidem Thomas Greene pater prefati Thomas Greene, fuit filius et Heres Thomas Greene Militis. D'm de Norton predicati, et Marie ux's ejus (filie) Ric'i D'm Strange de Blacmere, qui quidem prefatus Thomas filius predicati. Thome et Philippoe, obiit ix die Sept. An. dom. mili'mo cccclxii, et prefata Matilda una filiarum John'ni's Throcmorton, armigeri, quondam Subthesarauraii Angl. obiit . . . . die . . . . an. dom. millessimo cccc . . . . Quorum anemabus propitictur Deus. Amen."

Sir Thomas[10] died before his wife, Lady Matilda (called Maud), after the old English custom of nicknaming Matilda.

Sir Thomas[11] left an only son, Sir Thomas[12], the sixth lord in succession to be named Thomas, and the last Lord Greene. He had two daughters to whom Green's Norton passed. Boughton went to the Lord Montagues, through former marriages of daughters of the Greene line.

The last five Lord Greenes lived in the Bloody Century. There was bad blood between the Lancasters whose emblem was the red rose, and their royal cousins, the Yorks, who displayed the white rose. First one side and then the other gained the throne.

King Henry the VII, who never forgot he was of Lancaster, even though the War of the Roses was a thing of the past, had the meanness to throw the last Lord Greene into prison in 1506 on a charge of plotting treason. The infirm old man was then so near death that he died before the year was out.   He was released, but not until the grasping king was richer.

By the munificence of Queen Victoria and others, the church at Green's Norton was restored.   In the east window on the north side of the church there are thirteen coats of arms.   Here were the tombs of the six Sir Thomases, last Lords of the line, and their families.

The Lord Chief Justice's many estates had to be broken up, one by one, and reentailed.   It was in 1352 that he purchased Green's Norton—a part of the consideration by which Lord Thomas surrendered his birthright—and 1359 when Halstead speaks of the reentailment as fully completed.

No full list has been preserved of the many manors settled upon Henry, the younger son.   The more important and richest estates old historians list thus:

Buckworth,	Emerton,	Grafton,	Harringworth,	Islip,
Middleton,	Luffwich,	Harrowden,	Carlton,	Sudborow,
Raunds,	Isham,	Shipton,	Chalton,	Haughton,
Titmarsh,	Warrington,	Irtlingburg,	Alwincle,	Coats.
Ringstead,	Wolston,	Battershaseall,	Charlton,	
Pitchelery,	Cottington,	Warrington,	Hardwick,	

Halstead adds that through Henry's marriage with Matilda, sole heiress of her father, Lord Thomas Mauduit, the lordships of Werminister, Westburg, Lye, Grateley, Dychurch, "and other fair possessions" were added to his estates.

"And when the Conspiracies of divers of the turbulent and seditious Lords had obliged the King to condemn some and banish others, he conferred (1395) several parcels of their confiscated lands upon Sir Henry Greene, as the Manors of Kibworth, Cotgrave, and Preston Capes, that appertained to Thomas, Earl of Warwick, those of Knighton, Covelle, and Bulkington (this makes forty known manors that Sir Henry possessed, besides his town houses in London) in the County of Wilts, by reason of the attainer of Richard, Earl of Arundell; and the place of Lord Cobham in London with all its furniture.

Edward III died in 1377, leaving a grandson, Richard II, on the throne.   Time would fail to tell of Richard II's queer doings.   He was but sixteen when, in 1382, he married Princess Anne of Bohemia.   Queen Anne died in 1394 and Richard mourned her with almost a madman's outburst of grief.   Nevertheless, he married again the next year.   He was childless, and his cousins were plotting for his throne.   Instead of trying to secure an early heir, however, the one thing that could keep down his rivals' intrigues, in one of his follyfits he married Isabelle the daughter of the King of France, a pretty, dark-eyed child of eight, and put her in Windsor palace to be educated for her high duties.

Shakespear, who devotes much of Acts I and II of his Richard II to Sir Henry Greene, puts into the mouth of Bolinbroke, as these members of the Commission were brought before him, these words:

"Bring forth these men.—
Bushy and Greene, I will not vex your souls"
etc. (first two lines of the poem).

As with much else in this play, this harangue is probably purely fiction. Bolingbroke seems to have hustled them out without ceremony or the shadow of a trial, for no other crime than being loyal to their anointed king, to the market-place at Bristol. Sir Henry Greene[7] was beheaded September 2, 1399. The beheaded Sir Henry Greene[7] and Lady Matilda left seven children, Ralph, John, Thomas, Henry, Eleanor, Elizabeth and Mary. Two of the daughters married noblemen; Ralph and John were successively Lord Greene. The great estate, in the end, passed through the last heiress of John's line to the Earls of Wiltshire and Peterborough, her descendants. Of Henry, the youngest son of Sir Henry, we know no more. He probably died in some of the wars of the "Bloody Century," leaving no children. Thomas, the third son, was the ancestor of the Gillingham Greenes.

In the very first year of King Henry IV, Ralph[8], Sir Henry's oldest son, was restored to his title and estates, and received in after years particular honors from the king. As he left no children, the estate passed to his brother John[8], who left three children.

Lord Henry[9] next succeeded. He left an only daughter, who married John, Earl of Wiltshire, the second son of the Duke of Buckingham. Their only heir was Edward[10], Earl of Wiltshire, who died in 1501, while yet a young man, leaving no issue. The estate then reverted to the grandchildren of Lady Isabelle de Vere, a sister of Lord Henry[9]. None of the beheaded Sir Henry's line remained to bear the name of Greene, save the line of his son Thomas[8] alone. From him came the Gillingham Greenes, and from these again, came the Warwick and Quidnessett Greenes, two of the most important lines of that name in America. I have, therefore, taken pains to get all possible facts relating to the line of Thomas[8].

Between Thomas[8] and Robert[11], of Gillingham, two generations intervene. The name of the ninth of this line has not been preserved. All we can discover with certainty through the dark cloud that covers this period is a scene of horror and bloodshed, savage wars, and treacherous, dishonorable conduct in all parties.

His son is supposed to have been born about 1450. This son was John[10]. The signs of cadency, *i.e.*, descent of sons in order of birth, began to be added to coats of arms in the reign of Henry VII, 1485 to 1509.

In July, 1483, Richard III, one of the wickedest of England's several wicked kings, was crowned King, though his two nephews had the first right to the crown.

A son of John the Fugitive was Robert Greene, Gentleman. He purchased an estate at Gillingham, in Dorsetshire, which was called Bowridge Hill. On the old records it is usually spoken of as Porridge Hill, the local pronunciation of Bowridge Hill. His wife's name is unknown. Whoever she was, it is believed that by her came that extraordinary mathematical ability that has made the majority of her descendants "quick at figures," as we usually express it, and has every now and then since her day cropped out in one of those phenomenal cases of instantaneous calculators. Most of the subsidy rolls of that century have been destroyed. In the one of 1543, Robert Greene[11], of Gillingham, is listed. He was then an elderly man with grandchildren. He had five children: Peter, Richard, John, Alice and Anne. Peter died without heirs, and Richard inherited the estate. From Richard's[12] line came Surgeon John Greene[14], the head of the Warwick Greenes, and from the only other son, John, came John of Quidnessett[15], the head of a numerous Rhode Island family of Greenes. As these two were all of this family who came to the Colonies, we shall not attempt to give a full list of those who remained in England.

Richard[12] left a son, Richard[13], and a daughter. Richard[13] and wife Mary had five sons and four daughters. Of these the fourth son was Surgeon John Greene[14]. In most American genealogies he is called the son of Peter Greene, of Aukley Hall. This is a mistake. Peter was his oldest brother, the heir to Bowridge Hall.

EMIGRATION OF THE GREENES TO THE COLONIES, 1609-40

The forefathers are those emigrants who came to the American Colonies before 1650. From the first colonization to Cromwell's day, all emigration may be divided into three distinct periods: The early Virginia settlements on the James River, the first of all; the coming of the Pilgrim Fathers to Massachusetts, 1620-31, and the emigration of anti-laud men, the influx of which was at its greatest in the year 1635.

The New England Greenes may be divided into three groups: (1) Those of the Ruling Elder John Greene line; (2) the Gillingham Greenes; and (3) those whose ancestry is unknown.

By 1650 the Waites, Anthonys, Wardwells and Pierces, with whom the Greenes largely intermarried, were residents of the liberty-loving colony. Of the Greenes themselves there were three adult men. These all came about the same time, in the very earliest day of the colony (Rhode Island, then known as the Providence Plantations). Each was named John, and two of these three had wives named Joan. These three men were John of Newport, Surgeon John of Warwick, and John of Quidnessett. John of Newport's line yet continues. His family was never as extensive as the others, and kept to their own part of the country pretty well. So far as I have been able to trace them, his posterity did not intermarry with the other Greenes of Rhode Island at all. The other John Greenes were of the English Gillingham branch and were second cousins-german to each other. (The younger John's father was second cousin to Surgeon John, which would make the younger John third cousin to the Surgeon's children. He was, of course, more nearly related to the father than to the children, to whom he was mid-way between a second and third cousin, or as genealogists phrase it, a second cousin-german. German here denotes not nationality but degree of relationship.)

The older cousin was variously called John Senior, John the Elder, John of Salisbury, Chirurgeon John and Surgeon John, John of Providence and John of Warwick. / In these pages he is spoken of as Surgeon John of Warwick. Various dates have been given of his birth. His direct descendant, Henry Lehre Greene, who has studied the matter carefully, puts the date as 1585. He was born at Bowridge Hall, Gillingham, England, and was the younger son of Richard Greene, Gentleman, and Mary his wife. He was something of a bachelor when on November 4, 1619, he married Joan Tattersall (or Joane Tatarsole, as the old records have it), at St. Thomas' Church, Salisbury, England. (The St. Thomas' Church records are interesting. They give the baptism of "ye sonnes and daughters of Mr. John Greene and Mris. Joane Greene." "Mris." is an old abbreviation of Mistress. Our present John Greene is variously described as "Gentleman" and "Chirurgeon.") His home was at Aukley Hall, Salisbury. He was too strong an anti-land man to make it safe for him in England, so with his wife and five children, he set sail from Southampton in April, 1635, in the good ship *James,* and arrived at Boston, May 3 of the same year. He lived for a time at Salem and was among the first who followed Roger Williams to Providence. The latter showed his confidence in him by making him one of the trustees to whom Providence was deeded.

Surgeon John Greene was selected by the indignant Rhode Islanders to present their grievances to England. He got safely away in 1644, and made so favorable an impression in the mother country that he secured valuable concessions and privileges for Rhode Island. While in England he married a former Rhode Island friend, the widow Alice Daniels, who had returned to her old home. She lived but a short time, and after his return to Rhode Island he married a third wife, Philippa (or Phellix), who survived him. He died in 1659 at Warwick (Shawomet). He was buried at Conanicut (or Connimicut) by the side of his faithful Joan. As has already been said, his children for many years held high official positions under the government. Nevertheless, after his death, John of Quidnessett was the leading Greene of Rhode Island, and stands out in a plain clear light of his own.

But four of the Warwick Greenes left issue, Mary Greene-Sweet, Deputy-Governor John, James and Thomas. GEN. NA-THANIEL GREENE, THE GREATEST OF THE WARWICK GREENES, AND GREATEST, SAVE WASHINGTON, OF ALL THE REVOLUTIONARY WAR HEROES, was the great-great-grandson of Surgeon John (John[1], James[2], Jabez[3], Nathaniel[4], and Gen. Nathaniel Greene[5]).

(Page 54)   "KING'S PROVINCE IN NARRAGANSETT,
                                           21 July, 1679.
To All Whom This May Concern:
    I, John Greene, inhabiting in the Narragansett Country, called King's Province, I being a sworn Conservator of the Peace, do on my Oath affirme,

that forty years and more ago, Mr. Richard Smith that I then lived with, die first begin and make a settlement in the Narragansett, and byat by the consent and approbation of the Indian Princes and people, and did improve land mow meadows severall yeares before Warwick was settled by an English man; and I, being present did see and heare all the Narragansett Princes being assembled together give by livery and seizing some hundreds of acres of land about a mile in length, and so down to the sea; this being about thirty years agoe, many hundred Indians being present, consenting thereunto.

This I certify to be true as I am in Publique office, on oath and under my hand.

JOHN GREENE."

(Page 58)   Several times John of Quidnessett's name appears on the records as a witness to the transfer of land, etc.   March 24, 1682, he divided his land among some of his sons who remained in Rhode Island.   John Greene's wife was alive when these deeds were executed.   There are three old and dilapidated graves in what was once a part of John of Quidnessett's land.   Two of these rude head-stones bear the initials D. B. and R. G., and mark the graves of John of Quidnessett's son Daniel and his wife Rebecca.   The other gravestone, the oldest of all, is marked I. G. (evidently intended for J. G.   In olden times the two capital letters I and J were made almost exactly alike).   It is believed to mark the grave of Mrs. Joan Greene, wife of John of Quidnessett.

(Page 67)   The Quidnessett Greenes are, therefore, descended from one of these five brothers: Edward[2], John[2], Daniel[2], James[2], or Benjamin[2].

I have numbered the American generations from John Greene[1], of Quidnessett.   He was fifteenth from Lord Alexander de Greene de Boketon, who received his title in 1202; ninth from Sir Henry Greene, beheaded in 1399; and sixth from John the Fugitive.   His pedigree runs thus:

GREENE LINE.   Sir Alexander[1]; his son[2] and grandson[3], whose names are lost; Sir Thomas[4]; Sir Thomas[5], who married Lady Lucie de la Zouch, descended from the royal Capetian line; Lord Chief Justice Sir Henry[6]; the beheaded Sir Henry[7]; Thomas[8]; an unknown son[9]; John the Fugitive[10]; Robert of Gillingham[11]; John[12]; Henry[13]; Robert[14]; John of Quidnessett[15].

CAPETIAN LINE.   Robert the Strong[1], made Duke de France in 861; Duke Robert[2]; Count Hugh the Great[3]; Hugh Capet[4], King of France; King Robert the Pious[5]; King Henry[6]; Hugh Magnus[7], Count de Vermandois; Lady Isabel[8], married to Earl of Leicester; Earl Robert[9], Lord Chief Justice of England; Earl Robert[10]; Lady Margaret[11], married to Earl of Winchester; Earl Roger[12]; Lady Elene[13], married to Alan, Lord de la Zouch, Governor of Northampton; Lord Eudo de la Zouch[14]; Lady Lucie de la Zouch[15], who married the fifth Lord de Greene.

John of Quidnessett[1] was, therefore, twenty-fifth in descent from Robert the Strong; twenty-second from the king, Jugo Capet, and nineteenth from Hugh de Vermandois, the Great Crusader.

Those who like to get as far back as possible toward Noah, have only to count the generations between John of Quidnessett and themselves, and add to the above. This will show the number of generations in all, back to the fountain head.

John Greene, of Quidnessett, had nearly eight centuries of certified noble and royal blood behind him. There are lords, dukes, counts, and kings enough in his line to enthuse any title hunter.

John Greene (Surgeon John), 1597-1658, from England in the *James* to Boston, 1635. A founder with Roger Williams of Providence Plantation, where he lived till 1643. With twelve other men purchased Narragansett from the Indians; a founder of Warwick, 1643; magistrate, deputy commissioner, etc. Married in England, 1619, Joan Tattersall; married second, Alice Daniels; married third, Philippa, who died in 1687, aged 87 years. See "Compendium of American Genealogy," Vol. II, page 401.)

John Greene, Charlestown, Freeman, 1642, came to New England, 1632, born in London, he was an elder of the church, and died April 22, 1658. (See Alden's "Col. of Epitaphs." 2 Colt. His. Sec. II, page 179—His son Jacob in Artillery Co., 1650. See "Ancient and Honorable Artillery," by Whitman.)

John[4] (Richard[3], Richard[2], Robert[1]).

In 1642, John Greene bought land called Occupassnatuxet, or Minantouomi. This land remained in occupation of his heirs until 1782, when it was sold to John Brown, of Providence, and is now occupied by his heirs ("SPRING GREEN FARM"). September 12, 1643, he and ten others bought Minantouomi, for 144 farthings of wampum, tracts of land called Shawomet (Warwick). (See "Genealogical Dictionary of Rhode Island," by Austin, 1887.)

(Burke's "Royal Families," Vol. I [Pedigree LIV])
George William Blathwayt, Esq.

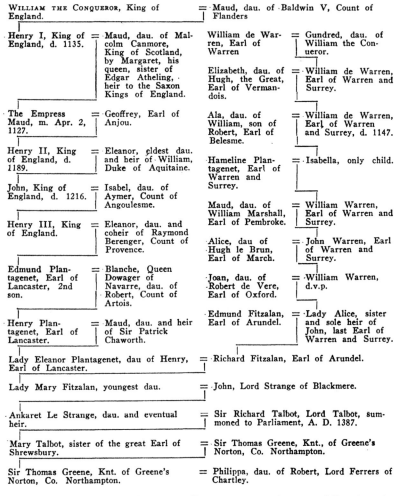

WILLIAM THE CONQUEROR, King of = Maud, dau. of Baldwin V, Count of
England. | Flanders

Henry I, King of = Maud, dau. of Malcolm Canmore, King of Scotland, by Margaret, his queen, sister of Edgar Atheling, heir to the Saxon Kings of England.
England, d. 1135.

The Empress = Geoffrey, Earl of Anjou.
Maud, m. Apr. 2, 1127.

Henry II, King = Eleanor, eldest dau. and heir of William, Duke of Aquitaine.
of England, d. 1189.

John, King of = Isabel, dau. of Aymer, Count of Angoulesme.
England, d. 1216.

Henry III, King = Eleanor, dau. and coheir of Raymond Berenger, Count of Provence.
of England.

Edmund Plantagenet, Earl of Lancaster, 2nd son. = Blanche, Queen Dowager of Navarre, dau. of Robert, Count of Artois.

Henry Plantagenet, Earl of Lancaster. = Maud, dau. and heir of Sir Patrick Chaworth.

Lady Eleanor Plantagenet, dau of Henry, = Richard Fitzalan, Earl of Arundel.
Earl of Lancaster.

Lady Mary Fitzalan, youngest dau. = John, Lord Strange of Blackmere.

Ankaret Le Strange, dau. and eventual heir. = Sir Richard Talbot, Lord Talbot, summoned to Parliament, A. D. 1387.

Mary Talbot, sister of the great Earl of Shrewsbury. = Sir Thomas Greene, Knt., of Greene's Norton, Co. Northampton.

Sir Thomas Greene, Knt. of Greene's Norton, Co. Northampton. = Philippa, dau. of Robert, Lord Ferrers of Chartley.

William de Warren, Earl of Warren = Gundred, dau. of William the Conueror.

Elizabeth, dau. of Hugh, the Great, Earl of Vermandois. = William de Warren, Earl of Warren and Surrey.

Ala, dau. of William, son of Robert, Earl of Belesme. = William de Warren, Earl of Warren and Surrey, d. 1147.

Hameline Plantagenet, Earl of Warren and Surrey. = Isabella, only child.

Maud, dau. of William Marshall, Earl of Pembroke. = William Warren, Earl of Warren and Surrey.

Alice, dau of Hugh le Brun, Earl of March. = John Warren, Earl of Warren and Surrey.

Joan, dau. of Robert de Vere, Earl of Oxford. = William Warren, d.v.p.

Edmund Fitzalan, Earl of Arundel. = Lady Alice, sister and sole heir of John, last Earl of Warren and Surrey.

1. LORD ALEXANDER DE GREENE DE BOKETON procured estate of Boughton in Northampton in 1202.

2. SIR WALTER DE BOKETON, listed in old rolls of 20th year of Henry III (1236), and 45th year of the same king (1261).

3. SIR JOHN DE BOKETON, Crusader, perished in Palestine in 1271, listed in a roll of the 7th year of Edward II (1314).

4. SIR THOMAS, the fourth Lord de Greene de Boketon, b. in closing years of the reign of Henry III.

5. SIR THOMAS, the fifth Lord, was b. in 1292; m. Lucie, dau. of Eudo de la Zouche and Millicent, one of the sisters and heirs of George de Cantelupe, Lord of Abergavenny (on the River Usk in Wales).

6. Sir Henry de Greene, only child of Sir Thomas and Lucie (de la Zouche). He was made Lord Chief Justice of England. He d. in 1370, a little under 60, and was bur. at Boughton. He early m. Katherine, the dau. of Sir John, and only sister of Sir Simon Drayton, of Drayton.
7. Sir Thomas de Greene, heir of Sir Henry⁶. He m. the dau. of Sir John Mablethorpe. Both were bur. at Greene's Norton.
8. Sir Thomas de Greene was b. in 1369 and d. in 1417.
9. Sir Thomas de Greene, m. Phillipa, dau. of Baron Ferrers. ⁽ˣ⁾See chart of lines from Greene to William de Warren and William the Conqueror.
10. John was supposed to have been b. about 1450. Called John the Fugitive.
11. Robert Greene, of Gillingham, in the year 1543, was an elderly man with grandchildren.
12. Richard Greene, son of Robert.
13. Richard Greene, who m. Mary ———.
14. Surgeon John Greene, of Warwick, fourth son of Richard and Mary Greene, b. in 1585, at Bowridge Hall, Gillingham, England. He m. Nov. 4, 1619, Joan Tattersall (Joane Tatarsole) at St. Thomas' Church, Salisbury, England. With his wife and five children he set sail from Southampton in Apr., 1635, in the good ship *James* and arrived at Boston, May 3, of the same year. He d. at Warwick in 1659. Children of John and Joan (Tatersall) Greene:
    John, bapt. Aug. 15, 1620.
    Peter, bapt. Mar. 10, 1622.
    Richard, bapt. Mar. 25, 1623.
    James, bapt. June 21, 1626.
    Thomas, bapt. June 4, 1628.
    Joan, bapt. Oct. 3, 1630.
    Mary, bapt. May 19, 1633.
15. Mary Green, of Narragansett, bapt. May 19, 1633; m. before June 6, 1671. Thomas Hungerford, b. 1648; d. 1714. Their third son named Green.
16. Thomas Hungerford, b. about 1673; d. 1750; m. 1699, Elizabeth, dau. of Mathew Smith and Mary Cutler, and had
17. Samuel Hungerford, b. about 1713; d. at New Fairfield, Conn.; m. June 23, 1746, Mary Graves, b. probably at Hatfield, Aug. 20, 1722, and had
18. Isaiah Hungerford, b. Jan. 23, 1757; d. June 16, 1833; m. Esther Mead, b. Aug. 11, 1760; d. Dec. 22, 1836, and had
19. Elizabeth Hungerford, b. Feb. 7, 1797; d. Jan. 7, 1878; m. Nash David Phelps, b. Oct. 4, 1796; d. Apr. 15, 1884, and had
20. Caroline Alexandra Phelps, b. July 3, 1840; d. Mar. 29, ʼ1921; m. Sept. 8, 1863, Horace Brayton Leach, b. Sept. 25, 1836; d. May 6, 1919, and had
21. Elizabeth May Leach, b. Jan. 7, 1866; m. Sept. 8, 1889, Oscar Herbert Rixford, b. Dec. 27, 1860; d. Sept. 11, 1926.
22. Oscar Adelbert Rixford, b. Aug. 4, 1890; m. Jan. 18, 1919, Mary Carolyn Hefflon, b. June 6, 1899.
23. Mary-Elizabeth Lenora Rixford, b. Oct. 6, 1922.
23. Oscar Theodore Rixford, b. July 21, 1925.

References: 1 to 14 generations—"The Greene Family and Its Branches, 861 to 1904," by Lora S. La Mance.
15 to 17 generations—"Thomas Hungerford and His Descendants," by F. Phelps Leach.
18 to 23 generations—Family Records.

("The Greene Family and Its Branches, 861 to 1904," by
Lora S. La Mance)

THE OLD GREENE TREE

Long years ago, "The old Greene Tree"
    Sank deep its roots in Albia's Soil;
Its branches spread and, banyan like,
    They bore to earth; thus no turmoil
Could shake this old and mighty tree.
    Was warfare on? Its branches then
Made stoutest staffs to slay the foe,
    And Lords de Greenes de Boketon's men,
Led by their fearless chiefs, became
    A scourging rod for those who dared
Oppose the will of England's king.
    But warrior Greenes their honors shared
With those of legal lore; and Lord
    Chief Justice Henry Greene we find
Was long supreme in Judges' Hall.
    His truly just and legal mind
Was tower of strength to Henry Third;
    And second son of this de Greene
Lives for all time, in Shakespeare's plays;
    And on the throne as England's queen,
A daughter of this line is seen.

The Greene Tree grew and "waxed strong"
    Nor would its sturdy branches bear
Unjust control; and thus it fell
    That men of Greene were those to dare
Oppose unjust, infamous Laud,
    Who sought with all his churchly power
To crush religious freedom out;
    But persecution proved a dower
Of Good unto those dauntless souls,
    Who, for religious liberty,
Forsook their dear ancestral homes
    And crossed the wide and stormy sea,
That they might live and worship God,
    In freedom, as their conscience taught.
But persecution was not o'er;
    The wilderness again was sought;
Again was fireside altar raised
    Where men were free. Thenceforth, they throve.

———

Their then have filled high place of trust
    In peace and war. Who does not love
This name of Greene? Who does not know
    And honor him, that stalwart son,
Branch of this tree, who, from the first
    Until the righteous war was done,
Undaunted led his brave men on
    To victory on many a field?
'Tis only to Great Washington's
    That fame of Greene doth yield.

                                —ATTIE A. STOWE.

("The Greene Family and Its Branches, 861 to 1904," by
Lora S. La Mance)

(Page 4)   One verse of the Poem.

At Norton's Hall, de Boketon's home,
High wassail reigned at Christmas-tide :—
The aged harper thumbed his strings,
Then drained the flagon by his side
And, when its contents warmed his blood
And roused his pride till wits were keen,
He voiced this lay, wherein he sang
Of Alexander, Lord de Greene.

GREGORY

Gregory is a very ancient English family. The coat of arms,
which appears to descend to the Gregorys of Connecticut is: Or,
two bars and a lo lion passant, in chief azure.
Gregory line may be summarized as follows:

1. JOHN GREGORY, Lord of the manors of Freseley and Asfordby, m. Maud,
   dau. of Sir Roger Moton, Knight of Peckleton, Leicestershire, England.
2. NICHOLAS.
3. ADAM GREGORY, or GREGOIRE, m. the dau. and coheiress of Ada Ormeston,
   County Lancaster, England. He was b. probably as early as 1450.
4. WILLIAM, son of Adam Gregory, m. Dorothy ———, dau. of Parre of
   Kempenhaugh, Lancashire.
5. HUGO, son of William Gregory, m. Maria ———.
6. THOMAS, son of Hugo Gregory, lived at Overbroughton, Nottinghamshire,
   England, on the borders of Leicestershire, north of Frisby and Asorby.
   He m. Dorothy Beeston.
7. JOHN, son of Thomas Gregory, was of De Broughton Sulney. He m.
   Alicia ———. Children: 1. *William;* 2. *John;* 3. *Edward;* 4. *Henry*
   ("de Boston in Nova Anglia" (New England), according to the
   ancient pedigree of the English family. (See "N. E. Reg.," July, 1869,
   page 306.)
8. HENRY, son of John Gregory, settled in Boston, Mass., as early as 1633,
   was at Springfield in that Colony in 1639. Removed few years later to
   Stratford, Conn. Estate distributed June 19, 1655, eldest son John
   being administrator. Children: *John* and *Judah.*
9. JOHN, son of Henry Gregory, lived at New Haven and settled at Norwalk.
   Had Lot 1 in Norwalk, the S. E. Towne Street Home; d. 1689.
10. JACHAN, of Norwalk, son of John Gregory first of the same, had *Mary,* b.
    1669; *John,* b. 1671; *Thomas,* b. 1673; *Samuel,* b. Mar. 19, 1676; *Sarah,*
    b. 1678; *Matthew,* b. 1680; *Jachan,* b. 1682.
11. SAMUEL GREGORY, son of Jachan, of Norwalk, b. Mar. 19, 1676, had dau.
    Rebecca, and probably others.
12. EZEKEEL² SANFORD, b. Mar. 6, 1668; m. Mar., 1696, at Chester Hill,
    Conn., Rebecca Gregory, dau. of Samuel.
13. EPHRAIM SANFORD, b. Feb. 12, 1708; d. Feb. 6, 1761-62; m. Oct. 7, 1730,
    at Fairfield or Reading, Conn., Elizabeth Mix, b. 1715; d. Jan. 21, 1777.
14. STEPHEN MEAD, b. 1728; d. Oct. 18, 1806; m. Oct. 31, 1751, probably at
    Reading, Conn., Rachel Sanford, b. July 23, 1733; d. probably 1800.
15. ISAIAH HUNGERFORD, b. Dec. 26, 1756, bapt. Jan. 23, 1757; d. June 16,
    1833; m. at New Fairfield, Conn., Esther Mead, b. Aug. 11, 1760; d.
    Dec. 22, 1836.

16. NASH DAVID PHELPS, b. Oct. 4, 1796; d. Apr. 15, 1884; m. Apr. 29, 1821, Elizabeth Hungerford, b. Feb. 7, 1798; d. Jan. 7, 1878.
17. HORACE BRAYTON LEACH, b. Sept. 25, 1836; d. May 5, 1919; m. at Stanbridge, Que., Sept. 8, 1863, Caroline Alexandria Phelps, b. July 3, 1840; d. Mar. 29, 1921.
18. OSCAR HERBERT RIXFORD, b. Dec. 27, 1859; d. Sept. 11, 1927; m. Sept. 8, 1889, at Sheldon, Vt., Elizabeth May Leach, b. Jan. 7, 1866; living May 6, 1931.
19. OSCAR ADELBERT RIXFORD, b. Aug. 4, 1890; living May 6, 1931; m. Jan. 18, 1919, at Montreal, Que., Mary Carolyn Hefflon, b. June 6, 1899; living May 6, 1931.   Children:
     Mary-Elizabeth Lenora, b. Oct. 6, 1922; living May 6, 1931.
     Oscar Theodore, b. July 21, 1925; living May 6, 1931.

References: "American Ancestry," Vol. I, page 33.
             "Genealogy—Connecticut," Vol. III, page 1432.
             1 to 15 generations—Records of Elizabeth M. Rixford.
             15 to 19 generations—Family Records.

SERVICES

Passingers wch. passed from Ye Port of London, Secondo January 1634, in the *Bonaventure* to Virginia.   Page 454—"John Gregory 204 acres land, 1 hired servant, 4 brought servants, and 85 Slaves."

See "Stevens Gen." (1891), Deed—Nat. Stephens 1734 R. Signed by John Gregory, Justice of the Peace and Samuel Gregory.

"History of New London," by Caulkins (1860), page 16—"First Settlers, Mathias St. John Sr. & Jr., John Gregory etc."

"Daughters of the 17th Century," page 231—"John Gregory d. 1689, Deputy from Norwalk, Conn., 1665, 1679, 1681.   Selectman 1669.   His son Jachin (———-1697-8), b. in Norwalk, Conn., Deputy 1695."

"History of Fairfield," Vol. I, page 67, by Scheneck—Among the Pequot Settlers, Samuel Gregory.   He lived near the foot of Golden Hill, near the street where it crosses the hill to Stratford, Conn.

Page 71—Samuel Gregory, soldier engaged in Pequot War 1637-1638, who settled at Fairfield.

HAINAULT

("Colonial Families," 1928, page 114)

Arms—Or, a lion rampant sable, armed and langued gules.

Crest—A conical hat barry per pale gules and argent counterchanged, surmounted by cock plumes sable.

Motto—*Haynault au noble comte.* (Haynault to the noble count.)

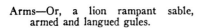

Ancient Counts
of
Hainault

The medieval Countship of Hainaut or Hainault is now included in Belgium and France. It passed to Burgundy in 1433, and afterwards shared the fortunes of the Belgian Netherlands. The parts acquired by France, in 1569 and 1678, are now included in the Department of Nord.

1. BALDWIN II, of Hainault, 1070-1126.
2. BALDWIN III, of Hainault, 1126-33.
3. BALDWIN IV, of Hainault, 1133-71; m. Alice, surname unknown.
4. BALDWIN IV, of Hainault, and VIII, of Flanders, 1171-95; m. Margaret, surname unknown.
5. BALDWIN IX, of Eastern Empire, 1195-1205; m. Mary, dau. of Count of Champagne.
6. MARGARET, second dau., held Hainault from 1244 to 1272; m. (1) Burchard, of Avesnes.
7. JOHN I, of Hainault, 1246-57; m. Adelaide, a descendant of the Counts of Holland and Namur.
8. JOHN II, of Holland and Hainault, 1257-1304.
9. WILLIAM I, of Hainault and Holland, 1304-37. Under Count William III and his successor.
10. PHILLIPA, m. King Edward III, of England. (See Royal Descent No. 28.)

   Mary-Elizabeth L. Rixford and Oscar Theodore Rixford are 30th in direct descent from (1) Baldwin II, of Hainault.

ROYAL LINES OF MARY-ELIZABETH L. RIXFORD AND
OSCAR THEODORE RIXFORD, GRANDCHILDREN
OF ELIZABETH M. RIXFORD

1. · HENRY I, King of England from 1100 to 1135, son of William the Conqueror, m. (1) Edith Matilda, of Scotland, dau. of Malcolm III and Margaret, by whom he had one dau., *Matilda*. He m. (2) Adela, dau. of the Count of Louvain, in Flanders.

2. · MATILDA (MAUD), dau. of Henry I and Edith Matilda, d. in 1167. She was accepted as Queen by the barons of England, but owing to the dislike they felt towards her husband, they finally turned against her, electing Stephen King in her stead. She fought many battles for her rights, and is one of the heroines of romantic history. She m. (1) the Emperor Henry V. She m. (2), in 1127, Geoffrey Plantagenet, Count of Anjou (see William the Conqueror III), and had a son, *Henry Plantagenet,* of whom further.

3. · HENRY PLANTAGENET, Henry II, King of England, son of Geoffrey Plantagenet and Matilda, was b. Mar. 25, 1133, and reigned in England as Henry II until 1189. He m., in 1152, Eleanor, of Aquitaine, and had a son, *John,* of whom further.

Henry II..
OF ENGLAND

4. ·JOHN PLANTAGENET, King John of England, son of Henry Plantagenet, was b. in 1167, and m. Isabella Taillefer, of Angouleme. (See Taillefer IX and Edward III of England.) They had a son, *Henry,* of whom further.

5. · HENRY PLANTAGENET, Henry III, King of England, m. in 1236, Eleanor, dau. of Raimond Berenger IV, of Province. (See Province VII.) They had *Edward,* of whom further.

6. · EDWARD I, King of England, son of Henry III, m. (1) Princess Eleanor, of Castile. He m. (2) Margaret, of France, and had *Edward II,* King of England, and another son, *Edmund,* of whom further.

7. · EDMUND PLANTAGENET, of Woodstock, Earl of Kent, youngest son of Edward I, King of England, and his second wife, Margaret; m. Margaret, dau. of John, Lord Baron Wake.

8. · JOAN PLANTAGENET, dau. of Edmund, of Woodstock, and Margaret Wake, was known as "the faire Maid of Kent." She m. Thomas Holland, second son of Robert, first Baron Holland. (See Holland II.)

9. · THOMAS HOLLAND, son of Thomas and Joan (Plantagenet) Holland, was Earl of Kent, Baron of Holland, Woodstock, and Wake, and Earl Marshal. He m. Alice Fitz-Alan, dau. of Richard, Earl of Arundel. (See Fitz-Alan VII.)

10. · THOMAS HOLLAND, son of Thomas and Alice (Fitz-Alan) Holland, was Earl of Kent, Duke of Surrey, Baron of Holland, Woodstock, Earl Marshal, and Lord Lieutenant of Ireland. He was taken prisoner and beheaded at the Battle of Cirencester in 1400, on account of his loyalty to his cousin, the deposed King Richard II. At the time of his death he was betrothed to Constance, dau. of Prince Edmund de Longley, fifth son of Edward III and Duke of York.

11. JOHN TOUCHETT, son of James Touchett, had livery of all his father's castles, lordships and lands. He was summoned to Parliament as Baron until his death. He m. (1) Margaret, dau. of William, Lord Roos, of Hamloke, by whom he had *John*, son and heir. He m. (2) Eleanor Holland, natural dau. of Thomas Holland, Earl of Kent, by Constance, dau. of Edmund de Longley, Duke of York. (See Holland V.) John and Eleanor (Holland) had three sons and three daus., of whom one was *Constance*, of whom further.

12. CONSTANCE, dau. of John and Eleanor (Holland) Touchett, m. as second wife, Sir Robert Whitney, Knight. (See Whitney English 'Pedigree X.) Sir Robert Whitney, son of Sir Eustace Whitney, was probably a a knight and was an active participant in the War of the Roses, and was attainted as a Yorkist in 1459. He was probably at the Battle of Mortimer's Cross in 1461. He was the subject of a poem by Lewis Glyn Cothi, on the occasion of his marriage to Alice, the great-grand-daughter of Sir David Gam. He m. (1) Alice Vaughan, dau. of Thomas Vaughan; (2) Constance Touchett, who was the mother of his sons. She was descended from William the Conqueror, through the wife of Edward I, King of England.

13. JAMES WHITNEY, son of Sir Robert Whitney, m. Blanche Milbourne, dau. and heir of Simon Milbourne. (See Milbourne IV.)

14. ROBERT WHITNEY, son of James Whitney, was of Icomb, and in charge of other confiscated estates. Died in 1541; m. Margaret Wye.

15. SIR ROBERT WHITNEY, son of Robert Whitney, m. Sybil Baskerville.

16. ROBERT WHITNEY, son of Sir Robert Whitney, m. Elizabeth, dau. of Morgan Guillims, or Duglim.

17. THOMAS WHITNEY, Gentleman, son of Robert Whitney, was of West-minster. He m. Mary Bray, dau. of John Bray, of Westminster.

18. JOHN WHITNEY, son of Thomas and Mary (Bray) Whitney, was b. in England in 1583, and d. June 1, 1673. He emigrated from London, England, in 1635, and settled in Watertown, Mass., the first of the name in America. He m. in England, Elinor ———, who was b. in 1599, and d. in Watertown, May 11, 1659. He m. (2), in Watertown, Sept. 29, 1659, Judith Clement, who d. before her husband.

19. JOHN WHITNEY, JR., son of John and Elinor Whitney, was b. in Eng-land in 1624; m. Ruth Reynolds, of Boston. He d. Oct. 12, 1692, and his wife d. later.

20. RUTH WHITNEY, b. Apr. 15, 1645; m. (1) a Shattuck; m. (2) Enoch Lawrence, Mar. 6, 1676-7. He was b. Jan. 5, 1648, and d. Sept. 28, 1744.

21. CAPT. DANIEL LAWRENCE, b. Mar. 7, 1681; d. 1777; m. Sarah ———, who d. probably at Canaan, Conn.

22. ISAAC LAWRENCE, SR., b. Feb. 25, 1704-5; d. Dec. 2, 1793; m. Lydia Hewitt, who d. Nov. 14, 1765.

23. ISAAC LAWRENCE, JR., of Canaan, Conn., m. May 8, 1760, Mary Brown, 7th child of Dea. Samuel Brown.

24. LYDIA LAWRENCE, b. 1761-2, d. Sept. 20, 1813; m. at New Haven, Vt., Phineas Phelps, b. Apr. 10, 1767; d. Apr. 20, 1813.

25. NASH DAVID PHELPS, b. Oct. 4, 1796; d. Apr. 15, 1884; m. Apr. 20, 1821, Elizabeth Hungerford, b. Feb. 7, 1798; d. Jan. 7, 1878.

26. CAROLINE ALEXANDRIA PHELPS, b. July 3, 1840; d. Mar. 29, 1921; m. Sept. 8, 1863, at Stanbridge, Que., Horace Brayton Leach, b. Sept. 25, 1836; d. May 6, 1919.

27. ELIZABETH MAY LEACH, b. Jan. 7, 1866; living Jan. 1, 1932; m. at Sheldon, Vt., Sept. 8, 1889, Oscar Herbert Rixford, b. Dec. 27, 1859; d. Sept. 11, 1926.

28. OSCAR ADELBERT RIXFORD, b. Aug. 4, 1890; m. Jan. 18, 1919, Montreal, Que., Mary Carolyn Hefflon, b. June 6, 1899; both living Jan. 1, 1932. They have two children (living Jan. 1, 1932):
    Mary-Elizabeth Lenora, b. Oct. 6, 1922.
    Oscar Theodore, b. July 21, 1925.

References: 1 to 18 generations—"Colonial Families," 1928.
19 to 23 generations—"Watertown, Mass., Bond," Vol. 1, 2nd Ed.
"Gen. Conn.," Vol. 2, pages 831-832.
"D. A. C.," Lineage of Elizabeth M. Rixford.
23 to 28 generations—Family Records.

HEYDON

("Colonial Families," 1928, page 42)

Arms—Quarterly, argent and gules, a cross engrailed counterchanged.
Crest—A talbot argent spotted sable.

The surname Heydon (or Haydon) originated from Haydon Parish, in the following family from Heydon (or Haydon) Parish in County Norfolk. Thomas de Heydon, clerk, in 1203, had to do with land in Heydon and London, and was a justice itinerant in 1221.

1. WILLIAM HEYDON, or Haydon.
2. WILLIAM HEYDON, son of William Heydon, was living at Heydon in the reign of Edward I (1274-1309).
3. SIMON HEYDON, was a son of William Heydon.
4. DAVID HEYDON, son (Noris says of Thomas, son of Simon) of Simon Heydon, m. Margaret, surname unknown.
5. WILLIAM HEYDON, son of Hugh and Alice (Loverd) Heydon, m. Elizabeth, dau. and heiress of Sir John Say.
6. HUGH HEYDON, son and heir of David Heydon, m. Alice Loverd, by whom he obtained the manor of Loverd.
7. ROBERT HEYDON, son of William and Elizabeth (Say) Heydon, m. Cecily, dau. and heiress of Robert Oulton, an eminent lawyer in the reign of Henry IV (1399-1413).
8. WILLIAM HEYDON, son of Robert and Cecily (Oulton) Heydon, m. Jane, dau. and heiress of John Warren, of Poynton.
9. ISABEL HEYDON, dau. of William and Jane (Warren) Heydon, m. William (4) Warren, son of Reginald and Adelia (de Mowbray) Warren. Reginald is the second son of William (3) de Warren, second Earl of Warren and Surrey, also the founder of the Warren Family, of Poynton. (See Warren 8-15, Stanley No. 11.)

Stella Frankie Buker and Elizabeth May Buker (named for Author), grandchildren of the Author's sister (Mrs. Charles J.) Alberta Leach Read, 34th in direct descent from (1) William Heydon.

JOHNSON

(HORACE BRAYTON LEACH'S ROYAL ANCESTRY, FATHER OF THE AUTHOR OF THIS GENEALOGY)

(Burke's "Royal Families," Vol. II)

1. RALPH NEVILLE, first Earl of Westmoreland, K. G., m. Margaret, dau. of Hugh, Lord Stafford, first wife. He m. (2) Joan de Beaufort, dau. of John of Gaunt, ancestor of Henry III, King of England.
2. PHILLIPPA NEVILLE, dau. of Ralph, Earl of Westmoreland, m. Thos. Dacre, Lord Dacre, of Gillesland.
3. SIR THOMAS DACRE, son and heir apparent, d.v.p., m. Elizabeth, dau. and heir of Sir William Bowet.
4. JOAN DACRE, dau. and heir, Baroness Dacre, m. Richard Fynes, *jure uxoris*, Lord Dacre, of Gillesland.
5. ELIZABETH FYNES, dau. of Richard, Lord Dacre, m. John Clinton, Lord Clinton and Say; d. 1488.
6. JOHN, LORD CLINTON, d. 1515; m. Elizabeth, dau. of Sir John Morgan, of Tredegar.
7. THOMAS CLINTON, Lord Clinton, d. 1517; m. Jane Poynings.
8. EDWARD CLINTON, first Earl of Lincoln, K. G.; m. Ursula, dau. of William, Lord Stourton.
9. HENRY CLINTON, Earl of Lincoln, d. 1616; m. Elizabeth Morison, relict of William Norreys, son of Hen., Lord Norreys.
10. THOMAS FIENNES, alias Clinton, third Earl of Lincoln. He had sons, *Theophilus* and *Charles*, and dau., *Arbella.* Theophilus was fourth Earl.
11. ISAAKE JOHNSON, Esqr., m. Lady Arbella, dau. of Thomas, third Earl of Lincoln.
    Humphrey Johnson, son of John and grandson of Isaac Johnson, who was one of the chief men in the founding of Roxbury. Humphrey Johnson resided in Roxbury many years, then removed to Hingham; was a man of affairs, a soldier in Capt. Isaac Johnson's Co. in the war against King Philip in 1675. Children: (1) Mehitabel Johnson, bapt. at Roxbury, Mar. 29, 1646. (2) Martha Johnson, bapt. Sept. 12, 1647. (3) Deborah Johnson, bapt. Jan. 20, 1649. ("Cheney Family," Part I, page 17.)

(Genealogy—"Connecticut," Vol. II, page 836)

12. (The Johnson Line)—JOHN JOHNSON, immigrant ancestor, was b. in England, and came to America in the fleet with Winthrop, accompanied by his wife Margery, who d. at Roxbury, June 9, 1655, and their sons, Isaac and Humphrey, and probably other children. Savage thinks there were three daus. Johnson was admitted a freeman May 18, 1630. He settled in Roxbury and was called a yeoman. He was chosen by the General Court, Oct. 19, 1630, constable of Roxbury and surveyor of all the arms of the Colony, and was a very industrious man in his place. He kept a tavern and was agent for Mrs. Catherine Sumpner, of London, in 1653. He was a man of wealth and much distinction. He was a deputy to the General Court in 1634 and many years afterwards. His house was burned Aug. 2, 1645, with seventeen barrels of his country's powder and many arms in his charge. At the same time the town records were destroyed. He was elected a member of the Artillery Company in 1658. He signed the inventory of Joseph Weld's estate in 1646. He d. Sept. 30, 1650, and his will was proved Oct. 15, following, dividing his property among his five children, the eldest to have a double portion. The estate amounted to six hundred and sixty pounds. He m. (2) Grace (Negus) Fawer, widow of

Barnabas Fawer. Her will was made Dec. 21, 1671, and proved Dec. 29, 1671, leaving all her estate to her brothers, Jonathan and Benjamin Negus. Children, all by first wife:

Isaac, m. Jan. 20, 1637, Elizabeth Porter; killed in the Narragansett fight in King Philip's War, Dec. 19, 1675.
Humphrey, mentioned below.
Mary, m. Roger Mowry, of Providence, who sold her share in the estate Oct. 12, 1659.
Two other daus.

13. · HUMPHREY JOHNSON, son of John Johnson, was b. in England. He came to America with his parents and settled in Roxbury as early as 1643, when his name appears on a deed. He was resident of Scituate in 1651. He m. (1) in 1642, Eleanor Cheney, of Roxbury, who d. at Hingham, Sept. 28, 1678. He m. (2) · Abigail ———.
Children of first wife:
Mehitable, b. 1644.   ·*Martha,* b. 1647.
John, b. 1653; drowned at Hingham, June 12, 1674.
Joseph, b. 1655; d. young.
Benjamin, b. 1657.   ·*Deborah,* b. 1661.
Margaret, b. 1659.   ·*Mary,* b. 1663.
Nathaniel, b. July, 1666; mentioned below.
·*Isaac,* b. Feb. 18, 1668.   ·*Joseph,* b. Sept. 6, 1676.
Children of second wife:
·*John,* b. June 8, 1680.   ·*Deborah,* b. February 19, 1682-3.

(See D. A. C. Records of Elizabeth M. Rixford, "Year Book," 1931.)

SERVICES

Humphrey Johnson (1603-1676), sergeant in King Philip's War, 1675.

References: "Soc. Col. Wars, Index and Honor Rolls" (1922), pages 271-272-273.

Humphrey Johnson was a captain in King Philip's War; born about 1620 in England and married in Roxbury; also resident of Scituate and Hingham.

References: "D. A. C. Lineage Book" (1929), page 92.

Humphrey Johnson, one of the original proprietors.

References: "History of Roxbury," page 56.

11. · MR. ISAAKE JOHNSON, Esqr. ("N. E. H. and Gen. Reg." [1921], page 236, Vol. LXXV); Lady Arbella his wife, dau. of Thomas Fiennes, third Earl of Lincoln, and sister of Charles, and Theophilus, fourth Earl of Lincoln.
12. HON. JOHN JOHNSON, b. in England, 1600; d. 1659; m. Margery ——— in England; had son, *Capt. Humphrey Johnson.*
13. · CAPT. HUMPHREY JOHNSON, b. in England about 1620; m. Mar. 20, 1642-3, Ellen Cheney, b. in England about 1626; had dau., *Mehitable Johnson.*
14. SAMUEL HINSDALE, m. Oct. 31, 1660, Mehitable Johnson, b. 1644; d. Aug. 4, 1689; had dau., *Mehitable Hinsdale.*
15. OBADIAH DICKINSON, m. Mehitable Hinsdale, b. Oct. 18, 1663, at Medfield; had dau., *Mehitable Dickinson.*
16. · NATHANIEL FRARY, b. Nov. 29, 1675; d. Apr. 30, 1737; m. Jan. 26, 1715-6, Mehitable Dickinson, b. 1696; had dau., *Eunice Frary.*

17. · AARON FIELD, b. Mar. 17, 1721-2; d. Mar. 17, 1800; m. May 26, 1743, Eunice Frary, b. Nov. 30, 1721; d. Oct. 28, 1813; had dau., *Chloe Field*.
18. · SAMUEL SHATTUCK, b. Sept. 18, 1741; d. Sept. 1, 1827; m. Nov., 1764, Chloe Field, b. Dec. 29, 1743; d. Apr. 10, 1781; had dau., *Chloe Shattuck*.
19. · EPHRAIM LEACH, b. Dec., 1761; d. Feb. 28, 1840; m. Nov. 17, 1785, Chloe Shattuck, b. Nov. 22, 1766; d. Jan. 22, 1845; had son, *Tertius Leach*.
20. · TERTIUS LEACH, b. Nov. 21, 1786; d. Feb. 4, 1864; m. Jan. 1, 1812, Sophia Hawley, b. Aug. 17, 1795; d. Jan. 7, 1879; had son, *Tertius Hawley Leach*.
21. · TERTIUS HAWLEY LEACH, b. Mar. 19, 1813; d. Sept. 19, 1881; m. Feb. 28, 1835, Orissa Fanton, b. May 1, 1812; d. June 24, 1890; had son, *Horace Brayton Leach*.
22. · HORACE BRAYTON LEACH, b. Sept. 26, 1836; d. May 6, 1919; m. Sept. 8, 1863, Caroline Alexandria Phelps, b. July 3, 1840; d. Mar. 29, 1921.

References: 1 to 18 generations—Records of Elizabeth M. Rixford.
           18 to 20 generations—"Lawrence Leach and His Descendants," by F. Phelps Leach.
           21 to 22 generations—Family Records.

("New England Historical and Genealogical Register," Vol. LXXV, 1921, page 236)

Leaders in the Winthrop Fleet, 1630; communicated by J. Gardner Bartlett, of Boston, Mass.

The following list of some of the leading men who came to New England in the fleet with Winthrop in 1630 is preserved in the Colonial Office Papers, Vol. 5, No. 78, in the Public Record Office, London.

A Note of the names of the principal undertakers for the plantation of the Massachusetts bay in Newe England that are themselves gonne over with theire wives and children.

Mr. Joh: Winthroppe Esqr: Governor, and three of his sonnes.
Sr Rich: Saltonstall Knight, three of his sonnes and 2 daughters.
Mr. Isaake Johnson Esqr and the Lady Arbella his wife Sister to the Earle of Lincolne.
Mr. Charles Fines the said Earles brother.
Mr. Dudley, his wife, 2 sonnes and 4 daughters.
Mr. Coddington and his wife.
Mr. Pincheon and his wife and 3 daughters.
Mr. Vassall and his wife.
Mr. Revell.

(Endorsed)
The names of the New plantators In New England.
For the right honorable the Lord Carleton.

This list raises a few interesting points. From various evidences it appears that the three sons brought by Governor Winthrop were Henry, Stephen, and Samuel. Sir Richard Saltonstall had four sons, Richard, Samuel Robert, and Henry. Probably the youngest son, Henry, was the one left in England, and he came later to New England. The daughters were Rosamond and Grace. Charles Fiennes, born about 1607, was the fifth son of Thomas Fiennes, alias Clinton, third Earl of Lincoln, and a younger brother of Theophilus Fiennes, fourth Earl of Lincoln. He entered Christ's College, Cambridge, in Easter, 1624, but did not proceed to a degree. He remained only a few weeks in New England, and then returned to England. ("Savage, in his 'Gen. Dict.,' has erroneously confused this passenger with another person of the same name.") The four daughters brought over by Thomas Dudley were Ann, Patience, Sarah, and Mercy. His son, Samuel Dudley, baptized November 30, 1608, is known to have come with his parents; but who was the other son referred to in the list? The father married April 25, 1603, Dorothy Yorke, and when elected deputy governor, May 17, 1637, is called "senior," a term which implies a son Thomas then living in New England. The records of Emmanuel College, Cambridge, show that a Thomas Dudley, pensioner, matriculated in Easter, 1624, and received his A.B. in January, 1626-7, and A.M. in April, 1630. This may well have been the eldest son of Governor Dudley, born probably about 1606 and receiving his master's degree just before sailing in the Winthrop fleet, of which some of the vessels did not leave England until the end of April, 1630. According to this list William Pyncheon's only son, John, did not come with his parents, as has been commonly supposed. William Vassall and his wife soon returned to England, but came back in 1635, bringing then their children.

WILLIAM LATHAM, MAYFLOWER PASSENGER

The names of those which came over first, in yᵉ year 1620, and were by the blessing of God the first beginers and (in a sort) the foundation of all the Plantations and Colonies in New-England; and their families.

Mʳ. John Carver; Kathrine, his wife; Desire Minter; & 2. manservants, John Howland, Roger Wilder; William Latham, a boy; & a maid servant, & a child yᵗ was put to him, called Jasper More.

William Latham—Marshfield, Mass., Member Marshfield Co. 1643. (See "Society of Colonial Wars," 1922, page 563.)

Robert Latham was probably the son of William. He married Susannah, daughter of John Winslow and brother of Governor Edward, 1649, and had Mercy, 1650 (at Plymouth), James, Chilton, Joseph, Elizabeth, Hannah, Sarah. Settled in East Bridgewater in 1657. His wife's mother was the famous Mary Chilton. He named his first two sons after her grandfather, James and Chilton. The third child, Joseph, after her father.

References: Bradford's History "of Plimouth Plantation," from the Original Manuscript, Appendix.
"History of Early Settlement of Bridgewater, Mass.," page 222.

Ancestry to William Latham may be summarized as follows:

1. WILLIAM LATHAM, b. in England, came in the *Mayflower* in 1620.
2. ROBERT LATHAM, b. in England; m. Susannah Winslow.
3. HANNAH LATHAM, dau. of Robert Latham and Susannah Winslow, m. Joseph Washburn.

4. HEPZIBAH WASHBURN, b. West Bridgewater, Mass.; d. Apr. 14, 1750; m. Sept. 8, 1702, No. 20 Benjamin Leach Esq., b. West Bridgewater, Mass.; d. July 13, 1764.
5. HANNAH LEACH, b. Mar. 4, 1725, at West Bridgewater, Mass.; m. at Greenfield, Mass., Aug. 6, 1743, Solomon Leach, b. Feb. 19, 1712.
6. EPHRAIM LEACH, b. Dec., 1761; d. Feb. 28, 1840; m. Nov. 17, 1766, at Greenfield, Mass., Chloe Shattuck, b. Nov. 22, 1766; d. Jan. 22, 1845.
7. TERTIUS LEACH, b. Nov. 21, 1786; d. Feb. 4, 1864; m. Jan. 1, 1811, Sheldon, Vt., Sophia Hawley, b. Aug. 17, 1795; d. Jan. 7, 1879.
8. TERTIUS HAWLEY LEACH, b. May 19, 1813; d. Sept. 19, 1881; m. Feb. 28, 1835, at Sheldon, Vt., Orisa Fanton, b. May 17, 1812; d. June 24, 1890.
9. HORACE BRAYTON LEACH, b. Sept. 25, 1836; d. May 6, 1919; m. Sept. 8, 1863, at Stanbridge, Que., Caroline Alexandria Phelps, b. July 3, 1840; d. Mar. 29, 1921.
10. ELIZABETH MAY LEACH, b. Jan. 7, 1866; living Jan. 1, 1932; m. Sept. 8, 1889, at Sheldon, Vt., Oscar Herbert Rixford, b. Dec. 27, 1859; d. Sept. 11, 1927.
11. OSCAR ADELBERT RIXFORD, b. Aug. 4, 1890; living Jan. 1, 1932; m. Jan. 18, 1919, at Montreal, Que., Mary Carolyn Hefflon, b. June 6, 1899; living Jan. 1, 1932. Children:
    Mary-Elizabeth Lenora, b. Oct. 6, 1922; living Jan. 1, 1932.
    Oscar Theodore, b. July 21, 1925; living Jan. 1, 1932.
    (Junior members of Vermont Society of Mayflower Descendants.)

References: 1 to 6 generations—"Lawrence Leach and His Descendants," by F. Phelps Leach, Volume 1.
    7 to 11 generations—Family Records.
    See: Supplemental Line of Elizabeth M. Rixford, in "Colonial Daughters of 17th Century," National No. 772. Supplemental Line of Elizabeth M. Rixford, National No. 2089, State No. 2, in "Daughters of American Colonists, Lineage Book," 1931, page 31.

COAT OF ARMS OF THE LAWRENCES

SIR ROBERT, of Ashton Hall, Lancashire, England, from his Sovereign, Richard Coeur de Lion, received his arms:

"Argent, a cross raguly gules," A. D. 1191. The same was the coat of arms of the Lancashire branch generally. There were distinctions, as "He beareth Ermine, a cross raguled gules, by the name of Lawrence, of Lancashire."

"Raguled" is a term to represent the rough-hewn stems of a tree from which the branches have been rudely lopped.

The Gloucestershire and Buckinghamshire branches had the same arms the crest "A demi turbot," or "tail inverted and erect"; or again, "The tail (or hindmost half) of a chub (fish) inverted and erect."

Other crests were used by these families, as, "Two laurel branches vert, forming a chaplet."

Also, "A wolf's head, couped, ppr." The Lawrences of Ives Co., Buckingham, and of St. Ives Co., Huntingdon, had, "Argent, a cross raguly gules; on a chief of the second a lion pass, guard or, "The crest," "a stag's head erased sa, platte attired or ducally gorgedor."

Lawrence.

FAMILY OF JOHN LAWRENCE
By John Lawrence, 1857

THE NAME

(Page 5)   Of Lawrence, as a personal and family name, it is sufficient to say, as to the orthography, that it is now almost universally spelled and written Lawrence, and not Laurence or Lawrance, as formerly was the case.

The derivation of this name of men may be traced to the Latin word Laurus—Laurentius.   Its signification has been thus given on the Town Records of Hingham, Mass., first page: "Christian names for men now most used with the signification, Lawrence—flourishing like a bay-tree."

ARCHBISHOP LAWRENCE

The first individual of this name who lived in England, yet ascertained, was Lawrence, the monk.   Collier, in his Dictionary, has the name Laurentius.   In Harris's "History of Kent," it is Lawrence. He came from Italy with Austin, who was sent to Britain for the propagation of Christianity in the island.

Upon the death of Austin, he succeeded him to the Archbishopric of Canterbury.   He is said to have been both learned and pious; and, at his death, was buried in the Abbey of St. Austins, A. D. 916.

THE ANCESTRAL LINEAGE OF JOHN LAWRENCE, OF WATERTOWN, MASS.

(Page 7)   The lineal ancestry of this stock of Lawrences in America, now found quite numerous in New England and other parts of the country, has been at length very satisfactorily ascertained.   As traced and determined, it originates in and derives from one ROBERT LAWRENCE, of Lancashire, England; born probably, as early as A. D. 1150, and the ancestor of the earliest families of the name in England.   Attending his Sovereign, Richard Coeur de Lion, to the war of the Crusades in the Holy Land, he so distinguished himself in the siege of Acre, that he was knighted, "Sir Robert, of Ashton Hall," and obtained for his arms, "Argent, a cross raguly gules," A. D. 1191.

The arms of Sir Robert, of Ashton Hall, conferred by Richard I, namely, "Argent, a cross raguly gules" were also those of the Lancashire branch generally.

THE ANCESTRAL LINEAGE OF JOHN LAWRENCE, OF WATERTOWN, MASS.

(Pages 8 and 9)   Also, "He beareth Ermine, a cross raguled gules, by the names of Lawrence, of Lancashire."   "Raguled" is a term used "to represent the rough-hewn stems of a tree from which the branches have been rudely lopped."

Proceeding with the successive generations of ancestry, we have in order of time, the first—Sir Robert Lawrence, of Ashton Hall.

THE SECOND GENERATION

Sir Robert, a son, and the immediate successor of the Knight of the Crusades, to the estate of Ashton Hall, married a daughter of James Trafford, Esq., of Lancashire; by whom he had a son and heir, James Lawrence.

THE THIRD GENERATION

James, of Ashton Hall, married, it is said, "in 1252," Matilda de Washington, daughter of John de Washington, an heiress. A son by this marriage, and the successor of James of Ashton Hall, was John Lawrence, said to have been living in the thirty-seventh year of Henry III.

Respecting the names "Lawrence" and "Washington," it may be noted that Lawrence Washington, a brother of the first President of the United States, was one of the earliest proprietors of Mount Vernon.

THE FOURTH GENERATION

John, of Ashton Hall, married Margaret, daughter of Walter Chesford; by whom he had a son, John Lawrence, his heir and successor.

THE FIFTH GENERATION

John, son of John and Margaret, married Elisabeth Holt, of Stably, in Lancashire; and died, it is said, A. D. 1360, leaving Robert Lawrence, his son and heir.

THE SIXTH GENERATION

Sir Robert, of Ashton Hall, married Margaret Holden, of Lancashire, and had:

I.   Robert.
II.   Thomas, the father of Arthur Lawrence, Esq., of Prior's Court, in Gloucestershire.
III.   William, b. 1425, or before, who fought under the Lancastrian banner at St. Albans in 1455, and, having fallen there, was bur. in the Abbey.
IV.   Edmund, who is said to have m. a dau. of Miles de Stapleton, a descendant of the distinguished family of that name of Norman extraction.

The Gloucestershire branch of the family had the same arms as already given; likewise the Buckinghamshire Lawrences. Thus, "Argent, a cross raguled gules, is borne by a family of the name of Lawrence in Buckinghamshire and Gloucestershire."—"Crest. The tail (or hindmost half) of a chub (fish) inverted and erect."

THE SEVENTH GENERATION

(Page 10) · Sir Robert, son of Sir Robert and Margaret Holden, of Ashton Hall, married Amphilbis, daughter of Edward Longford, Esq., of Longford, and had:

I.   JAMES, heir and successor to the estate of Ashton Hall, who m. Cecily, dau. of —— Botsler, Esq., of Lancashire. an heiress, and had issue, two sons and a dau.

II.   ROBERT, who m. Margaret, dau. of John Lawrence, Esq., of Lancashire, and had sons, *Robert* and *John,* the latter of whom commanded a wing of the English army, under Lord Stanley, in the Battle of Flodden Field; also *William,* who became a great landholder.

III.   NICHOLAS LAWRENCE.

THE EIGHTH GENERATION

NICHOLAS, son of Sir Robert and Amphilbis, was of Agercroft. He married, and had sons:

I.	THOMAS.	IV.	JOHN.
II.	NICHOLAS.	V.	WILLIAM.
III.	ROBERT.	VI.	HENRY.

VII.   OLIVER, the ancestor of the rich Orange branch of Lawrences. The son and successor of Sir Oliver Lawrence was *Edward,* who d. in 1601; leaving a son, Sir Edward, who was knighted in 1619, and d. about 1630.

THE NINTH GENERATION

JOHN, son of Nicholas Lawrence, of Agercroft, was ancestor of the Lawrences, of St. James Park in Suffolk, it is stated in the pedigree of the Lawrences, of Ashton Hall. He died in 1461; leaving THOMAS LAWRENCE, of Rumburgh, in Suffolk.

THE TENTH GENERATION

(Page 11) THOMAS, of Rumburgh, held lands in other places, as Holton, Wisset, and South Elmham. He married, and had:

I.   JOHN.   II.   RICHARD, of St. Ives.

The will of Thomas Lawrence is dated July 17, 1471.

THE ELEVENTH GENERATION

JOHN LAWRENCE, son of Thomas, of Rumburgh, married Margery ——, by whom he had a son, ROBERT. His will was made July 10, 1504, the year of his death; his wife died in 1507. Both were buried in church of Rumburgh.

THE TWELFTH GENERATION

ROBERT, son of John and Margery Lawrence, is named in his father's will, and wife in that of her mother-in-law. Their issue was a son, JOHN LAWRENCE.

THE THIRTEENTH GENERATION

JOHN, of Rumburgh, mentioned in the will of his grandmother, married Elizabeth ——, by whom he had:

I.	HENRY.	IV.	MARGARET.
II.	JOHN.	V.	KATHARINE.
III.	AGNES.		

VI.   WILLIAM, of St. James' Park, South Elmham; exiled during the reign of Queen Mary, he afterwards returned, and labored as a preacher at Fressingfield.

VII.   RICHARD, of Wisset and Rumburgh, whose will was dated Jan. 27, 1556.

THE FOURTEENTH GENERATION

(Page 12) JOHN, son of John and Elizabeth Lawrence, married Agnes ———, and had:

I. JOHN.
II. RICHARD, who d. in 1596.
III. SUSAN.
IV. ELIZABETH.
V. MARGARET.

His wife died January 22, 1583. His will bears date April 27, 1590. He was buried at Rumburgh, May 21, 1590.

THE FIFTEENTH GENERATION

JOHN, son of John and Agnes Lawrence, was of Wisset, in Suffolk, and married Johan ———. They had issue:

I. HENRY.
II. ROBERT, whose will, dated 1641, names his kinsman, Henry North, of Laxfield, a son of Sir Henry North, and grandson of Lord North.
III. MARGERY.
IV. KATHARINE.

The will of John Lawrence, of Wisset, is dated June 2, 1606. He was buried January 16, 1607.

THE SIXTEENTH GENERATION

HENRY, son of John and Johan Lawrence, married Mary ———; by whom he had JOHN, born at Wisset, and baptized October 8, 1609. The will of John Lawrence, of Wisset, the father of Henry, refers to him as having removed from Wisset to New England, and settled in Charlestown, Mass., in 1635, is the name of Henry Lawrence. Also, "In the first division of land on Mistick side, of ten acres to a house, five of which were given in for after-comers, made, as it appears, February 20, 1638, Henry Lawrence received five acres." A house-lot was granted him in 1635 by George Blott.

GENEALOGY OF JOHN LAWRENCE AND ISAAC LAWRENCE

("Of the Ancestors and Posterity of Isaac Lawrence," by Frederick S. Pease, of Albany—Pages 5 to 11, first to fifth generations)

FIRST GENERATION

(1) I. JOHN LAWRENCE, progenitor of Isaac Lawrence, probably came from England in the company which came over with Governor Winthrop in 1630. The place of his birth is not known; but as Governor Winthrop was from the county of Suffolk, it may be that Mr. Lawrence was from the same county.

The first account of him that can be relied upon as certain, is, that he was an inhabitant of Watertown, Mass., as early as 1635. The name of his wife was Elizabeth. Whether they were married in England or not, has not been ascertained. They had twelve children born at Watertown. He afterwards removed to Groton, Mass., at an early period of its settlement, his name being found in the records there in 1663. His wife died in Groton in 1663. He then married a widow—Susanna Batchelder, of Boston—the ceremony of which took place at Charlestown, November 2, 1664. By her he had two children. He died at Groton, July 11, 1667. He left children:

1-1.	JOHN, b. 14 d. 1 mo., 1635.	2-2.	NATHANIEL.
7-7.	ENOCH.	9-9.	ISAAC.
8-8.	SAMUEL.	10-10.	ELIZABETH.
3-3.	JOSEPH.	11-11.	JONATHAN.
4-4.	JONATHAN, d. young.	12-12.	ZACHARIAH.
5-5.	MARY.	13-13.	ABAGAIL.
6-6.	PELEG.	14-14.	SUSANNA

SECOND GENERATION

(2) II. ·ENOCH LAWRENCE (7-7), born 5 d. 1 mo., 1648-9, was married March 6, 1676-7, to Ruth, the widow of John Shattuck. Her maiden name was·Ruth Whitney. Her husband was drowned in crossing Charlestown ferry, September 14, 1675. He died September 28, 1744. He left children:

15-1.	NATHANIEL.	17-3.	ZACHARIAH.
16-2.	DANIEL, b. Mar. 7, 1681.	18-4.	JEREMIAH.

THIRD GENERATION

(3) III. ·DANIEL LAWRENCE (16-2), (Daniel Lawrence, father of Isaac and Daniel, lived and died in Canaan about seventy years ago. It is supposed that at the time of his death, he was with a son, John, who has since died in Norfolk. Isaac gave the use of a farm to his half-brother ·John as compensation for taking care of their father). Married Sarah ———. He left children:

19-1. DANIEL, b. Apr. 22, 1702.
20-2. ISAAC, b. Feb. 25, 1704-5 (4).

The foregoing facts in relation to the ancestors of Isaac Lawrence, have been chiefly derived from Butler's "History of Groton," recently published, and which is a highly valuable work, giving an account of about thirty families of the name of Lawrence which have lived in Groton.

ISAAC LAWRENCE AND HIS DESCENDANTS

FOURTH GENERATION

(4) IV. ISAAC LAWRENCE (20-2). It has always been said by his descendants that he came from Plainfield, Conn., to Canaan; but as there are no records in Plainfield to show that he or any of his family were ever there, the following facts are produced in proof of the assertion.—Groton was a frontier town, and much exposed to Indian depredations. The suffering was so extreme that the inhabitants became discouraged, and many of them removed from the town. Several families went to Plainfield, Conn., and others contemplated going to the same place. Among the latter was Daniel Lawrence, Joseph Lawrence, uncle of Daniel, and Zachariah Law-

rence, who was uncle or brother of Daniel. This took place in 1707, while Daniel, Jun., and Isaac, sons of Daniel, were young children. (Daniel Lawrence, Jun., was the grandfather of Mr. Isaac Fellows, on the maternal side. He was great-grandfather of Dea. Anson Lawrence and Nathaniel Lawrence.) As no record of them can be found in Groton after this event it may be taken as conclusive corroboration of the general belief on this point.

"Watertown, Mass., Gen." by Bond, says on page 124—Capt. Isaac Lawrence—Isaac and his family removed to *Hinesboro, Vt.;* which is an error, he moved to *Hinesburg, Vt.*

While he and his family were on their way to Canaan with a team composed of a yoke of oxen and a horse, they left the last house in New Hartford, about twenty-five miles from the place of their destination. The greater part of this distance they were obliged to cut their way through a heavily timbered forest. For several days after their arrival the family took up their quarters under a large oak tree, and slept in their wagon. Near this tree, which was on the south side of the river, near where the saw mill now stands (1848) and a few rods east of the house where Mr. Silas Beckley now lives, he built the house that he first occupied. He also built the house on the north side of the river, long known as the Lawrence tavern stand, where he died in the year 1751.

There is in the Dunham family a loom which was made of the identical oak tree under which Isaac Lawrence and his family took up their temporary residence on their first arrival. He arrived on June 2, 1738, and was one of the first settlers of the town.

He married *Lydia Hewitt.* The date of his death was December 2, 1793. His wife died November 14, 1765. His children were:

21-1. JONAS, b. 1728; m. Tryphena Lawrence, of Littleton, Mass., who d. Jan. 21, 1795, at West Stockbridge (5).
22-2. STEPHEN, b. ———; d. in infancy.
23-3. ISAAC, JUN., m. Mary Brown, Mar. 18, 1760 (6).
24-4. ASA, d. in infancy, July 24, 1750.
25-5. WILLIAM, d. young, Jan. 5, 1750.
26-6. ELIJAH, d. young.
27-7. SOLOMON, d. young, July 21, 1750.
28-8. AZUBAH, m. Samuel Hyde of Norwich, Conn., Oct. 25, 1750.
29-9. LYDIA, b. Dec. 2, 1747; d. Aug. 4, 1750.
30-10. AMY, m. Elijah Cobb, Mar. 30, 1760.
31-11. HANNAH, b. May 25, 1750; m. Willard Kingsbury.

PERSIS[3] CLEVELAND (Samuel[2], Moses[1]), born Chelmsford, Mass., April 21, 1683; married Stonington, Conn., October 24, 1706, Thomas Hewitt, born Stonington, February 3, 1685, a son of Thomas and Lydia (Utley). Children (some may have remained in Plainfield, Conn., but several are supposed to have gone to Westmoreland or Wyoming, Luzerne County, Pa.):

146. LYDIA[4] HEWITT, b. Nov. 4, 1707, Stonington; m. Dec. 19, 1727, Isaac Lawrence. On the doorstep of the Lawrence House, built 1751, and mentioned in Nathaniel Hawthorne's "American Note Book," are the names of their children:

Jonas⁵ Lawrence, rec. Dec. 1, 1728, in Canterbury, Conn.
Stephen⁵ Lawrence.   *Solomon⁵ Lawrence.*
Isaac⁵ Lawrence.   *Azubah⁵ Lawrence.*
Asa⁵ Lawrence.   *Anna⁵ Lawrence.*
William⁵ Lawrence,   *Lydia⁵ Lawrence.*
Elijah⁵ Lawrence.   *Hannah⁵ Lawrence.*
ELIZABETH⁴ HEWITT, b. Apr. 12, 1709, Stonington; m. July 24, 1734,
John Warren.
(See "Cleveland Family," E. J. and H. G. Cleveland, Vol. I, page
67.)

IMMORTAL SAILOR

The shortest and most desperate sea battle of the War of 1812 was fought off Boston Light, June 1, 1813. It was over in fifteen minutes. The "Chesapeake" struck her flag, but not before nearly all her officers were killed or wounded. Captain Lawrence had been but recently assigned to this boat. Mortally wounded, he said, "Tell the men to fire faster and not to give up the ship; fight her till she sinks." He was taken to Halifax a prisoner and died there June 5.

(Page 38)   President Grover Cleveland was a descendant of this family.

"GENEALOGY OF THE ANCESTORS AND POSTERITY OF ISAAC LAWRENCE"—F. S. Pease, page 14

(6) V. ·ISAAC LAWRENCE, JUN. (23-3), married ·Mary Brown, March 18, 1760. He removed from Canaan to Vermont, near Onion River, about 65 years since (1848). He had, before he left Canaan, four or five sons, namely: Elijah, Samuel, Isaac and Henry. Also several daughters, one of whom was named Lydia. Elijah, Samuel and Isaac, removed from Vermont to lower Canada, 40 or 50 years ago (1848) where it is supposed their families now reside. Their children were:

41-1.   LYDIA, b. Sept. 2, 1761 (or 2).
42-2.   ELIJAH, b. Oct. 17, 1763.
43-3.   SAMUEL, b. Nov. 19, 1765.
44-4.   ISAAC 3RD, b. Nov. 22, 1767; m. Debby Root.
45-5.   MARY, b. May 4, 1770.
46-6.   APAME, b. Dec. 7, 1772.
47-7.   HENRY, b. Feb. 25, 1778.
48-8.   ERASTUS, b. Mar. 11, 1780.
49-9.   PAMELIA, b. May 17, 1782.

"Colonial Daughters of the 17th Century." "Dau. American Colonists," page 30, 1931.

"NASH GENEALOGY" and "PHELPS GENEALOGY," by Phelps & Servin, page 252

Children of PHINEAS PHELPS and *Lydia Lawrence*—6th in descent from John Lawrence:

DAVID, m. Miss Elizabeth Hungerford.   PAMELIA.
POLLY, m. Joseph Wright.   TERESA.
ELKANAH, m. Miss Chappell.   LAWRENCE.
CAROLINE, m. William Norton.   DANIEL.

FAMILY OF JOHN LAWRENCE
By John Lawrence, 1857

The ancestral lineage of JOHN LAWRENCE, of Watertown, Mass., who was descended from an old and distinguished English family. As traced and determined, it originates in and derives from one, Robert Lawrence, of Lancashire, England, who attended his sovereign, Richard Coeur de Lion, to the war of the Crusades in the Holy Land, and so distinguished himself in the siege of Acre, that he was knighted "Sir Robert, of Ashton Hall," and obtained for his arms "Argent, a cross raguly gules," A. D. 1191. These arms were also those of the Lancashire branch generally.

The line of ancestry of the Watertown, Mass., Lawrences may be thus summarized:

1. SIR ROBERT, of Ashton Hall, Knight of the Crusades.
2. SIR ROBERT, a son, and the immediate successor of the Knight of the Crusades, to the estate of Ashton Hall, m. a dau. of James Trafford, Esq., of Lancashire, by whom he had a son *James.*
3. JAMES, of Ashton Hall, m. it is said, "in 1252," Matilda de Washington, dau. of John de Washington, an heiress. Had son *John.*
4. JOHN, of Ashton Hall, m. Margaret, dau. of Walter Chesford; by whom he had a son *John.*
5. JOHN, m. Elizabeth Holt, of Stably, in Lancashire, and d. A. D. 1360. He had a son *Robert.*
6. SIR ROBERT, of Ashton Hall, m. Margaret Holden, of Lancashire, and had *Robert, Thomas, William* and *Edmund.*
7. SIR ROBERT, of Ashton Hall, m. Amphilbis, dau. of Edward Longford, Esq., of Longford, and had: 1. *James;* 2. *Robert;* 3. *Nicholas.*
8. NICHOLAS, of Agercroft, who m. and had *Thomas, Nicholas, Robert, John, William, Henry, Oliver.*
9. JOHN, of Agercroft, ancestor of the Lawrences of St. James Park in Suffolk; he d. in 1461, leaving *Thomas,* of Rumburgh, in Suffolk.
10. THOMAS, of Rumburgh, in Suffolk, he m. and had *John, Richard,* of St. Ives. The will of Thomas Lawrence is dated July 17, 1471.
11. JOHN, m. Margery ———; d. 1504; wife d. 1507. Had son *Robert.*
12. ROBERT, m. and had son *John.*
13. JOHN, of Rumburgh, m. Elizabeth ———, by whom he had *Henry, John, Agnes, Margaret, Katharine, William* and *Richard.*
14. JOHN, of Wisset, in Suffolk, and m. Agnes ———. They had issue: *John, Richard,* d. 1596, *Susan, Elizabeth* and *Margaret.* His wife d. Jan. 22, 1583. He was bur. at Rumburgh, May 21, 1590.
15. JOHN, of Wisset, m. Johan ———, and had *Henry, Robert, Margery* and *Katherine.* Will of John dated June 2, 1606. He was bur. Jan. 16, 1607.
16. HENRY, son of John and Johan Lawrence, m. Mary ———; by whom he had *John,* b. at Wisset, in Suffolk, and bapt. Oct. 8, 1609. The will of John Lawrence, of Wisset, father of Henry, refers to him as having removed from Wisset to New England, and settled in Charlestown, Mass., in 1635, is the name of Henry Lawrence.
17. JOHN LAWRENCE, bapt. Oct. 8, 1609, in England; d. 1667, Groton, Mass.; m. Elizabeth ———, who d. 1663, Groton.
18. ENOCH LAWRENCE, b. Jan. 5, 1648-9; d. Sept. 28, 1744; m. Mar. 6, 1676-7, Ruth (Whitney) Shattuck, who was b. Apr. 15, 1645, and d. Mar. 6, 1676-7.
19. CAPT. DANIEL LAWRENCE, b. Mar. 7, 1681; d. 1777; m. Sarah ———, who d. probably in Canaan, Conn.

20. ISAAC LAWRENCE, SR., b. Feb. 25, 1704-5; d. Dec. 2, 1793; m. Lydia Hewitt, who d. Nov. 14, 1765.
21. ISAAC LAWRENCE, JR., of Canaan, Conn.; m. Mary Brown, 7th child of Dea. Samuel Brown, May 8, 1760.
22. LYDIA LAWRENCE, b. 1761-2; d. Sept. 20, 1813; m. Phineas Phelps at New Haven, Vt.; he was b. Apr. 10, 1767, and d. Apr. 20, 1813.
23. NASH DAVID PHELPS, b. Oct. 4, 1796; d. Apr. 15, 1884; m. Apr. 20, 1821, Elizabeth Hungerford, b. Feb. 7, 1798; d. Jan. 7, 1878.
24. CAROLINE ALEXANDRIA PHELPS, b. in St. Armand West, Que., July 3, 1840; d. Mar. 29, 1921; m. Sept. 8, 1863, in Stanbridge, Que., Horace Brayton Leach, b. Sept. 25, 1836; d. May 6, 1919, at Sheldon, Vt.
25. ELIZABETH MAY LEACH, b. in Bakersfield, Vt., Jan. 7, 1866; living May 6, 1931; m. Sept. 8, 1889, Oscar Herbert Rixford, b. in East Highgate, Vt., Dec. 27, 1859; d. Sept. 11, 1927.
26. OSCAR ADELBERT RIXFORD, b. Aug. 4, 1890; m. Jan. 18, 1919, Mary Carolyn Hefflon, b. in Montreal, Que., June 6, 1899. They have children:
27. MARY-ELIZABETH LENORA, b. in East Highgate, Vt., Oct. 6, 1922.
27. OSCAR THEODORE, b. in East Highgate, Vt., July 21, 1925.

References: "Gen. Washington Family," by Albert Wells.
1 to 18 generations—"Colonial Families," 1928.
19 to 27 generations—"Watertown, Mass., Bond," Vol. 1, 2nd Ed.
"Gen. Conn.," Vol. 2, pages 831-832.
"D. A. C.," Lineage of Elizabeth M. Rixford.

SERVICES

John Lawrence served in a garrisoned house during the trouble with the Indians.

John Lawrence, 1609-1667, born in England; selectman, Groton, Mass., 1664-1665; member of the Grand Jury of Cambridge; proprietor of Groton, Mass.; selectman and surveyor of highways.

References: "Colonial Daughters of the 17th Century" (1923), page 256.
"Daughters of the American Colonists" (1929), page 62.
"Genealogy of John and Isaac Lawrence," pages 5 to 11.
"Society of Colonial Wars," page 350.

Enoch Lawrence was a soldier in King Philip's War, Aug. 3, 1675; credited 02-00-00, under Capt. Nicholas Paige and His Troop.

References: "King Philip's War," page 86.

"King Philip's War," (page 274)—Credit to Capt. Daniel Lawrence, 1681-1777, Plainfield, Conn.; captain First Company, 1736; deputy, 1722.

"Mass. Archives," by Joseph Richardson (pages 184, 178)—Daniel Lawrence, one of the Original Patentees.

"History of Long Island"—1783, Daniel Jr. Lawrence, in the House of Assembly (page 265).

Isaac Lawrence, Jr., of Canaan, Conn. Fourteen days' service, one of the 92 men who rode horses to Canaan—State Library, War. No. 733—Capt. Uriah Stevens' Co. (page 244), Isaac Lawrence. two weeks' service. Campaign of 1757.

References: "Conn. Hist. Society Col. IX, French and Indian War, Rolls," Vol. I, page 228.

"Watertown, Mass., Gen.," by Bond, says on page 124—Capt. Isaac Lawrence—Isaac and his family removed to Hinesboro, Vt., which should be Hinesburg, Vt., which tends to show that Isaac Lawrence, Sr., was a captain.

"Society of Colonial Wars—Index of Ancestors and Honor Roll (1922)." (Page 289) Enoch Lawrence, 1648-1744, Watertown, Mass., in King Philip's War; in Groton Garrison, 1691-92; wounded, 1694, King William's War.

LISLE FAMILY

DUCHAL CASTLE

A few miles to the southwest of the city of Glasgow, in Scotland, lies the old barony of Lyle, or Duchal. In this barony stood Duchal Castle, the home for several centuries of the Lords Lyle. When the castle was built is not known, but in 1170, in a grant to the monks of Paisley, appears the signature of "Radulphus de Insula, Dominus de Duchal." A date so early as 1057 has had mention. From a book, "Much About Kilmalcolm," is taken an extract as follows:

"The great barony of Duchal, which for many ages was the chief property and place of residence of the ancient family of Lyle, was of great extent situated in the heart of the Parish on both sides of the Gryffe, but chiefly inland from it. The first mention of the family of Lyle (who are said to have been originally a West Highland family, and to derive their name from L'isle) occurs in the grant, etc."

In the same book appears:

"An eminent local antiquary holds that the castle (Duchal), surrounded on three sides by the stream, and the fourth by a fosse, which was crossed by a draw-bridge, is the Insula meant and that they took their name from the Island on which the fort was built."

In an old work in Edinburgh Library appears:

"The river Gryffe hath its rise in the moor and parish of Kilmalcolm, at the head of which stands the old castle and fort of Duchall, the ancient inheritance of the Barons Lyll of Douchalle, made Lords of Parliament by King James III, failed in the Reign of Queen Mary in the person of James, last Lord Lyle, who was dead about 1550."

The remains of Duchal Castle were described in 1792 "as very romantique in situation and strong in construction."

Says the *Imperial Gazeteer* of Scotland:

"The remains of the strong and romantic Duchal Castle stand upon the confluence of the Duchal with another rivulet. In 1710 a mansion was built about a mile east of this. The present (1848) mansion house was built in 1768. It stands on the right bank of the Gryffe and is well sheltered with wood."

At one time the castle was besieged. At this time the ruins are little distinguishable. In the nearby towns of Kilmalcolm and Kilbarchan are many of the Lyle name at this time. A small settlement was called Lylesland. Duchal is pronounced *Duck-all*.

The surname of L'isle, or Lyle, was first assumed by the proprietors of some of the Western Isles in the reign of Malcolm Canmore. They had also possessions in the County of Renfrew, where Duchal Castle was their principal seat.

From a letter written by William Robertson, the author of "Historical Tales and Legends of Ayrshire," the following extract is taken:

"The Lyles are a very old family. Old enough to have a wraith. That is, a duplicate of the head of the house who came to warn some relative that the master, or Lord, was about to die. The ballad 'Lord Lyle' is founded on Ayrshire traditions. As it is very old it may interest you, see pages 337 to 341."—"Historical Tales and Legends."

ALICIA LISLE, of Moyles Court in the County of Southampton, widow, 9 June 1682, with codicil of same date, proved 11 November 1689. To the poor of the parish of Ellingham two pounds within one year after my decease. The overplus (after payment of such debts) to my worthy friends, the said William Tipping and Mrs. Frances Tipping his sister, Richard Lloyd, citizen and linen-draper of London, and Triphena his wife, to hold forever upon this especial trust, etc., to discharge my funeral expenses and pay debts, etc., and to pay unto my daughter Anne twelve hundred pounds at the age of one and twenty years or day of marriage, to pay unto my granddaughter —————— Hore, daughter of my daughter Bridgett, now in New England, the sum of one hundred pounds at age of one and twenty or day of marriage, to pay unto my daughter Mary one annuity or yearly rent of six pounds during her natural life, but if said daughter Mary marry against their consent said annuity shall cease, to pay to daughter Mabella Lisle an annuity of forty pounds (under same conditions). The residue to be distributed among my daughters or daughters' children as they (the trustees) shall think fit.

Witnesses: Anne Tipping, William Withrington, John Swan and Abiah Browne.. Ent. 159.

(I am indebted to Henry Marillier, Esq., for the reference to the above will.)

Reference: "New England Historical and Genealogical Register," Vol. 39 (1885), page 62.

·HEZEKIAH USHER, JR., married 1686, Bridget, daughter of Lord John Lisle, one of Cromwell's Lords. She was the widow of Dr. Leonard Hoar (Pres. H. C.). He died s. p. July 11, 1697; and his widow died May 25, 1723. Their daughter Bridget m. Thomas Cotton.

Reference: "New England Historical and Genealogical Register," Vol. 23 (1869), page 410; Vol. 39, page 64.

JORDAN DE INSULA (OR LISLE)

Arms—Or, on a chief az. three lions rampant of the field.
Crest—A stag statant ar. attired or.
References: "Lisle Family," by Oscar K. Lisle, pages 99 and 100.
"The New England Historical and Genealogical Register," Vol. XXXIX, 1885, page 63.
Records of F. Phelps Leach,
Family Records.

Jordan de Insula lived in time of King Henry = Hawise ————.
I, and King Stephen.

Geffrey de Insula gave lands in francalmoine = ———— ————.
for the soul of Earl Baldlwin, of Devonshire.

Walter de Insula, in time of King John.   = Margaret ————.

Baldwin de Insula, Lord of Wodeton and = ———— ————.
Plompton in the Isle of Wight, lived in time
of Henry III.

John de Insula, a baron to the time of Edward I, and Governor of Carisbrooke Castle, ob. 32 Edward I. = ——— ———.

Walter de Insula, Lord of Wodeton. = Margaret ——— ——.

Walter de Insula, Lord of Wodeton. = Florence ———————.

William de Insula, Lord of Wodeton. = ——— ——— ——.

William de Insula, Lord of Wodeton, 44th Edward III. = ——— ——— ——.

Sir John de Insula or Lisle, Knt. = Margaret, dau. of John Bremshot, of Bremshot, in County Southampton.

George Lisle. = Anna, dau. of ——— Montgomery, of Calais.

Lancelot Lisle. = Anne, dau. of Sir Thos. Wroughton, Knt.

Thomas Lisle. = ———, dau. of ——— Moore, of Moore Court, Esq.

Anthony Lisle, of Wodeton, Esq. = Elizabeth, dau. of John Dormer, of Steeple Barton in County Oxon, Esq.

Sir William Lisle. = Bridget, dau. of Sir John Hungerford, of Down Ampney, in County Gloucester, Knt.

John Lisle, of Moyles Court, County Southampton; he was one of the judges who condemned King Charles the First, for which he was obliged to fly the kingdom, and ob. abroad. Second son. = Alice, dau. and co-heir of Sir White Beconsawe, Knt., beheaded at Winchester, 1685, by the order of Judge Jeffries.

Bridget Lisle, d. May 2, 1723. = Lenord Hoar, b. England, 1629-30; d. Nov. 28, 1675.

John[1] Hoar, b. Gloucester, England; d. Apr. 2, 1704. = Alice Lisle, b. England; d. June 5, 1696.

Mary Hoar. = Benjamin Graves, m. Oct. 21, 1668; b. Concord, Mass.

Benjamin Graves, b. Mar. 2, 1676-7; d. Dec. 30, 1752. = Mary Sterling; (2nd wife) Mary Haynes.

Mary Graves, dau. of Benjamin and Mary (Haynes) Graves, b. Jan. 20, 1728; m. June 23, 1746, probably New Fairfield, Conn. = Samuel Hungerford, b. abt. 1713; d. 1790.

Isaiah Hungerford, b. Dec. 26, 1756, bapt. Jan. 23, 1757; d. June 16, 1833; m. about 1777, at New Fairfield, Conn. = Esther Mead, b. Aug. 11, 1760; d. Dec. 22, 1836.

Elizabeth Hungerford, b. Feb. 7, 1798; d. Jan. 7, 1878; m. Apr. 29, 1821, at St. Armand, West, Que. = Nash David Phelps, b. Oct. 4, 1796; d. Apr. 15, 1884.

Caroline Alexandria Phelps, b. July 3, 1840; d. Mar. 29, 1921; m. Sept. 8, 1863, Stanbridge, Que. = Horace Brayton Leach, b. Sept. 25, 1836; d. May 6, 1919.

Elizabeth May Leach, b. Jan. 7, 1866; living; m. Sept. 8, 1889, Sheldon, Vt. = Oscar Herbert Rixford, b. Dec. 27, 1859; d. Sept. 11, 1927.

Oscar Adelbert Rixford, b. Aug. 4, 1890; living; m. Jan. 18, 1919, Montreal, Que. = Mary Carolyn Hefflon, b. June 6, 1899; living.

Mary-Elizabeth Lenora Rixford, b. Oct. 6, 1922; living.

Oscar Theodore Rixford, b. July 21, 1925; living.

HOAR FAMILY

("Lineage and Family Records of the Hoar Family," page 3)

Reference: "Hoar Family," 1898, by Alfred Wyman Hoar, pages 3, 4, 5, 6, 7, 8, 9, 15 and 16.

When or where our race or family first became known as a distinct family cannot be traced. Asia is regarded as the birthplace of man, and we may be said to have come from the Indo-Germanic race. Cæsar invaded England in B. C. 55. The inhabitants then were Celtic, kindred to the Gauls. It was not until A. D. 43 that Claudius began the real conquest. The Romans abandoned the country before the middle of the fifth century. In 449 the Anglo-Saxons, led by Hengist with his brother, Horsa, landed in England with 300 men and were employed against the Picts and Scots. Horsa is said to have been killed in battle A. D. 455.

The coat of arms of the "Hoare Family" of England is here shown more as an object lesson of the history of our race, than for personal use. "An eagle displayed with two heads within a brodure engrailed" is found on all the shields of the Hore, Hoore, Hoare and Hoar Families.

"The crest is the uppermost device of a coat of arms and is as ancient as devises on shields."

Ours in America is an eagle, head erased, a ring in its beak, or.

The eagle was at an early date adopted as the symbol of royal power. Xenophon relates that the kings of the Medes bore a golden eagle on their shields. From the time of Marius it was the principal emblem of the Roman Republic, and the only standard of the legions; first silver, then gold.

The double-headed eagle was in use among the Byzantine emperors to indicate their claims to the empire, both of the east and west. Afterwards the eagle was adopted by the Russian, Austrian, and German emperors. The German, under Albert First, became the double-headed eagle as the successors of the Roman emperors. The English heraldry dates from the Tournaments, found on tombs in the eleventh century, and became common in the twelfth century.

We have shown that our arms were the arms of dominion and sovereignty.

Our line came from Gloucester, England.

"Venit Hora" and *"In Ardua"* are mottoes that clearly express our character. Approbativeness is another trait of our ancestors. We wish to be well thought of at home and abroad. In size, of the German type, bald headed at quite an early age. Many are dark with piercing black eyes, but the majority are of a lighter complexion.

· Of the first Charles Hoare, of Gloucester, England, but little is known. He married Margery ———. He died in 1636 and left a will, which mentions Thomas, Margery, John and Charles, David, Leonard and Joan, last three minors in 1632. He appears to have been a person of note in that place. The "coat of arms" of the "Hoare Family" were used by the Gloucester family.

· His son, the second Charles, also lived in the same place. He was alderman of the city from 1632 to 1638. Sheriff in 1634. He left a will dated Sept. 25, 1638. "'Prerogative Court of Canterbury, Doctors Commons, Ad'ion granted Dec. 31, 1638, to Joane Hoare the relict." (Will with notes by G. F. Hoar.) He appears to have left quite a large estate and was a man much engaged in public affairs. His widow, with her five children, John, Daniel, Joanna, Leonard and Margerie came to this country in 1639-40, and settled in Braintree, Mass. About this date many families, who brought much wealth, came to New England. The cause of this emigration would appear to arise from the troublesome times in England. Charles I became king in 1625. Then came the long Parliament, and the Civil War began late in 1642. Charles I was condemned and executed in London, January 30, 1649. There is no doubt but that our line at the time of the second Charles Hoare belonged to the Parliament side and were strong supporters of the Protestant faith, and this line of the Hoar family would probably never have had to be recorded if Joane and her son John had remained in England. (See "The Hoar Family in America," by H. S. Nurse, 1899.) Joanna (Joane in will), the widow of the second Charles, died in Braintree, Sunday, December 20, 1661. The meaning of the name (grace of the Lord) seems very happily merited. She was buried in the old Quincy Cemetery with her son Leonard and his wife and daughter.

John Hoare, the first in our line in this country, first settled in Scituate, Mass., in 1643 (to 1655) and bore arms the same year. He was a lawyer, and noted "for his bold, independent mind and action." He had a farm on the west of Little Masquashart Pond. While here he appears to have been engaged in the business of the town, drafting deeds, bonds, etc.

Leonard returned with his wife to Boston, Mass., in July, 1672, and preached for a short time as assistant at the South Church. He was soon called to be president of Harvard College, December, 1672.

Mrs. Bridget Hoar, wife of Leonard, married second, Hezekiah Usher, 1686. They did not live together long. She went to England in 1687. She had two daughters, one died young. The other, Bridget, married in London, June 21, 1689, Thomas Cotton, who was born at or near Worthy, England, 1657; died 1730. Mrs. Bridget Cotton was willed by her stepfather, Mr. Usher, the tumbler with the "Arms of Hoare" engraved thereon.

Joane, sister of John, married Col. Edmund Quincy, July 26, 1648, Braintree, son of Edmund and Judith Quincy, who came to New England, September 4, 1633. They had eight children.

Margerie, sister of John, married first, —— Mathew; married second, Rev. Henry Flynt, of Braintree, Mass. He came to New England, 1635. Ordained church at Braintree, 1639.

John Quincy Adams was a descendant from her.

CHARLES HOARE, Gloucester, England; died 1636; married Margerie ——.

Children were:
1. THOMAS, b. ——; d. ——.
2. CHARLES.

3. ·DAU., m. Thomas Hill.
4. ·DAU., m. Leonard Tarne.
(Notes by author of "Hoare Family," say "3" and "4" were 3. Elinor,
4. Anna. Authority lost.)

CHARLES HOARE, Gloucester, England, born ———; died 1638;
married Joanna Hincksman or Henchman, born ———; died Braintree, December 20, 1661.
Children were:

1. ·THOMAS (mother uncertain), bapt. June 15, 1612.
2. ·JOHN.
3. ·DANIEL, b. Gloucester, England.
4. ·JOANNA, b. Gloucester, England; d. Braintree; m. Col. Edmund Quincy;
    he was b. 1627; m. July 26, 1648.
5. LEONARD, b. Gloucester, England, 1630; d. Nov. 28, 1675, Boston; m.
    Bridget Lisle, d. May 25, 1723, Boston.
6. ·MARGERIE, b. Gloucester, England; d. Mar. 10, 1687, Braintree; m. (1)
    ——— Mathewe; m. (2) Rev. Henry Flynt, Braintree; he d. Apr. 27,
    1668.

·JOHN HOARE, b. Gloucester, England; died Concord, Mass.,
April 2, 1704; married Alice Lyle in England (spelled Ales, Connecticut Register); died Concord, June 5, 1696. He was at Scituate,
in Plymouth Colony in 1643, moved to Concord, Mass., 1659, and
was the means of rescuing Mrs. Rowlandson from her captivity
among the Indians in 1676.
Children were:

1. ·ELIZABETH, b. Concord, Sept. 25, 1687; m. Jonathan Prescott, Concord,
    Dec. 23, 1675.
2. ·MARY, b. ———; d. ———; m. Benj. Graves, Oct. 21, 1668.

MARSHALL

("Colonial Families," 1928, page 28)

Arms—Per pale or and vert, a lion rampant gules, armed and langued
azure.

The family name Marshall is derived from the occupation of
marshal, originally that of farrier, but at length an office and official
military title, as master of horse or cavalry. William le Mareschal
is on record in the Hundred Rôlls of Cambridge, A. D. 1273.

1. ·GILBERT, surnamed Mareschal, with John, his son, in the reign of Henry I,
    were impleaded by Robert de Venviz and William de Hastings for the
    office of marshal to the King, but without success.
2. ·JOHN, surnamed Mareschal, son of Gilbert, sided with Maud, the Empress,
    against Stephen; therefore, on the accession in 1154 of Maud's son,
    Henry II, he had valuable lands in Wiltshire granted to him, and was
    the King's Marshal. He m. and had *John,* who was confirmed as King's
    Marshal; and at the coronation of Richard I bore the gilt spurs; but
    died in that reign without issue, leaving a brother William, and a
    nephew John, by another brother. The nephew was the head of
    Mareschal of Hengham, whose arms were: Gules, a bend lozengie or.
3. ·WILLIAM MARESCHAL or MARSHALL, second son of John, son of Gilbert,
    surnamed Mareschal, on the death of his brother became Lord Marshal

and did exploits in the reigns of Richard I, John, and Henry III; he quelled the Irish, foiled the French, and defended Normandy. He d. in 1219, and was bur. in the Temple Church, London. He m. Isabel, only dau. and heiress of Richard, Earl of Pembroke, through the favor of Richard I, at whose coronation he bore the royal sceptre of gold; and on the coronation of King John was invested with the Sword of the Earldom of Striguil or Pembroke, and confirmed in its possession. He had five sons and five daus. His sons were successively Earls, but all d. without issue.

4. ·SIBYL MARSHAL (as the name is now spelled), fourth dau. of William Mareschal, or Marshal, first Earl Marshal of Pembroke, m. William de Ferrers, seventh Earl of Derby. (See Ferrers 9, Beauchamp 4 to 7, Seymour 4 to 9, and Winslow No. 4.)

Horace Leach Cutler and Alberta Irene Cutler, only children of the Author's ·sister, Mrs. Homer James Cutler, is 30th in direct descent from (No. 1) Gilbert Mareschal.

MILBOURNE

Arms—Sable, a chevron between three escallops argent.
Crest—A griffin's head erased.

The surname Milbourne originated from the township of Milburn, parish of Ponteland, in County Northumberland, England.

Margaret de Milleburn is recorded in the Testa de Neville, County Northumberland, written 1216-74.

I.   ·PIERS MILBOURNE, of Burghill, County Hereford, m. Elizabeth Eynesford, dau. and heir of Sir John Eynesford (or Eylesford), of Burghill, member of Parliament ten times. Their only child was *John,* of whom further.

II. ·JOHN MILBOURNE, son of Piers and Elizabeth (Eynesford) Milbourne, m. Elizabeth Devereux, dau. of Sir Walter Devereux. They had one child, *Simon,* of whom further.

III. ·SIMON MILBOURNE, son of John and Elizabeth (Devereux) Milbourne, m. Jane Baskerville, dau. and heir of Ralph Baskerville. (See Baskerville XII.) They had thirteen daus., among whom was *Blanche,* of whom further.

IV. ·BLANCHE MILBOURNE, dau. of Simon and Jane (Baskerville) Milbourne, m. James Whitney, son of Sir Robert and Constance (Touchett) Whitney. (See Whitney English Pedigree XI.)

See Royal Descent Line No. 13. Elizabeth M. Rixford is 18th in direct descent from Piers Milbourne, of Burghill, County Hereford, England.

MOORE, LORD MOORE

(Marquis of Drogheda, in Ireland)

(Collins' "Peerage of England," Vol. 9, pages 1-4)

·This noble family is of French extraction, from which kingdom they came very early after the Conquest into England; and acquiring a good estate in the County of Kent, made the manor of "Moore-Court" their residence, until they removed to "Moore-Place," in Benenden, in the said county, which they held for many generations.

Mr. John Philipot, Somerset Herald, who drew the pedigree of this family in 1612, tells us, that their surname was assumed from the lands which they originally possessed at More Place, in "Rolvinden and Benenden," in Kent. But he should have said More-Court, in Iviechurch, in the same county.

He begins with Thomas De La More, Esq., who held the manor of More-Place, whence the name was variously written De More, De La More, Atte-More, until the general relinquishing of such prepositions before names was practiced, when it determined also in this family, which was about the time of Henry VI.

This Thomas was living in the reign of Henry II, as is proved by a deed, wherein his grandson is styled John, the son of Henry, son of Thomas de More, whereby he purchased from John, the son of Thomas de Iden, a certain croft abutting upon his own lands; and this deed bears date at More-Place, on St. Vincent's day, 1280, 9 Edward I.

HENRY DE MORE, his son aforementioned, as is proved by several deeds, had four sons, viz.:

1. JOHN, his heir.
2. THOMAS (who sold his lands to Henry Fitz-Geffery Coote; from him descended Matthew More, who held certain lands within the hundred of Blackburne, next to Rolvinden, by knight's service, and paid his aid for them 20 King Edward III, when the Black Prince was made a Knight, as appears by the records of the aid enrolled in the Exchequer).
3. STEPHEN (who disposed of his estate at Maplesden, in Kent, to his brother, Thomas).
4. CHARLES.

JOHN DE MORE, of More-Place, the eldest son (in some deeds written Atte-More), died about 7 King Edward II. He married Matilda, daughter of William Falkinden, by whom he had two sons:

1. THOMAS.
2. SCOLAND, who had lands confirmed to him by his uncle Charles.

THOMAS, who succeeded, by Joan his wife (who survived him and purchased lands 10 Edward III), had

JOHN, his heir, who lived in the time of Edward III and died seized of his paternal inheritance, leaving two sons:

1. THOMAS.   2. JOHN.

THOMAS DE MORE, the elder son, marrying Catharine, the co-heiress of the family of Benenden, of Benenden (whereof John de Benenden held a Knight's fee there 20 Edward III and bore for his coat armour, Azure, a lobster, Or, which is now quartered by the Marquis of Drogheda): his family, on that match, transplanted themselves to Benenden, where they built a house called Moore-Place, and possessed a fair estate, until John Moore, Esq., sold it to Mr. William Watts, in the first year of Queen Mary's reign. By her, who outlived him, he had two sons:

1. WILLIAM.   2. JOHN.

WILLIAM, the elder, married Catherine, daughter and heir to Anthony Aucher, Esq., and had issue:
2. THOMAS, his heir.   2. JOHN.

THOMAS, married Agnes, daughter and heir of Robert Austen and was father of William Moore, of Moore-Place, Esq., who married Margaret, daughter and coheir of John Brenchley, Esq., Lord of the manor of Benenden, by his wife, Margaret, daughter and heir to Richard Golding, 21 Henry VI, and with her he got the inheritance of Moat-Landa and Bettenham, in Kent. He lies buried in the church of Benenden, in Kent, with his father-in-law; as appears by this inscription in the chancel window on the north side: *"Orate pro animabus Johannis Brenchley et Willielmi More."*

WALTER MOORE, of Benenden, Esq., was his son, and recovered certain lands in Smallhide and Tenterden, which had been entailed upon the issue of his grandfather, Thomas, by Agnes Austen his wife, niece to Robert Jane, in case her said uncle should die childless, and proved that, contrary to his entail, the said Robert had given those lands to his bastard son, which of right belonged to him, who was the son of William, son and heir to Thomas More and Agnes Austen, cousin and heir to the said Robert Jane. This Walter's will is recorded in the office of wills at Canterbury, and shows that he died in 1504, 19 Henry VII, leaving by Alice his wife (who brought into the family lands in the parishes of Brokeland, Fayerfield, Brensett, and Snave, in Kent), two sons:
1. THOMAS, of Benenden, his heir.
2. WILLIAM, who m. Elizabeth, one of the three daus. and coheir of William Betenham, Esq., by whom he had the ancient seat of Betenham, in the parish of Cranebrooke, where he resided, and was father of *Nicholas Moore,* of Wingmore, in Elham, who m. Clare, dau. of John Toke, of Goddington and Great-Chart, in Kent, by Cicely, dau. of Sir Thomas Kempe, Knt., and dying in 1556, at Wingmore (4 Queen Mary), (there is a memorial for him in Elham church, by which, according to Hasted, it appears that he d. at Wingmore, May 8, 1577, ae. fiftynine—Hasted, III, 343), without issue, gave all his lands by will to the sons of his cousin, John Moore, of Pluckley.

THOMAS MOORE, of Benenden, Esq., eldest son of Walter, made his will in 1519, 11 Henry VIII, which is recorded in the prerogative court of Canterbury, and proves that he had three sons:
1. JOHN.
2. EDWARD.
3. THOMAS, whose posterity settled in Norfolk

JOHN, the eldest son, Alienated More-Courto to John Watts, 1st Queen Mary. He married Margaret, daughter, and at length heir to John Brent, Esq., widow of John Dering, of Surrenden, in Pluckley, by whom he had one daughter and six sons, the fourth being Sir Thomas, of Croghan, ancestor to the late Earl of Charleville.

("Collectanea Topographica and Genealogy," Vol. III, page 281)

(Note 1)   This Sir John Lawrence, about the year 1644, restored the inscription on Sir Thomas More's monument in Chelsea church; causing it to be recut on a handsome table of black marble. In "Faulkner," 1829, Vol. II, 132, he is incorrectly identified with Sir John Lawrence, Lord Mayor of London during the plague in 1665, whose coat of arms was differenced by a canton Ermines.

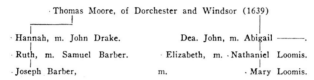

```
                 Thomas Moore, of Dorchester and Windsor (1639)
        ┌──────────────┘                              │
        │                                             │
   Hannah, m. John Drake.                   Dea. John, m. Abigail ──────.
        │                                             │
   Ruth, m. Samuel Barber.            Elizabeth, m. Nathaniel Loomis.
        │                                             │
   Joseph Barber,                     m.              Mary Loomis.
```

The ancestral line to Thomas De La More, Esq., of More-Place, may be summarized as follows:

1. THOMAS DE LA MORE, Esq., who held the Manor of More-Place. He was living in the reign of Henry II, as is proved by a deed.
2. HENRY DE MORE, son of Thomas De La More, as is proved by several deeds, had four sons, *viz.: John,* his heir, *Thomas, Stephen* and *Charles.*
3. JOHN DE MORE, of More-Place, the eldest son (in some deeds written Atte-More), d. about 7 King Edward II. He m. Matilda, dau. of William Falkinden, by whom he had two sons: *Thomas* and *Scoland.*
4. THOMAS DE MORE, who succeeded, by Joan his wife (who survived him and purchased lands 10 Edward III), had
5. JOHN DE MORE, his heir, who lived in the time of Edward III, and d. seized of his paternal inheritance, leaving two sons: *Thomas* and *John.*
6. THOMAS DE MORE, the elder son, m. Catharine, the coheiress of the family of Benenden. By her, who outlived him, he had two sons: *William* and *John.*
7. WILLIAM DE MORE, the elder, m. Catherine, dau. and heir to Anthony Aucher, Esq., and had issue: *Thomas,* his heir, and *John.*
8. THOMAS, m. Agnes, dau. and heir of Robert Austen, and was father of
9. WILLIAM MOORE, of Moore-Place, Esq., who m. Margaret, dau. and coheir to John Brenchley, Esq., Lord of the manor of Benenden, by his wife, Margaret, dau. and heir to Richard Golding, 21 Henry VI. He lies bur. in the church of Benenden, in Kent, with his father-in-law; as appears by an inscription in the chancel window on the north side.
10. WALTER MOORE, of Benenden, Esq., was his son. This Walter's will is recorded in the office of wills at Canterbury, and shows that he d. in 1504, 19 Henry VII, leaving by Alice his wife, two sons: *Thomas,* of Benenden, his heir, and *William.*
11. THOMAS MOORE, of Benenden, Esq., eldest son of Walter, made his will in 1519, 11 Henry VIII, which is recorded in the prerogative court of Canterbury, and proves that he had three sons: *John, Edward* and thirdly, *Thomas,* whose posterity settled in Norfolk.
12. THOMAS MOORE, b. in England; d. in Windsor, Conn., 1645.
13. HANNAH MOORE, d. Feb. 16, 1686; m. Nov. 30, 1648, John[2] Drake, who was b. in England, and came to Boston in 1630.
14. RUTH DRAKE, bapt. Dec. 6, 1757; m. Jan. 25, 1677, Samuel Barber[2], who was bapt. Oct. 1, 1648.
15. RUTH BARBER, b. July 24, 1683; m. Apr. 18, 1706, William Phelps, who was b. Feb. 4, 1668-9.
16. RUTH BARBER PHELPS, b. Jan. 23, 1713 at Harwington, Conn.; m. 1731, Lieut. Samuel[2] Phelps, b. Apr. 5, 1708; d. Aug. 14-17, 1754.
17. JOEL PHELPS, b. 1732, at Windsor, Conn.; m. Sept. 7, 1757, Jerusha Nash, b. Oct. 5, 1734; d. 1796.
18. PHINEAS PHELPS, b. Apr. 10, 1767; d. Apr. 20, 1813; m. Lydia Lawrence, b. Jan. 15, 1762; d. Sept. 20, 1813.

19. ·NASH DAVID PHELPS, b. Oct. 4, 1796, at New Haven, Vt.; d. Apr. 15, 1884; m. Apr. 21, 1821, at St. Armand West, Que., Elizabeth Hungerford, b. Feb. 7, 1798; d. Jan. 7, 1878.
20. ·CAROLINE ALEXANDRIA PHELPS, b. July 3, 1840; d. Mar. 29, 1921; m. Sept. 8, 1863, at Stanbridge, Que., Horace Brayton Leach, b. Sept. 25, 1836; d. May 6, 1919.
21. ·ELIZABETH MAY LEACH, b. Jan. 7, 1866; living Jan. 1, 1932; m. Sept. 8, 1889, at Sheldon, Vt., Oscar Herbert Rixford, b. Dec. 27, 1859; d. Sept. 11, 1926.
22. ·OSCAR ADELBERT RIXFORD, b. Aug. 4, 1890; m. Jan. 18, 1919, at Montreal Que., Mary Carolyn Hefflon, b. June 6, 1899; both living Jan. 1, 1932. They have two children:
    Mary-Elizabeth Lenora Rixford, b. Oct. 6, 1922; living Jan. 1, 1932
    Oscar Theodore Rixford, b. July 21, 1925; living Jan. 1, 1932.

References: 1 to 19 generations—Records of Elizabeth M. Rixford.
20 to 22 generations—Family Records.

SERVICES

Thomas Moore—1645, was in the first emigration from Dorchester, Mass., to Windsor, Conn., and a lot was granted him in 1639 on what is now Broad Street. He died in 1645.

References: "National Society Founders and Patriots," 1910-20, page 142.

List of Soldiers found on old Book of Ancient Records—John Bissell, Sr. and Jr., Thomas Moore, etc.

References: "History of Windsor," by Styles, page 196.

MOWBRAY

Arms—Gules, a lion rampant argent.

1. ·NIGEL DE ALBINI came into England as a leader in the army of William the Conqueror and obtained the lands forfeited by Robert de Mowbray, Earl of Northumberland, for treason. He m. (1) Maud, dau. of Richard de Aquila, by whom he had no issue. He m. (2) Gundred, dau. of Girald de Gornoy, by whom he had two sons.
2. ·ROGER, who assumed the name of Mowbray. He m. Alice de Gant.
3. ·NIGEL DE MOWBRAY, as he spelled the name, m. the dau. of the Earl of Clare.
4. ·WILLIAM DE MOWBRAY, m. Agnes, dau. of the Earl of Arundel.
5. ·ROGER DE MOWBRAY, son of William and Agnes, m. Maud. dau. of William de Beauchamp, of Bedford.
6. ·ROGER DE MOWBRAY, Baron Mowbray, and the first of the family to whom a valid writ of summons to Parliament is now on record, was called to Parliament in the eleventh year of Edward I (A. D. 1285) and continued in Parliament until the twenty-fifth year of Edward I. He m. Rose, great-granddau. of Richard de Clare, Earl of Hertford, and d. in 1298.
7. ·ADELIA DE MOWBRAY was, according to Berry's "County Genealogies," Bucleinghamshire, dau. of Roger de Mowbray (VI above), but in Bank's "Dormant and Extinct Baronage," she is recorded as the dau. of Roger de Mowbray (V above). She m. Reginald Warren. (See Warren 7-15, Stanley 11.)

Oscar Adelbert Rixford, son of the Author, is 35th in direct descent from Nigel de Albini.

PHELPS FAMILY
Descended from the Guelph Family, to which Queen Victoria belonged

The Phelps Family can be traced back to the middle of the twelfth century. They were a family of landed estates in Tewks-
bury, Worcestershire, England, and the name appears as Phylltpes and as Guelps, and is supposed to be of Italian origin. The superfluous letters were dropped during the reign of Edward IV, but the name was always pronounced Phelps. The surname Phelps is a variation of the spelling of Phillips, the latter originally meaning son of Philip. The spelling of the name has been varied, and a number of different family names are traced to the same origin. One family of Phelps claims to be descended from the Guelph Family, of Germany, to which Queen Victoria belonged. Some branches of the American family of Phelps are

descended from the ancient Phelps Family of Tewksbury, Gloucestershire, England. The coat of arms is described thus: Sable Lion chained and rampant. Various branches of the family in England bear coat of arms. (See "Genealogy Connecticut," Vol. III, pages 1569, 1699.)

The seat of the Phelps Family is still standing, occupied by Mr. Hooper. The family has eight various coats of arms. Their motto, "Truth without Fear." See "Doomsday Book No. 20," Cooper Institute, 1861. The American bearings of the family of Phelps are: Per pale or (gold) and argent (white), a wolf salient azure (blue) with an oric of eight crosses-crosslets fitchie gule (red) crest, a wolf's head erased (torn off), azure colored or, the collar charged with a marble sable (black).

James C. Phelps, Milton, Wiltshire, writes at "The Herald's Office to inform us that two coats of arms have been granted the Phelps Family, since the time of William the Conqueror."

The interpretation of the arms is as follows: The parting, per pale, indicates that a fortification has been placed, by ancestors in the face of an enemy. The wolf signifies courage and endurance, the crosses-crosslets fitchie, being emblems of the Second Crusade or Holy War, shows that in that campaign that arms were earned or acquired. The martle is the crest in the martin or swallows of Palestine, and indicates that an ancestor has been upon a pilgrimage to the Holy Land, in addition to having been in the Second Crusade.

The family has been of a number of centuries in the County of Stafford, England. Reference is made in our English correspondence to John Phelps, clerk of the Court that convicted Charles I. John Phelps who dwelt upon the Nether Thyme in England, the son of Francis Phelps, who died in the reign of Edward IV. John Phelps became private secretary to Oliver Cromwell. The Phelps Family opposed the High Church and Prerogative Party of Stafford and Bishopland. The original name of Phelps (Welf) Guelphs was a name assumed in Germany when the family came from the north of Italy. It is claimed that from the same stock with the House of Hanover, of whom Queen Victoria is a representative. The queen, it is well known, derives her lineage from the "Guelphs," of Germany, from the old Welfs, of Lombardy, Padua. The history of the Gulphs you will have no difficulty in tracing. The name was anciently spelled Phyllyppes, says Harper's "Pictoreal History of England," but has always been pronounced "Phelps." Although in the time of Edward IV the superfluous letters were dropped. First Phelps in the English form of "Guelphs"; 2nd, that Guelphs, German word of "Welf"; 3rd, that the Welf Family was princely in rank, the Guelphs being the leaders of the Papal Party in the famous conflict of the Pope with the German Princes. The parties Guelphs and Ghibellories, being like the Tories and Whigs in England. The present Royal House of England (Hanover), was one branch of Queen Victoria's ancestry.

> "Our Ancestors, a Gallant Christian Race,
> Patrons of every Virtue, every Grace."

Beside the old Tewksbury Abbey Church, Gloucestershire, England, founded by the Mexican Princess, Dukes Odo, and Dodo, two noble Saxon brothers, who flourished at the commencement of the eighth century. In the burying ground beneath the Sacred Shadow, lie interred some of our ancestors, others sweetly sleep in the cemetery of Dursley, in Gloucestershire. Others are interred in Purlock, Somersetshire, and Staffordshire.

Near Towbury Hill, in the parish near Tewksbury, there is a large encampment which Leland supposes was the site of the residence of the Mexican Princess, though there is no doubt of its having been a Roman Station. The old Phelps tombstones are at the northwest wall of the churchyard and the Viccorage Wall beneath the Sacred Shadows of Tewksbury Abbey Church.

References: "Phelps Genealogy," by Phelps and Servin, 1899, pages 12, 47 to 54.
"History of Royal Society," Vol. II, page 3.
Trumbell's "History of Connecticut."
"History of Tewksbury."
"Antiqueties of Tewksbury," by Dyde.
Burke's "Landed Gentry."
Burke's "Commons."
"Dyde Genealogy."

FIRST GENERATION IN AMERICA

WILLIAM² PHELPS (William, James, Richard), of Windsor, Conn., born in England; baptized Tewksbury Abbey Church, August 19, 1599. He married in England, first, Elizabeth ———; second, Mary Dover at Polluck, England; she died November 22, 1611. He resided for a time in Tewksbury, where his first child, Richard was born in 1619, and baptized in Tewksbury Abbey Church, December 26, 1619.

Soon after the birth of his first child (and the death of his father) he probably removed to one of the southern counties, either Somerset or Dorsetshire, as after the birth of his first child we find no reference to him in Tewkesbury, nor do I find any record of the birth of his five other children. He was the mayor of Tewksbury.

Mr. Phelps, his wife, six children, and brother George, then unmarried, emigrated to New England in the ship *Mary and John*, of four hundred tons burden, commanded by Captain Squeb, with one hundred and forty passengers. This company had been organized into a church and selected their ministers the day before sailing, as previously stated.

They sailed from Plymouth, England, March 29, 1630, arriving and landing in Nantasket (now Hull), Mass., May 30, 1630. This company settled in Dorchester, Mass., the first settlers and founders of that place. Dorchester claims the honor of being the first town in the Massachusetts Colony to organize a town government. Mr. Phelps took an active position in town matters, and during the first six months was made a freeman. In 1634, he was a representative to the General Court. May 14, 1634, he was one of a committee of four to view the ground at Mount Wollaston for the enlargement of Boston, and drew a plan then and reported at the next General Court. March 4, 1634, Mr. Phelps and Ensign Gibbs were appointed by the General Court to go with a committee of three to arrange the bounds between Boston and Dorchester, and explain what each town wants. May 5, 1635, he was a member of the General Court from Dorchester, held in Newton (now Charlestown). ("N. S. F. P. A.," page 20, No. 1526—Served as juryman in the first trial in New England.) He was a member of the first court ever held in Connecticut, 1636.

In the year 1635, Mr. Phelps' wife died. In the fall of 1635 the Rev. Mr. Warham, with sixty of his church in Dorchester, removed to the settling of Windsor, Conn. Mr. William Phelps and his family, and brother George, accompanied this expedition, though it is probable that Mr. Phelps did not go down to Windsor till the following spring. (See Records in Hartford, Conn., Adjutant General's Office.) William Phelps, q.v., was appointed on committee to prepare for war against the Pequots. A beautiful marble tablet placed in his honor in the upper entrance hall of the Library of the New England Historical and Genealogical Society, 9 Ashburton Pl., Boston.

Children by his wife Elizabeth:
1. RICHARD, bapt. Tewksbury Abbey Church, Dec. 26, 1619. He sailed for the Barbadoes, as previously stated, with Captain Burch and Gilbert Grimes; then unm.; all I know of him.
2. WILLIAM, b. England, about 1620; m. (1) Isabel Wilson; (2) Sarah Pinney.
3. SARAH, b. England, about 1620; m. William Wade, of Middletown, Conn., June 9, 1658.
4. SAMUEL, b. England, about 1625; m. Sarah Griswold.
5. NATHANIEL, b. England, about 1627; m. Elizabeth Copley.
6. JOSEPH, b. *England,* about 1629; m. (1) Hannah Newton; and (2) Mary Salmon.

Children by his second wife Mary Dover:
7. TIMOTHY, b. Windsor, Conn., Sept. 1, 1637; m. Mary Griswold.
8. MARY, b. Windsor, Conn., Mar. 2, 1644; m. Thomas Barber.

LIEUT. TIMOTHY PHELPS (seventh child of William and Mary [Dover] Phelps), born in Windsor, Conn., September 1, 1639; married Mary Griswold, Mach 19, 1661, daughter of Edward Griswold, of Killingworth, Conn.; she was born in Windsor, Conn.; baptized October 13, 1644. She died some years before her husband.

Mr. Phelps resided in Windsor, Conn., on the old homestead, on land purchased by his father from the Indians. He was propounded October, 1663, and made freeman May 2, 1664. May, 1690, "Thos. Allen chosen and allowed Capt. of Trainband in Windsor, and Timothy Phelps, Lieut., and are to be commissioned accordingly." May, 1696, "The soldiers at Windsor have chosen Timothy Phelps as their Capt. The Court approved their said choice and does order the said officers shall receive their commissions. Sgt. Timothy Phelps that went up to the Great Falls in Oct. last, ordered by Gov. and Council, 6 Feb., 1706-7, upon public service, shall be allowed 8 shillings apiece more than allowed them by Capt. Mathew Allen." He was appointed a Lieut. by the General Court, receiving his commission in 1709, and served under Col. William Whiting in Capt. Matthew Allyn's Co., in 1607, in the Queen Anne War. He died in 1719. His will, dated 2nd May, 1717, mentions all his children (except Mary who died young), and grandson Samuel Filer, son of his daughter Abigail. Timothy Phelps was commissioned Lieutenant of Captain Thomas Allyn's Company or trainband in Windsor, May 1690. Commissioned Captain of company or trainband in Windsor, May 1696." (See War Records in State House at Hartford, Conn.)

June 11, 1667, "to the Poor of other Colonies, Timothy Phelps 3s. 6d." ("Stiles' History.")

Capt. Matthew Allyn led a company from Windsor, in the unfortunate campaign against Quebec. From letters to his wife from the camp on Weeds Creek near Albany, that "Himself, Tim. Phelps, Obadiah Owen, Nat. Taylor and Bartlett are sick. Taylor the worst."

In a deposition taken at Hartford, Conn., March, 1682-3, he is mentioned as son of William, about forty-two years old.

Children were:
1. TIMOTHY, b. Windsor, Conn., Nov. 1, bapt. Nov. 7, 1663; m. Martha Crow.
2. JOSEPH, b. Windsor, Conn., Sept. 27, 1666; m. Sarah Hosford.
3. WILLIAM, b. Windsor, Conn., Feb. 4, 1669; m. (1) Abigail Mudge; (2) Ruth Barber.
4. CORNELIUS, b. Windsor, Conn., Apr. 26, 1671; m. Sarah Mansfield.
5. MARY, b. Windsor, Conn., Aug. 14, 1673; d. May 23, 1690, ae. 17.
6. LIEUT. SAMUEL, b. Windsor, Conn., Jan. 29, 1675; m. Abigail Eno.
7. CAPT. NATHANIEL, b. Windsor, Conn., Jan. 7, bapt. Jan. 13, 1677; m. (1) Hannah Bissell; m. (2) Abigail Pinney.
8. SARAH, b. Windsor, Dec. 27, 1670; m. David Marshall, of Hebron, Conn.
9. ABIGAIL, b. Windsor, Conn., June 3, 1682; m. Samuel Filer. He resided in Hebron, where he d. Sept. 13, 1710; and where his wife d. Jan. 28, 1709, leaving one child, referred to in the will of her father, Lieut. Timothy Phelps.
   Abigail (Filler or Filer), b. Hebron, Conn., before the death of grandfather, Lieut. Timothy Phelps.
10. HANNAH, b. Windsor, Conn., Nov. 2, bapt. Aug. 16, 1684; m. Thomas Phelps.
11. ANNE, b. Windsor, Conn., Oct. 2, 1686; m. David Porter.
12. MARTHA, b. Windsor, Conn., Nov. 12, 1688; m. Corp. Samuel Holcomb.

LIEUT. SAMUEL (sixth child of Capt. Timothy Phelps) was born January 29, 1675. He married Abigail Eno, who was born 1696. Samuel Phelps established and confirmed as ensign of company or trainband at Northwest Society in town of Windsor, May, 1728. Commissioned lieutenant of company or trainband in West Society in town of Windsor, October, 1729. (See Records in Adjutant General's Office, Hartford, Conn.) Lieut. Samuel and Abigail (Eno) Phelps had children.

Children born at Windsor, Conn.:

1. ABIGAIL, b. Mar. 8, 1707.
2. SAMUEL, b. Apr. 5, 1708-10.
3. JAMES, b. Aug. 12, 1713.
4. MATTHEW, b. Jan. 25-28, 1715.
5. MARY, b. Feb. 20, 1718.
6. JAMES, b. Jan. 23, 1720.
7. TABITHA, b. Jan. 18, 1721.
8. JOSHUA, b. Oct. 13, 1729.
9. HEZEKIAH, m. Lydia Griswold.

LIEUT. SAMUEL PHELPS 2nd (son of Lieut. Samuel [1] and Abigail Eno) was born April 5, 1708, and died August 14-17, 1754. He married in 1731, Ruth Phelps, daughter of William and Ruth (Barber) Phelps. She was born Jan. 23, 1713. Samuel Phelps 2nd established and confirmed ensign of 5th company or trainband in Windsor, October, 1736. (See Records in Adjutant General's Office, Hartford, Conn.) Lieut. Samuel 2nd and Ruth (Phelps) Phelps had Joel, born in Windsor, 1732, and other children. (See Records of F. Phelps Leach for other children.)

Children by first wife, all b. in Harwinton, except Joel.
1. JOEL⁷, b. 1732, at Windsor, Conn.
2. RUTH, b. Feb. 6, 1733.
3. SAMUEL, b. Sept. 15, 1736.
4. ZERUAH, m. Apr. 17, 1739.
5. THANKFUL, b. about 1740.
6. ABIGAIL, b. Nov. 1, 1741; m. Elkanah⁷ Phelps.
7. ANNA, b. about 1743; m. as 2nd wife, 532. Elkanah⁷ Phelps.

VERITAS SINE TIMORE

DAVID NASH PHELPS
(Original name Welf)

This ancestry is traced from the "House of Hanover" of whom Queen Victoria was a representative who derived her lineage from the old Welfs of Lombardy Padur.

(Authority for the above statement is based on the claim of some genealogists.)

8. SARAH, b. Apr. 6, 1744.
9. MATTHEW, b. June 6, 1746; m. Jerusha[7] Phelps.
10. OLIVER, b. 1748; d. Dec. 20, 1749.
11. ASENATH, b. Dec. 21, 1749.

Children by second wife:

12. OLIVER, b. June 7, 1753.
13. ELIZABETH, b. 1754; m. Samuel Hotchkiss.

· JOEL PHELPS (son of Lieut. Samuel Phelps 2nd and Ruth Phelps) was born in Windsor, Conn., in 1732. He married September 8, 1757, Jerusha Nash, who was born October 5, 1734, and died 1796. Joel Phelps enlisted August 26, 1776, as a private in Capt. Hezekiah Holcomb's in 18th Regiment, discharged September 25, 1776. This regiment was in service at New York, August to September, 1776, and was under command of Col. Jonathan Pettibone and was composed of companies from Simsbury. (See Records in Adjutant General's Office, Hartford, Conn.)

Joel and Jerusha (Nash) Phelps had children:

1. ABRIHAM, b. Goshen, Conn., 1758.
2. EBENEZER, b. Goshen, Conn.; m. Cynthia Soule, dau. of Joseph and Eunice (Hungerford) Soule. Ebenezer Phelps held nearly all the town offices in Fairfield, Vt., before 1813. He was surveyor, later collector, first constable and selectman for many years. The children recorded at Fairfield were:
    Charles J., b. May 28, 1798.
    Hiram Phelps, b. 1800.
    Perhaps other children. (Records of F. Phelps Leach.)
3. SAMUEL NASH PHELPS, b. Goshen, Conn., 1762; m. Phebe Darrow.
4. JOEL PHELPS, b. Norwalk, Conn., May 3, 17—.
5. PHINEAS, b. Norwalk, Conn., Apr. 10, 1767; m. Lydia Lawrence.
6. A SON, b. Norwalk, Conn., May 10, 1770; m. (1) Sarah Gilbert; m. (2) Widow Sarah Hogle.
7. MARTIN PHELPS, b. Norwalk, Conn., Sept. 10, 1772.
8. ———, b. Jan. 11, 1775; d. Oct., 1779.
9. ELKANAH, bapt. Norwalk, Conn., May 31, 1779; m. Mary ———.
10. LUCY, b. Norwalk, Conn., Oct. 11, 1780; m. Amiriah Smith.
    (Records of F. Phelps Leach.)

· PHINEAS PHELPS, born April 10, 1767; died April 20, 1813; married Lydia Lawrence, born 1761-2; died September 20, 1813. Children were:

1. DAVID PHELPS, m. Miss Elizabeth Hungerford (Nash David Phelps).
2. POLLY PHELPS, m. Joseph Wright.
3. ELKANAH PHELPS, m. Mina Chappell.   6. TERESA.
4. CAROLINE PHELPS, m. William Norton.   7. LAWRENCE.
5. PAMELIA.   8. DANIEL.

· NASH[10] DAVID PHELPS (Phineas[9], Joel[8], Lieut. Samuel 2nd[7], Lieut. Samuel[6], Capt. Timothy[5], William 2nd[4], William[3], James[2], Richard[1]) was born October 4, 1796, at New Haven, Vt.; d. April 15, 1884, at Stanbridge, Que.; married St. Armand West, Que., April 29, 1821, Elizabeth Hungerford, b. February 7, 1798; d. January 7, 1878.

Children were born at Stanbridge, Que.:

1. LYDIA, b. Dec. 2, 1825; d. Feb. 12, 1826.
2. LYDIA, m. Henry H. Bucklin.

3. ESTHER, m. Alexander Douglas; both d. at Stanbridge.
4. DAVID ALFRED, m. Victoria Sawyer.
5. EDGAR JOSIAH, b. Nov. 20, 1831; d. June 29, 1832.
6. ALMIRA EUDORA, b. Sept. 18, 1832; d. Jan. 7, 1913, at (Stone) North Stanbridge; m. Oct. 15, 1851, Asa Russell.
7. MARY ELIZABETH, b. Sept. 30, 1836; m. Apr. 20, 1853, Horatio Nelson Currie.
8. HELLEN ANN, b. Dec. 21, 1837; d. Oct. 27, 1920; m. (1) Heman Mitchell; (2) Samuel Fairfield, d. Oct. 21, 1914.
9. CAROLINE ALEXANDRA (mother of the Author of this Book), b. July 3, 1840; d. Mar. 29, 1921; m. Sept. 8, 1863, Horace Brayton[8] Leach, b. Sept. 25, 1836; d. May 6, 1919.
10. ALVIRA JANE, b. Sept. 30, 1843; m. Dec. 13, 1864, Arvide Henry Martin; d. and bur. at Clarenceville, Que.

MARY ELIZABETH PHELPS, daughter of Nash David and Elizabeth (Hungerford) Phelps, born September 30, 1836; married February 10, 1853, Horatio Nelson Currie, of Stanbridge, Que.

Children were:

1. ·EDWIN FRANCIS CURRIE, b. at Stanbridge, Que., June 17, 1854; m. at Bedford, Que., Alma Read. He was register for the County of Missisquoi, and mayor of Bedford, Que. They had children b. at Berford, Que.:
    1. *Mary Eliza Currie,* b. Nov. 19, 1891; graduate of Dunham Ladies' College; m. Nov. 19, 1914, Frank Erle Draper, M.D.C.M., who was b. on Jan. 28, 1887. Children b. at Bedford, Que.:
        1. ·Dennis Currie Draper, b. Feb. 23, 1921.
        2. ·Catherine Draper, b. May 22, 1926.
    2. *Francis Read Currie,* b. Feb. 18, 1893; m. Muriel Brydon, at Vancouver, B. C., where is prominent in the banking business; promoted to the head office in Toronto, 1932. Children b. in Vancouver:
        1. ·Francis Vaughan Currie, b. Sept. 22, 1925.
        2. ·Peter Edwin Currie, b. Nov. 18, 1927.
    3. *John Edwin Currie,* b. Sept. 24, 1894; m. Nora O'Donnell, Apr. 18, 1892. Served three years in the World War with Royal Mounted Rifles, 1st Division.
    4. *Lewis Nelson Currie,* b. Nov. 19, 1898; m. Mamie Reily, Sept. 27, 1921. Served four years with the 42nd Highlanders in the World War on the Staff of General McDonald; organist for several years at the Episcopal Church at Bedford.
    Edwin Francis Currie m. (2nd) Cora Hulburd, of Bedford, Que. They have two children b. at Bedford, Que.:
    1. *Isabel Hulburd Currie,* b. Jan. 11, 1914; a graduate and head girl at St. Helen's College, Dunham, Que., in 1931. She was head of the Green House, president of the Athletic Association, vice-president of the Literary Association and secretary-treasurer of the Girls' Auxiliary. She was one of the "Intelligentsia" of the form, and early showed herself a leader of the school. After graduating from St. Helen's College, she entered McGill University at Montreal, Que.
    2. ·*Heman Bruce Currie,* b. Sept. 21, 1916; a student of Bedford High School.
2. ·HATTIE JANE CURRIE, b. at Stanbridge, Que., Nov. 24, 1856; m. Andrew G. Johnston, of Beatrice, Neb., b. 1856; m. (2nd) 1915, O. L. Hulburd, of Oakland, Calif. Child by first marriage:
    1. ·*Nye Johnson,* b. at Bedford, Que., 1883.

(See Burke's "Royal Families," Vol. II, Pedigree CLII)

Eleanor, of Castile, 1st wife.	= EDWARD I, d. 1307.	= Margaret, of France, dau. of Philip IV, King of France, and grand-dau. of Louis; 2nd wife.

Edward II, d. 1327.	= Isabel, of France.	Thomas, of Brotherton, Earl of Norfolk, 2nd son, from whom, in the female line, the Howards descend.	Edmund, of Woodstock, Earl of Kent, 3rd son; beheaded 1329.	= Margaret, sister and heir of Thomas, Lord Wake.

21 generations from Edward I, King of England, to Edwin Francis Currie, Mayor of Bedford, Que.

The Phelps line is summarized as follows:

1. RICHARD PHELPS (then spelled Phylyppes), b. at Nether Teyne. (See Note, "Edward VI, 1547-1555," page 50.).
2. JAMES PHELPS, b. at Tewksbury, 1530; in Prerogative Court at Canterbury, A. D. 1587-1591. He m. Joan ———, who was given permission to administer on his estate, May 10, 1588. Children, bapt. in the Tewksbury Abbey Church, England.
   William, mentioned below.
   Thomas, Aug. 10, 1563.
   George (Giles), Sept. 5, 1566.
   Alice, Dec. 24, 1572; m. June 21, 1595.
   John Hope.
   Edward, May 10, 1578.
   Keneline, Oct. 16, 1583.
   Robert, July 18, 1584.
   Nicholas.
3. WILLIAM (1), son of James Phelps, was bapt. at Tewksbury Church, Aug. 4, 1560; m. Dorothy ———, who administered his estate and d. in 1613. He probably d. in 1611. Children, bapt. at Tewksbury:
   Mary, Sept. 4, 1587; d. young.
   Mary, Apr. 23, 1588.
   Thomas, June 24, 1590.
   Dorothy, Feb. 29, 1595.
   William, Aug. 19, 1599;
   James, July 14, 1601.
   Elizabeth, May 9, 1603.
   George, mentioned below.
4. WILLIAM (2) PHELPS, son of William (1), was b. in Tewksbury, England, Aug. 17, 1599; bapt. in Tewksbury Abbey Church, Aug. 19, 1599; and d. in Windsor, Conn., July 16, 1672. He was the mayor of Tewksbury, England, in 1607.
5. LIEUT. TIMOTHY PHELPS, son of William (2) and Mary Ann (Dover) Phelps, was b. at Windsor, Conn., Sept. 1, 1639; d. in 1719. He received his commission as lieutenant under Col. William Whiting, and served with Capt. Matthew Allyn in Queen Anne's War, in 1709. He m. Mary, dau. of Edward Griswold. ("Conn. Gen.," by Lewis Pub. Co., page 1699, Vol. I—William Phelps, governor's assistant, 1636-42; War 2nd Service.)
6. LIEUT. SAMUEL[1] PHELPS, b. Jan. 29, 1675, Windsor, Conn.; m. Abigail Eno, b. Mar., 1696; d. Mar., 1728. (See "D. A. C. Lineage Book," 1931.)
7. LIEUT. SAMUEL[2] PHELPS, b. Apr. 5, 1708; d. Aug. 14-17, 1754; m. 1731, Ruth Phelps, b. Jan. 23, 1713. (See "D. A. C. Lineage Book," 1931.)
8. JOEL PHELPS, b. at Windsor, Conn., 1732; m. Sept. 8, 1757, Jerusha Nash, b. Oct. 5, 1734; d. 1796.
9. PHINEAS PHELPS, b. Apr. 10, 1767; d. Apr. 20, 1813; m. Lydia Lawrence, b. 1761-2; d. Sept. 20, 1813.
10. NASH DAVID PHELPS, b. Oct. 4, 1796; d. Apr. 15, 1884; m. at St. Armand West, Que., Apr. 29, 1821, Elizabeth Hungerford, b. Feb. 7, 1798; d. Jan. 7, 1878.
11. ALFRED PHELPS (only brother of Caroline Alexandria Phelps), m. Victoria Sawyer; d. New Haven, Conn. He was b. and d. in Stanbridge, Que. They have children, all b. at Stanbridge, Que., as follows:
    1. *Ferdanand*, d. in Stanbridge, unm.

2. *Byron*, d. in New Haven, Conn.; children.
3. *Mira*, m. (1) Arthur Lewis; one child, Arthur; (2) George Button.
4. *Milton*, d. in New Haven, Conn., Feb. 1, 1922; two daus., Grace and Avis.

Reference:—Records of F. Phelps Leach and Elizabeth M. Rixford.

PORT

("Colonial Families," 1928, page 43)

Arms—Azure, a fesse engrailed cotised between three pigeons, each having in the beak a cross formee fitchee, all or.

From a dwelling at a portal the surname Port originated, or, as in the following, from a well-known port, probably at Portsmouth, in Hampshire, where are also Portsea, and Portchester Castle, built on the site of the Portus Magnus of the Romans, when in possession of Britain. Hugh de la Porte gave land to the Church of St. Peter at Gloucester, 1086. The arms blazoned herewith are those of Port, of Etwall, County Derby.

1. HUBERT DE PORT, held the manor of Mapledurwell in Hampshire, in the Domesday Survey, A. D. 1080.
2. ADAM DE PORT, of Mapledurwell, son of Hubert de Port, in the reign of Henry I, was Lord also of Kington, in Herefordshire. A charter granted by Henry I, at Easter, 1121, to the See of Hereford, is addressed to Adam de Port and Walter de Gloucester, implying that Adam was the principal officer of the county. He m. and left three sons.
3. ROGER DE PORT, of Mapledurwell, Lord of the Honor of Kington, and eldest son of Adam de Port, m. Sybil (surname unknown), who outlived him.
4. SIR HUGH DE PORT, second son of Roger and Sybil de Port, is called by Warren in the "Warren Family," Sir Hugh de Port, of Etwall; but Lyson's "Magna Britannia," Vol. V, County Derby, states that the Manor of Etwall, County Derby, was granted to Sir John Port, by Henry VIII, 1540; previously, lands of Welbeck Abbey. Sir John Port was a descendant of Sir Hugh de Port, bearing the same arms, but proof that Sir Hugh was of Etwall does not appear. Sir John's grandfather, Henry, was at (West) Chester, County Derby. Sir Hugh married, but the name of his wife is not known.
5. JOAN DE PORT, dau. of Sir Hugh de Port, m. John (2) Warren, son of Sir John and Alice (Townsend) Warren. (See Warren X.)

(Mrs. Frank) Beatrice Josie Young, dau. of F. Phelps Leach, 29th in descent from Sir Hugh de Port. She d. in 1919, and left one child, Kathleen Mary Young.

Families Directly Descended from all the Royal Families (40AD-1953) and Mayflower Descendents

The Relationship existing between Elizabeth M. Leach Rixford
and the two QUEENS VICTORIA

by John Wurts Esq., Philadelphia, Author of Magna Carta

1. VICTORIA (BOADICEA—PRASUTAGUS
2. Princess of Iceni—Meric
3. OLD KING COLE*
4. Athildis—Marcomir IV
5. Clodomir IV—Hasilda
6. Farabert
7. Sunno
8. Hilderic
9. Bartherus
10. Clodius III
11. Walter
12. Dagobert
13. Genebald I
14. Dagobert
15. Clodius I
16. Marcomir
17. Pharamond—Argotta
18. Clodio—Basina
19. Merovee—Verica
20 Childeric I—Basina
21. Clovis—St. Clothilde
22. Clothaire I—Ingonde
23. Blithildes—Ausbert
24. Arnolph—Oda
25. St. Arnolph—Lady Dodo
26. Anchises—Begga
27. Pepin d'Heristal—Alpais
28. Charles Martel—(1) Rotrude
29. Pepin—Bertha
30. CHARLEMAGNE—Hildegarde
31. Louis I—(1) Ermengarde
32. Lothaire—Ermengarde
33. Ermengarde
34. Regnier
35. Giselbert
36. Albreda
37. Ermentrude
38. Beatrice

*Colchester in Essex, Britain's Oldest recorded town, dates from about 40AD, and is said to be the home of the methodical Old King Cole, according to the British Travel Bureau.

Families Directly Descended from all the Royal Families (40AD-1953) and Mayflower Descendents

The Relationship existing between Elizabeth M. Leach Rixford and the two QUEENS VICTORIA

39. Geoffrey II
40. Fulk IV
41. Fulk V
42. Geoffrey Plantagenet—Matilda
43. Hameline Plantagenet—Isabel Warren
44. Isabella Plantagenet—Roger Bigod
45. Hugh Bigod—Maude Marshall
46. Isabel Bigod—Gilbert de Lacy
47. Maud Lacy—(2) Geoffrey de Genevill
48. Peter de Geneville—Joane Brune
49. Joane Geneville—Roger Mortimer
50. Edmund Mortimer—Elizabeth Badlesmere
51. Roger Mortimer K.G.—Philippa Montacute

52. Margery Mortimer—John Prideaux	Edmund Mortimer—Philippa Plantagenet
53. Percy Prideaux—Isabella Montacute	Roger Mortimer—Eleanor Holland
54. Sir John Prideaux—Joan Adeston	Anne Mortimer—Richard Plantagenet
55. Giles Prideaux—Miss Gunston	Richard Plantagenet—Cicely Neville
56. Sir John Prideaux—(3) Anne Shapton	Edward IV—Elizabeth Wydeville
57. William Prideau—(3) Alice Gifford	Elizabeth—Henry VII
58. Sir Fulk Prideaux—(2) Katherine Poyntz	Margaret—James IV of Scotland
59. Humphrey Prideaux—(2) Edith Hatch	James V of Scotland
60. Elizabeth Prideaux—Robert Drake	Mary, Queen of Scotland
61. William Drake—Philippa Denys	James I—Anne
62. John Drake—Elizabeth Rogers	Elizabeth—Frederick V
63. John Drake—Hannah Moore	Sophia—Ernest Augustus
64. Ruth Drake—Samuel Barber	George I—Sophia Dorothea
65. Ruth Barber—William Phelps	George II—Caroline
66. Ruth Barber Phelps—Lt. Samuel Phelps	Frederick—Augusta
67. Joel Phelps—Jerusha Nash	George III—Charlotte
68. Phineas Phelps—Lydia Lawrence	Edward—Victoria
69. Nash David Phelps—Elizabeth Hungerford	VICTORIA—Albert

70. Caroline Alexandra Phelps—Horace Brayton Leach
71. ELIZABETH MAY LEACH (Mrs. Oscar Herbert Rixford)
72. Oscar A. Rixford
73. Oscar T. Rixford—Mary-Elizabeth Rixford Selchow
74. Mary-Alice Selchow
74. Stephen Rixford—Bradley Rixford

Reference—Royal Families, pages 2 to 7.
Page 1, Pedigree A, also pages 231, 232, 233.

ROYAL LINE OF PORTUGAL

ROYAL ARMS OF

𝔓𝔬𝔯𝔱𝔲𝔤𝔞𝔩

A r m s — Argent, five inescutcheons azure, one, three and one, each charged with five plates, two, one and two, a bordure gules, charged with seven towers or, doors and windows azure.

Helmet—Affronte or, crowned of the same.

Crest—A dragon issuant, wings displayed or.

Supporters — Two winged dragons vert, each holding a banneret; the dexter argent, charged with the five inescutcheons of the arms, the sinister gules, with seven towers or, two, two, two, and one, doors and windows azure.

The origin of Portugal as a separate state was an incident in the Christian re-conquest of Spain from the Moors. Towards the close of the eleventh century crusading knights came from every part of Europe to aid the Kings of Northern and Central Spain in driving out the Moors. Among these adventurers was Count Henry of Burgundy, an ambitious warrior, who married Theresa, natural daughter of Alfonso VI. The County of Portugal, which had already been won back from the Moors (1055-64), was included in Theresa's dowry. His line is traced as follows:

1. ROBERT, King of the Franks or of France.
2. ROBERT, Duke of Burgundy, son of Robert, King of France.
3. HENRY, d. 1066; m. Sibylla.
4. HENRY, Count of Burgundy and later of Portugal, son of Henry and Sibylla, held the countship from 1093-1112. He m., in 1095, Theresa, dau. of Alfonso VI of Castile, who was also King of Leon. They were the parents of *Alfonso I* of Portugal.
5. ALFONSO I of Portugal, son of Henry, Count of Portugal, and Theresa, was b. in 1112, and d. in 1185. He became King of Portugal in 1139. He m. Matilda, dau. of Amedus of Maurienne.
6. URRACA, dau. of Alfonso I and Matilda, m. Ferdinand II of Castile. (See Castile 5; Royal Descent of Elizabeth M. Rixford No. 11; Henry I, King of England.)

Mary Eliza Draper (great-granddau. of Nash David and Elizabeth Hungerford Phelps), dau. of Edwin Francis Currie, of Bedford, Que., is 32nd in direct descent from Robert, King of the Franks or of France.

PROVINCE

("Colonial Families," 1928, page 113)

Arms—D'or au chev. d'azur acc. de trois batons ecotes de gu.   Or, a chevron azure between three batons raguly gules.

The name Province was applied to a province in the southeastern part of Ancient France, and dates back to the first entrance of the Romans into Gaul in B. C. 125, when after the Roman Conquest the territory between the Alps, the sea, and the Rhone, with the Province of Narbourne on the right bank of the river, were formed unto the "Provincia Romana." Later, when part of this section was added to other provinces, the name Provence remained with the territory between the Dauphine and Rhone and Lanquedoc, the Alps and the Mediterranean. It was attacked by the Visigoths at the beginning of the fifth century, conquered by the Saracens at the beginning of the eighth century, later came under Frankish rule, and at the time of the partition of Charlemagne's Empire (843), fell to the share of Lothaire I, from whom it passed to Emperor Louis II, who was also King of Italy. At his death (875) Provence passed to Charles the Bald. From Charles the Bald it passed to his brother-in-law, Duke Boso. After the middle of the tenth century the Countship of Provence passed to William and Rouband (Rotbold), sons of Boso. A descendant of Rouband was Douce, who married Raimond Berenger III, son of Raimond Berenger II, of further mention.

1. RAIMOND BERENGER II, of Barcelona, m. Matilda Guiscard, dau. of Robert Guiscard.
2. RAIMOND BERENGER III, d. in 1130. He m. Douce, heiress of Provence. (See Berenger.)
3. RAIMOND BERENGER IV, of Barcelona, d. in 1162. He m. Petronilla, of Aragon.
4. ALFONSO II, of Aragon, m. Sancia, dau. of Alfonso VIII, of Castile.
5. ALFONSO II, of Provence, 1196-1209.
6. RAIMOND BERENGER IV, of Provence (1209-1245), m. Beatrice, dau. of Count of Savoy.
7. ELEANOR, of Provence, m. Henry III, of England. (See Royal Descent XXV.)

Mary-Elizabeth L. Rixford and Oscar Theodore Rixford are 29th in direct descent from (1) Raimond Berenger II, of Barcelona.

ROGERS FAMILY

J. L. Chester, 1861

(Page 232) Having thus established, perhaps as clearly as it will ever be possible to do, the identity of the Martyr with John Rogers, the son of John Rogers, of Deritend, it will be interesting to learn something of his ancestors.

Among the Visitations of Dorsetshire, and other genealogical MSS., in the British Museum and elsewhere, dated 1565, 1612, and 1623, are several, varying in detail, but generally agreeing in the following lineage:

1. JOHN FITZ-ROGER, who m. a dau. of Sir Simon Furneup, descended from the Earls of Bush.
2. SIR JOHN FITZ-ROGER (or John Rogers), whose second wife was Anne, dau. and heir of Sir Thomas Etchingham, and widow of Doctor Audley.
3. SIR HENRY FITZ-ROGER (or Henry Rogers), of Henry Rogers), of Bryanstone, who m. Avice (or Amy), dau. of William, Lord Stourton (who d. in 1477).
4. THOMAS ROGERS, who appears to have had two elder brothers, *viz.*: Sir John Rogers, of Bryanstone (who d. in 1500); and James, a doctor of divinity; and also a younger brother, Richard.

This is supposed to be the Thomas Rogers who married Catharine, daughter of Sir William Courtenay, of Powderham, County of Devon (who died in 1485), by his wife Margaret, daughter of Lord Bonville. If this be so, he is identical with him known as Thomas Rogers, of Bradford, County of Wilts, who, with eight others, formed the call of sergeants at law, June 9, 1477. He had two wives: 1st, Cecilia, daughter and coheir of William Besyll, of Bradford (one of the principal men in Wiltshire, in the time of Henry VI), by whom he had one son, William, from whom is descended, among others, the family of Rogers, of Rainscombe, County of Wilts; the present representative of which is Rev. Edward Henry Rogers. 2nd, Catharine Courtenay (as above), by whom he had two sons, *viz.*: George Rogers, of Luppitt, County of Devon, from whom was descended Sir Edward Rogers, of Cannington, County of Somerset, Comptroller of the Household and one of the Privy Council of Queen Elizabeth; and, continuing the above lineage:

5. JOHN (or THOMAS) ROGERS, of Sutton Vallens, County of Kent, who appears to have been the first son by his second wife. This John (or Thomas Rogers), or possibly a son of his, was doubtless the "Rogers, of Sutton Vallens," the progenitor of the family described in the first two pedigrees discussed in these pages, and the father of
6 or 7. JOHN ROGERS, of Deritend, the father of
7 or 8. JOHN ROGERS, the Martyr.

The arms of Thomas Rogers, of Bradford, are nearly identical with those of John Rogers, of Deritend—the variations being such trifling ones as usually occur in different branches of the same family. It must be said that they are entirely at variance with those of Sir John Rogers, of Bryanston, which bore a fleur-de-lis and a mullet; but this may be accounted for on the presumption that, from some cause now unknown, and being a younger branch of that family, he assumed peculiar arms of his own (a document in the possession of the family of Rogers, of Rainscombe, states that he did assume these arms, at the time when he married into the family of Besyll, of Wiltshire), an ocurrence by no means uncommon.

Pursuing the maternal ancestry of the Martyr, we find that Sir William Courtenay, the father of the second wife of Thomas Rogers, of Bradford, was the eldest son of Sir Philip Courtenay (who died

in 1463), by Elizabeth, daughter of Walter, Lord Hungerford; Sir
Philip was the eldest son of Sir John Courtenay (who died before
1415), by Joan (or Anne), daughter of Alexander Champernowne,
of Beer Ferrers, and widow of Sir James Chudleigh, Knt.; Sir John
was the second son of Sir Philip Courtenay, Lord Lieutenant of
Ireland (who died July 7, 1406), by Margaret (or Anne), daughter
of Sir Thomas Wake, of Blisworth, County Northampton; Sir
Philip was the fifth son of Hugh de Courtenay, second of that name
Earl of Devon (who died in 1377), by the Lady Margaret de Bohun
(who died December 16, 1392); Lady Margaret was the second
daughter of Humphrey de Bohun, fifth Earl of Hereford and third
of Essex, Lord High Constable (who was slain at Borough Bridge
in 1321), by the Princess Elizabeth Plantagenet, sixth daughter of
Edward I, by Eleanor, daughter of Ferdinand, King of Castile.

It will probably satisfy most of the present generation to trace
their ancestry back thus far, but if there are any who desire to go
still further, they may be gratified to know that they may do so,
from Edward I through Henry III, John, Henry II, Henry I, and
William the Conqueror, even to Charlemagne. The great majority,
however, will overlook the fact that the blood of kings (although
by this time greatly diluted) flows in their veins, and be proud of
their lineage only as it embraces the simple man with the humble
name—John Rogers—who, obscure as his personal history has been
and still is, probably did more for the cause of Christianity in England than any other single man who ever lived.

(Page 222) ·JOHN ROGERS was born between the years 1500 and
1505, and probably at Detitend, although it is possible that his father
did not reside there until after his birth. The records of both uni-
versities give no information beyond the bare facts above mentioned.

There are in the British Museum two MSS. pedigrees, upon
which we must primarily rely in our endeavors to establish his identity. The first is contained in a volume (Harleian MSS. 1563, fol.
19 b) bearing this title, *viz.:* "The Visitation of the County of Warwick, made in Anno 1563, by Robert Cooke, Chester Herald, for
William Hervey, Clarenceux: continued and enlarged with another
Visitation of the same County; made in Anno 1619, by Sampson
Leonard, Blue Mantle, and Augustine Vincent, Rouge Rose, Officers
of Arms and Deputies to William Camden, Clarenceux." This pedigree commences with one "Rogers," who had two sons, *viz.:* Nicholas,
who had issue, William; and "John Rogers, of Detitend," in the
parish of Aston, County of Warwick, who married Margery Wyatt.
This John Rogers had three sons and two daughters, as follows:

1. JOHN, who. m. "Adryan Pratt, of Brabant."
2. WILLIAM.
3. EDWARD.
4. ELLENOR, who m. Roger Hylward, of Alnechurch, County of Worcester.
5. JOAN, also m., but the name of whose husband is not stated.

The children of John Rogers and "Adryan Pratt" are given thus:

1. DANIEL, of Sunbury, County of Middlesex, clerk of the Council to Queen Elizabeth (ob. 1591), who m. Susan, dau. of Nicasius Yetsworth, clerk of the Signet, and secretary for the French tongue.
2. JOHN, a proctor of the Civil Law, who m. Mary, dau. of William Leete, of Everden, County of Cambridge, D. C. L.
3. AMBROSE.
4. SAMUEL.
5. PHILIP.
6. BERNARD.
7. AUGUSTINE.
8. BARNABY.
9. SUSAN, who m. John Short, merchant, of London.
10. ELIZABETH, who m. James Proctor, chancellor, of Salisbury.
11. HESTER, who m. Henry Ball, physician.

The children of Daniel Rogers, of Sunbury, are Francis, and a daughter named Posthuma.

The children of John and Mary Rogers are Cassandra, Elizabeth, Heckuba, Constantine, John, Edward, Mary, and Varro (a son).

The volume containing the other pedigree (Harleian MSS. 1551, fol. 59 b). (Also see "N. E. Hist. and Gen. Register," 44:301), has this original endorsement on the first page, *viz.:* "In this book (are) Collections of Descents and Arms of the Gentry of Middlesex, whereof was no Visitation General of the same County before that made (A. D. 1634) by Sir Henry St. George, Richmond Herald, Deputy to his father (Sir Richard St. George), then Clarenceux; except seven Descents (Which) are entered in the old Visitation of Hertfordshire: .... all the rest are the collections of me, Richard Mundy." This pedigree follows the former one very closely, but has the following very important additions, *viz.:* The progenitor of the family is called "Rogers, of Sutton Vallens, in Kent"; 2. John Rogers, who married Adryan Pratt, is said to be of Birmingham, County of Warwick; and, 3. Francis, the son of Daniel Rogers, of Sunbury, is stated to have married a daughter of —— Cory, and to have a son, also named Francis, while his sister Posthuma was married to —— Spears.

The arms given in both MSS. are precisely alike, *viz.:* Argent; a chevron sable, between three stags statant sable; a crescent for difference or; crest, a stag's head sable, issuant from a ducal coronet or.

MEAD FAMILY, by L. E. W. (page 49 [Appendix]) Much has been written on the subject of the Rogers family and many claim descent from either John Rogers the Martyr or Thomas Rogers, a passenger of the *Mayflower*. In the Preface to the "Life of John Rogers the Martyr," by Joseph Lemuel Chester, we find that he married Adrian Platt and had eleven children: Daniel, John, Ambrose, Samuel, Philip, Bernard, Augustine, Barnaby, Susan, Elizabeth and Hester.

(Page 236 [Note]) The writer has been unable to discover any trace of the three daughters, after their respective marriages. James Proctor, named as the husband of Elizabeth, and represented as chancellor of Salisbury, does not appear in that capacity in the records of that cathedral. One of the same name occurs as archdeacon of Dorset, Diocese of Salisbury, in 1533, but he had resigned before 1537 and, in 1543, the archdeaconry was transferred to the See of Bristol. Elizabeth Rogers could hardly have been marriageable before 1560, when this James Proctor must have been advanced in years, and it seems quite improbable that he should have been the one indicated. (Dodsworth's "History of Salisbury Cathedral," 1814, page 239.)

(Page 249) Ezekiel Rogers, in his will, uses very significant language, decidedly averse to such a supposition. To give his precise words—after leaving legacies to "my loving nephew, Mr. Samuel Stone"—"my cousin, his son John"—"my loving niece, Mrs. Mary Watosius"—"my loving niece, Mrs. Eliza Cawton"—and "my cousin Rogers, of Billerica"—as if purposely to intimate to curious genealogists of the present day that the next legatee enjoyed no such near relationship, he adds—"Ezekiel Rogers, the son of Mr. Nathaniel Rogers, late Pastor of the Church of Ipswich, deceased." (See a copy of this will, in Rev. James Bradford's address, contained in Gage's "History of Rowley," Boston, 1840.)

(Page 154) (In the present portion of this work, it will be referred to only as it may serve to illustrate the account of the trial of the Martyr, and his personal history during the two weeks preceding his death.)

On Tuesday, the 22nd of January, 1555, Rogers was brought, a prisoner before the Privy Council. Gardiner seems to have abruptly intimated that he knew the object of the interview, and at once demanded if he was willing, then and there, to abandon his old faith, and acknowledge the Papal creed and authority. It will be noticed that the "Romish," or the "Roman Catholic" Church, was never spoken of: it was, invariably, the "Catholic" Church. Rogers claimed to be still a member of that Church, as he understood it and, therefore, replied to that effect, compelling Gardiner to express his meaning more definitely. He was then required, if he desired the favor of the authorities, to assent to the supremacy of the Pope. With true courage, he replied boldly that he recognized Christ as the only head of the Church, and declared his opinion that the "Bishop of Rome"—not the "Pope"—had no more or other authority in spiritual matters than any other of the numerous Bishops then living, etc.

(Page 414) Aman. The 8. of May, An. Do. 1554.

Robert Manauen, alias	Edwarde Crome.
Robert Ferrar.	John Rogers.
Rowlande Taylor.	Laurentius Saunders.
John Philpot.	Edmunde Lawrence.[1] (Note.)
John Bradforde.	I. P.
Joannes Wigorn and	T. M.
Glouc. Episcopus, alias Ioannes Hoper.	

To these thinges aboue said, do I Myles Couerdale, late of Exon, consent and agree with these my afflicted brethren, being prysoners, with mine own hand.

(*Note*) No other reference to an Edmund Lawrence is found in the histories of the times, and this is, perhaps, one of Foxe's errors. Strype calls him John Lawrence. One of that name, who had been a priest, had his examination on the 8th of February, 1555, was condemned on the 9th, and burnt at Colchester on the 29th of the same month. He had suffered so severely from ill treatment while in prison, especially from the effect of heavy irons on his legs, that he was carried to the stake in a chair, and burned while sitting in it.

ROGERS

("Colonial Families," 1928, page 175)

Arms—Argent, a chevron between three stags trippant sable.
Crest—A stag's head sable ducally gorged or.

Although this surname is generally acknowledged to have originated from the possessive form of the baptismal name Roger, used to designate Roger's son, as Henry, Roger's Harrison reminds us that "many an Irish Mac Rory, or Mac Rury, has Anglicized his name to Rogers or Rogerson." Many persons called Roger and Rogerus are recorded as tenants in the Domesday Book (1086). The Norman patronymical form is Fitz-Roger, and the Welsh ap Roger, became in some cases Prodger. The name was exceedingly common in the thirteenth century all over Great Britain, appearing in various forms, including the nicknames Hodge and Dodge.

1. THOMAS ROGERS, a descendant of John Rogers, the "martyr son" of Thomas Matthew and —— McMurds (or McMurcock) Rogers, was born in 1586, and died in Plymouth, England, in February, 1621. He and his eldest son, John, emigrated to America in the *Mayflower,* in 1620.

Children:
1. JOHN, d. between Aug. 26, 1691 and Sept. 20, 1692; m. in 1639, Ann Churchman. Children:
    1. *John,* b. 1640.
    2. *Abigail,* b. in 1642.
    3. *Ann.*
2. JOSEPH, who d. in 1678; m. Hannah, surname unknown.

Since John Rogers, mentioned below appears in the list of "Mayflower Descendants" (Vols. XIV, XV, and XVIII), he was probably a descendant of John, mentioned above (son of John, son of Thomas), who married three times.

1. JOHN ROGERS, married Sarah Rogers.

RUSSELL

("Colonial Families," 1928, page 175)

Arms—Argent, a lion rampant gules, on a chief sable three escallops of the first.

Crest—A demi-lion rampant gules.

Motto—*Che sara, sara.*

Russell as a surname belongs to that class of English surnames which had their origin in nicknames. It is derived directly from the cognomen Russell, the diminutive of Rous, a sobriquet for one with hair or complexion of a reddish-brown. Just as the old French *brun* (brown) took in English two diminutives, burnett and burnell, so *roux* (reddish-brown) found two diminutives, russet and russell. From nicknames these became hereditary surnames, and are all in existence today with the exception of Russet. The first entry of the name in English records of mediæval date occurs in the Hundred Rolls in the year 1273. It is recorded that the name Rozel (roz-castle, el—a synonym for water) was first given to a castle located in lower Normandy in 1045 and implied a tower or castle by the water. Hugh, son of William Bertrand, was invested with this stronghold and took its name, calling himself Hugh Rozel, from which came Rosel, Rousel, and Russell. The Bertrand ancestry traces to Norwegian Earls of the seventh century, whose descendants were in the train of William the Conqueror and received large grants of the public domain taken from the Saxons. They were founders of the English family of Russell.

Jennett Russell, married as first wife, Sir Eustace Whitney, son of Sir Robert Whitney. (See Whitney English Pedigree 4.)

ALMIRA EUDORA PHELPS, born September 18, 1832; died January 7, 1913, daughter of Nash David and Elizabeth Hungerford Phelps; married Asa Russell, October 15, 1851; died ———.
Children:

EDWARD CLARENCE RUSSELL, b. Oct. 10, 1852, at North Stanbridge, Que.; m. Dec. 19, 1882, Ida Hungerford, dau. of Samuel² Hungerford and sister of Samuel³ Hungerford (vice-president of the Canadian National Railways, Inc.).

ERNEST A. RUSSELL, b. June 27, 1854, at North Stanbridge, Que.; m. Affa Stone, of North Stanbridge, Apr. 13, 1898. He d. Nov. 20, 1917. He was a proprietor of the creamery at Stanbridge and won a premium for the best cheese at the World's Fair at Chicago, Ill., 1892.

IRVIN N. RUSSELL, b. June 17, 1858, at North Stanbridge. He was killed in a railway accident on Mount Washington, N. H., Oct. 10, 1882.

ELMER A. RUSSELL, b. Dec. 7, 1862, at North Stanbridge; m. Mary Hunter at North Stanbridge, Mar. 23, 1892.

Irvin Russell, son of Elmer Russell, b. Feb. 28, 1898; d. Mar. 7, 1917.

There are no other descendants of this branch of the Russell Family besides Irvin, son of Elmer, excepting Alice, Ethel, Beryl, and Stewart Hungerford, nieces and nephew of Mr. and Mrs. Edward Russell. (See Whitney Ancestry No. 4.)

Twenty generations in direct descent from children of Asa Russell and Almira Eudora (Phelps) Russell to Sir Eustace, of Whitney, son of Robert, of Whitney.

SEYMOUR

Arms—Gules, a pair of wings conjoined in lure or.
Crest—A pair of wings conjoined, the dester or, the sinister gules, surmounted by a ducal coronet per pale counterchanged.

The surname Seymour is usually a variation of St. Maur, originated from a commune of that name in Normandy; probably that in the Department of del 'Oise, Arrondissement Beauvais, though perhaps St. Maur des Bois, in Department de la Manche. Henry de Sancto Mauro is in the Hundred Rolls of Oxfordshire, A. D. 1273; Henry de St. Maur in Writs of Parliament about 1300; and Elizabeth Seyntmaur in Calendarium Inquisitionum post mortem. Camden and others agree that the St. Maur Family entered England during the reign of William the Conqueror, but the earliest and most certain information concerning this family and the place of their residence is given by Camden in his "Britannia" (in Monmouthshire) in these words: "Not far from Coldecot are Woundy and Penhow, the seats formerly of the illustrious family of St. Maur, now called Seymour." About 1235-40 Gilbert Marshall, fourth Earl of Pembroke, and William St. Maur decided to wrest Woundy (or Undy) out of the hands of the Welsh Morgan of Howell, Lord of Caerleon, They agreed that when they had acquired the manor they should divide it equally between them; that the Earl should pay William St. Maur lbs. 10 of the whole manorial rent, but that St. Maur should remain in possession. He had already assured his position in the country by marrying the third daughter of William Marshall, first Earl of Pembroke, of the second creation. St. Maur enlarged the Castle of Penhow, his manorial residence, and the old tower of the castle stands, with some alterations, as it was first built by William St. Maur.

1. WILLIAM ST. MAUR had two sons: *William,* the older, living in 1270, became Lord of Penhow; *Roger,* the younger, held Undy, but as William presumably d. childless, Roger's family came also into possession of Penhow.
2. ROGER ST. MAUR, son of William St. Maur, senior, had a son, *Roger.*
3. ROGER ST. MAUR, son of Roger St. Maur, was holding both Penhow and Undy in 1314. He m. Joan, dau. of one of the Damarels, of Devonshire, leaving two sons: *John,* the elder, held Penhow and d. in 1385, leaving a son, Roger, ae. 18; but his only dau., Isabel, m. about 1382, John Bowler, or Bowlay, and carried Penhow castle into the Bowlay Family.

4. ·SIR ROGER ST. MAUR, or SEYMOUR, younger son of Roger and Joan (Damarel) St. Maur, left Monmouthshire, which was not formally transferred from Wales to England until the reign of Charles II and settled at Even Swindon in Wiltshire. He m. Cecily, dau. of John de Beauchamp, third Lord of Beauchamp, of Hache, in Somersetshire. (See Beauchamp VII.) This marriage brought him into union with one of the most noble and wealthy families in the Kingdom, and in 1363, on the death of her brother John, without heirs, Cecily became coheiress, with her sister, to all the Beauchamp estates. Sir Roger and Cecily had five children, descended not only from the Marshalls, Earls of Pembroke, by both parents, but by their mother, from Ferrars, Earls of Derby.

5. ·WILLIAM ST. MAUR, or SEYMOUR, elder son of Roger and Cecily (Beauchamp) St. Maur, m. Margaret, dau. of Simon de Brockburn, and lived for the most part at Undy. He d. in 1390, before his mother.

6. ·ROGER SEYMOUR (Harleian MSS. calls him Sir John), (note change in spelling of name), son of William, inherited his father's estate, and also the property of his grandmother, Cecily, on her death in 1383. He was b. in 1366, and d. in 1420. He m. Maud, dau. and coheiress of William Esturmy, Lord of Wolf Hall in Wiltshire, the fearless Speaker of the House of Commons, best known as the leader of the Layman's Parliament of 1405.

7. ·JOHN SEYMOUR, son of Roger and Maud (Esturmy) Seymour, became sheriff of Southampton, and held many important offices in Wiltshire, including that of sheriff. He m., in 1424, Isabel Williams, dau. of Mark Williams, of Bristol. He d. in 1464.

8. JOHN SEYMOUR, son of John and Isabel (Williams) Seymour, m. Elizabeth Coker, dau. of Robert Coker, of Lydiard, St. Lawrence, in Somersetshire, and d. in 1463; leaving sons, *Sir John* and *Humphrey*, the former being grandfather of Edward, first Duke of Somerset, and of Lady Jane Seymour, third wife of King Henry VIII.

9. ·HUMPHREY SEYMOUR, son of John and Elizabeth (Coker) Seymour, and Lord of Even Swindon, m. Elizabeth, dau. and coheiress of Thomas Winselowe, Esq., of Burton, in Oxfordshire. (See Winslow 4.)

Mary-Elizabeth L. Rixford and Oscar Theodore Rixford are 25th in direct descent from William St. Maur (1).

DE SPINETO

Arms—Sable, a chevron argent between three crescents or.

The surname de Spineto originated in a village or manor in Warwickshire, and is the Latinized form of its English name, Spine, and appears on record in 1282, by intermarriage with the coheir of Coughton, anciently Cocton.

1. ·WILLIAM DE SPINETO, m. Johanna, dau. and coheiress of Simon de Cocton, Knight, and Constantia, dau. of William de Parcọ. They had two sons : *Roger;* and *William,* of whom further.

2. ·WILLIAM DE SPINETO, son of William and Constantia (de Cocton) de Spineto, was Lord of Cocton and had two sons : *Nicholas;* and *William,* of whom further.

3. ·WILLIAM DE SPINETO, son of William de Spineto, held, in 1317, the half-knight's fee in this manor of Cocton, from Guy de Beauchamp, Earl of Warwick, and d. in 1318. He m., and had a son, *William.*

4. ·WILLIAM DE SPINETO, son of William de Spineto, had various notable offices in the county, and bore the arms heretofore described. He m., and among his children was Sir Guido, or Guy, of whom further.
5. SIR GUIDO, or GUY, DE SPINETO, son of Sir William de Spineto, succeeded as Lord of Coughton. He m., and had two daus.
6. ·ELEANOR DE SPINETO, dau. and coheiress of Sir Guido, or Guy, de Spineto, m. John, son of Thomas and Agnes (Besford) Throckmorton. (See Throckmorton 3-4, and Winslow No. 3.)

Mary-Elizabeth L. Rixford and Oscar Theodore Rixford are 19th in direct descent to William de Spineto (1).

SMITH AND GEORGES FAMILY

"Fairbanks Heraldry": Gorges, a greyhound's head (erased), or, collared, gu. Pl. 43, cr. 11.
Smiths, Yorks: Out of a ducal coronet, or, a boar's head, az., tusked and crined, of the second langued, gu. Pl. 102, cr. 14.

· SIR ARTHUR GORGES, Chelsea; Knighted 1597; died 1625. He built a house on the site of (Stanley house) for his residence. "As Queen Elizabeth passed the faire new building, Sir Arthur Gorges presented her with a faire jewell." Sidney papers, letter from Roland White to Sir Robert Sidney, November 15, 1599. Sir Arthur was the intimate friend of Spencer, who made a beautiful elegy on the first Lady Gorges, daughter of Viscount Bindon, who died 1590, entitled "Daphnaida," and her husband is meant by Alcyon, Sir Arthur's second wife was Lady Elizabeth, daughter of Henry, Earl of Lincoln, by which marriage he became Lord Chancellor, possessed of Sir Thomas Moors House, which in 1619 he conveyed to Lionel, Lord Cranfield. He left by his second wife six chidlren, *viz.*: Arthur (1), first son and heir, age then 25 (1625); Timeleon (2); Egremont (3); Carew (4); Henry (5); Elizabeth (6).— No. 18, N. H. G. R., age 120—Sir Arthur Gorges married Elizabeth daughter of the Earl of Lincoln.
· Elizabeth, 6th child, married Sir Henry Smith and came to New England, 1630.

SMITH FAMILY TO EPHRAIM SMITH READ

· Sir Henry Smith (son of Sir Hugh Smith, of Ashton, Somerset, England) with his wife Elizabeth Gorges came to New England, 1630, as chaplain in charge of fleet with Governor Winthrop. (See "Compendium of American Genealogy," Vol. III, page 683.)
Rev. Henry[1] Smith was born in England. Some say he was the son of Robert Smith of London, while others claim he was the son of Erasmus Smith, born about 1540, at Whitcock; died 1616; m. 1576 his second wife, Marjery (Cecil) Cave, widow of Roger Cave, daughter of Wm. Cecil, Lord Burleigh, Lord High Treasurer of Queen Elizabeth. He came to Watertown, Mass., removed to

Wethersfield, Conn., and became the first settled pastor of the church there in 1636. He married first in England, but we know nothing about his wife. He married second, Dorothy, who after his death, married John Russell, father of Rev. John Russell, who succeeded Henry Smith as minister at Wethersfield. They moved to Hadley, Mass., where she died in 1694. Henry Smith was appointed by Governor Winthrop a member of the General Court of Connecticut in 1636. He was a soldier in the Pequot War, 1637. He died August 9, 1648. (See "Bassett Preston Ancestry," page 257.)

Thomas Watson, Esq., one of the principal secretaries to our most dread Sovereign, Lady Queen Elizabeth and of her Highness most Honorable Privy Council, May 18, 23 Eliz., proved July 19, 1582. Buried without any charge my good and loving friend Sir Francis Washington, Knight, brother-in-law, Sir William Winter, Knight, and Matthew Smith, Esq., my cousin. (See "Genealogical Gleanings in England," Vol. I, page 854.)

SIR HENRY SMITH

Sir Hugh Smith, of Ashton, Somerset, England.

Sir Henry Smith, son of Sir Hugh, with his wife Elizabeth Gorges, came to New England, 1630, as chaplain in charge of fleet with Governor Winthrop.

Smith, Matthew 3, 4, 5.

Ralph 1. Inhabitant 1636.

Henry 2. Married Dorothy ———; both admitted church July 10, 1637; perhaps he was the Rev. Henry, of Wethersfield, and probably was the same Henry who embarked in the *Elizabeth* with wife Dorothy, aged 45; daughter Mary, aged 15; and son John, aged 12, 1635.

Matthew 3. Probably the same who embarked at Sandwich, County Kent, with wife Jane and four children, 1635; shoemaker; inhabitant, 1637, Charlestown, Mass., with his son Matthew, herdsman, 1649 and 1655; town crier, 1657; aged about 72, 1682. Estate—Had grant of house-plot and four acres beyond Menotomy.

Matthew 4. Son of Matthew 3; admitted church 1 (5) 1643; town crier 1 (11), 1648-9; married (2) Alice Loader (3), July 14, 1655 or 1665. Issue:

I. Elizabeth, b. Sept. 15, 1658; m. Humphrey Miller (24).
II. Matthew, b. Sept. 2, 1659, at Woburn. Besides others.

Estate—On the list, 1680-1; taxes, 1688. Sells. (See "Charlestown Genealogies and Estates," by Wyman, K-Z, page 622, Loader, John 1, m. Elizabeth ———. Issue: John, b. May 20, 1689. John 2 [Loder], m. Mary Ann Goodwin. Alex 3, m. Matthew Smith [4],

1665.) ("King Philip's War," page 132—Captain Loader, Commander on a Voyage to Jamaica, Oct. 2, 1691.)

1. SIR HUGH SMITH, of Ashton, Somerset, England.
2. HENRY SMITH, m. in England, Dorothy ———; both admitted church July 10, 1637.
3. MATTHEW SMITH, b. in England; m. in England, Jane ———.
4. MATTHEW SMITH, b. in England; d. probably in Woburn, Mass.; m. (2) Alice Loader.
5. MATTHEW SMITH, b. Sept. 2, 1659, son of Matthew and Alice (Loader) Smith; m. Mar. 2, 1682 or June 20, 1684, probably at Woburn, Mass., Mary Cutler, b. Mar. 5, 1663.
6. ELIZABETH SMITH, dau. of Matthew and Mary (Cutler) Smith; m. Thomas Hungerford, who was b. about 1673, and d. 1750.
7. SAMUEL HUNGERFORD, b. about 1713; d. 1790; m. 1746, probably at New Fairfield, Conn., Mary Graves, b. probably Aug. 20, 1722.
8. ISAIAH HUNGERFORD, b. Jan. 23, 1757; d. June 16, 1833; m. at New Fairfield, Conn., Esther Mead, b. Aug. 11, 1760; d. Dec. 22, 1836.
9. ELIZABETH HUNGERFORD, b. Feb. 7, 1798; d. Jan. 7, 1878; m. Apr. 29, 1821, at St. Armand West, Que., Nash David Phelps, b. Oct. 4, 1796; d. Apr. 15, 1884.
10. CAROLINE ALEXANDRIA PHELPS, b. July 3, 1840; d. Mar. 29, 1921; m. Sept. 8, 1863, at Stanbridge, Que., Horace Brayton Leach, b. Sept. 25, 1836; d. Mary 5, 1919.
11. ALBERTA LOUISA LEACH, b. at Bakersfield, Vt., July 27, 1868; d. at East Fairfield, Vt., May 31, 1904; m. at Fairfield, Oct. 21, 1891, Charles J. Read, b. Oct. 31, 1866, at East Fairfield; living Jan. 1, 1932. Children (surname Read) b. at East Fairfield:
    1. *Ephraim Smith*, b. Aug. 8, 1902. Graduate of Fellers Institute; supt. Fletcher Schools, two years.
    2. *Henrietta Frankie*, b. Aug. 2, 1902; m. Howard Buker. Children:
        (1) Stella Frankie Buker.
        (2) Elizabeth May Buker, b. Apr. 15, ———.
        All living Jan. 1, 1932.
12. EPHRAIM SMITH READ, b. Aug. 8, 1901; attended school at Brigham Academy; m. 1924, Frances Maynard, b. Aug. 17, 1898, a graduate of University of Vermont, dau. of Frank and Martha (Davis) Maynard. Children:
    1. *Charles Richard Read*, b. Feb. 23, 1924, Jeffersonville, Vt.
    2. *Alberta Martha Read*, b. 1925, Jeffersonville, Vt.
    3. *David Maynard Read*, Jeffersonville, Vt.
    4. *Robert Frank Read*, Jeffersonville, Vt.

SMITH GENEALOGY

Mrs. Sophia (Smith) Martin, of Hartford, Conn.

(Page 3—Introduction) In the old records the name is spelled Smith, Smithe, Smeith and Smyth. It is one of the very oldest surnames, giving precedence to none, unless it be King.

There is no doubt that the ancestors were of English origin, and the Matthew which I have designated as 1st came to America from England, in 1637, and in direct descent there appear nine by that name alone, the ninth dying unmarried.

FIRST GENERATION

(Pages 5, 6 and 7) MATTHEW SMITH, a cordwainer (a shoe maker), came from Sandwich, County of Kent, England, in 1637, with his wife Jane and four children, and was said to have been admitted inhabitant of Charlestown, Mass., the same year. His wife became a member of the church October 22, 1639, and he in May, 1643. The names of the children could not be ascertàined. In 1658, he was a householder, under the title of Good-man. The time of the death of Matthew and Jane does not appear. ("The Planters of the Commonwealth," by Banks, page 190—Came in the *Hercules,* Matthew Smith, of Sandwich, cordwainer, Charlestown; Mrs. Jane Smith, Matthew Smith, —— Smith, —— Smith, —— Smith.) ("Charlestown Genealogies and Estates," page 871—Shoemaker and inhabitant, 1637. His son Matthew, herdsman; town crier, 1657.)

SECOND GENERATION

MATTHEW SMITH, of Woburn, Mass., undoubtedly son of Matthew, of Charlestown, Mass., was born in England, and had seven children.
Children:

I.   ELIZA, b. Sept. 15, 1658.
II.   MATTHEW, b. Sept. 2, 1659.
III.   JOHN, b. June 16, 1661; and d. young.
IV.   SAMUEL, b. Apr. 29, 1662; and d. young.
V.   SAMUEL, b. July 26, 1663.
VI.   HANNAH, b. Oct. 21, 1664.
VII.   JOHN, b. Mar. 28, 1667.

THIRD GENERATION

MATTHEW 3RD, son of Matthew 2nd, grandson of Matthew 1st, born September 2, 1659; married March 2, 1682, or June 20, 1684, Mary Cutler (daughter of Jòhn Cutler), who was born March 5, 1663, in Woburn, Mass., and had at least four children.
Children:

I.   MATTHEW, b. in 1684, in Lyme, Conn.
II.   THOMAS.
III.   MARY.
IV.   ELIZABETH.

Matthew and Thomas settled at Mt. Parnassus, in the central part of East Haddam, Conn., about 1706, each receiving a deed of a tract of land of Rev. Stephen Hosmer, bearing date October 14, 1708, which was the beginning of the "Smith Homestead." Thomas, in 1708 or 1709, enlisted to go on an expedition to Albany, N. Y., to make the quota of Connecticut, 350 men, required for the reduction of the French. Ninety of the number never returned, Thomas being one of them.

Elizabeth married Thomas Hungerford, and lived on a farm by the Eight Mile River, in East Haddam, Conn. Mary was unmarried, as appears by the following agreement: COPY—

"Be it known to all to whom it may concern:—We, Thomas Hungerford, and Elizabeth Hungerford, my wife, and Mary Smith, all of Haddam, on the east side of the great river, in ye County of Hartford and colony of Connecticut, for ourselves, our heirs, executors, administrators and assigns, do hereby mutually agree with our loving brother, Matthew Smith, of the town and county aforesaid, concerning ye distribution of ye estate of our brother, Thomas Smith, late of said Haddam, deceased, that is to say, he, the said Matthew Smith, is to pay all the just debts due from said estate, and to enjoy the lands belonging to ye estate of ye said Thomas Smith, his heirs and assigns forever: the remainder of the estate to be divided after the following method: Ye said Matthew Smith is to have one undivided for half part of the movables to his own proper use and behoof forever: ye said Thomas and Elizabeth Hungerford and said Mary Smith are to have the other half of ye movable estate of ye said Thomas Smith, deceased, equally divided between them, upon the receipt whereof we, the said Thomas Hungerford, Elizabeth my wife, and Mary Smith, do hereby engage fully and wholly to acquit and discharge ye said Matthew Smith, his heirs and assigns forever; and, whereas the said Thomas Smith was out in the late expedition to Albany, the said Matthew Smith is to take care to get his wages, and it is to be divided in the same manner with the rest of ye movables, they all bearing an equal share in the charges.

In witness whereof, we, the said parties above named, have hereunto set our hands, this 25th day of November, A. D. 1709.

his
THOMAS X HUNGERFORD.
mark.
ELIZABETH HUNGERFORD.
her
MARY X SMITH.
mark.
MATTHEW SMITH.

Witnesses:—JOHN BOODGE, WILLIAM SPENCER."

STANLEY FAMILY

Stanley

The English family.—In the County of Stafford, in the heart of England, there was in very ancient times an old Saxon manor called STONELEY, a name compounded of Stone and Leah or Ley (modern, lea), meaning a stony meadow or field. There is still in that county a considerable town named Stone, which very probably, like the former, may bear a remembrance of the rugged surface of what is now one of the chief mining districts of the island. At the time of the conquest, the estate belonged to Saxon Sir Henry de Stoneley, the place of his residence in that day supplying the surname of the owner.

Among the Norman knights who accompanied William the Bastard into England in 1066, were Adam de Alditheley and his two sons, Lydulph and Adam. These received, as did others of William's associates, large possessions from the conquered lands as a reward for their services. Lydulph, the elder son, had a son Adam, and Adam, the younger, had a son William. These two young Normans, Adam and William, both married wives of the Saxon family De Stoneley.

Adam de Alditheley married Mabella, daughter of Sir Henry de Stoneley, and received with her as her marriage portion the two adjacent estates of Stoneley and Balterley. They were ancestors of the noble family of Audley, so called by a shortening of their name from Alditheley to Aldethley and Audley.

William de Alditheley married Joan, daughter of Thomas de Stoneley, a kinsman of Sir Henry, and received with her as a dowry the manor of Thalk, in the same county. Afterwards he exchanged this estate with his cousin Adam for Stoneley and half of Balterley, and made Stoneley his family residence; and in honor of his lady, and the great antiquity of her family, of noble Saxon descent, who flourished many years before the conquest, he assumed the surname of Stanley, and became the recognized founder of the Stanley family. This was in the reign of Henry I, A. D. 1100-1135.

The ancestral line of the Stanley Family may be summarized through to the early English ancestors as follows:

1. SIR WILLIAM DE (ALDITHELEY) STANLEY, who m. Joan de Stoneley, and had
2. SIR WILLIAM STANLEY, who had *John*, d. childless, and *Adam*.
3. SIR ADAM STANLEY, had
4. SIR WILLIAM STANLEY, who m. Joan de Bamvile, eldest dau. of Sir Philip de Bamvile, heiress of Stourton, by which alliance he became possessed of the manor and bailiwick of Wyrral Forest, near Chester, and thereupon assumed the armorial bearings since used by all branches of the family, *viz.*, three stags' heads, or, on a bend, az. They had a dau.; son *John*, of Stourton; and son *Adam*.
5. SIR JOHN STANLEY, Lord of Stourton, etc., m. Mabella Hausket, dau. of Sir James Hausket. They had *William*, of Stourton, and another son *John*, of Greswithin.
6. SIR WILLIAM STANLEY, Lord of Stourton, etc., m. Alice, dau. of Hugh Masey, of Timperley. They had a dau.; son *William*, of Hooton; son *John*, Lord-Deputy of Ireland; *Henry*.
7. SIR JOHN STANLEY, of Greswithin, Cumberland County, was a member of Parliament for Carlisle in the time of Edward III, A. D. 1347. The line of succession in this family as descended from him was as follows (I give little more than the bare names):
8. JOHN STANLEY, of Greswithin.
9. NICHOLAS STANLEY, 1345.
10. THOMAS STANLEY, 1431.
11. JOHN STANLEY, of Hallthwaytes.
12. WILLIAM STANLEY.
13. THOMAS STANLEY, of Hallthwaytes.
14. JOHN STANLEY.
15. WILLIAM STANLEY.
16. ROGER STANLEY.
17. JOHN STANLEY, of Arnaby, County of Cumberland, who had sons, *Christopher Thomas*, d. childless; *Richard*, who m. the widow of Doctor Burcott, who had before m. his brother Thomas, Richard was of Fittleworth, Sussex County.
18. CHRISTOPHER STANLEY, captain in Boston Militia, b. 1603; d. 1646. He m. Susanna ———, who d. probably in Boston. She was b. 1604 in England.
19. ZECHARIAH FIELD, b. in England, came to America in 1629. He d. in June, 1666; m. Mary, dau. of Christopher Stanley, of Boston.
20. SAMUEL FIELD, b. about 1651; d. June 24, 1697; m. in Hatfield, Mass., Aug. 9, 1679, Sarah Gilbert, b. Feb. 19, 1655-6; d. Feb. 4, 1712.
21. EBENEZER FIELD, b. Mar. 17, 1687-8; d. Sept. 12, 1723; m. in 1714, Elizabeth Arms, b. about 1695; d. Oct. 1, 1772-7.
22. AARON FIELD, b. Mar. 17, 1721-2; d. Mar. 17, 1800; m. May 26, 1743, in Deerfield, Mass., Eunice Frary, b. Nov. 30, 1721; d. Oct. 28, 1813.
23. SAMUEL SHATTUCK, b. Sept. 18, 1741; d. Sept. 1, 1827; m. Nov., 1764, in Greenfield, Mass., Chloe Field, b. Dec. 29, 1743; d. Apr. 10, 1781.
24. EPHRAIM LEACH, b. Dec., 1761; d. Feb. 28, 1840; m. Nov. 17, 1785, probably in Greenfield, Mass., Chloe Shattuck, b. Nov. 22, 1766; d. Jan. 22, 1845.
25. TERTIUS LEACH, b. Nov. 21, 1786; d. Feb. 4, 1864; m. Sheldon, Vt., Jan. 1, 1812, Sophia Hawley, b. Aug. 17, 1795; d. Jan. 7, 1879.
26. TERTIUS HAWLEY LEACH, b. Mar. 19, 1813; d. Sept. 19, 1881; m. Sheldon, Vt., Feb. 28, 1835, Orissa Fanton, b. May 1, 1812; d. June 24, 1890.
27. HORACE BRAYTON LEACH, b. Sept. 25, 1836; d. May 5, 1919; m. at Stanbridge, Que., Sept. 8, 1863, Caroline Alexandria Phelps, b. July 3, 1840; d. Mar. 29, 1921.

28. OSCAR HERBERT RIXFORD, b. Dec. 27, 1859; d. Sept. 11, 1927; m. Sept. 8, 1889, at Sheldon, Vt., Elizabeth May Leach, b. Jan. 7, 1866; living May 6, 1931.

29. OSCAR ADELBERT RIXFORD, b. Aug. 4, 1890; living May 6, 1931; m. at Montreal, Que., Mary Caroline Hefflon, b. June 6, 1899; living May 6, 1931. Children:
    Mary-Elizabeth Lenora, b. Oct. 6, 1922; living May 6, 1931.
    Oscar Theodore, b. July 21, 1925; living May 6, 1931.

References: "Stanley Family," 1887, pages 8, 9, 10 and 11.
            1 to 23 generations—Records of Elizabeth M. Rixford—"D. A. C. Lineage Book," 1931, page 30.
            23 to 25 generations—"Thomas Hungerford Genealogy" and "Leach Family Genealogy," by F. Phelps Leach.
            26 to 29 generations—Family Record.

SERVICES

Capt. Christopher Stanley was a captain of Boston Militia; member of the Ancient and Honorable Artillery Company of Mass., 1640.

References: "History of the A. and H. A. Co.," Roberts, Vol. 1, page 110.
            "Savage's Gen. Dict.," Vol. 4, page 164.
            "Year Book, Society of Colonial Wars," 1897-8, page 55.
            See "D. A. C. Lineage Book," 1931, page 30.

THROCKMORTON

Arms—Gules, on a chevron argent three bars gemel sable.

Throckmorton

From Throckmorton Chapelry in Fladbury Parish, Worcestershire, the surname Throckmorton originated. Lower quotes from Shirley's "Noble and Gentle Men," "John de Trockmerton was dwelling there about the year 1200."

1. JOHN THROCKMORTON, Lord of Throckmorton in 1339, m. Agnes, or Anne, dau. and heiress of Sir Richard Abberbury, of Abberbury, in Oxfordshire.

2. THOMAS THROCKMORTON, son of John and Agnes (Abberbury) Throckmorton, was of the retinue of Thomas Beauchamp, Earl of Warwick in 1397, escheator of Worcestershire in 1042, and constable of Elmley Castle in 1405. He m. Agnes Besford, an heiress.

3. JOHN THROCKMORTON, son and heir of Thomas and Agnes (Besford) Throckmorton, made a distinguished figure in the reigns of Henry V and Henry VI, and in the latter reign bore the title of Under Treasurer of England. He d. in 1452. He m. Eleanor, dau. and coheiress of Sir Guido, or Guy de Spineto, Lord of Coughton, in Warwickshire. (See de Spineton VI.) Children:
   1. *Thomas*, ancestor of the present Baronet of Coughton.
   2. *John*, m. Isabel Breges, and gained estates in County Gloucester.
   3. *Eleanor*, m. Richard Knightly, of Fawsley, County Northampton.
   4. *Maud*, m. Sir Thomas Green, of Norton, County Northampton.
   5. *Margaret*, m. John Rous, Esq.
   6. *Agnes*, of whom further.
   7. *Elizabeth*, m. Robert Russell, Esq.

4. AGNES THROCKMORTON, fourth dau. of John and Eleanor (de Spineto) Throckmorton, m. John Winselowe, or Winslow, Esq. (See Winslow English Pedigree 3.)

Mary-Elizabeth L. Rixford and Oscar Theodore Rixford are 21st in direct descent from John Throckmorton, Lord of Throckmorton in 1339. (1.)

TAILLEFER

("Colonial Families," 1928, page 112)

Arms—Azure, six bendlets indented argent.

Taillefer was the surname of a bard and warrior of the eleventh century, who accompanied the Norman army to England in 1066, and obtained permission from William to strike the first blow at the Battle of Hastings. He fought valiantly and was killed in the battle. Some of his valorous deeds are depicted on the Bayeux tapestry. The family were early Counts of Angouleme. (See Angouleme.) The Taillefer mentioned above was William, son of Geoffrey, fourth in the pedigree given below.

1. WILLIAM TAILLEFER succeeded Aldwin as Count of Angouleme. He was succeded by his son Armand. (See Angouleme II.)
2. ARMAND TAILLEFER, son of William Taillefer, was Count of Angouleme. He m. Hildegarde.
3. WILLIAM TAILLEFER, Count of Angouleme, who is said to have built the Chateau de Taillefer, d. in 1028. He m. Girberge or Gilbergue, dau. of the Count of Anjou.
4. GEOFFREY TAILLEFER, son of William Taillefer, d. in 1040. He m. Petronille d'Archiac. Children:
   1. *William*, called Chassard or Le Chauser. He accompanied William the Conquerer to England and was given permission to strike the first blow at the Battle of Hastings. He was killed in that battle.
   2. *Foulques*, of whom further.
5. FOULQUES TAILLEFER, Count of Angouleme, was living in 1089. He m. Condo.
6. WILLIAM TAILLEFER, son of Foulques Taillefer, Count of Angouleme, d. in 1130. He m. ——— de Vitapoi.

7. WILLIAM TAILLEFER, Count of Angouleme, d. in 1178. He m. (1) Emma, surname unknown; m. (2) Margareta, surname unknown.
8. ADOMAR (or AYMER) TAILLEFER, son of William Taillefer, by his first wife, was Count of Angouleme. He m. Alix, surname unknown.
9. ISABELLA TAILLEFER, dau. of Adomar (or Aymer) Taillefer, m. King John of England. (See Royal Descent No. 24.)

Mary-Elizabeth L. Rixford and Oscar Theodore Rixford are 33rd in direct descent from (1) William Taillefer.

VERMANDOIS

Arms—Chequy azure and or, on a chief of the first three fleurs-de-lis of the second.

From Vermand, a county named from its capital in Picardy, now Department Aisne in northeastern France, seat of the Veromandui, of Roman times, the surname or title de Vermandois originated. The house of Vermandois is one of the most ancient and famous of the early French noble houses, and is descended in direct male line from the Emperor Charlemagne. The records of the counts go back to Herbert, grandson of Bernard of Italy. From 1045 to 1083, the counts possessed also the Valois. In 1102, Raoul de Vermandois was the reigning count, probably son of Hugh de Vermandois. Hugh the Great, Earl of Vermandois, was one of the leaders of the First Crusade and died at Tarsus in Cilicia in 1102.

1. HUGH, son of Henry I, King of France, and Anne, of Russia, was m. to Adela, dau. and heiress of Herbert, fourth Earl of Vermandois, and through her right became fifth Earl of Vermandois. (See House of Capet VI, and Warren Pedigree B, VII.)
2. ELIZABETH (sometimes recorded Isabel), dau. of Hugh, Earl of Vermandois, and of Adela, his wife, m. William (3) de Warren, second Earl of Surrey. (See Warren 6 and Warren Pedigree B, No. 8 and Stanley 11.)
Claude Clesson Macy, m. Aug. 22, 1897, Edith Alice Leach, dau. of F. Phelps Leach, 29th in direct descent from Henry I, King of France. She has three children:
    1. *Fern Alice Macy*, b. July 13, 1918.
    2. *Keith Sherwood Macy*, Beverly.
    3. *A dau.*, d. young.
Mrs. Macy was a graduate of Franklin High School. She taught school until 1919.

WARREN

Arms—Chequy or and azure.

𝕸𝖆𝖗𝖗𝖊𝖓

Warren family history is exceeded in interest and antiquity by that of no ancient English house. The surname is of Norman-French origin, and is derived from Gareme or Garrenne, a small river in the old County of Calais or Caux, in Normandy, which gave its name to the neighboring commune. There is at present a village called Garenne in the same district, and it is here that the origin of the family has been fixed by historians. The ancient baronial seat of the de Warrenes stood on the west side of the River Garrenne, and as late as the year 1832 some of the ruins were standing. The surname has assumed different forms from time to time—Gareyn, Warreyn, Waryn, Warin, Waring, Warynge, Warying, and Warren. It first appears in England with William the Conqueror, to whom he was related both by marriage and common ancestry. An ancient genealogy of the family traces the lineage of this William de Warren back to A. D. 900, when his Scandinavian ancestors are said to have settled in Normandy. The Scandinavian origin of the Norman family is acceded by eminent genealogists, and is embodied in the pedigree of the English house as drawn up by W. Flower, "Norroy, King of Arms," and R. Glover, "Somerset Herald," of England, in 1580. The following account of the early family is taken from the work of the late Rev. Dr. Israel Perkins Warren, of Portland, Me.:

The family of Warren has been traced by English writers to a Norman baron of Danish extraction. The Normans and Danes were united in their efforts to make a settlement in the northern part of France and ultimately succeeded in obtaining a footing in that part of the country from which the Normans took the name of Normandy. One of these barons became connected by marriage with considerable families, as is related in the following account of an English author:

The Danish knight had Gunnora, Herfastus, Wevia, Werina, Duvelina, and Sainfra. Of these, Gunnora married Richard, Duke of Normandy, who had Richard, the father also of Richard, who dying without issue was succeeded in the dukedom by his brother Robert, the father of William the Conqueror, who by Maud, daughter of Baldwin, Earl of Flanders, had Robert, Duke of Normandy; Richard, Duke of Bernay, in Normandy; William, King of England; Henry, King of England; and several daughters, one of whom, Gundred, was married to William, the first Earl of Warren and Surrey. Werina, according to a large pedigree drawn up and signed by W. Flower, "Norroy," and R. Glover, "Somerset Herald," in 1580, married Asmundde Commitiis villa . . . Gundred, wife of William, first Earl of Warren and Surrey, in England, was a descendant of Charlemagne, and the fourth daughter of William the Conqueror and his wife Maud, daughter of Baldwin, Earl of Flanders. We may, therefore, believe that William de Warrenne was one of the principal and confidential auxiliaries of William, from whom he had received the title of Earl before coming to England. He took an important part in the Battle of Hastings, A. D. 1066, and in payment for his services, which were evidently highly estimated by the Conqueror, received immense land grants. He is mentioned in the Domesday Book as possessing lands in almost every county in England, comprising in all, according to Hume, three hundred lordships. He had lands in Shropshire, Essex, Suffolk, Oxford, Hants, Cambridgeshire, Bucks, Huntington, Bedfordshire, Norfolk, Lincoln, and York. He selected his residence in the village of Lewes, County Surrey, and there erected his beautiful castle, the ruins of which are still to be seen standing on an eminence surrounding the town. Although the principal parts are demolished, its gates are still standing, showing the massive construction. William, Earl of Warren and Surrey, and his wife Gundred, erected the priory in the town of Lewes, and he continued his benefactions to it during his life. Gundred died on May 27, 1085, and was buried in the chapter house of the Priory of Lewes, County Surrey. Her tombstone is still in existence. William died June 24, 1088. His epitaph is still in existence, although the gravestone is lost or destroyed. In 1845 the coffers containing the bones of the Earl and Countess were disinterred and are now in the Church of St. John the Baptist, Southover.

Between William, first Earl of Warren and Surrey, and Richard Warren, of the *Mayflower,* the American progenitor, seventeen generations elapse.

THE WARREN PEDIGREE

Showing the alliances with Gundred, daughter of William the Conqueror, and Isabel, member of the noble French house of Vermandois.

1. A DANISH KNIGHT, the progenitor, was among those who succeeded in obtaining a footing in Normandy, and became allied through marriage with some of the foremost families of noble lineage in Europe. He was the father of:

   1. *Gunnora.*
   2. *Herfastus,* mentioned below.
   3. *Wevia.*
   4. *Werina.*
   5. *Duvelina.*
   6. *Sainfra.*

2. HERFASTUS, son of the progenitor.

3. A DAUGHTER, who m. Walter de Saint Martin.

4. WILLIAM DE WARREN, Earl of Warren, in Normandy, m. a dau. of Ralph de Torta.

5. WILLIAM (2) DE WARREN, son of William (1) de Warren, m. Gundred, dau. of William the Conqueror, and became the first Earl of Warren and Surrey, in England. (See William the Conqueror II.)

6. WILLIAM (3) DE WARREN, son of William (2) de Warren and Gundred, dau. of the Conqueror, succeeded his father in his title and lands, and became the second Earl of Warren and Surrey. He m. Isabel (sometimes recorded as Elizabeth), dau. of the fifth Earl of Vermandois, in France. (See Vermandois II and Pedigree B VIII.)

7. REGINALD WARREN, son of William (3) de Warren and Isabel, his wife, m. Adelia, dau. of Roger de Mowbray. (See Mowbray VII.)

8. WILLIAM (4) WARREN, only son and heir of Reginald and Adelia (de Mowbray) Warren, m. Isabel, daughter of William Heydon, Knight. (See Heydon IX.)

9. SIR JOHN WARREN, only son and heir of William (4) and Isabel (Heydon) Warren, m. Alice, dau. of Roger Townsend, Esquire.

10. JOHN (2) WARREN, son and heir of Sir John and Alice (Townsend) Warren, m. Joan, dau. of Sir Hugh de Port, Knight. (See Port V.)

11. SIR EDWARD WARREN, son of John (2) and Joan (de Port) Warren, m. Maud, dau. of Richard de Skeyton.

12. SIR EDWARD (2) WARREN, son of Sir Edward (1) and Maud (de Skeyton) Warren, m. Cicely, dau. of Nicholas de Eaton, Knight. (See Eaton III.)

13. SIR JOHN (3) WARREN, only son of Sir Edward (2) and Cicely (de Eaton) Warren, m. Agnes, dau. of Sir Richard de Wynnington, Knight. (See Wynnington II.)

14. SIR LAWRENCE WARREN, only son and heir of Sir John (3) and Agnes (de Wynnington) Warren, m. Margery, dau. of Hugh Bulkeley, of Ware, in Shropshire, the ancestor of the Bulkeleys of New England. (See Bulkeley IX.)

15. JOHN (4) WARREN, eldest son of Sir Lawrence and Margery (Bulkeley) Warren, m. Isabel, dau. of Sir John Stanley, Knight. (See Stanley 14.)
    Mary-Elizabeth L. Rixford and Oscar[4] Theodore Rixford, grandchildren of the Author, 34th generation from (1) A Danish Knight, founder of the Warren line.

16. SIR LAWRENCE WARREN, of Poynton, son of John (4) and Isabel (Stanley) Warren, m. Isabel, dau. of Robert Legh, Knight.

17. WILLIAM (5) WARREN,, seated at Caunton, in Nottinghamshire, m. Anne, surname unknown; he d. in May, 1496.

18. JOHN (5) WARREN, m. Elizabeth ———; and d. in 1525.

19. JOHN (6) WARREN, of Headborough, was of the parish of Ashbutton, in Devonshire.

20. CHRISTOPHER WARREN, of Headborough.

21. WILLIAM (6) WARREN, of Headborough, m. (1) Anne, dau. of Thomas Mablie, of Calstocke, in Cornwall; she m. (2) William Cutting, of Woodland, in Devonshire.

22. CHRISTOPHER WARREN, of Headborough, only son and heir of William (6) Warren, m. Alice, dau. of Thomas Webb, of Sidham, in Devonshire, and among their children was *Richard,* who was a prosperous mer-

chant of Greenwich, County Kent, England, and in 1620 sailed with the historic *Mayflower* Company which founded Plymouth, Mass.

23. RICHARD WARREN, of Greenwich, England, who came to New England in the *Mayflower,* in 1620, and participated in the fight with the Indians at the field of the first encounter. He m. Elizabeth Maych, in England, and had

24. SARAH WARREN, who m. John Cooke (son of Francis Cooke), Mar. 28, 1634, and had

25. MARY COOKE, who m. Philip Taber, and had

26. BETHIAH TABER, who m. John Macomber, and had

27. WILLIAM MACOMBER, who m. Lusanna Hicks, and had

28. PATIENCE MACOMBER, who m. James Soule, and had

29. JAMES SOULE, who m. Nancy Wellman, and had

30. JOHN J. SOULE, who m. Mary Ann MacLauren, and had

31. MARY ELIZABETH SOULE, who m. Vollie H. Griffith, Danby. Children: Caroline, Florence Mary, John B. and Elizabeth.

Mrs. Griffith is treasurer of the Vermont Society of Mayflower Descendants, charter member and registrar Highgate Colony New England Women, and town clerk of Danby for several years.

Mr. Albert Read, of Manchester, Vt., charter member, State No. 5, Gen. No. 2957; Mrs. Jacob P. Marshall, of New York, State No. 69, Gen. No. 10583; Mr. Owen Johnson, Manchester, N. H., State No. 78, Gen. No. 11011; Mrs. E. R. Campbell, State No. 99, Gen. No. 11671, members of the Vermont Society of Mayflower Descendants, are descended from Richard Warren of the *Mayflower,* who was 23rd in descent of William, first Earl of Warren; A Danish Knight.

WASHBURN FAMILY

WILLIAM, SONNE OF SAMPSON, LORD OF WASSEBOURNE

WASHBURNE

Burke in his "Commoners," III, pages 621-622, says:

"The Washbournes or Washbornes were generation after generation of knightly degree previous to the time of Edward I (1274-1307) and ranked in point of descent with the most ancient families of the kingdom."

"The Book of Family Crests," I, 54, speaks of the Washbournes as
"a name of Norman descent, the founder having been knighted on the field of battle by the Conqueror and endowed by him with the lands and manors of Great and Little Washbourne."

Dr. A. B. Grosart goes back further and speaks of the family as reaching back into the Saxon period in Edward the Confessor's time before the Conquest. Perhaps there is not so much contradiction in this as appears. At any rate, it would seem as if the Domesday Book should throw some light on such a question. But whether a family of Knights Washbourne can or cannot be found in the Domesday Book (1086-7) existent in Saxon times, it appears certain, from the antiquary Sir Thomas Habington's quotation from the Bishop of Worcester's Domesday Book (1108-18) that there were Washbournes or Wassebornes holding land in one of these villages as early as when its statistics were gathered, which, as we shall see, was very early. The quotation is as follows (Survey of Worcestershire c. 1640) :

"Where the Bishop of Worcester's Domesday Book beginneth '*Quatuor decem hides, ex hiis tenet Willielmus fillius Sampson in Wasseborne 3 hides g.* Theare are 14 hydes (in) that guild, of which William the sonne of Sampson holdeth 3 hydes in Washbourne, and Sampson of him.' Wheather the ancient family of Washborne is descended from this Sampson or not, I am vincertaine; for fewe of the englishe at thys tyme had surnames."

And again :

"You may read in Bredon (*i.e.,* in the Bishop's Domesday Book's account of Bredon, an adjoining parish), that William the sonne of Sampson was lord of thys Washborne in the raygne of Henry the second; but knowing not how to unyte them (*i.e.,* Sampson and William) to these (the later family of knights, Sir Roger and Sons) I omit them here" (in the account of Sir Roger's family).

The interesting point in this extract from the Bishop of Worcester's Domesday Book is, that if this William, Lord of Wassebourne, and his father, Sampson, were living and holding land at the time the "inquisitions" for this book were made, *viz.*, in 1108-18 and before, they were but only twenty or thirty years removed from the last years of William the Conqueror; and the father, Sampson, might well have been a subject of Edward the Confessor before 1066, and William may well have been holding his lands from the Conqueror's times, or even before. But no record of descendants of Sampson and William permits us to link them with the next family of de Wassebournes that comes into view from that village a little more than a century later. And hence they are not brought into the pedigree of that family with which hereafter we shall be concerned.

Summary of the ancestral line of the Washburn Family to the early English ancestors :

1. SIR ROGER DE WASSEBOURNE, Knight, b. about 1239 or before, and d. probably 1297. He had wife, Joan ———, and son, *John.*

2. SIR JOHN DE WASSEBORNE, Knight, before father's death called John de Dufford. He m. Isabella (Cassy or Kassy). They had one son, *Roger* the heir, and probably other children.
3. SIR ROGER was confirmed heir and entered on possession of the Washourne title and estates of his father in 1319. He m. in 1316, Margaret ———. They had two sons, both named *John.* The elder and heir m. Katharine Thromwin and d. without issue.
4. JOHN, as mentioned above, Roger had two sons named John. After the death of the first without issue "Roger, Lord of Washborne, Knight, did confirm to John his son in Ao. Ed. 3. 9" (1336) (College of Arms) the right of inheritance to his titles and estates, but he did not come into possession until 1358. John m. Isabelle ———, and had at least one son, Peter.
5. PETER, m. Isolde, dau. of Thomas Hanley, of Hanley-William in 29 Ed. III (1355) according to two pedigrees of the College of Arms. They had two sons, *John* and *William.* The date of Peter's death is not known.
6. JOHN, m. Jane Musard, dau. of John Musard, Knight, and Katherin (Thromwin), and after her death, about 1397, Margaret, dau. and coheir of John le Poher. By the first of these marriages he had a dau., *Isolde.* By the second marriage he had *Norman, John* and *Elynor.*
7. NORMAN, m. Elizabeth Knivton, dau. of Henry Knivton of an ancient Derbyshire family. She perhaps d. in 1454. He d. before 1479. He had several children: *John,* his heir; *Eleanor,* who d. in 1505; a dau. who m. John Vampage; *Elizabeth,* and a fourth dau., who m. John Hungerford, of Dixton, Gloucestershire.
8. JOHN, probably b. before 1454. He made his will May 3, 1517, and d. on the 6th following. John m. Joan Mitton, dau. of William Mitton, Lord of Weston, a village in Staffordshire. By her he had four sons: *Robert,* eldest and heir; *John,* the ancestor of the American Washburns, who migrated from Wichenford to Bengeworth, a suburb of the ancient town of Evesham; *Walter;* and *Francis,* who has not been traced. After the death of Joan Mitton, first wife, John m. Elizabeth, dau. of George Mornington, of Butters Co., Hereford. By her he had two sons, *Anthony* and *Richard,* and dau., *Ann.*
9. JOHN, m. Emme ———. She d. in 1547. They had children: *Katharine, Alix, John* and *William.* John's burial is recorded Jan. 8, 1546, and Emme's, May 13, 1547.
10. JOHN, son of John and Emme, m. (1) Jone Bushell, by whom he had son, *John.* She d. in 1556-7. He m. (2) May 8, 1561, Jone Whitehead who d. in 1567. John apparently m. a third wife before 1577-8, by whom he had three children: "*Radigone,* bapt. Feb. 21, 1578; *Daniell,* bapt. June 17, 1582; and *Mary,* dau. of John Washborn, bapt. Dec. 7, 1584."
11. JOHN, son of John and Jone Bushell, m. July 6, 1596, Martha Stephens and had at least two sons, one dau., who m. Isaacke Averell, and *Jane,* who probably d. unm. Will dated Aug. 3, 1624.

References: "Ebenezer Washburn—His Ancestors and Descendants," pages 17-18, 21-26.

THE FAMILY IN AMERICA

"Original List of Persons of Quality who went from England to American Plantations," by J. C. Hotten (page 257)—John Washborne age 25 in the *Jonathan,* 1619. (Page 57)—In the *Elizabeth and Ann,* Mr. Roger Coop (Coŏper) Master, xiij° Aprilis 1635, Margerie Washborn age 59, John Washborne age 14, and Philipp Washborne age 11 (2 sons).

Hon. John Washburn, first secretary of Massachusetts Bay Colony.

12. JOHN¹ WASHBURN was b. at Evesham, County of Worcester, England, and came to Duxbury in 1631, and d. at Bridgewater, Mass., before 1670. His wife, Margery (aged 49), and two sons joined him at Duxbury in 1635, coming on the ship *Elizabeth;* and they went to Bridgewater about 1665. He and his sons, John and Philip, were included in those able to bear arms, 1643, and his name is among the first freemen of Duxbury.

John Washburn and his son John were two of the fifty-six original proprietors of (the town of Bridgewater) the thousands of acres of land bought in 1645 of the old Indian chief, Massasoit (King Philip's father), by Capt. Myles Standish, Samuel Nash and Constant Southworth, for the use of those proprietors.—"History of Bridgewater, Mass.," John and sons Joseph, etc., with Church in battle in King Philip's War.

Children of John¹ and Margery Washburn, b. in Evesham, England:

John, b. in England about 1621.

Philip, b. in Evesham, England, about 1624; d. unm.

13. JOHN², b. in England about 1621; m. at Duxbury, 1645, Elizabeth Mitchell, b. 1629, whose father, Experience Mitchell, was with the forefathers of the Colony, was with the Pilgrims at Layden, and came to Plymouth on the ship, the *Anne,* 1623. He lived at Duxbury some years but removed before 1670 to Bridgewater, and made his will in 1686.

Children of John²:
1. *John³,* m. Rebeckah Laphram.
2. *Thomas³,* m. (1) Abigail Leonard; (2) Deliverance Packard.
   Children:
   1. Nathaniel⁴.   5. Patience⁴.
   2. Thomas⁴.   6. Deliverance⁴.
   3. Timothy⁴.   7. Elizabeth⁴.
   4. Hepzibah⁴.
      (Per will in 1729.)
3. *Joseph³,* m. Hannah Latham, granddaughter of Mary Chilton, and great-granddaughter of Francis Cooke, two of the *Mayflower* passengers.
   Children:
   1. Joseph⁴.   6. Edward⁴.
   2. Jonathan⁴.   7. Benjamin⁴.
   3. Ebenezer⁴.   8. Hepzibah⁴.
   4. Miles⁴.   9. Hannah⁴.
   5. Ephraim⁴.
      (Per "American Ancestry," Vol. XII, 1900, page 169, and "Genealogical Notes of the Washburn Family," by Mrs. Julia Chase Washburn, pages 26 and 27.)
4. *Samuel³,* b. 1651; m. Deborah Packard.
5. *Jonathan³,* m. Mary Vaughn, of Middleboro, Mass.
6. *Benjamin³,* d. in Phipps' expedition against Canada.
7. *Mary³,* m. in 1694, Samuel Kinsley.
8. *Elizabeth³,* m. (1) James Howard; (2) Edward Sealey.
9. *Jane³,* m. William Orcutt, Jr.
10. *James³* m. Mary Bowden.
11. *Sarah³,* m. 1697, John Ames.

14. JOSEPH WASHBURN, b. 1655, in Bridgewater, Mass.; m. at East Bridgewater, Mass., Hannah Latham.

15. HEPZIBAH WASHBURN, b. West Bridgewater, Mass.; d. Apr. 14, 1750; m. Sept. 8, 1702, at Bridgewater, Mass., Benjamin Leach, Esq., b. at West Bridgewater, Mass.; d. July 13, 1764.

16. HANNAH LEACH, dau. of Benjamin and Hepzibah (Washburn) Leach, b. at West Bridgewater, Mass., Mar. 4, 1725; m. Aug. 6, 1743, at Bridgewater, Solomon Leach, b. Feb. 19, 1712.

17. EPHRAIM LEACH, b. Dec., 1761; d. Feb. 28, 1840; m. Nov. 17, 1785, at Greenfield, Mass., Chloe Shattuck, b. Nov. 22, 1766, and d. Jan. 22, 1845.
18. TERTIUS LEACH, b. Nov. 21, 1786; d. Feb. 4, 1864; m. Jan. 1, 1811, at Sheldon, Vt., Sophia Hawley, b. Aug. 17, 1795; d. Jan. 7, 1879.
19. TERTIUS HAWLEY LEACH, b. May 19, 1813; d. Sept. 19, 1881; m. Feb. 28, 1835, at Sheldon, Vt., to Orisa Fanton, b. May 17, 1812; d. June 24, 1890.
20. HORACE BRAYTON LEACH, b. Sept. 25, 1836; d. May 6, 1919; m. Sept. 8, 1863, at Stanbridge, Que., Caroline Alexandria Phelps, b. July 3, 1840; d. Mar. 29, 1921.
21. FRANKIE ORISA⁶ LEACH, b. Oct. 11, 1870; m. in Fairfield, Vt., June 5, 1895, Homer Jessie Cutler, b. Jan. 5, 1870.
    Children (surname *Cutler*) b. at East Highgate, Vt.:
    1. *Horace Leach*, b. Apr. 19, 1898.
    2. *Alberta Irene*, b. Mar. 2, 1904.
    Mr. and Mrs. Cutler and both children living Jan. 1, 1932.

References: "Society Colonial Wars," 1922, page 513—John Washburne, Sr., 1585-1670, Duxbury, Mass., first secretary of Massachusetts Bay Colony. In expedition against Narragansetts in 1643, under Captain Myles Standish.
    "Journal of American Genealogy," Vol. 24, page 96—John Washburne, Sr., one of the List of Settlers in Plantation of Accawmcoke in Virginia.
    1 to 12 generations—Records of Elizabeth M. Rixford.
    12 to 18 generations—"Leach Genealogy," by F. Phelps Leach.
    19 to 21 generations—Family Records.

Mr. Edward Bentley Huling, of Chicago, Ill., m. Dec. 25, 1893, Sara Julia Hawks, dau. of Hon. William E. Hawks, of Bennington, Vt. She is a member of the Vermont Society of Mayflower Descendants, State No. 30, Gen. No. 9425, 21st in direct descent from Sir John de Wasseborne. Children: Three daughters.

Offices held by Mrs. Huling include the following:

National: Curator National, National Society United States Daughters of 1812; Councillor National, National Society Daughters of Founders and Patriots of America; National Color Bearer and Organizing Secretary of New England and New York, National Society of New England Women; Treasurer, Association of State Presidents and Charter Members United States Daughters of 1812.

State Presidents: Honorary Organizing President Vermont Chapter, National Society Daughters of Founders and Patriots of America; Organizing State Regent Vermont Chapter, National Society Daughters of American Colonists; State Regent of New York, National Society Magna Charta Dames; State President, Highgate, Vermont Colony, National Society of New England Women; Honorary State President Vermont Branch, National Congress of Mothers and Parent-Teacher Associations; Honorary State President, National Society United States Daughters of 1812.

MRS. EDWARD BENTLEY HULING
nee SARA J. HAWKS
AND HER THREE DAUGHTERS
KATHARINE, ELIZABETH and FRANCES
OF
BENNINGTON, VT. and LARCHMONT MANOR, N. Y.

RAVENSWORTH CASTLE

Built about 1030 by Thorfin the Dane, Earl of Orkney Isles, and also called Lord of Tanfield.   The founder of
the Washington Family in England.

DERIVATION

of

"THORFIN, THE DANE,"

Earl of the Orkney Isles,

Founder of the Washington Family in England

Circa A. D. 1030-35,

from

ODIN,

First King of Scandinavia, B. C. 70.

The pedigree and history of the Washington Family, derived from Odin, the founder of Scandinavia, B. C. 70, by Albert Welles, president of the American College for Genealogical Registry and Heraldry, 1879, pp. 3 to 9:

(PREFACE.) My position as president of the American College for Genealogical Registry and Heraldry enables me to obtain correct pedigrees and history of foreign families, and as the English history of the Washington family, by several authors, has been confessedly suppositious, it is deemed important that a correct and authentic volume should be written that would become the standard for reference on the subject.

My correspondent in London, from whom I have obtained the material for the Washington pedigree in England, is a lineal descendant of the progenitor in England, and has been engaged over thirty years in gathering evidence. He thus writes: "If I had not taken upon myself the great labor of examining those inestimable records, the 'Common Pleas Rolls,' the truth of that great man's lineage would not have been revealed. They are of immense value, and I hope you will make them known to your countrymen by the publication of the Washington History. The pedigree I now send I can establish by legal evidence."

The uncertainty hitherto existing in regard to the English progenitors of the Washington family, which has led to the numberless and fruitless controversies among the genealogists, will be entirely removed and cleared up by this volume. Beginning with Odin, the founder of Scandinavia, B. C. 70, the history is followed down through the royal line of Denmark in the thirty-two generations to "Thorfin, the Dane," nat. circa A. D. 1000, whose ancestors were of Schleswig, Denmark. He settled in Yorkshire, England, prior to the Norman Conquest. The descent is traced in Denmark and England, from father to son, down through the centuries, including branches in different shires, to John Washington, the great-grandfather of General George Washington, in twenty generations from Thorpin; with interesting personal matter regarding nearly 500 members of the family and their alliances in England and America.

The family of Washington derives its name from the village of Wassington, juxta Ravensworth (now called Wharleton), in the parish of Kirkby-Ravensworth, in the North Riding of Yorkshire. Originally Evervicscire—the Eboricure of the Romans, or Evereux—afterwards Ebor, at the time of the Conquest, and lastly Yorkshire.

The people of this part of the country were all of Scandinavian descent, and spoke the same language with the Normans themselves, which was the language of the ancient Angles. The Saxons never settled here, and were of a different race. The city of York having been long before that time especially a Danish city, and the chief city in all England.

With respect to the Anglo-Saxons, there were no Saxons in these parts, which was settled by the Angles, who spoke the same language as is spoken this day in these parts of Yorkshire; and all those Saxon inscriptions, about which so many wonders are made, is simply plain Yorkshire. The Angles were a branch of the Danes, who lived in Schleswig (a seaport town of Denmark), and came over to England, men, women, children, beasts, etc., and left that country desolate for 300 years, as is confirmed by the Saxon chronicles.

The 174 manors given to Earl Alan by the Conqueror, were only so many shadows. There were only about six manors really attached to the Earldom of Richmondshire; of all the others he was merely nominally the chief Lord; and each was held by an owner whose ancestors held for many generations before the Conquest.

There was never in Richmondshire above six families descended from Norman ancestors; and they acquired their lands by marrying heiresses.

The growing importance and value of such a work as this, is illustrated by the increasing interest in everything pertaining to General Washington, and it is, in fact, the only genealogy and family history of national importance in this country.

The Bible is a history of the earliest races of mankind; and a record of the Jewish lineage—religion, the science of immortality—genealogy cognate with both, inasmuch as it is a study embracing the present life, combined with departed generations, giving results of vast import in the future, and may, therefore, be considered next only in importance to religion and Bible history.

The songs with which the northern bards regaled the heroes at their "feasts of shells" were but versified chronicles of each ancestral line, symphonied by their stirring deeds.

Through the oak fire's uncertain flame, the chieftain saw descend the shadowy forms of his fathers; they came from the Halls of Odin, as the harper swept the strings, and deployed before their descendant, rejoicing in the sound of their praise. No parchment told his lineage to the warrior of those days, but the heroic names were branded each night upon his swelling heart by the burning numbers of the bards.

Thus did the northman chronicle his ancestry in those unlettered times. Afterward, when the oak fire was extinguished, the shell thrown by, and the night came no more with songs; when we reach the age of records we find this love of lineage availing itself of the new method of commemoration. This strong ancestral spirit of the northman may be traced, partly to the profound sentiment of perpetuity which formed the principal and noblest element of his character, and partly to the nature of the property to which he was linked by immemorial customs of the race.

The family history, or record, of the Sovereigns of the World before Christ, furnishes almost the only histories of the countries over which they reigned, as Egypt, Chaldea, Babylonia, Greece, etc. The Chinese annals, the most ancient known, were written with the most perfect exactness, and preserved with the greatest care; composed originally by order of the Emperors—each of whom, on his accession to the throne, commanded the acts of his predecessors to be written by some learned philosopher—so that the whole form one uniform continued series of the history of the ancient Chinese Empire, from the beginning of the monarchy (Fo Hi B. C. 2538), for some thousands of years. And thus was the history of China obtained and preserved more correctly, and for a longer period than that of any other nation in the world. Had not the Hebrew race cherished this love of kindred and lineage we should not have any Bible today, and to this feeling we owe our knowledge of the history of the most ancient kingdoms of the world and most of our modern history. The English registers have for upwards of a thousand years, been the protection and authority of many families; and the means of preserving large property interests.

iii

Ancestry of Washington Family may be summarized as follows:

Page v. ODIN, the son of Fridulf, supreme ruler of the Scythians, in Asaland, Turkestan, between the Euxine and Caspian Seas, in Asia. He reigned at Asgard, whence he removed in the year B. C. 70, and became the first King of Scandinavia. He died in the year B. C. 50, and was succeeded by his sons, who reigned in different parts of Scandinavia. His son

Page vii. SKIOID became King of Zealand and Jutland, B. C. 50, and died B. C. 40. His son was

Page viii. FRIDIEIF, who became first King of Denmark, B. C. 40. He died B. C. 23. His son was

Page viii. FRODE FREDIGOD, who became King of Denmark, B. C. 23. He died A. D. 35. His son was

Page viii. FRODE II, who became King of Denmark, A. D. 59. He died A. D. 87. His son was

Page viii. VERMUND, THE SAGE, who became King of Denmark, A. D. 87. He died A. D. 140. His son was

Page viii. OLAF, THE MILD, who became King of Denmark, A. D. 140. He died A. D. 190. His

Page viii. DAUGHTER, became Queen of Denmark, and

Page viii. DAN MYKILLATI, her husband, became King of Denmark, A. D. 190. He died A. D. 270. His son was

Page ix. FRODE III, who became King of Denmark, A. D. 270. He died A. D. 310. His son was

Page ix. HALFDAN, who became King of Denmark, A. D. 310. He died A. D. 324. His son was

Page ix. FRIDIEIF III, who became King of Denmark, A. D. 324. He died A. D. 348. His son was

Page ix. FRODE IV, who became King of Denmark, A. D. 348. He died A. D. 407. His son was

Page ix. HALFDAN II, who became King of Denmark, A. D. 456. He died A. D. 457. His son was

Page ix. ROE, who became King of Denmark, A. D. 460. He died A. D. 494. His son was

Page x. FRODE VI, who became King of Denmark, A. D. 494. He died A. D. 510. His son was

Page x. FRODE VII, who became King of Denmark, A. D. 522. He died A. D. 548. His son was

Page x. HALFDAN III, who became King of Denmark, A. D. 548. He died A. D. 580. His son was

Page xi. IVAR VIDFADME, who became King of Denmark, A. D. 588. He died A. D. 647. His daughter

Page xi. AUDA DIUPHRAUDZA, Queen of Holmgard, married RERICK, King of Holmgard. Her son was

Page xi. HARALD HILDETAND, who became King of Denmark, A. D. 647. He died A. D. 735. His son was

Page xv. THROUD, King of Frondheim, who married A. D. 750, daughter of SIGURD HRING. His son was

Page xv. EISTEN, King of Frondheim, born about A. D. 755. Married A. D. 780. His son was

Page xv. HALFDAN, King of Frondheim, born about A. D. 785. Married A. D. 810. His son was

Page xv. EISTEN GLUMRU, King of Thrandia, born about A. D. 815, became King of Thrandia, A. D. 840. His

Page xv. DAUGHTER married, A. D. 850, IVAR, Earl of Upland. Their son was

Page xv. EISTEN GLUMRU. He was living A. D. 870. His son was

Page xv. ROGVAID, who was Earl of Moere, A. D. 885. His son was

Page xx. EINAR, Earl of the Orkney Isles. His son was

Page xx. TORFIDUR, who was Earl of the Orkney Isles, A. D. 942. His son was

Page xx. LODVER, who was Earl of the Orkney Isles. His son was

Page xx. SIGURD, who was Earl of the Orkney Isles. His son was

Page xxii. THORFIN, THE DANE," Earl of the Orkney Isles, also called TORKILL, of Richmondshire, England, Baron, and Lord of Tanfield, Founder of the Washington Family of England.

For later lineage see Vol. I, pages 147 to 151.

WASHINGTON FAMILY
("History of the Washington Family"—Albert Welles)

The following, from "Burke's Armory," will show the Coat Armorial as granted to branches of the Washington Family in several shires of England:

WASHINGTON COAT OF ARMS

YORKSHIRE

Arms—Vert (green), a lion rampant, argent (silver), within a bordure gobonated or (gold) and azure (blue).

Crest—Out of a ducal coronet, or (gold), an eagle, wings addorsed, sable (black).

Motto—*Exitus acta probat.*

LANCASHIRE, LEICESTERSHIRE, NORTHAMPTONSHIRE, BUCKINGHAMSHIRE, WARWICKSHIRE, AND KENT

Arms—Argent (silver), two bars gules (red), in chief three mullets (stars) of the second, gules (red).

Crest—A raven with wings addorsed, sable (black), issuing out of a ducal coronet, or (gold).

The second variety above described was the Coat Armour used by George Washington, but the Yorkshire Escutcheon was the original Arms of the family.

CHARTER

Charter of land on River Eure, at East Witton, Yorkshire.

"Conan, Duke of Brittany and Count of Richmond, his Steward, his Constable, his Chamberlain and Bailiffs, and all others, French and English; All take notice that I have given, and that this paper confirms the donation of land to Roger de Ask, which was made to certain Barons of mine, to the Church of St. Andrew's of Marring, and the fees of two villains, near the termination of the Barony, and me and my heirs do grant and give and confirm in wood, in field, in pasture, in moor or water, in crop or in seed, and all other places in and belonging to the Barony. I prohibit the Churchmen or Laymen, and all others from disturbing or molesting the grantees, nor any other man shall receive it for debt. And I commend all the Barons of mine and all others in love and duty to see this maintained. If any do injury, I command all ministers to see that full redress be made. Witnessed by Henry fil Acheris, Alan the Constable, Walter fil Acheris, Nigello the Chamberlain, Henry son of Henry, Conan de Ask, Thomas his brother, Radulpho the Chamberlain, and many others. Given at Richmond." Seal of white wax (dependent by a silk string), a Knight on horseback.

This was Conan the 4th, Duke of Richmond, called le Petit, grantor of Jourvaulx Abbey, whose founders were sons of Bardolf and Bodin.

This is the territory granted to the Monks on River Eure at East Witton, where they removed in 1166 from Wandleysdale, the original sige of Jourvaulx Abbey. St. Mary's and St. Andrew's were the same as Jourvaulx Abbey, with only change of locality.

The Family of Washington was founded in England by:

1. ·THORFIN THE DANE, whose ancestors came from Schleswig, in Denmark, and settled in ancient Ebor or Yorkshire, prior to the Norman conquest. The name of "Washington" was derived from a village juxta Ravensworth, called originally, "Wessyngton."

    The name is of Saxon origin, and it existed in England prior to the Norman conquest. The village "Wassyngton" is mentioned in a Saxon Charter, as granted by King Edgar in 973, to Thornby Abbey. ("Collectanea Typographica," Vol. 6, p. 55.)

    This village is now called "Wharlton," and is in the parish of Kirkby Ravensworth, in the North Riding of Yorkshire. This Torfin was a great man, of Danish-Scandinavian descent, as were all of the great men of these parts.

    "In Ravensworth of the Geld, Torfin had one manor, and land, the whold was 1 league in length and a half broad. temp. Edward the Confessor." The above is from "Domesday Book," and is a translation of that portion respecting the North Riding in Yorkshire, including the district of Wharleton alias Washington, about 1070 to 1080.

    THORFIN THE DANE, Earl of the Orkney Isles, also called Torkill, of Richmondshire, England, Baron and Lord of Tanfield, founder of the Washington Family in England, was b. about A. D. 1010, and settled in Yorkshire, England, about 1030-35. Obit. about A. D. 1080. Two sons of Torfin were:

    2. ·*Bodin,* b. in Ravensworth, Yorkshire, about 1040.

    2. ·*Bardolf,* b. in Ravensworth, Yorkshire, about 1045.

2. ·BARDOLF, "Lord and Monk of Ravensworth," was b. about 1045. He was second son of Torfin the Dane. Bardolf possessed Ravensworth with divers other fair lordships in Richmondshire, in the time of King William the Conqueror, but, desiring in his age, to end his days in the devout service of God, forsook the world, and, with his brother Bodin, took upon him the habit of a monk of the Abbey of St. Marie's at York. Whereunto, at the especial instance of Bodin, he gave the churches of Patrick-Brompton and Ravensworth, in pure Almes. To this Bardolf succeeded his son and heir. Children:

    3. ·*Alaris,* Lord of Ravensworth, b. at Ravensworth about year 1080.

    3. ·*Henry,* Lord of Ravensworth, b. at Ravensworth about year 1090.

    The manor of Eggington, Derbyshire, was held at Doomsday Survey, by Azelm, under Geffrey de Alselyn, or Aseline. Bardolf m. the heiress of Hanselyn, of this baronial family, and she carried the manor to the Bardolfs.

SULGRAVE MANOR, ENGLAND

Ancestral home of George Washington.

3. ·AKARIS or Akar, or Akary, called also Akary fil Bardolf, or Fitz Bardolph, Lord of Ravensworth, b. about 1080, first son and heir of Bardolf, Lord and Monk of Ravensworth, in Richmondshire, second son of "Torfin the Dane." "And Bardolf, whose son Akar was the pious founder of 'Jourvaulx,' a famous Abbey of the Cisterian Order in the Northern tract. To this Bardolf succeeded Akaris, his son and heir, who in 5 Stephen, 1139, founded an Abbey at Fors, in Wenslay-dale in Com. Ebor, then called the 'Abbey of Charity.' He departed this life in Ann. 1161, 7 Henry II." He gave 3 carucates of land in Wharton, and 1 carucate and a half in Fors, to the abbey, where he was buried, leaving nine sons, of whom only five are mentioned ("Dugdale's Baronage," Vol. 1, p. 403) :

    4. *Hervey Fitz Akaris,* b. at Kirkby Ravensworth, about 1120.
    4. ·*Walter fil Akaris,* b. at Kirkby Ravensworth, about 1122.
    4. ·*Robert Fil Akery de Ashton,* b. at Kirkby Ravensworth, about 1125.
    4. ·*Heresculfus fil Akery,* b. at Kirkby Ravensworth, about 1127.
    4. ·*Bondo Fitz Akaris,* b. at Kirkby Ravensworth, about 1130.

    Akaris was one of the great Vassals of Stephen, Earl of Richmond, and, as such, appears upon the great Pipe Rolls in 1st Henry 2 (1154). He was the father of Hervey fil Akary, who was Lord of Ravensworth and ancestor of the Lords Fitz Hugh of that place, and of Bondo, Lord of Oualsington, juxta Ravensworth, which was given to him by his father, King Stephen.

4. BONDO FIL AKARIS, a younger son of Akaris, was b. at Ravensworth about 1122. Lord of Wessynton, juxta Ravensworth, Richmondshire Co., York, which manor was given to him by his father in the time of King Henry II (1154 to 1189). He is called sometimes Bondo de Washington, and sometimes Bondo de Ravensworth. These two places join each other. His sons were:

    5. *William fil Bondo,* b. at Wassington, about 1150.
    5. *Conan de Washington,* b. at Washington, about 1155.
    5. *Walter fil Bondo,* b. at Washington, about 1160.
    5. *Ralph fil Bondo de Ravensworth,* b. at Washington, about 1165.
    5. *Robert de Washington,* b. at Washington, about 1170.

Gen. George Washington, first President of the United States, was a direct descendant of these five generations.

5. WALTER FIL BONDO DE WASHINGTON, third son of Bondo fil Akaris, was b. at Wassington, about 1160. Walter was Lord of Milburn in Westmoreland, in right of his wife Agnes, in the time of King John (1199-1216). Walter de Washington acquired large estates in the counties of Northumberland and Westmoreland, in right of his wife Agnes, Lady of Milburn, dau. and heiress of Ivo de Welleburne, county Westmoreland, and resided at Welleburne, in Westmoreland. He had issue by wife Agnes:

    6. · *Robert de Washington,* b. at Welleburne, about 1195.
    6. · *William de Washington,* b. at Welleburne, about 1200.

His second wife Julianna, who survived him, claimed dower in his estates, and was living, 30 Henry III (1245). She claimed dower in the lands of her husband, in Northumberland and Westmoreland, and amongst others, she claimed, against Robert de Washington, the third part of the manor of Milleburne (or Welleburne), county Westmoreland, 20 Henry III (1245).

6. PETER DE WASHINGTON, second son of William de Washington, b. at Wassington, about 1178. He was seized of lands in Dalton Travers, Lancashire, 25 Henry III (1240). He had issue:

    7. *John de Washington,* b. at Wassington, about 1215.
    7. *Robert de Washington,* b. at Wassington, about 1220.

7. JOHN DE WASHINGTON, first son of Peter de Washington, second of William, first of Bondo, second of Akaris, first of Bardolf, second of Torfin the Dane, was b. at Dalton Travers, Lancashire, about 1215. Robert de Travers claimed against him common of pasture, in Dalton Travers, Lancashire, in 30 Henry III (1245). Had issue, only child: 8. • *Matilda,* b. at Dalton Travers, Lancashire, about 1230.

8. MATILDA WASHINGTON, dau., heiress and only child of John de Washington, first of Peter, second of William, first of Bondo, second of Akaris, first of Bardolf, second of Torfin the Dane, was b. at Dalton Travers, Lancashire, about 1230. She m. in 1252, James, son of and successor to Sir Robert Lawrence, of Ashton Hall, Lancashire, whose father, Sir Robert accompanied the lion-hearted Richard to Palestine, and distinguished himself at the siege of Acre, in 1191, and was made Knight Banneret, and obtained for him arms "Argent, a cross raguly gules." James Lawrence acquired by his marriage the Manor of Washington (change from Dalton), Sedgwick, etc., in that county. His son and successor was:

9. JOHN LAWRENCE, who levied a fine of Washington and Sedgwick, in 1283. He m. Margaret, dau. of Walter Chesford, and was father of:

10. JOHN LAWRENCE, who presented to the church of Washington, in 1326, and d. about 1360, leaving by Elizabeth, his wife, dau. of Holt of Stably, Lancashire, a son and heir.

11. SIR ROBERT LAWRENCE, Knight, who m. Margaret Holden of Lancashire; four sons, *viz.:*
    1. *Sir Robert,* his son and heir.
    2. *Thomas,* whose son Arthur was ancestor of Sir John Lawrence, of Chelsea, who was created a Baronet in 1628. Now extinct.
    3. • *William,* b. 1395, served in France, and afterward joining Lionel, Lord Welles, fought under the Lancastrian banner at St. Albans, in 1455, where he was slain, and bur. in the Abbey Church.
    4. *Edward,* b. about 1400 (or Edmund).

12. SIR ROBERT LAWRENCE, of Ashton Hall, mar. Amphilbis, dau. of Edward Longford, Esq., of Longford; and had: 1. *James,* 2. *Robert,* 3. *Nicholas.*

13. NICHOLAS LAWRENCE, of Agercroft, who m. and had *Thomas, Nicholas, Robert, John, William, Henry,* and *Oliver.*

14. JOHN LAWRENCE, of Agercroft, ancestor of the Lawrences of St. James Park in Suffolk, d. in 1461; leaving *Thomas,* of Rumburgh, in Suffolk.

15. THOMAS LAWRENCE, of Rumburgh, in Suffolk. He m. and had: *John, Richard* of St. Ives. The will of Thomas Lawrence is dated July 17, 1471.

16. JOHN LAWRENCE, m. Margery ———; d. 1504; wife d. 1507; had son, *Robert.*

17. ROBERT LAWRENCE, m. and had son, *John.*

18. JOHN LAWRENCE, of Rumburgh, m. Elizabeth ———, by whom he had: *Henry, John, Agnes, Margaret, Katharine, William* and *Richard.*

19. JOHN LAWRENCE, of Wisset, in Suffolk, m. Agnes ———. They had issue: *John; Richard,* d. 1596; *Susan; Elizabeth* and *Margaret.* His wife d. Jan. 22, 1583. He was bur. at Rumburgh, May 21, 1590.

20. JOHN LAWRENCE, of Wisset, m. Johan ———, and had: *Henry, Robert, Margery* and *Katherine.* Will of John, dated June 2, 1606. He was bur. Jan. 16, 1607.

21. HENRY LAWRENCE, son of John and Johan Lawrence, m. Mary ———; by whom he had *John,* b. at Wisset, in Suffolk, and bapt. Oct. 8, 1609. The will of John Lawrence, of Wisset, father of Henry, refers to him as having removed from Wisset to New England, and settled in Charlestown, Mass., in 1635, is the name of Henry Lawrence.

22. JOHN LAWRENCE, bapt. Oct. 8, 1609, in England; d. 1667, Groton, Mass.; m. Elizabeth ———, who d. 1663, Groton.

23. ENOCH LAWRENCE, b. Jan. 5, 1648-9; d. Sept. 28, 1744; m. Mar. 6, 1676-7, Ruth (Whitney) Shattuck, who was b. Apr. 15, 1645 and d. Mar. 6, 1676-7.
24. CAPT. DANIEL LAWRENCE, b. Mar. 7, 1681; d. 1777; m. Sarah ——, who d. probably in Canaan, Conn.
25. ISAAC LAWRENCE, SR., b. Feb. 25, 1704-5; d. Dec. 2, 1793; m. Lydia Hewitt, who d. Nov. 14, 1765.
26. ISAAC LAWRENCE, JR., of Canaan, Conn., m. Mary Brown, 7th child of Dea. Samuel Brown, May 8, 1760.
27. LYDIA LAWRENCE, b. 1761-2; d. Sept. 20, 1813; m. Phineas Phelps at New Haven, Vt. He was b. Apr. 10, 1767, and d. Apr. 20, 1813.
28. NASH DAVID PHELPS, b. Oct. 4, 1796; d. Apr. 15, 1884; m. at St. Armand West, Que., Apr. 20, 1821, Elizabeth Hungerford, b. Feb. 7, 1798; d. Jan. 7, 1878.
29. CAROLINE ALEXANDRIA PHELPS, b. July 3, 1840; d. Mar. 29, 1921; m. Sept. 8, 1863, at Stanbridge, Que., Horace Brayton Leach, b. Sept. 25, 1836; d. May 6, 1919.
30. ELIZABETH MAY LEACH, b. Jan. 7, 1866, living May 6, 1931; m. Sept. 8, 1889, at Sheldon, Vt., Oscar Herbert Rixford, b. Dec. 27, 1859; d. Sept. 11, 1927.
31. OSCAR ADELBERT RIXFORD, b. Aug. 4, 1890; m. Jan. 18, 1919, at Montreal, Que., Mary Carolyn Hefflon, b. June 6, 1889. They have two children:
    Mary-Elizabeth Lenora, b. Oct. 6, 1922.
    Oscar Theodore, b. July 21, 1925; both living May 6, 1931.

This Lawrence line traces back to CERDIC, founder of the West Saxon Kingdom, or Wessex, who in the year 495 landed with his son Cynric in Hamptonshire, England.—See Records of Elizabeth M. Rixford.

References: 1 to 8 generations—"History of Washington Family," by Albert Welles.
9 to 26 generations—Records of Elizabeth M. Rixford.
26 to 31 generations—Family Records.

WINNINGTON (WYNNINGTON)

Arms—Argent, an orle sable within eight martlets in orle of the second.

1. · RICHARD DE WYNNINGTON, Knight, of Winnington, Cheshire, in the twenty-second year of Richard II (1399), m. Agnes, surname unknown. They had three sons and a dau.
2. AGNES DE WYNNINGTON, dau. of Sir Richard and Agnes de Wynnington, m. Sir John (3) Warren. (See Warren 13-15, and Stanley 11.)

Viola Beatrice, James, Jr., and Conrad Allard, children of (Mrs. James) Hazel May Allard, dau. of F. Phelps Leach, are 23rd in direct descent (No. 1) Richard de Wynnington.

GOVERNOR THOMAS WELLES

GOV. THOMAS WELLES, ancestor, was born in 1598, being descended from "a family of high rank in Normandy and England, with royal intermarriages for over seven centuries"; came to America with his kinsman, Lord Say and Seal, in 1636; occupied the most important offices in Connecticut, including that of governor; died January 14, 1660; married first, in England, Elizabeth Hunt. Their son, John Welles (1621-59), married 1647, Elizabeth, daughter of John Curtiss. Their son, John Welles (born 1647; died March 24, 1714), married 1669, Mary, daughter of Lieut. John and Joanna (Treat) Hollister. Their daughter, Sarah Welles (born January 2, 1674), married Ambrose Thompson. (See "Gen. Conn.," Vol. III, page 1453.)

Gov. Thomas Welles (Robert, Thomas), was born in England; died at Wethersfield, Conn., January 14, 1659-60. He married first, in England, soon after July 5, 1615, Alice Tomes, who died in Connecticut probably not later than 1646, daughter of John Tomes; and secondly, in Connecticut, about 1646, Elizabeth (Deming) Foote, who died between August 16, 1682 and September 3, 1683, sister of John Deming and widow of Nathaniel Foote, both of Wethersfield.

Gov. Thomas Welles was probably related to William Shakespeare's family, as Dame Elizabeth, wife of Sir John Barnard, the grandmother of Shakespeare, bequeathed in her will £50 to be given to her cousin Thomas Welles, of Carlton, Bedford, England. ("American Ancestry," Vol. 7, page 216.)

He emigrated to New England with his six children after August 20, 1635 and before April 5, 1636. He was with his wife in Boston, Mass., June 9, 1636, and perhaps had a house at Cambridge, Mass., February 8, 1635-6. He settled at Hartford, Conn., his home lot being opposite that of Gov. George Wyllys, on what is now Governor Street. The first mention of Gov. Thomas Welles in the Connecticut Colony Records is under date of March 29, 1637, when he was a member of a court held at Hartford. After that his name appears on almost every page of the Connecticut Colony Records until his death in 1659-60. He acted as magistrate at the General Court held May 1, 1637, and was a magistrate every year thereafter until his death. He was elected treasurer of the Colony in 1639 and served until 1641, and was again elected to this office in 1648, and served until 1652. He was secretary from 1640 until 1648, and commissioner of the United Colonies in 1649 (in Boston).

He was chosen governor in 1655 and 1656; the next year he was deputy governor and in 1658 was reelected governor of the Colony. The following year he was deputy governor again, and that ended his eminently successful and honorable public career. Governor Welles went to Wethersfield to live.

A writer says of the Governor:

"Governor Welles possessed the full confidence of the people, and many of the most important of the early laws and papers pertaining to the founding of the Colony were drafted by him. The successful issue of Connecticut from her difficulty concerning the fort erected at Saybrook on one side and the Dutch enchroachments on the other was largely due to his skill and wisdom." (See "The Governors of Connecticut," by Frederick Calvin Norton, pages 19 to 21.)

Concerning the exact spot where the Governor's remains lie buried, there has been considerable controversy among the historians. Benjamin Trumbull, the eminent historian, wrote regarding this:

"Though Governor Welles was first buried at Wethersfield, his remains were afterwards removed to Hartford. Four of the first governors of Connecticut, Haynes, Wyllys, Welles and Webster, lie buried at Hartford without a monument. Considering their many and important public services this is remarkable. But their virtues have embalmed their names and will render their names venerable to the latest posterity."

Albert Welles, a biographer of the Governor, says that his remains were buried

"on the top of the hill near the fence on the south side of the old yard, in the rear of the meeting-house, where the remains of the Welles family for many generations now lie grouped."

One of the very best authorities on this question contends that the Governor was buried at Wethersfield and was never removed from that town. This seems to be the general belief. (See "The Governors of Connecticut," by Frederick Calvin Norton, pages 19 to 21.)

Children, by first wife, born in England:

I.   JOHN.
II.   THOMAS.
III.   SAMUEL.
IV.   MARY, d. in Connecticut, probably before Nov. 7, 1659, for her father, in his will of that date, bequeathed to "My Daughter Maryes Children."
V.   ANN, d. before Oct. 19, 1680; m. (1) Apr. 14, 1646, Thomas Thompson, who d. Apr. 20, 1655; m. (2) Anthony Hawkins, who was later one of the patentees of the Connecticut Charter. Thomas Thompson was a deputy to the General Court in 1650 and a constable in 1653.
VI.   SARAH, b. about 1631; d. Dec. 12, 1698, ae. 67 (gravestone) ; m. in Feb., 1653-4, Capt. John Chester, of Wethersfield.

References: "The New England Historical and Genealogical Register," pages 300, 301, 302.
"The Governors of Connecticut," pages 19, 20 and 21.

Descendants of Gov. Thomas Welles as follows:

1. Gov. THOMAS WELLES (England—Jan. 14, 1659-60), m. in England soon after July 5, 1615 Alice Tomes (1619—1646) ; m. 2nd, Anthony Hawkins.
2. THOMAS THOMPSON (bapt. Oct. 1, 1610—Apr. 20, 1655), m. Apr. 14, 1646, Ann Welles (d. before Oct. 19, 1680).
3. SAMUEL HAWLEY (1647— ———), m. May 20, 1673, Mary Thompson (bapt. June 7, 1653— ———).
4. MATTHEW[1] HAWLEY (Nov. 7, 1680— ———), m. ——— ——— (——— — ———).
5. MATTHEW 2ND HAWLEY (Feb. 16, 1720—May 31, 1790), m. Bethia ——— (Mar. 19, 1728—Jan. 24, 1786).
6. JAMES HAWLEY (1760—Apr. 14, 1836), m. Feb. 12, 1793, Martha (Stevens) Waterhouse (May 12, 1761— ———).
7. TERTIUS LEACH (Nov. 21, 1786—Feb. 4, 1864), m. Jan. 1, 1811, Sophia Hawley (Aug. 17, 1798—Jan. 7, 1879).
8. TERTIUS HAWLEY LEACH (May 19, 1813—Sept. 19, 1881), m. Feb. 28, 1835, Orisa Fanton (May 17, 1812—June 24, 1890).

9. HORACE BRAYTON LEACH (Sept. 25, 1836—May 6, 1919), m. Sept. 8, 1863, Caroline Alexandria Phelps (July 3, 1840—Mar. 29, 1921).
10. OSCAR HERBERT RIXFORD (Dec. 27, 1859—Sept. 11, 1927), m. Sept. 8, 1889, Elizabeth May Leach (Jan. 7, 1866—living May 6, 1931).
11. OSCAR ADELBERT RIXFORD (Aug. 4, 1890—living May 6, 1931, m. Jan. 18, 1919, Mary Carolyn Hefflon (June 6, 1899—living May 6, 1931).
    Children:
    Mary-Elizabeth Lenora (Oct. 6, 1922—living May 6, 1931).
    Oscar Theodore (July 21, 1925—living May 6, 1931).
    Reference: Records of Elizabeth M. Rixford.

WHITNEY

("Colonial Families," by New York Historical Society, 1928, pages 168-179)

Arms—Azure, a cross chequy or and gules.

Crest—A bull's head couped sable, armed argent, the points gules.

Motto—*Magnanimiter crucem sustine* (Gallantly uphold the cross.)

The surname Whitney was originally a place name. The parish from which the family takes its name is located in County Hereford, England, upon the extreme western border, adjoining Wales, and is traversed by the lovely Wye River. The name of the place doubtless comes from the appearance of the river, meaning in Saxon, white water, from "hwit," white, and "ey" water. The English ancestry of JOHN WHITNEY, the immigrant, who settled at Watertown, Mass., has been established by Henry Melville and presented in an exquisitely printed and illustrated volume. Very few American families have their English genealogy in such well authenticated and satisfactory form. An abstract of the English ancestry is given below:

1. TURSTIN "the Fleming," otherwise known as Turstin de Wigmore, probably also as Turstin, son of Rolf, and Turstin "the White," was a fol-

lower of William the Conqueror. He was mentioned in the Domesday Book as an extensive landholder in Herefordshire and the Marches of Wales. He m. Agnes, dau. of Alured de Merleberge, a Norman baron of Ewias Castle, in the Marches of Wales.

2. ·EUSTACE, son of Turstin, was a benefactor of the monastery of St. Peter in Gloucester. He or one of his immediate descendants took the surname de Whitney from Whitney of the Wye, in the Marches of Wales, where his principal castle was located. The estate comprised over two thousand acres, and remained in the family until 1893, when it was sold, there being no member of the family to hold it. The castle has entirely disappeared, but it is believed to be in ruins under the Wye, which has in the course of years changed its path. The castle was probably built on an artificial mound, surrounded by a moat fed by the river, which gradually undermined the castle, which was at last disintegrated.

3. ·SIR ROBERT DE WHITNEY, a direct descendant of Eustace, was living in 1242, and was mentioned in the "Testa de Nevill." Three or four intervening generations cannot be stated with certainty.

4. SIR EUSTACE DE WHITNEY, son of Sir Robert, gave deed to the monastery of St. Peter in 1280, referring to and confirming the deed of his ancestors above mentioned. He was Lord of Pencombe, Little Cowarn, and Whitney in 1281; was granted free warren by Edward I in 1284; summoned to wars beyond the seas in 1297; tenant of part of the manor of Huntington in 1299; in Scotch War in 1301. He was possibly grandson instead of son of Sir Robert.

5. SIR EUSTACE DE WHITNEY, son of Sir Eustace, was knighted by Edward I in 1306, and was a member of Parliament for Herefordshire in 1313 and 1352.

6. SIR ROBERT DE WHITNEY, son of Sir Eustace, was one of the two hundred gentlemen who went to Milan in the retinue of the Duke of Clarence on the occasion of the latter's marriage in 1368. He was a member of Parliament for Herefordshire in 1377, 1379, and 1380, and sheriff in 1377.

7. SIR ROBERT WHITNEY, son of Sir Robert, was sent abroad to negotiate a treaty with the County of Flanders in 1388; member of Parliament for Herefordshire in 1391. He was sent to France to deliver the castle and town of Cherbourg to the King of Navarre in 1393; was knight marshal in the court of Richard II; sent on King's business to Ireland in 1304. He was killed, together with his brother and most of his relatives at the Battle of Pilleth, 1402.

8. SIR ROBERT WHITNEY, son of Sir Robert Whitney, was granted the castle of Clifford, and lordships of Clifford and Glasbury by Henry IV in 1404 on account of the services of his father. He was sheriff of Herefordshire in 1413-28-33-37; member of Parliament, 1416-22. He fought in the French War under Henry V, and was captain of the castle and town of Vire in 1420. He was named as one of the five knights in Herefordshire in 1433, and d. Mar. 12, 1441.

9. SIR EUSTACE WHITNEY, son of Sir Robert Whitney, was b. in 1411. He was head of a commission sent to Wales by Henry VI in 1455, and was a member of Parliament for Herefordshire in 1468. He m. (1) Jennett Russell; (2) Jane Clifford.

10. SIR ROBERT WHITNEY, son of Sir Eustace Whitney, was probably a knight and was an active participant in the War of the Roses, and was attainted as a Yorkist in 1459. He was probably at the Battle of Mortimer's Cross in 1461. He was subject of a poem by Lewis Glyn Cothi, on the occasion of his marriage to Alice, the great-granddaughter of Sir David Gam. He m. (1) Alice Vaughan, dau. of Thomas Vaughan; (2) Constance Touchett, who was the mother of his sons. She was descended from William the Conqueror, through the second wife of Edward I, King of England. (See Touchett IV.)

11. JAMES WHITNEY, son of Sir Robert Whitney, was appointed receiver of Newport, part of the estate of the Duke of Buckingham, confiscated by Henry VII in 1522. He m. Blanche Milbourne, dau. and heir of Simon Milbourne. (See Milbourne IV.)

12. ROBERT WHITNEY, son of James Whitney, was of Icomb, and in charge of other confiscated estates, He was sheriff of Gloucestershire, 1527-28-29-30. He was nominated Knight of the Bath by Henry VIII at the coronation of Anne Boleyn in 1531; was granted part of income of monastery of Brewern in 1535; furnished forty men to put down rebellion in 1536; and was named to attend upon the King's person. He d. in 1541, and his will was proved June 11, 1541. He m. Margaret Wye. (See Wye.)

13. SIR ROBERT WHITNEY, son of Robert Whitney, was knighted the day after Queen Mary's coronation in Oct., 1553. He was summoned before the Privy Council in 1555 and 1559. He was member of Parliament for Herefordshire in 1559, and d. Aug. 5, 1567. He m. Sybil Baskerville, a descendant of William the Conqueror through the first wife of Edward I.

14. ROBERT WHITNEY, son of Sir Robert Whitney, was mentioned in the will of his father, and also in an inquisition taken after the latter's death. He m. Elizabeth, dau. of Morgan Guillims, or Duglim.

15. THOMAS WHITNEY, gentleman, son of Robert Whitney, was of Westminster. He was bur. at St. Margaret's, Apr. 14, 1637. He m. Mary Bray, dau. of John Bray, of Westminster; she was bur. at St. Margaret's, Sept. 25, 1629.

    Children:
    1. *John,* American emigrant.   4. *Richard.*
    2. *Nicholas.*   5. *Margaret.*
    3. *William.*   6. *Anne.*

    Among those of the family who have attained distinction in this country are: William Dwight Whitney, an eminent philologist, who became professor of Sanskrit, at Yale; and Joseph Dwight Whitney, a geologist of the first rank who became head of the State Geological Survey of California.

16. JOHN WHITNEY, son of Thomas and Mary (Bray) Whitney, was b. in England in 1583, and d. June 1, 1673. He received for the times a good education in the Westminster School, now known as St. Peter's College, and on Feb. 22, 1597, at the age of fourteen was appointed by his father to William Pring, of the Old Bailey, London, a freeman of the Merchant Tailors' Company. At the age of twenty-one, Mar. 13, 1604, John Whitney became a full-fledged member of the Merchant Tailors' Company. He made his home in Isleworth-on-the-Thames, eight miles from Westminster, and there three of his children were born. There also his father apprenticed to him his younger brother, Robert, who served seven years. Soon after termination of the apprenticeship of his brother Robert, John Whitney left Isleworth, and doubtless returned to London and lived in Bow Lane, near Bow Church, where his son Thomas was born. In Sept., 1631, he placed his eldest son John in the Merchant Tailors' School, where, according to the registers, he remained as long as the family was in England. Early in Apr., 1635, John Whitney registered with his wife Eleanor, and sons John, Richard, Nathaniel, Thomas and Jonathan as passengers on the ship *Elizabeth and Ann,* landing a few weeks later in New England. He settled in Watertown in June, and bought a sixteen-acre homestall of John Strickland on what is now Belmont and East Common Streets. He was admitted a freeman Mar. 3, 1635-36, and was appointed constable June 1, 1641. He was selectman from 1638 to 1655, inclusive, and town clerk in 1655; was the grantee of eight lots, and was one of the foremost citizens of Watertown for many years. He d. June 1, 1672. He m. (1) in England, Eleanor, surname

unknown, who was b. in 1599, and d. in Watertown, May 11, 1659. He m. (2), in Watertown, Sept. 29, 1659, Judith Clement, who d. before her husband. His will was dated Apr. 3, 1673.

Children of first marriage:
1. *Mary,* bapt. in England, May 23, 1619; d. young.
2. *John,* b. in England, 1620; m. Ruth Reynolds, of Boston.
3. *Richard,* b. in England in 1626.
4. *Nathaniel,* b. in England in 1627.
5. *Thomas,* b. in England in 1629; d. Sept. 20, 1719; m. Jan. 11, 1654, Mary Kedall or Kettle.
6. *Jonathan,* b. in England in 1634.
7. *Joshua,* b. in Watertown, July 12, 1640.
8. *Caleb,* b. in Watertown, July 12, 1640.
9. *Benjamin,* b. in Watertown, June 6, 1643.

"WATERTOWN, MASS."—Bond, 2nd Edition, Vol. I, pages 642-643

WHITNEY.—1. Embarked at Ipswich, England, April, 1635, for New England, in the *Elizabeth and Ann,* Roger Cooper, master, JOHN WHITNEY, aged 35; wife Ellin (Eleanor), aged 30; sons John, aged 11; Richard, aged 9; Nathaniel, aged 8; Thomas, aged 6; and Jonathan, aged 1 year. He was admitted freeman March 3, 1635-36; was selectman several years between 1638 and 1655, inclusive, and was town clerk 1655. In 1642 his homestall lot of 16 acres (where he continued to reside), was bounded E. and S. by William Jennison; W. by Martin Underwood; N. by Isaac Mixer (See 60). He at the same time owned eight other lots, amounting to 212 acres. The Registry of Deeds shows that he made additions to these possessions. His early admission as a freeman, and his early election as selectman, show that he held a respectable social position. His wife, Eleanor, died May 11, 1659, and he married (2), September 29, 1659 Judah (Judith) Clement. He died a widower, June 1, 1673, aged 74. His will, dated April 3, 1673, attested by William Bond, Sr., and Sarah Bond, Sr., mentions sons John, Richard, Thomas, Jonathan, Joshua and Benjamin. Inventory, dated June 4, 1673, 50 acres dividend land, £25; 3 acres of Beaver Brook meadow, and 1½ acres upland £60; 1 acre plain meadow, £10. He had probably previously distributed much of his estate in the settlement of his sons. See his son Benjamin (60).

Children of John and Eleanor Whitney.
1. JOHN, b. in England, 1624.
2. RICHARD, b. in England, 1626.
3. NATHANIEL, b. in England, 1627; not mentioned in his father's will, probably d. young.
4. THOMAS, b. in England, 1629.
5. MARY, b. Apr. 29, 1650; unm. in 1693.
6. JOSHUA, b. in Watertown, Feb. 15, 1635-6.
7. CALEB, b. in Watertown, July 12, 1640; not mentioned in his father's will, probably d. young.
8. BENJAMIN, b. in Watertown, June 6, 1643.

JOHN WHITNEY, JR., was admitted freeman May 26, 1647, then aged 23; was selectman 1673, '74, '75, '76, '78 and '79. He married Ruth, daughter of Robert Reynolds, of Boston. (The will of Robert

Reynolds, of Boston, dated April 20, 1658, mentions his daughter Ruth Whitney, and her eldest son; his daughter Sarah Mason, and her son Robert.) He died October 12, 1692, and adm. granted to widow Ruth, and sons John and Benjamin. Inventory, dated October 26, 1692, taken by Elnathan Beers and Thomas Hammond. It embraced 18 lots or parcels of land, amounting to about 210 acres, and prized at £197/15. It embraced one lot of 17 acres, "purchased of father Arnold."

Children of John, Jr., and Ruth Whitney:

1. JOHN, b. Sept. 17, 1642, (?) of Rox.; admitted freeman May 7, 1684; was he the one who m. Sarah, dau. of Richard Havén, of Lynn?
2. RUTH, b. Apr. 15, 1645; m. (1) June 20, 1664, John Shattuck (9); 4 children. He was drowned Sept. 14, 1675; and she m. (2) in Wat., Mar. 6, 1676-7,·Enoch Lawrence, son of John Lawrence, q.v.; 4 children. Her descendants are very numerous.
3. NATHANIEL, b. Feb. 1, 1646-7; d. in Weston, Jan. 7, 1732-3.
4. SAMUEL, b. July 28, 1648; m. Feb. 16, 1683-4, Mary Bemis (3). Children:
    1. *Mary*, b. Sept. 30, 1689; m. July 13, 1715, John Knapp (5-1), of Newton.
5. MARY, b. Apr. 29, 1650; unm. in 1693.
6. JOSEPH, b. Jan. 15, 1651-2; d. Nov. 4, 1702.
7. SARAH, b. Mar. 17, 1653-4; m. Oct. 18, 1681, Daniel Harrington.
8. ELIZABETH, b. June 9, 1656; m. Dec. 19, 1678, Daniel Warren.
9. HANNAH, unm. 1693.
10. BENJAMIN, b. June 28, 1660.

For Royal Line, see pages 4 to 5.

WILLIAM THE CONQUEROR
("Colonial Families," 1928, pages 40-42)

Arms—Gules, two lions passant guardant or.

𝕎illiam the Conqueror

1. · WILLIAM OF NORMANDY, later known as William the Conqueror, was b. in 1027 or 1028, bastard son of Robert, Duke of Normandy, sometimes called Robert the Devil, and of Arietta, dau. of a tanner of Nalaise;

and grandson of Richard II, Duke of Normandy. In 1034 Robert of Normandy induced his barons to acknowledge William as the successor. The following year he d., on the return journey from Jerusalem, and the barons kept their promise by acknowledging the lordship of the boy William. The conquest of England in 1066 and the years immediately following gained for William the title of Conqueror, as well as that of King William I of England. Recent authorities state that though in England many legends survive of arms borne by the Conqueror and his companions, nothing is more certain than that no armorial bearings appeared on either side of the Battle of Hastings. The arms described herewith are as recorded by Burke in his "Royal Armory."

William I, m. Matilda (sometimes recorded as Maud), dau. of Baldwin V, of Flanders, who traced descent in the female line from Alfred the Great.

2. GUNDRED, dau. of William the Conqueror, m. William (2) de Warren. (See Warren 5 to 15 and Stanley 11 to Elizabeth M. Rixford 27th in descent from William of Normandy [William the Conqueror].)

WINSLOW

Arms—Argent, on a bend gules seven lozenges conjoined or.

Crest—A stump of a tree with branches proper encircles with a strap and buckle.

Motto—*Decoptus floreo.*

Record is not made by Bardsley in his compendium of "English and Welsh Surnames," of the origin of the patronymic Winslow. But in Frank R. Holmes' "Director of Ancestral Heads," is found the following paragraph, which would seem to prove that "Winslow" is a place, or local name:

"Winslow, a place-name from the town of Winslow in Buckinghamshire. England. Original family seat in Worcestershire, England."

The preceding heraldic device is entitled to be borne by the descendants of Kenelm Winslow.—"Colonial Families," 1928, pages 14-15.

THE FAMILY IN ENGLAND

1. WILLIAM WINSLOW, or WYNCELOW, seems to have been the first of the name, of whom little is known except that to him were born two sons:
   1. *John,* of London, afterwards of Wyncelow Hall; was living in 1387-8; m. Mary Crouchman; d. in 1409-10, styled "of Crouchman Hall."
   2. *William, Jr.,* of whom further.
2. WILLIAM WINSLOW, or WYNCELOW, JR., second son of William Winslow, or Wyncelow, m. and to him was born a son, *John.*
3. JOHN WINSELOWE (note change in spelling), son of William Winslow, or Wyncelow, Jr., was living in 1400-20. He m. Agnes Throckmorton, dau. of John Throckmorton. (See Throckmorton IV.)
4. THOMAS WINSELOW, ESQ., of Burton, County Oxford, son of John and Agnes (Throckmorton) Winselow, was living in 1452. He m. Cecilia (or Agnes), dau. and coheiress of —— Tansley. His dau., Elizabeth, m. Humphrey Seymour. (See Seymour IX.)
5. WILLIAM WINSLOWE, son of Thomas, Esq., and Cecilia (Tansley) Winselowe, was living in 1529.
6. KENELM WINSLOW (note change in spelling), son of William Winslowe, had a large estate called Clerkenleap, in Kempsey Parish, County Worcester, and in 1559 bought from Sir Richard Newport an estate called Newport's Place, in Kempsey. He d. in 1607, leaving a widow, Katherine, in the parish of St. Andrew, County Worcester.
7. EDWARD WINSLOW, son of Kenelm and Katherine Winslow, was b. in the parish of St. Andrew, Oct. 7, 1560, and d. before 1631. He m. (1) Eleanor Pelham, of Droitwich, County Worcester. He m. (2), at St. Bridis Church, London, Nov. 4, 1594, Magdalene Ollyver. Records of his family in the parish register of St. Peter's, Droitwich, England, show the following:
   Children, b. in Droitwich, England:
   1. *Richard,* b. in 1585-6; d. May 20, 1659; m. Alice (Hay) Hurdman.
   2. *Edward,* b. Oct. 18, 1595; d. May 8, 1655, Governor of Plymouth Colony.
   3. *John,* b. Apr. 16, 1597; d. in Boston, Mass., in 1694.
   4. *Eleanor,* b. Apr. 22, 1598; lived in England.
   5. *Kenelm,* b. Apr. 29, 1599; d. in Salem, Mass., Sept. 13, 1672.
   6. *Gilbert,* b. Oct. 26, 1600; in Massachusetts, in 1620, returned to England.
   7. *Elizabeth,* b. Mar. 6, 1601-2; bur. Jan. 20, 1604-5.
   8. *Magdalen,* b. Dec. 26, 1604; lived in England.
   9. *Josiah,* b. Feb. 11, 1605-6; d. Dec. 1, 1674, in Marshfield, Mass.

1620   1920

MARY CHILTON
THE ONLY MAYFLOWER PASSENGER
WHO REMOVED FROM PLYMOUTH TO BOSTON
DIED HERE IN 1679
JOHN WINSLOW AND MARY CHILTON
WERE MARRIED AT PLYMOUTH ABOUT 1624
CAME TO BOSTON ABOUT 1657
AND BOUGHT A HOUSE ON THIS SITE IN 1671
JOHN WINSLOW DIED HERE IN 1674
AS A PASSENGER ON THE MAYFLOWER IN 1620
MARY CHILTON CAME TO AMERICA
BEFORE ANY OTHER WHITE WOMAN
WHO SETTLED IN BOSTON

THIS MEMORIAL ERECTED BY THE
MASSACHUSETTS SOCIETY OF
MAYFLOWER DESCENDANTS

THE FAMILY IN AMERICA

8. JOHN WINSLOW, son of Edward and Magdalene (Ollyver) Winslow, b Apr., 1597, in Droitwich, England; d. 1673-4. He m. Dec. 10, 1624, Mary Chilton, of the *Mayflower*. She d. in Boston in 1679 and is bur. in Kings' Chapel Burying Ground.

The graves of John Winslow and Mary Chilton are near the center of "Old Kings' Chapel Cemetery," Boston. The graves are marked with a large tomb with the Winslow coat of arms.

In commemoration of the Signing of "The Compact" on the *Mayflower,* at Cape Cod Harbor, now Provincetown, Mass., and in memory of Mary (Chilton) Winslow, the *Mayflower* Passenger, who removed from Plymouth to Boston, and was a member of the Old South Church from July 16, 1671, until her death in 1679, a memorial service was held at the Old South Church, Copley Square, Boston, on Sunday evening, Nov. 22, 1931, at half-past seven o'clock.

The sermon was preached by Rev. Russell Henry Stafford, D.D., minister of the Old South Church, and a member of the Massachusetts Society of Mayflower Descendants.

"The Compact" was read according to custom.

"History of Fairfield, Conn.," Vol. II, by Schenck—John Winslow, Esq., the Commander-in-chief of the Army, by order of Governor Shirley, of Massachusetts.

9. SUSANNAH WINSLOW, dau. of John and Mary (Chilton) Winslow, m. in 1649, Robert Latham.

10. HANNAH LATHAM, dau. of Robert and Susannah (Winslow) Latham, was b. in Bridgewater, Mass. She m. at East Bridgewater, Joseph Washburn, who was b. July 7, 1683.

11. ·HEPZIBAH WASHBURN, dau. of Joseph and Hannah (Latham) Washburn, was b. in Bridgewater, Mass., where she m. Sept. 8, 1702, Benjamin Leach, and d. there Apr. 14, 1750. Benjamin Leach was b. in West Bridgewater, Mass. He d. July 13, 1764.
12. HANNAH LEACH, dau. of Benjamin and Hepzibah (Washburn) Leach, was b. Mar. 4, 1725. She m. at Bridgewater, Mass., Aug. 6, 1743, Sergt. Soloman Leach, who was b. Feb. 19, 1712.
13. EPHRAIM LEACH, son of Sergt. Soloman and Hannah Leach, b. Dec., 1761; d. Feb. 28, 1840; m. at Greenfield, Mass., Nov. 17, 1785, Chloe Shattuck, b. Nov. 22, 1766; d. Jan. 22, 1845.
14. TERTIUS LEACH, son of Ephraim and Chloe (Shattuck) Leach, b. Nov. 21, 1786; d. Feb. 4, 1864; m. at Sheldon, Vt., Jan. 1, 1811, Sophia Hawley, b. Aug. 17, 1795; d. Jan. 7, 1879.
15. TERTIUS HAWLEY LEACH, son of Tertius and Sophia (Hawley) Leach, b. May 19, 1813; d. Sept. 19, 1881; m. at Sheldon, Vt., Feb. 28, 1833, Orisa Fanton, b. May 17, 1812; d. June 24, 1890.
16. HORACE BRAYTON LEACH, son of Tertius Hawley and Orisa (Fanton) Leach, b. Sept. 25, 1836; d. May 6, 1919; m. at Stanbridge, Que., Sept. 8, 1863, Caroline Alexandria Phelps, b. July 3, 1840; d. Mar. 29, 1921.
17. ELIZABETH MAY LEACH, dau. of Horace Brayton and Caroline Alexandria (Phelps) Leach, b. Jan. 7, 1866; living Jan. 1, 1932; m. at Sheldon, Vt., Sept. 8, 1889, Oscar Herbert Rixford, b. Dec. 27, 1859; d. Sept. 11, 1926. Charter Member No. 18 and Secretary of the Vermont Society of Mayflower Descendants.
18. OSCAR ADELBERT RIXFORD, b. Aug. 4, 1890; m. at Montreal, Que., Jan. 18, 1919, Mary Carolyn Hefflon, b. June 6, 1899. They have two children: *Mary-Elizabeth Lenora,* b. Oct. 6, 1922.
    Oscar Theodore, b. July 21, 1925; all living Jan. 1, 1932.
    Oscar Adelbert, Charter Member No. 22; Mary-Elizabeth, Junior Member No. 43; Oscar Theodore is Junior Member No. 73 of the Vt. Society of Mayflower Descendants.

References: "Colonial Families," by New York Historical Society, 1928, pages 14, 15.
1 to 8 generations—Records of Elizabeth Rixford.
8 to 14 generations—"Lawrence Leach and Some of His Descendants," Vol. 1, by F. Phelps Leach.
15 to 18 generations—Family Records.
"Mayflower Descendants," Vol. 1, Vol. 2.
Records of Elizabeth M. Rixford.

WYNE

("Colonial Families," 1928, page 173)

Arms—Vert, three eagles displayed in fease or.
Crest—An eagle displayed or.

Wyne, a name which is variously spelled Winne, Wynne, Wyne, also without the final "e," is of ancient Welsh origin, being derived from "gwyn," meaning white. Burke's "Peerage" has this to say of the English family: "To the House of Gydir, now represented maternally in one of its branches by the Williams-Wynns, of Wynnstay, must be conceded the first rank in Cambrian genealogy. This eminent family deduces male descent through their immediate ancestor, Rhodri, Lord of Anglesey, younger son of Owen Gwynedd,

Prince of North Wales, from Anarawd, King of North Wales, eldest son of Rhodri Mawr, King of Wales. This last monarch, the descendant of a long line of regal ancestors, succeeded to the crown of Powys on the demise, in 843, of his father, Mervyn Vrych, King of Powys, and by inheritance and marriage acquired the kingdoms of North Wales and South Wales."

Rhodri ap Owen Gwynedd, Lord of Anglesey, mentioned in the preceding paragraph, was born about the middle of the twelfth century, and married Agnes, daughter of Rhys ap Griffith ap Rhys ap Tewdyr Mawr, King of South Wales. Tenth in descent from this couple was John Wynne ap Meredith, of Gwydir, County Caernarvon, who died in 1559. He seems to have been the first to bear the name of Wynne in its present form. His grandsons, Sir John Wynn, of Gwydir, born in 1553, was the well-known author of the "History of the Gwydir Family." Burke, in his "General Armory" of England, Scotland, and Ireland, records thirty-two coats of arms for the Wynn and Wynne families, a large number of which are those of Welsh families. Those described herein are the Welsh royal arms Wynn, of Gwydir.

   1. JACOB WYNE, of German ancestry, was b. in New York State, where he was a cooper. He m. Ann Cook, of New Jersey. Had son, *George M.*

INDEX

DE STANLEY Sir William 135
DE STAPLETON Miles 91
DE ST. MAUR Henry 127
DE STOCKPORT Cicely 51
Joan 51
Sir Richard 51
DE STONELEY Joan 134
Mabella 134
Sir Henry 134
Thomas 134
DE TORTA Ralph 141
DE VALLIBUS William 52
DE VAUS Margaret 100 102
DE VEGA Lope 48
DE VENVIZ Robert 104
DE VERDON Bertram 51
Maud 53
Rhys 53
DE VERE Alberic 27 28
Alphonzo 27
Hawise 28
Hugh 27 28
Isabel 27 28 29 71
Joan 76
John 27
Robert 27 29 32 76
Sir Aubrey 27 28
Sir Robert 27 28
DEVEREAUX Katherine 11
Walter 11
D'EVEREUX Alice 42
Isabel 42
Sir William 42
Stephen 42
William 42
DEVEREUX Agnes 42
Anne 42
Cecilie 42
Edward 41
Elizabeth 42
Geruld 41
John 42
Katherine 42
Margery 42
Mary 42
Sir Walter 42 105
Sir William 42
Walter 41 42
DE VERMANDOIS Hugh 138
Raoul 138
DE VESEY William 52
D'EVREUX Eustace 42
Reginald 42
Robert 41 42
Walter 41
William 42
William 42
DE VIVONIA Cecily 11 12 52
William 11 52
DE WARENNE Alice 54
Joan 54
John 54
William 54 140 141
William 5 6 17 76 84 138 139 159
DE WASSEBORNE Alix 144
Ann 144
Anthony 144
Daniell 144
Eleanor 144
Elizabeth 144
Elynor 144
Emme 144
Francis 144

DE WASSEBORNE cont'd
Isabelle 144
Isolde 144
Jane 144
John 144
Katharine 144
Norman 144
Margaret 144
Peter 144
Radigone 144
Richard 144
Robert 144
Sir John 144 146
Sir Roger 144
Walter 144
William 144
Joan 143
John 143
Sir Roger 143 144
DE WASHINGTON John 91 97 149 150
Juliana 149
Matilda 91 97 150
Peter 149 150
Robert 149
Walter 149
William 149
DE WELLEBURNE
Agnes 149
Ivo 149
DE WHITNEY Eustace 155
Sir Eustace 155
Sir Robert 155
DE WYNNINGTON Agnes 141 151
Sir Richard 141 151
DICKINSON Mehitable 17 86
Obadiah 17 86
DODA 1
DODGE Nathan 60
DORMER Anne 36
Sir William 36
DOTEY Edward 23
DOUGLAS Alexander 43 116
Alexander (Mrs) 38
Alfred 43
Alfred E 43
Bertha 43
Caroline 43
Charles A 43
Elizabeth 100 103
Ester 43
Greta 43
John 43
Herbert 43
Ida 43
Leslie 43
Mabel 43
Nancy 43
DOVER Mary 112 113
DRAKE Alice 47
Bernard 49
Elinor 45 46
Enoch 47
Gilbert 47
Hannah 47
Henry 45
Job 47
Johan 47
John 44 45 46 47 48 49 108
John Esq 46 47
John Jr 47 50
Louis Stoughton 43
Richard 44
Robert 45 47 49
Ruth 47 50 108
Sir Barnard 45
Sir Francis 48

DRAKE cont'd
Sir John 45 46
Sir William 46 49
Thomas 47
DRAPER Catherine 116
Dennis Currie 116
Frank Erle 116
Mary Eliza 117
DRAYTON Katherine 68, 77
Sir John 68 77
Sir Simon 68 77
DUDLEY Ann 88
Samuel 88
Sarah 88
Thomas 87 88
Mercy 88
Patience 88
DUNCH Edmund 35
Hungerford 35
DUVELINA 140 141
DYFNWAL 3

EALHMUND 2
EARNLEY Michael Esq 36
EATON Francis 23
EDGAR 3
EDGINA 3
EDITH Matilda 3
EDMUND "Ironsides" 3
the Elder 3
EDWARD "the Elder" 2 3
"the Exile" 3
I of England 4 11 12 16 29 49 82 83 117 122 155 156
II of England 4 82 117
III 70 81 82
IV 40
VI 16
EDWY 3
EGBERT I of England 2 27 28
ELDRED 3
ELEANOR dau of Berenger IV 4 76 82 120
of Aquitaine 1 3 76 82
of Castile 4 15 16 49 82 117 122
dau of Richard 1
ELFLEDA 3
ELFRED 3
ELFRIDA 3
ELIZABETH of Vermandois 76 138
ELLIOT Rev John 18 19
ELPHIDE 1
EMMS John F 53
ENGAINE Elizabeth 16
Sir John 16
ENGLISH Thomas 23
ENO Abigail 114 117
EOFA 2
EOPPA 2
ERMENGARD 9
ERSKINE Sir Alan 102
Sir Robert 102
ESTURMY Maud 128
William 128
ETCHINGHAM Anne 121
Sir Thomas 121
ETHELBALD 2
ETHELBERT 2
ETHELRED 2 3 24
ETHELWULF 2
EVERINGHAM Adam 10
Joan 10
EYNESFORD Elizabeth 105
Sir John 105

.SALISBURY CATHEDRAL CITY

The Litany is sung in procession by the Cathedral Choir (British Official—B.C. 9841.
The Crest was taken from St. George 1611.
The Hungerford Arms are still to be seen in the Flemish glass windows.

(British Official photograph—B.C. 9864.)

The Choristers at Play in Their Playing Field Near the Cathedral

Tribute, unsolicited, paid to Mrs. Rixford by the Mayor of Salisbury, England: "Your Genealogy 'Families Directly Descended from all the Royal Families of Europe and Mayflower Ancestry 495-1932,' is a most wonderful work, in fact I have never seen anything like it before and I expect it is quite unique. I should very much like to know how it could possibly have been done and should be grateful if you could be so good as to write and inform me." R. I. Gorden, Mayor of Salisbury, England, Council House. Salisbury, England.

Royal and Colonial Ancestry

For ancestry of the following name, see "300 Colonial Ancestors" and Supplements I-II-III-IV.

The Author has 200 lines to the National Society of the Daughters of the American Colonists; 47 to the Colonial Daughters of the 17th Century; 12 to the National Society Daughters of the American Revolution; and 4 to the United States Daughters 1812.

Arms
Baker
Barber
Barstow
Bidwell
Bird
Birdseye
Bissell
Brackett
 (Capt. Richard)
Brown (Abraham)
Brown (Peter)
Burt
Butterfield
Canfield
Chamberlain
Chapin
Cheney
Chilton
Clesson
Cleveland
Cole
Collier
The Compact
Presidents and their
 Mayflower Ancestry
Cooke
Comstock
Copley
Crane
Currie
Cushman
Cutler
Cutting
Daniel
Davenport
*Davis
Dean
Dickinson
*Douglas
*Drake
Eggleston
Eno
Fanton
Ferguson
Field
Flint

Ford
Frary
French (Lieut.)
Fuller
*Fulwood
*Gallup
Gilbert
Goodenow
Goodspeed
*Graves
*Greene
*Gregory
Griswold
Gull
*Gunn
Hall
Hawkins
Hawks
*Hawley
Haynes
Heald (Hale)
Heaton
Hewitt
Hildreth
Hinckesman
Hinds
Hinsdale
Hoar
Holbrook
Holcomb
Howe
*Hungerford
Husted
Hyde
*Johnson (Capt.)
Kellogg
*Lake
*Latham
*Washington-Law-
 rence
Leach
*Lisle
Lead
Merrill
Miller
Mitchell
Mix

*Moore (Lord Moore)
Nash
Nutting
*Palmer
Patterson
*Phelps
Platt
*Read
*Reynolds
Rigby
Rixford
Russell
St. John
Sanford
Seabrook
*Shattuck
Shelley
Sherwood
Smith
Soule (George of the
 Mayflower)
Spaulding
Stallion
*Stanley
*Stephens (Capt. John)
Stevenson
Stone
Terry
*Thompson
*Tomes
Tomlinson
Turner
*Vicars
*Warren
Washburn
*Watson
Wells
Wheeler
White
*Whitney
Willard
Wilmot
Wilson
*Winslow
Wynn
Index

Their Lineal Descendant

ELIZABETH M. LEACH (MRS. OSCAR HERBERT) RIXFORD
East Highgate, Vermont

Names marked with a star traced to Royal ancestor by the Author of this Supplement.

Supplement

References for this supplement can be found in

GENEALOGY: FAMILIES DIRECTLY DESCENDED FROM ALL THE ROYAL FAMILIES IN EUROPE
(495-1932)
AND MAYFLOWER DESCENDANTS

Compiled by

Their Lineal Descendant

MRS. OSCAR HERBERT (ELIZABETH M. LEACH) RIXFORD in 1932

The Genealogy consists of:

A large chart of the family Lineage in front of Genealogy.
Old chart about 1000 to the Kings of Jerusalem in the Town of Courtenay.
Pedigree CCIII Burks "Royal Families," 44, to Old Mayor Austrasia, d. 639.
Pedigree A, Founder of West Saxon Kingdom to 495, 49.
Pedigree IV, Royal Lines of Portugal.
Pedigree CCIII, 25.
Pedigree A, Cedric Founder, 48.
Pedigree B, Danish Knights, 35.
Pedigree V, Houses of Capet, 30.
Pedigree D, Wm. Conqueror, 45.

Pedigree LIV, Double Chart { Wm. Conqueror, King of England, 36.
{ Baldwin V, Count of Flanders, 32.

Double Chart { Robert Bruce, King of Scotland.
Pedigree CLXXXV, Burks "Royal Families" { Henry III, King of England.

ROYAL FAMILIES

Angouleme, 36
Anjou (Anc. Counts), 38
Baskerville, 27
Beauchamp, 28
Berenger, 29
Bray, 27
Bulkeley, 29
Capet, 34
Castile, 32
Cheney, 20
Courtenay, 27
De Vere (by John S. Wurts), 27
Deverous, 32
Drake, 20E
Eaton, 26
Farleigh Hungerford, 27
Ferrer, 37
Fitz-Alan, 27
Flanders (Anc. Count), 30
Graves, 21
Greene, 36
Gregory, 20
Hainault (Anc. Comita), 20
Henry, King of Eng., 28
Heydon, 35
Insula, Jordan D. (or Lisle), 27

Johnson, 25
Latham, Mayflower Line
Lawrence-Washington, 31
Marshall, 31
Milbourne, 20
Moore, 23
Mowbray, 36
Neville, 25
Phelps (Eng. & America)
Port (Hubert De), 31
Portugal, 33
Russell, 22 (Pedigree 4)
Seymour, 25
Spineto (DE) 19
Stanley, 30
Stephens, 44
Taillefer, 33
Throckmorton, 21
Vermandois, 30
Warren (Pedigree & Branches), 31
Washburn, 22
Whitney, 48
Winnington (Wynnington), 24
Winslow (Wyncelow), Mayflower Line
(Eng. & American), 19
Wm. the Conqueror (Normandy), 29

Number after names are for Generations.
Mayflower Compact — Several Mayflower Lines — Several Colonial Lines.

The Four Supplements bound together in blue buckram.
Price—$5.50, less 15% to libraries.

DICTIONARY OF ROYAL FAMILIES

Burke, "Peerages." ·

1. PRINCE HUGH, THE GREAT, CRUSADE COMMANDER, 1096; m. Adelheid, dau. of Herbert, IV, Count de Vermandois, whose dau.:
2. ISABEL DE VERMANDOIS, m. (1st) Robert de Beaumont, Earl of Leicester, whose dau.:
3. ELIZABETH BEAUMONT, m. Gilbert, younger son of Gilbert de Clare and Adeljza de Claremont, whose son:
4. RICHARD DE CLARE (Strongbow), conquered Ireland; m. Eva, dau. of Dermot MacMurrogh, last King of Leinster, whose only child:
5. ISABEL DE CLARE, m. William le Marshall, whose dau.:
6. ISABEL MARSHALL, m. her distant cousin, GILBERE DE CLARE, M.C.B., son of RICHARD DE CLARE, M.C.B., and Amecia Meullent. Their son:
7. RICHARD DE CLARE, m. Maud, dau. of JOHN DE LACIE, M.C.B., and Margaret, dau. of Robert, son of SAIRE DE QUINCEY, M.C.B., whose 2nd son (Burke, "Extinct Peerages," 1831, pp. 121-3):
8. THOMAS DE CLARE, Governor of London, m. Amy, dau. of Maurice FitzRaymond, whose son:
9. THOMAS DE CLARE, II, of London, whose dau.:
10. MAUD DE CLARE, m. Robert, Baron Clifford, of Appleby, killed at Banockburn, 1314, whose dau.:
11. IDONIA CLIFFORD, m. Henry, 2nd Lord Percy, 1299-1352, whose dau.:
12. MAUD PERCY, m. Sir John Neville, K.G, Baron of Raby Castle, whose son (Burke, "Extinct Peerages," 1831, pp. 386-90):
13. SIR RALPH NEVILLE, K.G., M.P. 1389-96, created Earl of Westmoreland; m. (2nd) Joan, dau. of John of Gaunt, K.G., son of King Edward III, of England, K.G. (founder), whose younger son:
14. WILLIAM NEVILLE, m. Joan, dau. of Sir Thomas Fauconberg, becoming through · her, Neville, Lord Faunconberg, whose dau.:
15. DIONESIS DE FAUCONBERG, de Neville, d. 1437; m. Sir Thomas Brocket, of Brockett Hall, d. 1435, whose son ("Brocket Chart," by E. J. Brocket, published in England, 1860, also Burke, "Peerage," 1929, pp. 1959):
16. SIR THOMAS BROCKET, m. Elizabeth, dau. of Sir William Ashe, whose son:
17. SIR EDWARD BROCKET, of Brocket Hall, m. Elizabeth Thwaites, of Loftus, Yorkshire, England, whose son:
18. SIR JOHN BROCKET, Sheriff of Hertshire and Essex, 1507/8; m. Lucy, dau. of John Pulter, of Hicham, whose younger son:
19. EDWARD BROCKET, of Lechworth, m. Margaret Micelfield, whose son:
20. WILLIAM BROCKET, of Wildhill, m. Anne, dau. of Edmund Bardolphe, whose son:
21. JOHN BROCKET, of Quidicots, living in 1634, m. Dorothy, dau. of Robert Pen, of Cudicot Bury (evidently the disinherited Puritan son), whose son (younger):
22. RICHARD BROCKET (or Brackett), b. 1610; d. 1690; captain and deacon, came to America as a Puritan and took the oath in Boston, May 25, 1636; m. Alice ——, whose dau.:
23. JOHN BRACKETT is the son of Richard Brackett, d. Mar., 1690.
24. MARY BRACKETT is the dau. of John Brackett, d. Mar. 9, 1674; m. Hannah French, d. May 9, 1674.
25. JOSIAH SPAULDING is the son of Edward Spaulding, b. Sept. 16, 1663; m. Nov. 27, 1683 to Mary Brackett, b. Feb. 12, 1668; d. Dec. 8, 1704.
26. MARTHA SPAULDING is the dau. of Josiah Spaulding, d. Oct. 4, 1759; m. Dec. 4, 1710 at Plainfield, Conn., to Sarah Warren, Mar. 3, 1689; d. before Oct. 4, 1759.
27. PHOEBE HOWE is the dau. of Samuel Howe, b. June 24, 1718; m. Oct. 30, 1740 to Martha Spaulding, b. Oct. 25, 1723; d. 1757.
28. MARTHA STEVENS is the dau. of Capt. John Stevens, b. Oct. 19, 1737; d. Nov. 20, 1801; m. Jan. 2, 1759 to Phoebe Howe, b. Aug. 12, 1741; d. 1811, Shaneateler, N. Y.

29. Sophia Hawley is the dau. of James Hawley, b. 1760; d. Apr. 14, 1830; m. Feb. 12, 1793 to Martha Stevens, b. June 12, 1761; d. 1851.
30. Tertius Hawley Leach is the son of Tertius Leach, b. Nov. 21, 1786; d. Feb. 4, 1864; m. Jan. 1, 1811 at Sheldon, Vt. to Sophia Hawley, b. Aug. 17, 1795; d. Jan. 7, 1879.
31. Horace Brayton Leach is the son of Tertius Hawley Leach, b. May 18, 1818; d. Sept. 19, 1881; m. Feb. 28, 1835 at Sheldon, Vt. to Orisa Fanton, b. May 17, 1912.
32. Horace Brayton Leach, of Bakersfield, b. Sept. 25, 1836; d. May 6, 1919; m. Sept. 8, 1863 at Stanbridge, Que. to Carolina Alexandria Phelps, b. July 3, 1840; d. Mar. 29, 1921.
33. Elizabeth May Leach Rixford, b. Bakersfield, Jan. 7, 1866; m. Sept. 8, 1889 to Oscar Herbert Rixford.
34. Oscar Adelbert Rixford, b. Aug. 4, 1890; m. Jan. 8, 1919 to Mary Carolyn Hefflon, b. June 6, 1899 in Montreal, Que. (both living). They have two children:
35. Mary-Elizabeth Lenora Rixford, b. Oct. 6, 1922.
    Oscar Theodore Rixford, b. July 21, 1925.

References: Supplement II to "Three Hundred Colonial Ancestors and War Service" and "Her Papers to Daughters of the American Colonists," by Mrs. Elizabeth M. Rixford.

FITZROBERT-NEVILLE

Burke, "Landed Gentry and Commoners," Vol. 2, p. 238.

1. John FitzRobert, M.C.B., m. Ada, dau. of Hugh Baliol, whose son:
2. Roger FitzJohn, whose son:
3. Robert, Baron FitzRoger, m. Margaret la Zouche, whose dau.:
4. Anastasia (or Euphemia), m. Ranulph (Ralph) Neville, whose son:
5. Ralph Neville, II, m. Alice, dau. of Hugh d'Audley and Margaret, dau. of Gilbert de Clare and Princess Joan, dau. of King Edward III, of England (Gilbert, 1st son of Richard de Clare and Maud de Lacie).

DE ROOS-FAUCONBERG-NEVILLE LINEAGE

Burke, "Extinct Peerages," 1831, p. 452.

1. Robert de Roos, M.C.B., m. Isabel, dau. of King William, the Lion, King of Scotland, whose son:
2. William de Roos, m. Lucy, dau. of Reginald FitzPiers (desc. of Robert FitzRobert, M.C.B.) and his 1st wife, Alice ———. Their son:
3. Robert de Roos, II, m. Isabel, dau. of William, son of William D'Albini, M.C.B., and Marjory d'Umfraville, of Belvoir Castle. Their dau. ("Extinct Peerages," 1831, p. 390):
4. Isabel de Roos, m. Sir Walter Fauconberg, whose son:
5. Walter Fauconberg, II, m. Anastasia, dau. of Ralph Neville, and d. in 1313. Their son:
6. John Fauconberg, d. 1349, Sheriff of Yorkshire, whose son:
7. Sir Walter Fauconberg, III, d. 1362; m. (1st) Maud, dau. of John John, Lord Patshull, of Bletso, whose son:
8. Thomas, Lord Fauconberg, whose only child and heir:
9. Joan Fauconberg, m. William Neville.

HOUSE OF BOHAN

1. Henry I, King of France, m. Anne of Russia.
2. Prince Hugh Magnois, m. Princess Adelheid of Vermandois.
3. Isabel de Vermandois, m. William, Earl of Warren.

4. ADE DE WARREN, m. Prince Henry, son of King David I.
5. MARGARET DE HASTINGS, m. Humphrey de Bohan, 4th Baron de Bohan.
6. HENRY DE BOHAN, Earl of Hersford, Constable of England.
7. HUMPHREY DE BOHAN, called the "Good" Earl of Hersford and Essex, m. Maud d 'En.'
8. HUMPHREY DE BOHAN, Governor of Castile, m. Eleanor Braose.
9. HUMPHREY DE BOHAN, 3rd Earl of Hersford, m. Maud de Finnes.
10. HUMPHREY DE BOHAN, 4th Earl of Hersford and Essex, Lord High Constable, m. Princess Elizabeth Plantagenet, dau. of Edward I, King of England;' m. (1st) Princess Eleanor, of Castile.
11. ELIZABETH DE BOHAN, m. Richard Fitz-Alan, Earl of Arundale.
12. LADY ALICE FITZ ALAN, m. Sir Thames de Holland, 2nd Earl of Kent, son of Sir Thomas de Holland, K.G., and his wife, Lady Joan Plantagenet was known as the fair maid of Kent, dau. of Edward Plantagenet.

Reference: See pages 4 and 5, "Families Directly Descended to all the Families of Europe," 1932, for 18 generations to author's grandchildren.

BEAUMONT-BROASE-BRAMPTON-THROCKMORTON-WINSLOW
Compiled by W. Ross Cooper.

1. ROBERT DE BEAUMONT, m. Isabel de Vermandois (her 1st), whose dau.:
2. ELIZABETH BEAUMONT, m. Gilbert de Clare, Earl of Pembroke, whose son:
3. RICHARD DE CLARE, 2nd Earl (Strongbow), m. Eva MacMurrogh, whose dau.
4. ISABEL DE CLARE, m. William Marshall, whose dau.: ·
5. EVA MARSHALL, m. William, 6th Baron de Broase, whose dau.:
6. MATILDA (Maud) DE BROASE, m. (1st) Roger, 6th Baron Mortimerl; m. (2nd) Sir Brian, Lord Brampton, Knight. By the 2nd marriage was a son:
7. SIR BRIAN, II, Lord Brampton, Knight, m. Alice dau. of William de Remeville, Knt. Southampton, whose son:
8. SIR BRIAN, III, m. Emma, dau. of Sir Thomas Corbet, of Caus Castle, Co. Salop, whose son:
9. SIR WALTER, Lord Brampton, m. Johanna, Lady of Ewilley, whose son:
10. SIR BRIAN, Lord Brampton, d. 1294; m. Eleanor, heir of Robert de Hereford; whose dau.:
11. MARGARET BRAMPTON, m. Sir Robert de Harley. She was b. 1287/8. Their son:
12. SIR ROBERT, Lord Harley, m. Joan, dau. of Robert Corbet; whose dau.:
13. JOAN HARLEY, m. John de Besford, 1341, whose son:
14. SIR ALEXANDER BESFORD, Lord of Black Nauton, M.P. 1398, d. 1403, whose dau.:
15. AGNES BESFORD, m. Thomas de Throckmorton, and inherited Black Nauton, whose son:
16 JOHN THROCKMORTON, Under Treasurer of England, m. Alainore de la Spineto; whose son:
17. THOMAS THROCKMORTON, Lord of Black Nauton, b. 1412; d. 1472; m. 1446, Margaret Olney, whose children:
   1. *John*, the heir.
   2. *Robert* (or Ralph), b. 1452; d. 1520.

Addenda

16. SIR JOHN THROCKMORTON, m. Alainore de Spineto who also had the daughters:
   1. *Maud*, m. Sir Thomas Greene, of Greene's Norton.
   2. *Agnes*, m. William Winslow. (For Mrs. Rixford see Royal line of Winslow line, p. 160, "Families Directly Descended from All the Royal Families of Europe," by Elizabeth M. Leach Rixford, 1932.)

References: Jordon, "Your Family Tree," p. 233.
"Notes and Lineage," by Mrs. Mackenzie.
Burke, "Peerage, etc."

BIGOD-GENEVILLE-CHERLTON-PULESTON

1. HUGH BIGOD, M.C.B., m. Maud, dau. of William Marshall (sister of Eva). their dau.:
2. ISABEL BIGOD, m. John FitzGeoffrey, whose dau.:
3. MAUD FITZJOHN, m. Peter, Lord Geneville, whose dau.:
4. JOAN DE GENEVILLE, m. Roger Mortimer, 1st Earl of March, whose dau.:
5. MAUD MORTIMER, m. John, Lord Cherleton, whose dau.:
6. JANE CHERLETON, m. John, Baron le Strange, whose dau.:
7. ELIZABETH LE STRANGE, m. Gruffydd ap Madoc Vychan, Lord of Glyndyfrdwy, whose son:
8. GRUFFUDD VYCHAN, IV, Lord of Glyndyfrdwy; whose dau.:
9. LOWRY VYCHAN, m. Robert Puleston, whose son:
10. ROGER PULESTON, whose dau.:
11. ALICE PULESTON, m. Sir Robert, Lord of Harley, Knight, whose son:
12. SIR RICHARD HARLEY, d. 1287; m. Burgo de Willey, dau. of Andreas Fitz Nicholas, Lord of Willey, whose son:
13. SIR ROBERT HARLEY, m. Margaret Brampton. (See No. 11.)

Reference: Jordon, "Your Family Tree," pp. 136-37.

EARL OF HERFORD

1. RICHARD DE CLARE, Baron.
2. GILBERT DE CLARE, Baron.
3. RICHARD DE CLARE, m. Maud Lacia, dau. of John de Lacie.
4. GILBERT DE CLARE, m. Joan of Acre, dau of King Edward I.
5. MARGARET CLARE, m. (2nd) Hugh Audley.
6. MARGARET AUDLEY, m. Ralph Stafford, K.G.
7. MARGARET STAFFORD, m. John Stafford.
8. RALPH STAFFORD, m. Maud Hastings.
9. JOAN STAFFORD, m. Nicholas Beke.
10. ELIZABETH BEKE, as above, m. Robert Swinnerton.
11. MAUD SWINNERTON, m. John Savage.
12. JOHN SAVAGE, m. Eleanor Brereton.
13. MARGARET SAVAGE, m. Randall Mainwaring.
14. MARGARET MAINWARING, m. Randall Grosvenor.
15. RANDALL GROSVENOR, m. Anna Charlton.
16. ELIZABETH GROSVENOR, as above, m. Thomas Bulkeley.
17. REV. EDWARD BULKELEY, m. Olive Irby.
18. SARAH BULKELEY, m. Oliver St. John.
19. MATTHIAS ST. JOHN, m. Elizabeth ——, b. England; d. 1669.
20. MATTHIAS ST. JOHN, m. Elizabeth ——, b. 1630; d. 1728/9.
21. JAMES ST. JOHN, b. 1674; d. 1754; m. Mary Comstock, b. 1671; d. 1747.
22. HANNAH ST. JOHN, b. 1703; d. 1746; m. 1725 Jeremiah Mead, b. 1702; d. 1742.
23. STEPHEN MEAD, b. 1728; d. 1806; m. 1751, Rachel Sanford, b. 1708; d. 1800.
24. ESTHER MEAD, b. 1760; d. 1836; m. about 1777, Isaiah Hungerford, b. 1756; d. 1833.
25. ELIZABETH HUNGERFORD, b. 1798; d. 1878; m. 1821, Nash David Phelps, b. 1796; d. 1884.
26. ELIZABETH MAY LEACH, b. 1866 (living Jan. 1, 1944); m. Sheldon, Vt., Sept., 1889, Oscar Herbert Rixford, b. 1859; d. 1926.
27. OSCAR ADELBERT RIXFORD, b. 1890; m. 1919, Montreal, Que., Mary Carolyn Hefflon, b. 1899, both living.
28. MARY-ELIZABETH LENORA RIXFORD, b. 1922.
    OSCAR THEODORE RIXFORD, b. 1925.

Other Royal Lines of St. John's Family are:
HUMPHREY D. BOHUN, King of England.
SAIRE DE QUINCY, Baron.
ROBERT DE BUKLOGH, Lord of the Manor of Buklogh.
ROBERT BEAUCHAMP, First of the Somerset Family.

GREEN LINEAGE

1. ALAN, "Dapifer Dolensis," Steward of Dol, Brittany.
2. FLAALD (Flathald or Fleance), m. dau. Warine of Shropshire, or m. Nesta, dau. Griffith ap Llewellin, Pr. N. Wales.
3. ALAN FITZ FLAALD, m. Avelina, dau. Ernulf de Hesdin.
4. WALTER FITZ ALAN, m. Eschina, dau. THOMAS OF LONDON.
5. WALTER FITZ ALAN, m. dau. Alan, Earl of Brittany.
6. ALEXANDER DE BOKETON, m. a sister of William de Cantilupe, Senechal of King JOHN's household.
7. SIR WALTER, Crusader, d. 1272; m. Isabel (Alice?), dau. JOHN FITZALAN and Isabel d'Albini.
8. JOHN DE BOKETON, d. 1271, in Palestine; his wife was thought to have been a de la Zouche.
9. SIR THOMAS DE BOKETON, Sheriff of Northampton, m. Isabell, dau. of Thomas de Boltsham of Braunston.
10. SIR THOMAS DE GRENE, DE BOKETON, Sheriff of Northampton, m. Lady Lucie, dau. Eudo de la Zouche, etc.
11. SIR HENRY DE GRENE, of Boughton, Lord Chief Justice, 1361-65; m. Lady Katherine, dau. Sir John de Drayton.

References: "The Green Family and its Branches," by Lora S. Lee Lance.
"The Dictionary of National Biography," English.
"The Journal of American History," Vol. XII.
Mrs. La Mances' latest manuscripts.
Henry K. Elliott, "Genealogist at Boughton, Northampshire."
"Studies in Peerage and Family History," by J. H. Round.
"The Family of Greene," by T. R. Marvin & Son.
"Families Directly Descended from All the Royal Families in Europe," by Elizabeth M. Leach Rixford.

There is a book called "Halstead's Genealogies" of which only a few copies are extant. It was compiled by the second Earl of Peterborough in 1685, and gives a long history, illustrated, of the Greene family. There is not a copy in this country. Baker's "History of Northamptonshire gives quite a history of the family.

We are descendants of the John Greene who came over, and was with the Roger Williams company in Rhode Island.

From a book entitled "Americans of Royal Descent," by Charles E. Browning, 1891, page 259 *et sec.*, I copy the following:

1. HENRY I, King of France, had by his first wife, Anne of Russia.
2. PRINCE HUGH MAGNUS, Count de Vermandois.
3. LADY ISABEL DE VERMANDOIS, who m. (1st) Robert, Baron de Bellamont, Earl of Mellent, created Earl of Leicester.
4. ROBERT, second Earl of Leicester, Lord Chief Justice of England, m. Aurelia de Waer, dau. of Ralph. Earl of Norfolk.
5. Robert, third Earl of Leicester, Steward of England, d. 1196; m. Petronella, dau. of Hugh de Grentermemeil.
6. LADY MARGARET DE BELLAMONT, m. Saier de Quincey, created 1207 Earl of Winchester, d. 1219, one of twenty-five Magna Charta barons.

7. ROGER, second Earl of Winchester, Constable of Scotland, d. 1264; m. (1st) Helen, dau. of Elan, Lord of Galloway.
8. LADY ELENE DE QUINCEY, m. Sir Alan, Lord Zouche of Ashby, Constable of the Tower of London, Governor of the Castle at Northamptonshire.
9. ENDO C. ZOUCHE, second son, m. Lady Millicent Canteluke, widow of John de Nonalt.
10. LACY C. ZOUCHE, m. (1st) Thomas de Grene, b. 1292 (son of Sir Thomas de Grene, Lord of Boughton), Northamptonshire.
11. SIR HENRY DE GREENE, only child of Sir Thomas and Lucie de la Zouche. He was made Lord Chief Justice of England. He d. in 1370, a little under 60, and was buried at Boughton. He early m. Katherine, the dau. of Sir John and only sister of Sir Simon Drayton, of Drayton.
SIR HENRY DE GRENE, Lord of Greens-Norton, Northamptonshire, Lord Chief Justice of England, 1353 m. Catherine, dau. of Sir John Drayton.

At Greens-Norton is an old church, St. Bartholomew's, built in pre-Norman times, and much mutilated at times, but it has been greatly repaired and everything restored that could be. The rector, Rev. R. A. Kennaway, has sent me pictures of the exterior and interior, and a drawing of Sir Henry Greene's tomb, and a notice of the restorations and the service of November 13, 1891. The tomb is of alabaster, and is one of the finest yet remaining in England.

Reference: Seventeen (17) generations from here to grandchildren of the author. See "Families Directly Descended from All the Royal Families in Europe," p. 77.

HUNGERFORD-CLIFFORD LINEAGE
Burke, 1831, "Extinct, Dormant and Suspended Peerages," pp. 282-283.

1. SIR EDMUND HUNGERFORD, 1165; m. ——, whose son:
2. SIR ROBERT HUNGERFORD, m. Joane ——, whose son:
3. SIR WALTER HUNGERFORD, m. Elizabeth, dau. of Sir Adam St. John, whose son:
4. SIR THOMAS HUNGERFORD, m. Joane, dau. of Sir Edmund Hussie, Knight. Their dau., Gracia, m. Sir John Stourton. They also had a son:
5. SIR WALTER HUNGERFORD, Knight of the Garter, m. (1st) Catherine, dau. of Sir Thomas Peverel, and m. (2nd) Margaret, dau. of Sir Thomas Courtenay, whose son:
6. SIR ROBERT HUNGERFORD, m. Margaret Botreaux, whose son:
7. SIR ROBERT HUNGERFORD, m. Alainore, dau. of Sir William Molines (Molineaux), whose 2nd son:
8. SIR WALTER HUNGERFORD, m. Jane, dau. of Sir William Bulstrode, whose son:
9. SIR EDWARD HUNGERFORD, m. (2nd) Alice, dau of William, Lord Sandys, whose son:
10. SIR ANTHONY HUNGERFORD, m. ——; whose dau.:
11. —— HUNGERFORD, m. Sir Henry Clifford, of Barscombe, Wiltshire.

MOELS-COURTENAY LINEAGE
Burke, 1831, "Extinct, etc., Peerages," p. 251.

1. NICHOLAS DE MOELS, m. Hawise, dau. of James de Newmarch (Neufmarche), whose son:
2. ROGER DE MOELS, d. 1294; m. Alice, dau. of William de Preux, whose son:
3. JOHN DE MOELS, d. 1311; m. ——, dau. of John, Lord Grey of Ruthven, whose son:

4. NICHOLAS DE MOELS, m. Margaret, dau. of Sir Hugh Courtenay and Eleanor, dau. of Hugh Despencer, Earl of Winchester, whose 2nd son:
5. JOHN DE MOELS, m. Joan, dau. of Sir Richard Luvel (Lovell), of Castle Carey, whose dau.:
6. MURIEL DE MOELS, m. Sir Thomas Courtenay.

Reference: See Old Chart, p. 36, "Families Directly Descended from All the Royal Families of Europe," by Elizabeth M. Leach Rixford.

Zedekiah (whose name was changed from Mathanica by the King of Babylon), King of Judah, 619-587 B.C. being the last of the kings; his daughter Tea Tephi, who flourished in 580, married Heremon Eochaid, King of Ireland (grandson of the Egyptian Pharaoh mentioned in the Exodus, whose daughter Scota married Milesius, father of Heremon Eochaid, who reigned fifteen years; took the Stone of Scone with her (the pillow of rock used by Jacob when he had his famous dream) and which today remains with her descendants, the Kings of Great Britain and Ireland.

(The Stone of Scone is sometimes called "The Stone Chair" and rests at Westminster beneath the throne chair of the English monarchs—all the kings of Judah, Israel, Ireland, Scotland [except Mary Queen of Scots], England 'from Edward I to the present day have been crowned upon this famous stone.)

LECHE OF CARDEN

JOHN HURLESTON LECHE, O.B.E., of Carden Park and Stretton Hall, Cheshire, educated at Eton and Royal Military College, Sandhurst, 2nd Secretary Diplomatic Service, Lieutenant Special Reserve, late 12th Lancers, served on Staff in Grear War, 1914 (despatches twice, medal and star), has Order of the Crown of Belgium, born 21 November, 1889; married 28 June, 1916, Amy Violet, youngest daughter of Clement, Wm. Joseph Unthank, J.P., of Intwood Hall (see that family).

Lineage.—JOHN LECHE, living in the reign of Henry IV, a scion of the family of Leche, of Chatsworth County, Derby, married Lucy, daughter and co-heir of Wm. DeCawarden, of Carden, County Chester, and was father of

JOHN DE L'LECHE, living temp. Henry IV, father, by Maud, his wife, of John Leche, of Cardon, whose name, with that of his wife Isabel, dau. and heir of William Johnson, of Farndom, occurs in a deed I Edward IV. His son and successor:

JOHN LECHE, of Carden, married 14 Edward IV, Margaret, daughter and sole heir of George Mainwaring, of Ightfield, and had other issue:

1. JOHN, his heir.
2. HENRY, who m. Mary, dau. of Andrew Wilson, and was father of John, who. s. his uncle at Carden.
3. GEORGE, Aldermen of Chester, ancestor of the Leches of Mollington.

The eldest son and heir:
JOHN LECHE, of Carden, survived until 6 Edward VI, as appears

by his will, dated in that year, and, dying without issue, was s. by his nephew:

JOHN LECHE, of Carden, married before 27 Henry VIII, Jane, daughter of Robert Fitton, was was s. by his son:.

JOHN LECHE, of Carden, baptized 1548; married Ursula, daughter of Rev. John Mainwaring, of Drayton, and had (with two daughters, Mary, the elder, married Thomas Bebington, of Chorley; and the younger married John Hinde, of Stanney) a son and heir.

JOHN LECHE, of Carden, married 1613, Alice, daughter of William Aldersee, Alderman, of Chester, and dying 1567, s. by his son:

JOHN LECHE, of Carden, aged 50, 29 July, 1664; married (1st) Elizabeth, daugther of John Newton, of Highlev, in Salop, and by her (who died 1654) had four sons and four daughters. He married (2nd) 20 April, 1665, Elizabeth, daughter of —— Best, and relict of Richard Alport, of Overton, by whom he had one son and one daughter. He was s. by his eldest son:

JOHN LECHE, of Carden, married 23 September, 1674, Grace, daughter of Hugh Currer, of Kildwick, County York, and had with other issue:

JOHN LECHE, of Carden, High Sheriff of County Chester, 1719, married Sarah, daughter and heiress of Thomas Hargrave, of Helsby, and was s. by his eldest son:

JOHN LECHE, of Carden, High Sheriff, 1753, married 7 May, 1728, Mary, 2nd daughter of John Hurleston, of Newton, and co-heir of her uncle, Charles Hurleston, and by her (who died 29 December, 1763) left her at his decease (with three daughters: 1. Penelope, married Thomas Puleston, of Emral, but d. s. p.; 2. Sarah; 3. May, married Thomas Roberts, of Mollington). Several sons, all of whom d. s. p. except

WILLIAM LECHE, of Carden, High Sheriff for County Chester, 1774, married 26 April, 1805, Hannah, daughter of James Newell, by whom he left at his decease, 8 May, 1812, aged 83, a son:

JOHN HURLESTON LECHE, of Carden, born 23 May, 1805, High Sheriff of County Chester, 1832; married 25 May, 1826, Elizabeth Antonia, eldest daughter of Anthony Innys Stokes, of St. Botolph's, County Pembroke, and died 30 November, 1844, leaving with other issue:

JOHN HURLESTON LECHE, of Carden Park and Stretton Hall, County Chester, J. P. and D. L., High Sheriff 1851, late Captain Cheshire Militia, born 25 February, 1827; married (1st) 18 July, 1850, Caroline, youngest daughter of Edward Corbett, of Darnhall, County Chester, and by her (who died 1853) had two daughters:

1. CAROLINE MAUDE, b. 23 July, 1851; d. 7 Sept., 1867.
2. FLORENCE ANN (Llanerch Panna, Ellesmere, Co. Flint), b. 27 Apr. 1853; m. 21 Oct., 1875, the Hon. George Thomas Kenyon, and son of Lloyd, 3rd Baron Kenyon of Gredington, Co. Flint, by his wife, Hon. Georgiana de Gray, dau. of Thomas, 4th Lord Walsingham. He d.s.p. 26 Jan., 1908.

He married (2nd), 18 June, 1855, Eleanor Frances (who died 7 August, 1916), 2nd daughter of Capt. Charles Stanhope Jones of the 58th Regiment, and died 21 June, 1903, having had issue by her:

1. JOHN JURLSTON, J.P., b. 19 Nov., 1858; m. 13 Nov., 1888, Kathleen Marie, eldest
   dau. of Charles Donaldson-Hudson, M.P. of Cheswardine, Co. Salop; and
   d.v.p. 4 Mar., 1894, leaving issue:
   1. *John Jurleston,* now of Carden Park.
   2. *Charles Wilbraham,* b. 20 Mar., 1891; d. 1894.
   3. *Ermintrude Eleanor Augusta.*
   4. *Gwendoline Mary.*
   5. *Violet Alice,* m. 19 Nov., 1889, Frederick William Hayes, 3rd son of
      William Hayes. He d. Dec., 1908, leaving issue.

Arms: Erm., on a chief indented gu. three ducal coronets or. Crest—On a ducal
coronet or, a cubit arm ppr. the hand grasping a snake vert. Motto—Alla Corona
fidissimo.

Seats: Carden Park, near Chester; and Stretton Hall, Malpas. Official Residence—
H. M. Embassy, Rio de Janeiro.

Coat of Arms: The same as on cover of "F. Phelps Leach's Genealogy," Vol. III.

Reference: Burke's "Landed Gentry of Great Britain," 929.72 B92.

STEPHENS FAMILY
AMERICAN
STEPHEN OF TREGONY

1. JOHN.
2. THOMAS, of Duln, m. Joane Collicotts.
3. THOMAS, their son Tregony living 1620, he m. Jane, dau. of Thomas Cock, of
   Bodman, in Cornwall. Their children were (so recorded):
   1. *Henry Stephens.*
   2. *John.*
   3. *Arthur.*
   4. *Rafe.*
   5. *Richard.*
   6. *Elizabeth.*
   7. *Agnes.*

The great home of the Stephens family in England is in Cornwall
as descended from the Ancient Stephyns of St. Ives in the reign of
Edward IV. St. Ives was erected into a borough by Philip and Mary
in 1558. In 1731, the Stephens family, long stewards of the Earls of
Buckingshire, began to assert itself.

Reference: See Stephens Ancestry, Supplements I and II.

THE ANCESTRAL LINES OF WILLIAM WARREN

THE FRANKISH-CHARLEMAGNE LINE
(Thirty-five generations are omitted)

36. BELI MAWR
    to
    CLODIMIR III
42. Marcomir
43. Athildis, m. ......CLODIMIR IV
    to
51. CLODIMIR V
    to
56. Argotta, m. PHARAMOND

THE SALIAN FRANKS

CLODION, Earliest Ruler
Marovaeus, Founder that Dynasty
CLOVIS, Founder Frankish Monarchy
CLOTAIRE OF SOISSONS
to
Pepin D'Landen
Andegisus, m. Bega
PEPIN D'HERISTAL
Charles Martel
Pepin the Short
CHARLEMAGNE
Louis I of France
Charles the Bald
Louis II
Charles the Fat, m. ......
Gisela, m.

THE NORTHMEN AND SAXONS

WODEN
to
CEDRIC, First King
to
Aethelswuth
ALFRED THE GREAT and ETHELRED (No. 22)

THE NORMAN DUKES

(71) ROLF THE VIKING
72. William Longsword
73. Richard the Fearless
74. Richard the Good
75. Robert the Devil
76. WILLIAM THE CONQUEROR
77. Gundreda (See No.31)   ALFRED THE GREAT   EARL MERCIA
Edward the Elder, m. Aethelswith
......Eadgufu

THE RUSSIAN-TURKISH LINE

RURIK, Russian
Ignor the Brave
Sylastolof
Vladimir, m.
Yaroslav, m.
......ANNE OF RUSSIA

ALFRED THE GREAT
Alfrith

THE CHARLEMAGNE-ITALIAN LINE

66. CHARLEMAGNE
67. Pepin of Italy
    to
70. Pepin, Count D'Vermandois
71. Heribert I, Count
    to
76. Heribert IV
77. Adela, Countess, m. ......

THE CAPETIAN-GERMAN LINE

66. ROBERT THE STRONG   OTTO, 1st Duke Saxony
67. Robert II   Henry the Fowler
70. Hugh Magnus, m.   Hedwig
71. HUGH CAPET
    Robert the Pious
76. Henry I, m. ......
    HUGH THE GREAT
77. ISABEL, Countess D'Vermandois, m. William, 2nd Earl Warren

THE FLANDERS LINE

Charles the Bald
......Judith
BALDWIN OF FLANDERS, m. ......   ALFRED THE GREAT
Baldwin II, m. ......   Alfrith
Baldwin IV
MATILDA OF FLANDERS

1. WILLIAM DE WARREN, m. Isabel de Vermandois, of whom you know.
2. GUNDRED DE WARREN, m. Roger de Bellomont de Newburgh.
3. WALDERAN DE NEWBURGH.
4. ALICE DE NEWBURGH, m. William de Mauduit.
5. ISABEL DE MAUDUIT, m. William Beauchamp.
6. WILLIAM DE BEAUCHAMP.
7. ISABEL DE BEAUCHAMP, m. Hugh le Despenser.
8. JOAN LE DESPENSER, m. Thomas, Lord Furnival.
9. MAUD FURNIVAL, m. John, Lord Marmion.
10. AVICE MARMION, m. John, Lord Grey.
11. ROBERT MARMION, alias Grey.
12. ELIZABETH MARMION, m. Henry, Lord FitzHugh.
13. WILLIAM, Lord FitzHugh.
14. LORA FITZHUGH, m. Sir John Constable.
15. MARGERY CONSTABLE, m. Robert Holme.
16. JOHN HOLME.
17. WILLIAM HOLME.
18. ANNE HOLME, m. William Cheney.
19. WILLIAM CHENEY.
20. JOHN CHENEY.
21. WILLIAM CHENEY, the American immigrant (12 generations to author's grandchildren).
22. MARGARET CHENEY, m. Deacon Thomas Hastings.
23. JOHN HASTINGS.
24. JOHN HASTINGS.
25. HANNAH HASTINGS, m. David Farnsworth.
26. HANNAH FARNSWORTH, m. John Tarbell.
27. PETER TARBELL.
28. WALTER TARBELL.
29. CAROLINE RELIEF TARBELL, m. Franklin G. Humiston.
30. HELEN ENSWORTH HUMISTON, m. Gilbert David Kelley.
31. DAVID HUMISTON KELLEY.

References: Generations 1-8—several sources, including Browning's "Americans of Royal Descent," Burke's "Peerage," the encyclopedia, and other easily available sources.

Generations 8-14—"The Extinct and Dormant Peerages of the Northern Counties of England."

Generations 14-18—Foster's "Pedigrees of the County Families of Yorkshire," Glover's "Visitations of the County Families of Yorkshire"—but both of these sources say Sir John Constable m. Lora, dau. of Henry, Lord FitzHugh, as does the "Extinct and Dormant Peerages of the Northern Counties of Eng." under Constable—but it gives it as shown under FitzHugh.

Generations 18-21—Glover's "Visitations of Yorkshire" and your book, but 21 is only in your book.

Generations 21-25—Hastings genealogies.

Generations 25-26—Farnsworth Memorial.

Generations 26-27—Tarbell genealogy in the "New Eng. Hist. and Gen. Reg.," Vol. 61.

Generations 27-29—Hartwell genealogy.

Generations 29-30—"Town Hist. of East Jaffrey, N. H."

Generations 30-31—My birth certificate.

LINEAGE OF THE WIFE OF RICHARD WARREN, MAYFLOWER IMMIGRANT

Burke, "Peerages, etc."

1. KING EDWARD I, of England, whose dau.:
2. PRINCESS JOAN, m. Gilbert, 9th Earl of Clare, whose dau.:
3. MARGARET DE CLARE, m. Hugh d'Audley, Earl of Gloucester, whose dau. (Burke, "Extinct Peerages," 1831, pp. 386/8):
4. ALICE D'AUDLEY, m. Sir Ralph Neville, d. 1367, whose son:
5. SIR JOHN NEVILLE, K.G., m. Maud, dau. of Henry Percy and Idonia Clifford, whose 2nd son:
6. SIR THOMAS NEVILLE, m. Joan, dau. of Sir William Furnival, whose dau. (Burke, "Peerages," Ed. 1929, pp. 2123.)
7. MAUD NEVILLE (Lady Maud de Furnival, via her mother's estates), m. Sir John Talbot, 1st Earl of Shrewsbury, whose son:
8. SIR JOHN TALBOT, 2nd Earl of Shrewsbury, m. (2nd) Elizabeth, dau. of James Butler, 4th Earl of Ormonde, whose 5th son:
9. SIR GILBERT TALBOT, d. 1518, P.C., K.G., created 1496, Knight of Grafton, High Sheriff, County Worcester, fought at Bosworth, 1485, and Stoke in 1487; m. (2nd) Ethelreda (or Audrey, dau. of William Landwade Cotton, of Cambridge, Eng. Their son:
10. JOHN TALBOT, Knight of Grafton and Albrighton, d. 1555; m. Frances, dau. of Sir John Gifford, Knight, whose dau.:
11. MARY TALBOT, m. Thomas Poole, of Poole, living 1560. Their son:
12. JOHN POOLE, the heir, d. 1618; m. Mary, dau. of Sir Rowland Stanley of Hooton, whose dau.:
13. CICELY POOLE, m. Robert Bellyn (was this Boleyn, per W. R.? C.?). Their dau.:
14. MARGERY BELLYN, m. in 1578 William Jewett (or Jouett), Alderman and J.P., and Maior (Mayor). Was it their dau.:
15. ELIZABETH JOUETT (Jewett), b. about 1583; m. before 1611 (her 2nd) Richard Warren, Mayflower immigrant.

References: See "Jewetts of America," by Frederic Clarke Jewett, Introduction, pages XIV, etc. Taken from the Harlean Society records, Vol. XVIII, "Jewetts of England and America."

"MYSTERY CITY" FOUND UNDER SOVIET BUILDING

LONDON.—A Soviet expedition has discovered, 1943, a "mystery city" that flourished from the first to the twelfth century, when it was razed by Genghis Khan, under an electric power station in Russian Turkestan, the *Soviet War News,* published in London, said recently.

No reference to the city appears in any available historical material. However, the excavation, carried out by the Soviet Institute of History of Material Culture, revealed a troubled history, dating from the seventh and eighth centuries, with traces of destruction coinciding with the Arab conquest of central Asia.

Below the city's strata Soviet scientists have found traces of a still older civilization of the Anau type belonging to the thirtieth or twentieth century before Christ.

RARE BOOKS, MANUSCRIPTS FOUND IN RUINED ITALIAN CHURCH

With the Fifth Army in Italy, April 30th.—Rare books, manuscripts and pamphlets of the 15th and 16th centuries worth millions of dollars have been discovered, 1944, in a ruined church in the front-line town of Minture on the American-held sector of the Fifth Army front.

Included were ·many original drawings by Leonardo De Vinci. The almost priceless collection, crated in 170 boxes, was discovered and identified by Capt. Allan J. Oppenheim, 3045 Jackson St., San Francisco, Calif., and 1st Lt. Vincent H. Naramore, Orwell, Vt., after they were led to the ruined church by Sgt. Calvin Timmons, 2959 Parker Ave., Dearborn, Mich.

THE BURT FAMILY

1. Henry Burtt, of Harberton, County Devon, clothier, the testator of 10 July, 1617, died between 10 July, 1617, when his will was dated, and 10 September, 1617, when the inventory of his estate was taken. He married Isett (or Isott) ——,· who survived her husband and died between 14 March, 1629/30, when she declared her nuncupative will, and 8 July, 1630, when the inventory of her estate was taken.

He was a prosperous clothier and landholder, who had his own flock of sheep and owned at his death a considerable stock of cloth and yarn. The value of his estate according to the inventory was £602 7s. 9d. In his will he gave 30s. to the poor of the parish of Harberton, and bequeathed to his wife Isett, his sons Henry and John, his daughters Raddegan (under twenty-one), Allies (Alice), Agnes, and Elizabeth (these three under twenty), another daughter, Johan, who was the wife of Christine (Crispin) Saunder(s), his grandchildren Joseph and Samuel Saunders, his brothers' and sisters' children, and others. His son John was apparently his executor.

His widow, Isott Burte, in her nuncupative will of 14 March, 1629/30, or thereabouts, gave all her goods to her daughters Agnes Burte and Elizabeth Burte, whom she made her executors. Her estate (personal) was appraised at £9 13s. 4d.

Children:

1. John, eldest son.
2. Henry, living 1617.
3. Johan, living 1629.
4. Raddegan, living 1617.
5. Allies (Alice), living 1617.
6. Agnes.
7. Elizabeth.

2. Henry Burtt (probably son of Henry Burtt, of Harberton, County Devon, clothier, the testator of 1617), of Harberton, County Devon, and of Roxbury and Springfield, Mass., born probably about

1595; died at Springfield, 30 April, 1662. He married at Dean Prior, County Devon, 28 December, 1619, Ulalia (or Eulalia) March, who died in New England 29 August, 1690, daughter of Richard and Joan Martyn (?) March (*vide infra,* March pedigree).

Henry Burt was taxed on land at Harberton in the subsidy of 1624, the bequest of lands and houses made by Henry Burt, the testator of 10 July, 1617, to his son Henry. He emigrated to New England, probably in the winter of 1638/39 or in the spring or summer of 1639, and probably also with his wife and his seven surviving children, two children having died in England.

References: For American ancestry, see "Three Hundred Colonial Ancestors," by Elizabeth M. Rixford.
"New Eng. Historical Genealogical Register," pp. 217, 218 and 219.

THE MARTIN (MARTYN) LINE
Arms: Argent, two bars gules.
Crest: An estoile gules.

Martyn, as a surname, is baptismal in origin, and means "the son of Martin" or "Martel." Other forms of the name are Martins and Martinson. Both as a personal designation and as a surname, it is very widely spread in all the countries of Western Europe as well as in America. In France it is Martineau, in Spain it is Martinez, and in Italy it is Martinelli and Martini. In the English Hundred Rolls of 1273, we find listed William fil. Martin, of County Cambridge, and Mariota fil. Martini, of County Hunts.

Reference: "Americana," Vol. XXXVII; Third Quarter; No. 3; Year 1943.

FROM PARISH REGISTERS, COUNTY DEVON

1630 Luke Burt, son of Henry Burt, baptized.

CREDITON
1634 Anna, daughter of Samuell Saunders and Ulalaiah, 1 June.
1636 Samuel, son of Samuell Saunders and Ulalie, 18 June.
1638 John, son of Samuell Saunders and Ulalie, 24 March (1638/9).
1645 Susannah, daughter of Samuel Saunders and Ulalie, 8 June.

DARTMOUTH (St. Saviour's Church)
1604 Joan, daughter of Henry Byrt, baptized 19 April.
1607 Anna, daughter of Henry Byrt, baptized 11 December.

DEAN-PRIOR
Baptism
1571 Allen, son of John Berd, 2 September.

Marriages
1619 Henrie Burt and Ulalia March, 28 December.
1646 George March and Sibell Taylor, 14 April.

Burial

1582 John, son of Henry Berd, 6 March (1582/3).

HARBERTON

Baptisms

1620 Sarah, daughter of Henry and Eulalia Burt, 14 January (1620/1).
1624 Samuel, son of John Burt, — April.
1624 Jonathan, son of Henry Burt and —— (his wife), 23 January (1624/5).
1628 John, son of John Burt and Wilmote, his wife, — February (1628/9).
1629 David, son of Henry Burt and Ulalia, his wife, 18 October.
1632 Mary, daughter of Henry Burt and Ulalia, his wife, 2(7) April.
1632 Nathaniel, son of John Burt and Wilmote, his wife, 15 April.
1635 Mary, daughter of Henry Burt and Ulalia, his wife, 13 April.
1637 Nathaniel, son of Henry Burt and Eulaliah, his wife (on or after 23) March (1637/8).
1638 Elizabeth, daughter of Henry Burt and Ulaiah, his wife, 4 December.
1650 John, son of Nicholas Marche and Elizabeth, his wife, 21 January (1650/1).

Marriage

1649 Nicholas March and Elizabeth Voysey, 26 December.

Burials

1612 Christian, daughter of Henry Burt, 11 November.
1625 Samuell, son of Henry Burt, 21 November.
1629 Isack Burt, 13 March (1629/30).
1634 Mary, daughter of Henry Burt, 18 July.

Reference: "New Eng. Historical Genealogical Register," pp. 82 and 83.

II. THE MARCH ANCESTRY

The March family seems to have been in the neighborhood of Sherford, County Devon, as early as September, 1569, when a John Marche was charged in the court of the manor of Stokenham, County Devon, with diverting the water at Allymore from its right course, so that it could not run to the mill of the lord of the manor. The same charge against John Marche is found in the records of the court of the manor of 30 September, 1470. On 3 January, 1580/1 William Marche, son of John Marche, is mentioned in the court rolls of the manor, and on 9 October, 1587, Peter Marche, a stranger, son of John Marche, appears in the rolls, as does Peter March, a stranger, probably the same man, in 1599-1601. Moreover, on 29 March, 1602, Robert Marche and Richard Marche of Alvington, County Devon, were distrained to answer to the lord for hunting in Stokenham manor. Since the parish registers of Sherford being late (in 1713), probably because Sherford was formerly a chapelry of Stokenham, where the registers begin in 1578, the exact relationship of these early Marches to the family to which Ulalia (March) · Burt belonged has not been determined; but it seems likely that the John Marche of 1569 and 1570, who had sons William (1580/1) and Peter (1587, 1599-1601), was the great-grandfather of Ulalia March, the wife of Henry Burt, John's son William being probably identical with William Marche, the elder, the testator of 1612, with whom the following pedigree begins.

RICHARD MARCHE (WM.), of Sherford, County Devon, died before 29 April, 1612. ˙ He married Joane —— (? Martyn), the testatrix of 21 May, 1616, who died between that date and 10 June, 1616, when the inventory of her estate was taken. She was probably a sister of Rev. Henry Martyn, vicar of Rattery, County Devon, the testator of 13 November, 1619, or of his wife, Lucy Martyn, administration on whose estate was granted 20 September, 1639, for, since Elizabeth March, of Rattery, spinster, daughter of Richard and Joane Marche, in her will proved 14 May, 1619, called Mr. Henry Martyn her uncle, there can be little doubt that Elizabeth's mother was Henry Martyn's sister or sister-in-law.

Wm. Marche, father of Richard Marche, in his will dated 29 April, 1612, had bequeathed to each of his seven children of his (the testator's) son Richard, deceased, 6s. 8d., and had made his daughter-in-law, Joane Marche, his residuary legatee and executor. In her own will, dated 21 May, 1616, and proved 21 June, 1616, Joane Marche of Sherford, widow, disposed of an estate appraised (according to inventory of 10 June, 1616) at £140 7s. including apparel.

Reference: "New Eng. Historical Genealogical Register," pp. 249.

DANIEL ANCESTRY

The name Daniell appears among the earliest settlers of various parts of New England. Of those who settled in the vicinity of Boston were: Robert Daniell, of Watertown, about 1636.

1. ROBERT DANIELL, probably from England, settled in Watertown, Mass., previous to 1636. He was grantee of five lots, and purchased the "homestall" of Nicholas Jacob, 13 acres of land, lying not far from the present site of the U. S. Arsenal. He was admitted freeman March 14, 1638/9. His wife Elizabeth died October 2, 1643. In 1651 he removed to Cambridge, where he married Reana Andrews, May 2, 1654. He was released from training April, 1655, and died July 6, 1655. His son Samuel was executor of his will. His children were:

    i. ELIZABETH, b. 1630; m. May 17, 1655, Thomas Fanning; d. Jan. 27, 1722. Children: 1. Elizabeth, b. Apr. 15, 1656; d. Apr. 25, 168—. 2. Mary, b. Nov 12, 1657; d. next Dec. 3. Mary, b. Oct. 27, 1662; m. Benoni Learned of Sherborn. 4. Sarah, b. July 18, 1665; d. Aug. 24, 1691.

2. ii. SAMUEL, probably b. about 1633; d. about 1695.

   iii. JOSEPH, b. about 1635. Perhaps bought land in Cambridge of D. Fiske, May 30, 1662, and possibly removed to Medfield.

iv. SARAH, b. about 1640.
v. MARY, b. Sept. 2, 1642; m. June 14, 1660, Samson Frary, of Medfield, and
had: 1. Mary, b. July 24, 1662. 2. Hitte, b. Jan. 16, 1664. 3. Susanna,
b. 1668. 4. John, b. 1669. 5. Nathaniel, b. 1675. Removed to Deerfield, Frary being the first English planter there. He was killed by
Indians Feb. 29, 1704. She was taken captive and killed on the way
to Canada. (See Morse's "Gen. Sherborn and Holliston.")

MORSE ANCESTRY

"15 April, 1635. These parties hereafter expressed are to be
transported to New England, imbarqued in the "Increase," Robert
Lea master, having taken the oath of allegiance and supremacy as
being conformable to the orders and discipline of the Church of
England, thereof they brought testimony per certificate from the
justices and ministers where their abodes have lately been, Samuel
Morse, husbandman, aged 50, Elizabeth Morse, aged 48, Joseph
Morse, aged 20."

On August 15, 1636, there was a covenant adopted which had been
drawn up for a company of twelve men to whom the Great and General Court of the Massachusetts Bay Colony had granted a tract of
land lying south of the Charles River for a new settlement and
among these twelve was Samuel Morse, whose·name stood third on
the paper, with those of Daniel Morse, who signed as the twenty-
eighth, Joseph Morse as the twenty-ninth, and John Morse as the
thirty-fourth, with one hundred and twenty-two others. At first they
named this new place "Contentment," but, on September 10, 1636,
the General Court decreed that it should be changed to that of
Dedham.

While forming this new colony "they took care to look after the
rights of the natives, for every part of the territory was purchased of
the Indians before it was assigned to the settlers." At a meeting
of the new proprietors in Watertown, September, 1636, Samuel Morse
was appointed collector of the money to be paid out as occasion should
arise. By an early law of the Massachusetts Colony, every settler
was obliged to build his house within half a mile of the site chosen
for the meeting house; each man received a home lot of eight or twelve
acres of land conveyed to him according to his being a single or a
married man, together with a share in a large inclosure, called the
Commons, which was to be cultivated by all the people "in common."

November 8, 1638, a church covenant was prepared and on the
30 May, 1641, Samuel Morse with others, members of the First
Church in Watertown, were received into the newly organized church
of Dedham. In the first Board of Townsmen (afterwards called the
selectmen) or "the Seven Men," Samuel Morse was the third man
chosen for the important office.

As their numbers increased, they, following the law that each
family should be within a certain distance from the "meeting house,"
set about forming a new township, and Samuel Morse there received
a home lot and built a house in the place which received the name of
Medfield. On February 21, 1675, in the general rise of the Indians

against the settlers, his house was fired; a new house arose on the ground and this never passed from the possession of his descendants.

1. SAMUEL MORSE was born in 1587, died 1654.

In the register of Dedham, England, was found: "Richard Morse married February 15, 1586, Margaret Symson, and their son Samuel was baptized July 25, 1587. At the time of Samuel's decease in Dedham, Mass., in 1654, he was 67 years of age, whence it is argued that this Samuel is more likely to have been the son of Richard and Margaret Morse than of Rev. Thomas Morse, whose will Rev. Abner Morse, placed on record as promising to have been that of the father of Samuel of Dedham, Mass. Samuel Morse married, before he left England, Elizabeth *Jasper* who was born in 1587; d. 1654.

They had children:

2. I.   JOHN, b. in 1611.
3. II.   DANIEL, b. in 1613
4. III. JOSEPH, b. 1615.
5. IV.   SAMUEL.
6. V.   JEREMIAH.
7. VI.   MARY, m. Aug. 10, 1641, Deacon Samuel Bullen, of Medfield, who first settled in Watertown, Mass., in 1636, and was at first a tenant of his brother-in-law, Daniel Morse, he d. Jan. 16, 1691; she d. Feb. 14, 1691.

TOMLINSON ANCESTRY

1. GEORGE TOMLINSON and Maria Hyde were married in January, 1600, at St. Peter's Church, Derby, Derbyshire, England.

2. HENRY TOMLINSON, wife Alice and two or three children at Watertown, Mass., 1644. At Milford, Conn., 1652. At Stratford, Conn., 1656. At Derby, Conn., 1668. Keeper of the ordinary at Stratford. Henry was baptized 1606. From England he brought an illuminated coat of arms—"Three ravens, rising argent." The motto was "Non Sibi Sed Patriae." Abraham died 1662. Henry Tomlinson's will mentions daughter Mary Pierson, with others. In his will he advises his children to "To live in love and peace, and the God of love and peace will be with you."

The data above is from "Henry Tomlinson and his Descendants in America, with a Few Additional Branches of Tomlinsons, later from England," by the Rev. Samuel Orcutt. Published 1891.

Henry and wife Alice and probably two or three children came to America from Derby and in 1652 settled in Milford, Conn. Do not know exact year or ship he came in, but tradition says he came to New Haven, then to Milford. In 1656 with family moved to Stratford, Conn. In 1668 bought Indian lands at Derby, where his descendants lived several generations. Henry died at Stratford, March 16, 1681, leaving a widow, two sons and five daughters, all married except Agur, his younger son. His widow Alice married John Birdsey, Sr., 1688. John B. died April 4, 1690, age 74; and Alice died June 25, 1698, past 90 years.

Children of Henry and Alice: Abraham; Jonas; Margaret, b. 1642; Mary; Tabitha; Phoebe, b. 1656; Agur, b. November 1, 1658; Bathsheba, b. 1661; Abraham, b. 1662.

This information from "History of Stratford and Bridgeport, Conn., Henry Tomlinson family," by Samuel Orcutt. I have four Tomlinson bars.

WAR SERVICE OF THE MEN INCLUDED IN THE SUPPLEMENT

This is the Town of North Canaan (P. O. Canaan), formerly a part of the Town of Canaan (P. O. Falls Village). All records prior to 1858 are in the old town. I shall have to refer you there for the information that you wish.

FRANK F. STEVENS,
Town Clerk.

The only record we can find of a Moses Hawkins is as follows: "Moses Hawkins—Granger Co.—Date of enlistment May 20, 1777, for the term of the war. Taken prisoner June 30, 1777."
This was the second regiment of the Connecticut line.

MARION MACALLEN,
Assistant Town Clerk and Reg.

Army records, regarding Daniel Lawrence, Col. Henry Jackson's Regiment, 1777-83, Capt. Samuel Ransom's Company. A Wyoming Valley Company, Daniel Lawrence reported killed at Wyoming Massacre, July 3, 1778. "Record of Conn. men in the War of the Revolution," pages 264-266.

Town Clerk of Canaan, Conn.